Conflict in Colonial Sonora

Map by Paul Mirocha

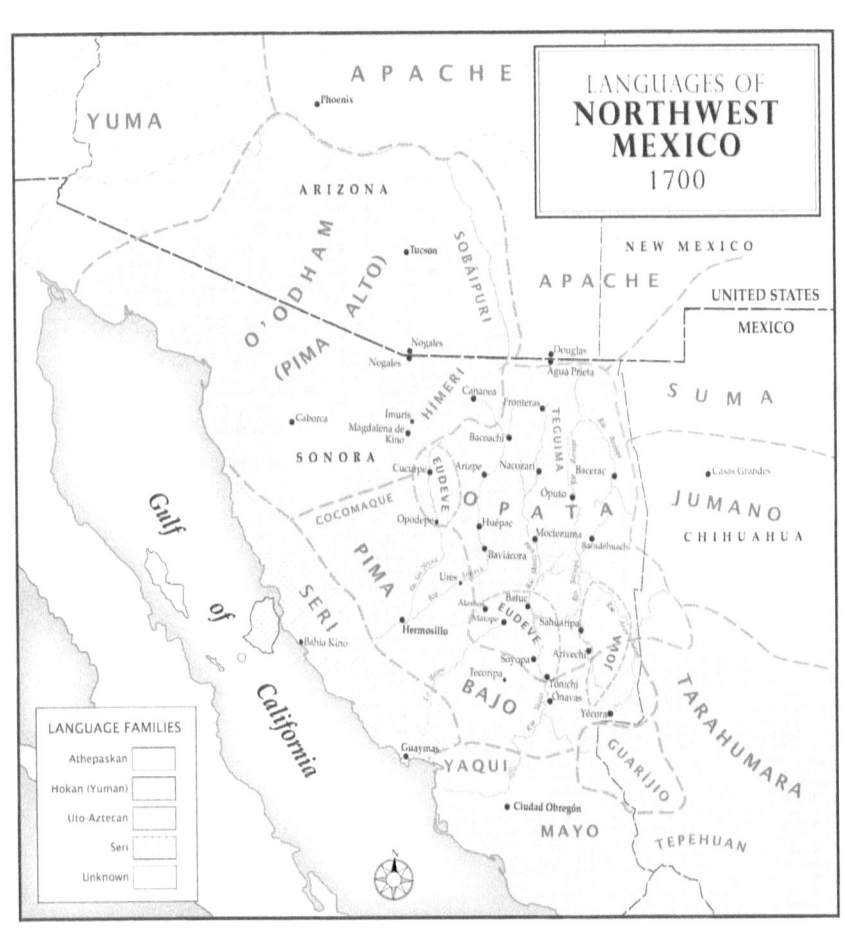

Map by Paul Mirocha

CONFLICT *in* COLONIAL SONORA

Indians, Priests, and Settlers

David Yetman

University of New Mexico Press ✦ Albuquerque

© 2012 by the University of New Mexico Press
All rights reserved. Published 2012
Printed in the United States of America

LIBRARY OF CONGRESS CATALOGING-IN-PUBLICATION DATA

Yetman, David, 1941–
Conflict in colonial Sonora : Indians, priests, and settlers / David Yetman.
    p. cm.
Includes bibliographical references and index.
ISBN 978-0-8263-5220-0 (cloth : alk. paper) — ISBN 978-0-8263-5222-4 (electronic)
1. Indians of Mexico—Missions—Mexico—Sonora (State)
2. Indians of Mexico—Mexico—Sonora (State)—History—Sources.
3. Indians of Mexico—Mexico—Sonora (State)—Social conditions.
4. Jesuits—Missions—Mexico—Sonora (State)—History—Sources.
5. Frontier and pioneer life—Mexico—Sonoroa (State)—History—Sources.
6. Sonora (Mexico : State)—History—Sources.
7. Sonora (Mexico : State)—Social conditions. I. Title.
F1219.1.S65Y47 2012
972'.17—dc23
                                    2012017367

BOOK DESIGN
Composed in 10.25/13.5 Minion Pro Regular
Display type is Electra LT Std
COMPOSITION
Maya Allen-Gallegos

Contents

Introduction
1

CHAPTER ONE
Pedro de Perea, His Heirs, and the Colonization of Sonora
26

CHAPTER TWO
Father Canal Calls in the Troops
54

CHAPTER THREE
The Conspiracies of 1681
72

CHAPTER FOUR
Sorcery in Eastern Sonora
122

CHAPTER FIVE
Father Guerrero Nails Simón García
140

CHAPTER SIX
Father Januske and the Indians Take On the Vecinos and Their Livestock: 1715
168

CHAPTER SEVEN
Sonora in 1771: Does the Conflict Deepen or Subside?
195

Appendix: The Tuape Indians' Legal Struggle to Regain Their Lands
210

Notes
229

Glossary
265

References
266

Index
272

Introduction

✣ IN THIS BOOK I DESCRIBE CONFLICTS AMONG THREE DISTINCT SOCIAL groups—Indians, religious orders of priests (primarily Jesuits), and settlers (including military personnel)—in the Northwest of Mexico over a period of about one hundred thirty years, beginning in the 1640s. Each side had its own interests and frequently struggled to defend them. Indians were usually aligned with Indians, priests with priests, and settlers and soldiers with settlers and soldiers. At times, however, the sides were riven with internal friction and conflict and sought alliances with their purported adversaries. Priests strove to pacify Indians, who in turn resisted the missionary clergy's hegemony through a variety of strategies. Sometimes, however, Indians found the missionaries to be their allies. Settlers often encountered opposition from priests to their entradas and operations and found Indians willing to side with them against the clerics. Settlers also sought to dominate Indians, take over their land, and, when convenient, exploit them as servants and laborers. Indians struggled to maintain control of their traditional lands and their cultures and persevere in their ancient enmities with competing indigenous peoples, with whom they often squabbled and fought wars, sometimes allying themselves with priests and settlers against other Indians. The missionaries faced conflicts within their own orders; between orders (Jesuits and Franciscans); and between the orders and secular clergy, and settlers took advantage of this interclerical conflict.[1] Some settlers championed Indian rights against the clergy, while others viewed Indians as ongoing impediments to economic development and viewed the priests as obstructionists.

Settlers, above all, demanded land. In this they had the strong backing of the Crown, which placed a high value on colonizers as carriers of the royal torch. Once colonizers were settled and producing from their farms and ranches (usually with Indians' labor), they would provide a cheaper security system for opposing foreign expansion and resisting Indian hostilities than expensive presidios staffed with paid soldiery. While settlers were expected to form local militias, their ties to their own land would lead them to establish roots and a permanence more reliable than could be expected from mere soldiers. Both their ethnic heritage as Spaniards and the fact that their land became theirs through the largesse of the king would guarantee loyalty to the Crown.[2] Many soldiers, Spanish authorities assumed, would double as settlers and remain as colonizers in the frontiers following their terms of service. Their land and holdings would provide vigorous incentives to defend their property from all takers.[3]

The short- and long-term interests of all three groups resulted in shifting alliances and changing opponents. Still, at the beginning of the 1630s, when the colonial era takes shape in Sonora, the three groups can conveniently be viewed as roughly univocal forces with mostly clear interests. As long as all three laid claim to the same territory, clashes and conflicts were inevitable. Yet without Indians, Jesuits would be without an assignment. And to some extent only the elimination, ejection, or marginalization of the other two groups could fully satisfy the goals and desires of Indians and settlers. In the end, settlers emerged triumphant. Jesuits and their Franciscan successors disappeared from the religious scene and Indians were for the most part pushed into the background.

Each of chapters 1 through 7 is based upon a manuscript, a file of manuscripts, or several folders of manuscripts. I chose these because each permits a distinct glimpse into a conflict pivotal in the social evolution of Mexico's Northwest, especially the state of Sonora. Each conflict underscores a different perspective and reveals the contradictions inherent in the three viewpoints. I came upon some of these manuscripts during research for an earlier book on the Ópatas. Others I discovered while working my way through microfilm copies of files. Still others I found while leafing through documents housed in the Archivo de Indias in Seville, Spain. The documentary foundation for chapter 3, the conspiracies of 1681, came from Luis Navarro García, who described them in his important book *Sonora y Sinaloa en el siglo XVII*. Using his references, I located the original documents in the Archivo de Indias and was able to read them closely. In so doing I arrived at conclusions that differed somewhat from those of Navarro García.

These chapters focus mostly on Ópatas, peoples who spoke the Eudeve and Teguima (Ópata) languages and lived in what is now northeastern Sonora. This is not an arbitrary decision on my part, since for much of the seventeenth century in northwest Mexico, the focus of conquest and pacification lay with Indians of the region Spaniards called the Opatería. Only later, in the final decade of the seventeenth century, would the attempts at evangelization of the Pimas Altos move into full force with the entradas of Father Eusebio Kino.[4] Furthermore, scholarly treatment of the archival basis for each of these chapters has been minimal or confined to Spanish language publications, whereas the later conflicts involving Pimans and Seris on one hand and settlers and priests on the other have received wide treatment in English. I have confined my search to Sonora of the seventeenth and eighteenth centuries because the archives of that region and that time period have received little attention.

The Missionary Agenda: Jesuits in Mexico's Northwest

The most general description of initial conflicts between Natives of the Americas and Spanish conquerors involves military operations in which the more powerful side defeated the other. The European forces nearly always prevailed. In the case studies in this book (and in most struggles in the Americas between Natives and Europeans), the conflicts were subtler. The most important complicating factor in Mexico's Northwest was the presence of missionaries affiliated with religious orders, primarily Jesuits.

The setting and conditions that gave rise to the conflicts described in this book have been widely elaborated elsewhere but bear repeating.[5] In the first hundred years after the conquest of Tenochtitlán in 1521, Spaniards subdued nearly all of Mexico's peoples and brought the bulk of New Spain under the Crown's control. By the time of the hundredth anniversary of the fall of the Aztecs, the largest remaining unvanquished territory lay in the Northwest, including most of the present state of Sonora. The Crown's policy for exploration and conquest of that distant territory was no longer based on sheer military power. Military victories there did not result in the bestowing of vast encomiendas, or feudal estates, on worthy Spaniards, as had been the case in central and southern New Spain. Instead, Spain supported the forays of a handful of evangelizing Jesuit priests, backed up by a strong military presence, rather than a show of military might alone. This strategy for overcoming resistance by Natives was codified in the Comprehensive Ordinances of

1573, which forbade the entry of unauthorized persons into Indian territory, required priests to be in the forefront of expeditions of "pacification," and prohibited the use of military forces against Indians living on the frontiers.[6]

Initially, at least, clergy and soldiery united as allies in the mission to conquer the pagan Indians, subdue and Christianize them, and "open up" the Northwest to economic development. The marriage was one of convenience, however, for although the clerics may have viewed the military as allies in their initial entradas, priests and soldier-settlers inevitably clashed. The soldiers represented the authority of *"ambas majestades"*—both majesties—king and God, with special deference to the king, who often granted them titles to land as a reward for service. When they became miners, as they often did, the Crown offered them special incentives and rights, including land grants; hence their first loyalty was to the king. The priests paid homage to the king (usually couching their written references to him with "May God protect him") but viewed themselves first as soldiers of God. The different interests of the two groups were bound to collide.

The Jesuit Order bore authorization from the Crown to clear the way for Spaniards by incorporating all Natives in what would come to be called Sonora into settled mission communities, from agriculturalists to hunters and gatherers and the many gradations in between. Sonora would be Jesuit territory. The order possessed both the necessary rigorous hierarchical organization and the manpower to carry out the imperial design. Recruiting individual secular priests to do the same job would not have been possible. Through the Jesuits, the king could funnel money and orders through one person, the *general*, and be assured that his orders would be carried out as well as was humanly possible. The Jesuits constituted a highly organized, authoritarian army, the perfect apparatus for the king's use.

The missionaries and their military support entered the Northwest from the south, working their way northward through Sinaloa, creating *reducciones* (reductions), mission communities where Indians were relocated to live in the vicinity of the church. The Black Robes slowly worked their way up the coast, subduing and converting as they advanced, always closely followed or even preceded by soldiers. The Crown allocated the priests ten years after founding the reducciones to convert and educate the Indians, to transform them from pagan barbarians into pious peasants. After that period, they were to become tithe- and tax-paying subjects.[7] Just when the clock measuring the onset of the ten-year grace period began ticking was never specified. At any rate, the presence of the religious order as part of the strategy of conquest inserted a third party lacking in other areas of Mexico. Franciscans and Dominicans had participated in campaigns of conquest elsewhere, but as part of the military strategy, not apart from it.

The earliest Spanish sallies to the Northwest followed the coast primarily because it seemed easier to negotiate a long journey by that route.[8] Coastal explorers had only to contend with dense thornscrub; wide, often deep rivers; swarms of ectoparasites; and fiery heat in the summer. While Natives were often unreceptive or hostile, they tended to be settled agriculturalists, more easily dislodged or defeated by traditional military maneuvers than the guerrilla warriors of the nomadic peoples east of the Sierra Madre, where the topography and arid climate rendered permanent agriculture more difficult. The Spaniards' initial choice of the coastal route to the Northwest, then, made good sense. East of the Sierra Madre, water sources were less reliable, food sources scarcer, the terrain more challenging, and Indians more mobile and more likely to harbor warlike inclinations.

The coastal route had seen imperial action at an early date. The voracious slave raider Nuño de Guzmán carried out a raiding expedition up the coast as far as Culiacán, Sinaloa, in 1531, pretty much destroying all Native peoples in his path. From there he dispatched a raiding party led by his nephew, Diego de Guzmán, which reached Sonora as early as 1533. The expedition of Francisco Vásquez de Coronado passed through Sonora in 1540. In spite of these successful penetrations of lands still under Native control, Native peoples continued to resist Spanish occupation of northern Sinaloa. After more than sixty years of skirmishes and battles, Spanish forces of occupation finally reached the Río Fuerte, where they established a permanent settlement at a place they called Montesclaros. There they constructed a fort, which they completed around 1610. It became a base from which to launch military expeditions and missionary enterprises to the northeast and northwest. Until roughly 1691, it was the sole source of regular soldiers to fight Indians all the way north into what is now Arizona. As we see in chapter 2, the great distances the soldiers needed to cover to address military problems in the Opatería posed a huge problem for priests and settlers alike.[9]

By now, Jesuit missionaries always accompanied the soldiers and Indian mercenaries. Military forces protected the clerics and softened any potential opposition until the army reached central Sonora in 1618, as always, putting on a massive display of military strength. At that point the priests seemed confident that word of the Spaniards' military might had been broadcast well into the hinterlands, steeling their confidence to set out on their own.

Still, though, they seldom strayed far from military backup, even if it was only a local militia. The first *alcalde mayor*, or chief magistrate, for Sonora was appointed in the early 1640s. When priests on the upper Río Sonora in the mid-1640s found their progress obstructed by two resistant villages, they called on the second alcalde mayor from the nearby mining town of Santiago to organize a militia and punish the upstarts (see chapter 2).

The priests' progress was slow, not merely because some groups of Natives resisted, but also because the Jesuits were unable to provide missionaries in the numbers they felt they needed to supervise the Indians and administer the burgeoning missions. Mayos of southern Ostimuri (now Sonora) appear to have requested missionaries as early as 1605, but none were available until 1614. Yaquis requested missionaries in 1610, but the first Jesuits did not arrive in Yaqui country until 1617–1618. Though itinerant priests began baptisms in 1622 in the Opatería (the northeast quadrant of Sonora), the first resident priest only arrived in 1628.[10]

By this time in the period of Spanish expansion, the military and religious leaders had a century of experience in conquering Native peoples and had for the most part become pragmatic about further conquests. After disastrous battles in the sixteenth century with Indians to the south in Jalisco and Durango in which casualties were enormous among Indians and considerable among Spaniards, royal authorities had sought a less violent solution to the Crown's imperialistic aims. For example, the Tepehuanes of Durango, relatives of present-day O'odham of the American Southwest, unleashed an organized rebellion against the conquerors in 1616. In the ensuing violence, Tepehuanes killed ten priests and more than two hundred Spaniards before Spanish forces managed to complete the conquest, killing as many as four thousand Indians in the process.[11]

The Crown understood that wherever Spaniards in New Spain encountered Native peoples unfamiliar to them, some degree of clash was inevitable. That was the price of conquering and civilizing the barbarians. Still, royal authorities hoped that Jesuits working in tandem with soldiers could minimize such violence. Spaniards would continue to demand immediate capitulation and subjugation to both king and pope, of course, and Natives often questioned the wisdom of either choice. By this time, however, the Crown had decided that assigning to priests rather than military leaders the initial role of convincing the Natives of the prudence of conversion and submission would result in the least possible loss of life (and the enhanced availability of Indians to work the ore bodies, herd cattle, and tend to the

Spaniards' needs). If that velvet glove approach failed, military backup was usually an option. And while Jesuits preferred a peaceful approach to conversions, they knew the importance of having reinforcements with weapons in the event of irrational Native resistance, as becomes clear in chapter 2. Even so, they quite naturally became leery of soldiers' proclivity for settling problems with Native peoples by fighting. On the other hand, soldiers, many of whom hoped to become settlers—ranchers and miners—easily became impatient with the slow progress and lenient policies of the clergy and with the way the priests considered the Indians their personal property.

The resolution of the conflicts with Indians took on many forms and left the vanquished Native peoples in varying stages of domination. Since each Indian group had its distinct social, cultural, and geographical makeup, each resisted in a distinct fashion. While some groups retained a barrier of hostility and fought to the death against the Spaniards, others demonstrated little resistance, at least initially. To some extent their different reactions can be attributed to the degree of mortality the Natives experienced from epidemics of European-based diseases. The rampages of disease frequently decimated entire peoples, leaving the few survivors poorly suited for resisting the Spanish onslaught. At least some peoples' early perceptions of Spaniards led them to believe that the Europeans might prove valuable allies in their clashes with traditional enemies or might help them combat disease.[12] In such cases they might welcome, rather than resist, the newcomers.

The Mayos of what is now southern Sonora present a case in point. Representatives of their heavily populated region appeared at the Río Fuerte (which formed the extreme southern boundary of their ancestral lands) in about 1605, well before construction of the fort at Montesclaros was completed. At that time, Mayos were in more or less constant battle over national boundaries with Yaquis to the north and west and seem to have viewed the Spaniards as a potential boon to their side in this ongoing conflict. This at least partially explains why the Spanish captain Martínez de Hurdaide experienced no difficulty in recruiting two thousand Mayos to join his fifty Spaniards in a planned invasion of Yaqui territory in about 1609. In other words, allying themselves with Spaniards represented a military advantage the Mayos had long sought.

As massive as the combined forces were, however, the warlike and well-organized Yaquis had no difficulty defeating them, which must have produced deep disappointment among the Mayos. The following year, Hurdaide launched a second campaign against the Yaquis, who defeated the Spaniards and an even greater collection of Mayos a second time in a decisive battle from which the Spaniards were lucky to escape with their lives. Then, in 1610, quite inexplicably, the Yaquis sent a delegation to the recently completed Fort Montesclaros on the Río Fuerte requesting missionaries.

In 1614 the Jesuits were finally able to send Father Pedro Méndez to evangelize the Mayos, who had been clamoring for missionaries for nearly a decade. Méndez described his widely announced encounter with the Mayos as a joyous reception. The Mayos had erected arches of greenery and donned festive garments at his arrival, volunteering in droves for baptism, at least according to the padre's reports.[13]

Later events may cast a less joyous aura over the proceedings, however. Father Méndez expressed concern about the Mayos' high death rate and the peculiar fact that Mayos, even those who had been converted, emigrated from their lands in droves, depopulating villages. All over the Northwest, Native peoples were reeling from catastrophic losses to their numbers. People of all ages succumbed, defenseless to the onslaught of the plagues. Noting that Spaniards suffered less during the epidemics, the Natives made the reasonable conclusion that the religion and baptism the Spaniards offered had something to do with resistance to disease. This troubled some Jesuits, probably Padre Méndez included, and rendered less than satisfactory the Jesuit reduction of the Mayos. Furthermore, the padre's enthusiasm over his reception must be tempered by the historical conditions that gradually unfolded amid the easy and enthusiastic conversion of the Mayos: their long history of fighting with Yaquis.

Captain Martínez de Hurdaide's principal task as head of the presidio of Montesclaros was to open up lands to the northwest for economic exploitation by Spaniards. In 1618 he organized an expedition to the north of Yaqui territory (his forces skirted Yaqui country so as to avoid any unnecessary battles with the fierce Yaquis) to punish Indian groups who had failed to show proper respect to some missionaries. At times only a strong military showing would dissolve obstacles to Spanish progress. Along the way, Hurdaide met with varying degrees of resistance. His forces numbered probably no more than fifty Spaniards but included at least one thousand Indians, many of them Zuaques, Cáhita speakers of the Río Fuerte who were previously defeated by Hurdaide and were reputed to be nearly as fierce as the Yaquis.[14] The mere presence of this massive armed force would put huge pressure on food resources and certainly would have created a lasting, if not entirely positive, impression on the Natives. The show of force succeeded in subduing local resistance to Spanish intrusion among the Native Nébomes, peoples of the middle Río Yaqui, who are now referred to as Pimas Bajos. And reports of the Spaniards' strength and their dastardly war machines undoubtedly reverberated northward into the Opatería, the land of the Ópatas. Hurdaide led his forces northward into the Sahuaripa Valley, probably occupied at the time by Ópatas and by Jovas, a group only distantly related to the Ópatas.

In spite of huge population losses to disease, the Natives often managed to pose spirited resistance to the Spaniards' offensives. The Sahuaripans, however, seem to have accepted the Spaniards' arrival without armed opposition. In the face of such a large force, it is not surprising that in 1628 the same Father Pedro Méndez who had ministered the Mayos experienced no resistance at all. He arrived among the Sisibotaris, as he called the people of Sahuaripa, and reported that they received him with a warm welcome, warmer even than he had received from the Mayos. The Indians were probably sufficiently astute to note that the Spaniards did not suffer equally from diseases and suspected that they might have something to offer in the way of prevention, and that this something might be baptism, a cheap boost to the immune system.

And thus the Jesuits came to establish themselves as pioneering clerics in the Opatería, as they would come to call the region. From Sahuaripa they fanned out to the north and northwest. By 1678 Jesuits had founded twenty-eight missions serving seventy-two Indian villages in Sonora.[15] Fourteen of these missions served the Opatería. Those missionaries forging northward from the south remained mostly west of the Sierra Madre, restrained from eastward expansion by geography and by stout Native resistance. The Native peoples of the northern Sierra Madre and the eastern foothills tended to be warlike, mobile, and nomadic sorts who resisted settlement and interference with their way of life. The more settled agriculturalist and semiagriculturalist Pimans and Opatans (as I shall refer to the language group that includes Ópatas and Eudeves; see p. 14) lived concentrated in the river valleys and uplands of Sonora. The two groups, especially the Opatans, appear to have been more amenable to reduction than the eastern nomads. The Opatans may have already lived in large towns with a developed infrastructure.[16] The Pimans staged major revolts on two occasions. The Ópatas did not rebel in large numbers until well into the nineteenth century.[17]

Jesuits supposedly held the Sonoran missionary franchise, while Franciscans exercised exclusive rights in New Mexico. Jesuits dominated the missionary efforts among agricultural peoples of the Sierras (Tarahumaras and Tepehuanes), while Franciscan priests were active among more nomadic peoples to the east of the Sierras (including Conchos, Janos, Jocomes, Jumanos, Mansos, and Sumas). By the 1630s Jesuits had established their presence in several of the river valleys of Sonora that constituted their turf: the lower Río Bavispe, the Río Mátape, the Río Sonora, the Río Sahuaripa, and the Río Moctezuma (the latter two both tributaries of the Río Yaqui). Other drainages would have to wait, but the Black Robes considered all these lands their legitimate and exclusive sphere of influence.

Settlers and the Economic Penetration of the Northwest

The Crown was unleashing more than religious imperialists into the Northwest of New Spain, however. The king of Spain seemed acutely aware that all wealth originates in the ground. By his fiat, he owned all the subsoil and the riches therein and was entitled to one-fifth of all the precious metals extracted from the ground of New Spain. To preserve his opulent life-style and carry on expensive wars and conquests, it was worth the king's while to promote mining on any scale. To this end the king encouraged prospecting and mining in general and provided special regulations and protections for itinerant miners. Miners could stake claims that gave them exclusive rights to exploitation as long as they worked the claims. They might own and operate as many as six mines. The Crown established assaying and refining facilities in every *real*, or mining town. Nearly everyone had the right to claim and work mines, except for mining officials (who routinely ignored this proscription) and (by their own rules) priests. In mining regions the Crown also appointed an alcalde mayor, primarily (though by no means exclusively) to deal with the administration of mining claims and rules governing mining, to collect the king's royal fifth, and to settle conflicts among miners.[18]

Usually, though, the lure of gold and silver, seams, outcrops, and alluvial deposits appearing in scattered locations was sufficient motivation for prospectors to penetrate the farthest corners of the empire. At an early date prospectors on the east slope of the Sierra Madre had probed northward into the mountains. With their eyes on the ground, the prospectors gradually worked their way west across the Sierras into the same Sonoran lands where Jesuits penetrating from the south were busy setting up their missions and reductions. And thus a second wave of Spaniards arrived in Sonora. Clerics entered from the south, miners from the east, and by the late 1630s their paths began to cross. The players were now in place and confrontation among priests, settler-soldiers, and Indians could hardly be avoided. And thus the setting for this book fell into place.

Lone prospectors had been sniffing around Sonora from the time of Coronado's expedition. The official entrada into Sonora from the east occurred around 1637 or slightly thereafter. Its leader was Captain Pedro de Perea, who is usually credited with being the first Spanish settler in Sonora. Unlike the prospectors who preceded him, he bore with him documents officially granting him settler status and authorization to found a *villa*, or town, recognized by the Crown. Pedro left little doubt that settling an area meant mining it. Ore lay in the ground and mineralization had no respect for aboveground activity. The location of Indians' settlements may have coincided with locations where settlers could most conveniently live and mine. Miners needed food and basic materials, which had to be produced locally in fields and pastures. And thus settlers tended to push Indians aside when their interests collided—not too far aside, though, since Indians were often the only source of labor for mine, field, and homestead and, at least initially, for corn, beans, and squash sufficient to tide the settlers over until they could harvest their own crops.

Settlers and clerics were not always at odds. In 1678 an early Jesuit *visitador*, Padre Ortiz Zapata, expressed his hope that mining would speed civilized development. "Proximity to Spanish settlement [would be] . . . a definite help in the process of civilizing the natives."[19] But usually the two parties recognized their conflicting goals and gradually developed an adversarial, even hostile, relationship. Miners wanted Indians out of the way, but they also craved their labor in extracting ore. Priests required Indian labor to work mission fields, construct and maintain mission buildings, and attend to their priestly needs but also enjoyed the revenue derived from sales of commodities to miners. They also needed examples of successful evangelizing to establish their credibility as pacifiers and converters of Indians, and the most powerful indicator of such success was a flourishing mission with a fine chapel, prosperous fields, and devout Indians. Miners accused Jesuits of treating the Indians as slaves.[20] They concocted new and creative ways to attract—or kidnap—Indians to work their holdings, while priests struggled to contain them and prevent them from leaving the reach of the missions. Each side accused the other of crass exploitation of Native Americans, both with plausible evidence on their side.

Nonreligious representatives of the king were well aware that conflicts from serving "ambas majestades," i.e., both king and Church, were inevitable but sought to minimize them, often expressing a pious demeanor when referring to the clergy. Still, they viewed themselves above all else as subjects of the king, and his desire to extract his one-fifth of the value of precious metals always lingered high in the awareness of his subjects. Sonora lay many days' journey from the political seat of the province of Nueva Vizcaya, originally Durango, then around 1630, Parral, located in the foothills of the eastern Sierra Madre.[21] The latter location shortened the distance to Sonora but was still a tough three-week journey away from convenient supervision by the Crown's minions.

Foul play and corruption in the remote provinces could easily jeopardize the king's rightful takings. To determine the state of affairs in such outlying regions, provincial governors appointed local magistrates, the alcaldes mayores. In addition, from time to time the king's administrators dispatched inspectors to evaluate local conditions, the behavior of alcaldes mayores, and compliance with royal statutes in the far-flung reaches of the empire and bring back supposedly objective reports. The relationships between the inspectors and the alcaldes could be adversarial, since the inspectors were expected to inspect and enforce compliance, while alcaldes were notoriously corrupt and easily bribed, as we shall see in chapters 5 and 6.

One inspector's report was the result of an inspection of Sonora submitted by the semiretired captain Antonio Bezerra Nieto, head of the presidio at Janos (now in Chihuahua), who at the governor's request visited much of settled Sonora in 1717–1718.[22] He visited mostly mining towns, not missions, which remained under the regulatory domain of Jesuit hierarchy. The captain posed a list of questions to officials in every settlement, ranch, and mining town in Sonora. Included were inquiries about the treatment of Indians (including proof that they were being paid and not treated as slaves), the appropriate order of land titles and cattle brands, the correct operation of weights and measures, and the orderly application of rules for the operation of mines. At each stop, Captain Bezerra Nieto ordered Indians into his presence and questioned them (through an interpreter) about the treatment they were receiving from their Spanish masters, usually in a most perfunctory and rote manner that omitted detail. In all his many stops, he recorded only a few negative responses from the Indians, at least concerning Spaniards (they did complain about the depredations of Seri Indians). Their only major complaint involved the Spaniards' livestock, which was invading their lands and destroying their crops.

The Indians' unanimity in their endorsement of their Spanish masters, including the absence of complaints of mistreatment, seems implausible today, especially since several Jesuit priests had written to previous provincial governors a nearly unending litany of Spaniards' abuse of Indians. In 1718, during the time of the Bezerra Nieto inspection, the governor had found Spaniards' mistreatment of Indians so widespread that he had ordered all Spaniards who were not clerics out of mission communities (see chapter 6). Still, the archive appears to show Captain Bezerra Nieto blind or indifferent to the injustices being heaped on the Indians. He read aloud the requisite questions to the Indians through an interpreter, hardly leaving room for any Indian to lodge a complaint. But he had little real interest in Indians' or priests' welfare. He wanted to check on the mines and ranches to make sure they were operating lawfully and beneficially for the king. Behind his back, or perhaps with his full awareness, some of the greatest corruption in the history of New Spain was plaguing the development of Sonora.

Indians as They Encountered Priests and Settlers

Archival materials from the colonial era reflect the viewpoints or observations of priests, military men, or other people of European background. Indian voices for the most part can only be inferred and ethnographic descriptions are sparse. What Indians were up to at that time and before their contact with Europeans and their impressions of the invaders can only be surmised from archaeological findings, oral histories, and interpretations of events and Indian activities scattered throughout archival documents. In chapters 1 and 6 we find extensive testimony from Indians, but only to reinforce the position of the Jesuits, who, they maintained, sought to protect them from exploitation and damages from *vecinos*.

Archaeological studies over the last several decades document the ongoing conflicts among pre-Columbian indigenous peoples of the American Southwest.[23] Such documentation for Sonora is scarce. The principal indigenous groups living there in the seventeenth and eighteenth centuries were Opatans, Pimans, Seris, and Jovas.[24] Opatans (Eudeves and Teguimas) were the most numerous, numbering perhaps sixty thousand.[25] They inhabited the eastern half of Sonora. Pimans (a variety of peoples including those the Spaniards referred to as Cocomaques, Hímeris, Nébomes, Piatos, Pimas, Sobaípuris, and Sibúpapas) include present-day peoples who refer to themselves as Ob (Mountain Pimas),[26] Tohono O'odham, and Hia'Ched O'odham.[27] These were agricultural to semiagricultural peoples who inhabited the western half of Sonora and a narrow belt that ran southeastward into the Sierra Madre and included such present-day Sonoran towns as Tubutama, Ures, Tecoripa, Ónavas, and Yécora.[28] Seris (Comcáac) were hunters and gatherers, an ancient race inhabiting the drier desert regions of the lower Río Sonora and the eastern coast of the Gulf of California ranging from the mouth of the Río de la Concepción to Guaymas.[29] They resisted reduction and became a major impediment to the Spanish colonization of central and western Sonora well into the nineteenth century. Jovas were peoples of the western foothills and canyons of the Sierra Madre in extreme eastern Sonora who appear to have migrated into Opatan towns in the early seventeenth century. Though their numbers were far smaller than those of the Opatans and Pimans, Jovas figured prominently in missionary efforts, especially in the region of Sahuaripa, a primarily Teguima (Ópata) town (see chapter 5).

In addition to Pimans, Opatans, and Seris, other peoples frequented the north and east portions of the Opatería, though their presence appears to have been ephemeral. Among these were Conchos, Janos, Jocomes, and Sumas, who appear to have been largely nomadic and became intermittent raiders, but who also worked in mines in the region.[30] Sumas may also have been part-time agriculturalists. Their raids became so sufficiently widespread that by the late seventeenth century, Spaniards recruited Ópatas to quell the Sumas' warlike tendencies (see chapter 3).[31] At this time, Apaches also appear in documents from the Opatería and thereafter become of great importance in the history of Sonora, while the Conchos, Janos, Jocomes, and Sumas fade into obscurity.

By the mid-twentieth century, speakers of Opatan languages appear to have disappeared completely.[32] Seri speakers still number around six hundred, and their use of their language remains robust. While speakers of Piman languages are dwindling in Sonora, many thousands in Arizona speak Akimel or Tohono O'odham. Jova speakers disappeared by the mid-twentieth century.

Linguists classify the languages spoken by Jovas, Opatans, and Pimans as Uto-Aztecan. Opatan languages are sometimes classified with Mayo and Yaqui languages into the Opata-Cahitan subfamily, while Pima and related languages are grouped into Tepiman, another subfamily. Jova appears to be Uto-Aztecan, though linguistic evidence is sparse.[33] Seri is a linguistic isolate, meaning it is unrelated to any other known language.[34]

The events described in this book take place primarily in the Opatería (northeastern Sonora) and hence concern mostly Opatans. I use this term to refer to two linguistically distinct groups whose speakers dominated the Opatería in the seventeenth and eighteenth centuries. Spaniards often referred to them as Eudeves and Teguimas. David Shaul suggests that the Eudeve language was a creole language, a Pima adaptation to Teguima, but he continues to classify Opatan along with Cahitan as a separate subfamily of Uto-Aztecan languages.[35] Late in the seventeenth century, the name *Ópata* first appears as applying to peoples residing on the upper Río Moctezuma (see chapter 3, note 62). Spaniards gradually came to use the name *Ópata* for peoples in all those areas where Natives spoke Teguima. The origin of the name *Teguima* is obscure, but it first appears in documents in the early eighteenth century. Prior to these times, priests used a variety of terms to refer to the languages spoken in villages of the Opatería. In very early documents, priests referred to Eudeve (or Doheme or a close approximation) as the language spoken in Batuc, Cucurpe, Mátape, Tuape, and several smaller villages. They considered it a different language from the Teguima (Hoba, Hore, Ova, and Ore) spoken in other towns.[36] By the mid-nineteenth century, authorities generally referred to Natives of the Opatería as Ópatas, lumping the two linguistic groups together.

At the time of contact with Spaniards, Sonoran languages presented a confusing distribution (see map of languages, frontispiece). The linguistic affiliation of some of the peoples (notably the Conchos, Janos, Jocomes, and Sumas) remains unknown. The boundaries among various ethnic groups were fluid and conflicts between peoples were common. Spaniards encountered a changing linguistic landscape and lacked any means of providing a clear description of differences and similarities among the peoples they found there, nor could they understand the interethnic dynamics that were taking place. Still, a manifestation of the interethnic strife of the seventeenth century was the ease with which Spaniards recruited indigenous warriors to carry out their wars of "pacification" as they advanced northward and westward. This is evident in chapter 2 in the rapid and apparently enthusiastic response to Captain Simón de la Vega's order to missions whose Natives spoke Eudeve, Pima, or Teguima to furnish large numbers of Indian troops to join the campaign against two rebellious towns north of Arizpe. More than eight hundred men joined in the campaign, arriving from missions throughout the Opatería and the Pimería to the southwest.

Further historic descriptions of pre-Columbian conflict in Sonora abound. When the shipwrecked Álvar Núñez Cabeza de Vaca passed through the region in 1536, an entire village of Nébomes followed him southward and relocated in Sinaloa.[37] A likely explanation for the mass evacuation is that the Nébomes were being squeezed from the north by Opatans and from the south by Yaquis. Much later, the Ópatas of Sahuaripa described to a priest their ongoing battles against Jovas, whom they usually defeated.[38] The Ópatas in particular valued warrior qualities in their young men. Baltasar Obregón described the streets of the town of Oera, possibly Opatan, as lined with dismembered limbs of enemies.[39] Ópata warriors proudly flourished the severed hands of their vanquished enemies.[40] Conflict in the Opatería was abundant and probably ongoing prior to the arrival of the Spaniards. Obregón reported ongoing fighting between Opatan towns, as did Adolph Bandelier, three centuries later.[41]

The Opatans appear to have developed a more sophisticated social structure than the other peoples of Sonora and thus may have had larger and better-organized armies. Many who lived on the Río Sonora dwelt in towns that appear to have been organized under a hierarchy of authority, with semimonumental defense works included.[42] These large settlements may have experienced a constant need to expand their resource base and could have done so at the expense of neighboring peoples.

Directly to the north and west of the Opatería, archaeological records and descriptions from seventeenth-century Europeans document an extensive history of conflict among Native peoples. In pre-Columbian conflicts, Hohokams, who constructed elaborate infrastructure along the Gila and Salt Rivers, were engaged repeatedly in wars, apparently with the Pimans from the south, who succeeded them (and possibly ousted them from their agricultural lands).[43] Following the arrival of Europeans and livestock, conflicts between Pima-speaking peoples and raiders from the east and northeast became commonplace.[44] Livestock became an easy source of meat and hides and a magnet for raiders.

Indians, then, were involved in the same expansionist and defensive struggles as peoples in Europe. How they interpreted the arrival of the Spaniards' spectacular weapons of war can only be surmised. They were at an enormous disadvantage in the face of Spanish weapons of mass destruction and the diseases Spaniards spread in advance of their arrival.

Indians, Priests, and Settlers in Conflict

In these essays I illustrate the conflicts that broke out among the three parties—Indians, priests, and settlers. Each essay is based on an archival document or series of documents from the colonial era in Sonora. In chapter 1, Indians recount the arrival of Captain Pedro de Perea and how he wrested their lands from them. Only with their priests' assistance could they regain control over their traditional fields and springs. Faced with written complaints from Indians and nudging by the priests, Spanish civil authorities were forced to adjudicate the Indians' claims, much, we must suppose, to the Spaniards' discomfort. Even with the restitution of lands to some Indians, others, especially those on the Río Sonora and around the mines at Nacozari on the upper Río Moctezuma, did not fare as well, and settlers founded large estates along the rivers and on farmlands that rightfully belonged to Indians. (We learn in chapter 6 that by the early eighteenth century, large ranch estates with thousands of cows were common in the Opatería.)

Because the archival narrative of Pedro de Perea's interaction with the indigenous folk of Sonora contains many revealing details, I have translated a large portion of it and included it as an appendix to chapter 1.

In chapter 2, we find a shift in the relations among the three parties. Here, in the late 1640s, a priest of questionable missionary skills, Father Gerónimo de la Canal, found himself forced to resort to military backup while attempting to bring two villages on the northern Río Sonora into the fold of Catholicism. Father Canal (and most subsequent historians of a sympathetic bent) seems to have been reluctant to credit the military forces, which included some of the same settlers who accompanied Pedro de Perea into Tuape, with the pacification of the towns. We are fortunate, however, that current reports preserve a parallel account of the padre's need to resort to military force, namely, documents dictated by Captain Simón Lazo de la Vega, who led the assault on the apostate villages. One of the ironies of Captain Lazo's account lies in his success in recruiting more than eight hundred Indian allies to assist in subduing the recalcitrant Native peoples of the two villages. While Father Canal's reports have received considerable attention, the parallel description of his missionary activities north of Arizpe has remained largely obscure.

The success of Captain Lazo's campaign against the recalcitrant Natives to the north seems to have enticed more settlers into the region. A series of discoveries of precious metals and productive pastureland made the Opatería a magnet for settlers. By 1657 the San Juan Bautista mine had produced enough gold to warrant making the mine into a real (official mining town) and the capital of Sonora. It boasted a population of roughly fifty miners, plus their families and other administrators, a huge population gain for the Spanish tilt of the province.[45] Nacozari and Tepache, both mining towns, were the sites of *mercedes*, or land grants, to modest numbers of settlers as well.[46] Yet the settlers' numbers were tiny compared with those of indigenous people, as they well knew.

Even with the influx of more settlers into the province and the assertion of Spanish and Jesuit control—the last mission in the Opatería was founded in the 1650s[47]—security for settlers and priests alike was by no means guaranteed. In 1680, during a time of general ferment in northern New Spain, several of the pueblos of the northern Río Grande Valley united in a sudden and effective revolt. The Indians struck quickly, taking the Spanish forces and their sympathizers by surprise, killing many priests and settlers and driving the remainder from northern New Mexico to El Paso. The effect of the Pueblo Rebellion on specific Indian groups beyond northern New Mexico has not been documented, but as Indians testified during the crackdown in Sonora, word quickly spread west of the Río Grande and must have produced immeasurable excitement among Indians, many of whom had long entertained dreams of doing precisely what the Pueblo Indians managed to accomplish. Spaniards meanwhile remained tense and nervous, wondering when the rebellion would spread to other indigenous groups and erupt into similar violence.

The jitters that became a part of life for settlers probably led to the detection of the Opatan conspiracies of 1681, which I discuss in chapter 3. The revelations of seditious activity appeared as an outgrowth of that suspicion and fear but also probably involved some Indians who were loyal to Spaniards and who brought the alleged conspiracy to their attention. Still, settlers feared Indians and, for at least a few years, they tended to view every Indian as a potential assassin. In this lengthy episode from a thick file of documents, priests fade into the background and the clash becomes a strictly bilateral confrontation between settlers and Indians, with only token intervention by priests on the side of Indians, and then mostly on procedural grounds. The documents that describe the period are entirely one-sided.

Once dissident and rebellious Indians had been silenced or subdued, the perceived conspiracy unmasked, and the supposed perpetrators exposed and executed or punished, the missions returned to their apparent tranquility. Gradually, all or nearly all the Indians of the agricultural valleys of the Opatería were reduced, forced to dwell in the vicinity of the churches where they were required to attend Mass and work on mission facilities. Despite this major accomplishment, the priests still faced enormous challenges in bringing the Indians to understand Christianity and its mysteries, and even greater challenges in forcing them to internalize Catholicism and its teachings. In addition to protecting the Indians from the onslaught of physical and moral assaults and temptations from the outside, priests were dedicated to eradicating paganisms from the Indians in their missions—some behaviors more than others. Two practices they found especially reprehensible were polygamy and *curandismo*, or Native curing. These customs invariably topped the list of Native institutions to be eradicated, along with proscribed sexual practices. Polygamy was relatively simple to stamp out—it required only vigilance and stern suppression on the part of the priests, with drastic punishments for violators or backsliders.[48] Curandismo was more difficult, since it was pervasive, often subtle, and could easily be carried on beyond the watchful eyes of the clergy.

The priests were not as concerned with actual curing, at least within the limits tolerated by their medical conceptions. The deeper problem lay in the Indians' conception of medicine, which often made no distinction between healing and sorcery. Healers would often use spells and arcane rituals to heal and would use similar techniques to inflict spells on others. Priests came to believe that the Indian curers, especially Opatans, were also *hechiceros* (sorcerers), masters of dark arts, and servants of the devil. The priests' attitudes toward curing varied greatly from mission to mission, but for some, *curanderos* were hechiceros and were unequivocally capable of murder at a distance. And thus the case of Marcos Humuta in Bacerac in chapter 4 is especially revealing. Marcos's priest, Jesuit Father Horacio Polici, was a longtime missionary on the upper Bavispe, and his unwillingness to become involved in a furious dispute over accusations of witchcraft among his charges is instructive. Civilian authorities ultimately resolved the case, which became a criminal matter when the priest refused to assert his authority and settle the dispute.

As if instilling sufficient catechism were not a daunting task, priests faced a major challenge enforcing the Spanish rules against Indians leaving the missions. Some of the padres discovered to their dismay that without tough enforcement of rules against wandering, their parishes could become depopulated as Indians departed to work for settlers in their homes, mines, and fields. If on the one hand the priests were too lax with the rules, the Indians would flee on a whim and thumb their noses at the priests. On the other hand, if the clerics applied too heavy a punishment, as Spanish authorities permitted them to do, Indians would have all the more reason to flee and would also develop a hatred for the priests. The padres' task was rendered all the more difficult by tactics perfected by miners, such as arriving in mission settlements and offering the Indians inducements to leave the sphere of religion—and the autocracy of the priests—and enjoy a life of freedom in the much more libertine and lively mining towns. Work in the mines may have been hard and dangerous, but Indians did not fear the lash for failure to attend Mass and priests could not pry into their private affairs.

Priests were expected to refrain from involvement in political issues. These were civil and criminal matters and were to be adjudicated by Spanish civil authorities such as the governor of the province, the alcalde mayor (chief magistrate) of the jurisdiction, *justicias* (judges), and individual appointments by the governor that included responsibility for enforcing royal ordinances. From time to time, though, priests found they could not restrain their indignation and became directly involved in so-called civilian matters. A prime example is a 1722 letter from Padre Caitano Guerrero of Mátape to his visitador (father superior). Padre Guerrero angrily reported the murder of an Indian *mayordomo* (foreman) from his congregation who worked on the estate of a Spaniard. The Spaniard and his sons killed the Indian in a dispute over territory the settlers had claimed. The padre fumed that the Spaniards demonstrated no remorse about the murder and continued their brazen theft of lands that properly belonged to the mission and its Indians.[49] Father Guerrero wrote that complaints he forwarded to Alcalde Mayor Álvarez y Tuñón were met with silence. The alcalde was not about to intervene on the side of the Jesuits when a Spaniard was simply staking out a new land claim.

And, from time to time, the distinction between religious and civilian matters blurred, as when Padre Miguel Guerrero of Bacadéhuachi made a complaint to the governor of Parral in 1707 concerning the absence of Indians from his mission. Dismayed by a dwindling census in his congregations, he petitioned the governor to use the military to force wayward Indians to return to Bacadéhuachi. The governor agreed, all too readily, it would turn out. The consequences were more than Father Guerrero could have anticipated, as we see in chapter 5. When the (initially reluctant) governor ordered truant Indians back to their mission, he dispatched a military squadron to enforce his orders and the resulting confrontation pitted Spaniard against Spaniard, priest against priest, and, ultimately, Indians against Father Guerrero. In this case, settlers seemed to side with Indians against the priest.

Perhaps the most scathing confrontation was between priest and Spaniard, between the padre visitador and the captain whose troops were rounding up the illegal immigrant Indians.

Mining posed a related and perhaps even more insidious threat to the survival of mission Indians. The influx of ore diggers and their relaxed views toward morals and religion was a serious threat to the spiritual atmosphere of the missions. Even worse, the in-migration created a new demand for beasts of burden—burros, horses, and mules—both for riding and for hauling goods and carrying ore. In addition, miners seemed to offer an insatiable market for beef and beef products, including tallow for candles to illuminate their mines and homes; hides for clothing, for the manufacture of bellows to stoke the fires of the myriad small smelters, and for the large leather bags used for hauling ore and draining water from the mines; and meat, fresh as well as jerked, as a basic food for the miners. The burgeoning demand for livestock products led many miners to double as ranchers.[50] The Indians' struggles against the cattlemen and the intervention of their priests is the theme of chapter 6.

Fencing was nonexistent on the wild frontier, and while Spanish regulations limited the number of cattle a rancher might run on his ranch, the ranchers ignored the rules. They simply branded their cattle and released them to run free until the time came to capture and sell them, counting them only as a banker counts investments. Almost overnight, Indians found their *milpas* (cornfields) and *frijolares* (bean fields) invaded by hungry, stamping cattle that could destroy a year's crop in a few minutes. In addition, as the Indians testified in chapters 1 and 6, cattle thronged around springs and artesian wells, fouling the water, trampling the soil, destroying the protective vegetation, and causing springs to dry up. Severe droughts in 1715–1717 made the situation even more desperate. Several priests had lodged protests with Spanish authorities concerning the environmental and economic destruction brought on by livestock, but it was Father Daniel Januske, a Bohemian Jesuit, who devoted much of his career to challenging the right of settlers to allow their cows, horses, burros, goats, sheep, and pigs to roam unattended, savaging the Indians' fields of corn, beans, and squash. Father Januske ran into powerful and spirited opposition among the settlers and in so doing seemed to force everyone involved in the conflict between settlers and priests to take sides. His arguments against the settlers provoked a legal battle. The ensuing investigation provides some insight into the judicial processes of the colonial era and the involvement of Indians in these proceedings. It also underscores the vulnerability of Indians to the ecological alterations that accompanied the imposition of the Spanish way of life on Indian cultures. The mere diminution of deer herds through grazing competition by herds of cattle, as well as intense hunting by settlers, increased Indians' nutritional vulnerability, a need that Spanish beef could not supplant. The habitat transformation engendered by the rise of ranching can hardly be overestimated.

An equally vexing problem confronted Sonoran priests as the eighteenth century waned: attacks from gentile Indians. The Jesuits faced serious problems in converting their Indian subjects into the model Europeans they envisioned. Their tasks were immeasurably complicated by the infusion of settlers into Sonora and the raft of problems they brought—epidemic diseases and moral depravity were just two. Even more troubling, however, were the attacks of Pimans from the north and west; Mountain Pimas from the east; Apaches, Conchos, Janos, Jocomes, and Sumas from the north and east; and Seris from the coast to the west. Raids from nomadic peoples to the east and northeast began in the late seventeenth century and became increasingly violent as Apaches, Sumas, and others expanded into the Opatería from New Mexico and Chihuahua, while Seris from the west became serious raiders as well. Somewhere between 1690 and 1692 the Crown created a presidio at Corodéhuachi, roughly forty kilometers south of present-day Douglas, Arizona, to defend the burgeoning settler population against attacks from Apaches, Pimans, and Sumas. The presidio would later come to be known as Fronteras.

The antiraiding efforts and the location of the presidio were well conceived, but from the very outset the presidio lacked qualified and sufficiently armed soldiery to carry out any sort of organized threat to the raiders. At times Fronteras housed virtually no soldiers at all, since the commanders often used the few soldiers stationed there as workers on their estates, leaving the forts devoid of armed personnel. The presidio's military leaders were notoriously corrupt and often the military force existed on paper only, while the commanders pocketed the phantom soldiers' salaries.[51] For two hundred years Apaches terrorized the region, seemingly impervious to the most sophisticated and massive armed strategies hurled at them by the Spaniards, even after serious military expeditions emerged to combat them in the mid-eighteenth century.

From time to time, Spanish forces, staffed primarily by Indian allies, most of them Opatans, inflicted what they considered crushing defeats on the raiding Apaches and others. For a short period of time, a few months to even a few years, settlers and non-Apache Indians could live in peace. Inevitably, however, the Apaches would regroup, often joined by the warlike Seris and unrepentant Pimans in making life miserable for Spaniards and their Opatan allies. Decade after decade, Sumas, and later on Apaches, Pimans, and Seris, would conduct raids, sometimes coordinated among the various Native peoples. So great were the depredations by Apaches and other raiders that at times large portions of Sonora were virtually depopulated of Spaniards, while Native numbers plummeted as well.[52] Whenever Spanish developers hoped to open up the Northwest of New Spain to orderly expansion, the rebels and raiders interfered with their speculative enterprises.

By the latter third of the eighteenth century, some Spaniards perceived that royal forces were gaining the upper hand against the Native rebels. Spanish and Opatan forces had inflicted heavy defeats on the Sumas by the beginning of the century and the latter had disappeared by the 1780s.[53] Relentless military campaigns of the 1760s demoralized the Pimans and Seris, and their attacks gradually became more sporadic.

The political situation in New Spain, especially in the Northwest, had also altered drastically in 1767 with the expulsion of the Jesuits. The Crown, in the person of visitador José de Gálvez, had come to agree with secular critics that Jesuits wielded too much power and commune-based Indian missions constituted a blockage to economic development. Along with the expulsion, Gálvez instituted a variety of reforms, including the removal of impediments to modest capitalist development. Missions as institutions gradually disappeared and private property on former mission lands became the norm. Gálvez also organized major offensives against rebellious Indians.[54]

In spite of the efforts of Gálvez and his appointees, however, the violent attacks, now increasingly against private property, showed no sign of letting up. A few promoters or speculators, downplaying the violence and perhaps having a vested interest in suppressing stories of Indian raids, published glowing accounts of economic opportunity in the Northwest. It was this situation that the governor of Durango confronted in 1771, and this is the topic of chapter 7. With the assistance of two knowledgeable Franciscan priests from Sonora, Governor Joseph Fayni compiled a file of written descriptions of attacks on Spaniard and Indian alike and in so doing helped deflate the speculative efforts of the promoters. The priests' dramatic testimony underscores an unusual alliance among priests, settlers, and settled Indians against nomadic or semiagriculturalist Apaches, Pimans, and Seris. It also demonstrates that missionaries and settlers were forced to unite against common

Indian enemies and recruit settled Indians (primarily Opatans) to assist in the antiraiding campaigns.

Gradually, the tripartite nature of the conflicts merged into a bilateral struggle. The Jesuits' replacements came first from the ranks of Franciscans, later from the secular clergy, few of whom felt any loyalty or ideological sympathy toward missions or Indians. The vision of missions as religious communities of catholicized Indians faded as governments permitted former mission lands to be distributed to settlers and their heirs and priests came more and more to minister to the needs of the settlers and their many offspring, while Indians were more or less relegated to the religious and social periphery of Sonoran history.[55] The conflicts thereafter tended to lapse into simple Indian versus non-Indian struggles over land and power, with the Indians usually losing, as they did throughout the Americas.

The demise of the missions was hardly the singlehanded result of scheming by settlers, however. The Laws of the Indies had always envisioned the missions as temporary institutions intended to pacify and evangelize Natives. After ten years, the missions' task would be accomplished—Indians would have become rationalized, tax-paying subjects of the king—and the missions would be phased out. The Jesuits, and to a lesser extent the Franciscans, however, gained political power and forgot or chose to ignore the original ten-year limitation, extending it to nearly two centuries. Settlers, however, and their representatives at all levels did not forget and waged an ongoing struggle against the hegemony of the religious orders, not for religious reasons, but in order to gain access to land and resources formerly under first Indian, then mission, control. In this they were largely successful. By the end of the colonial era, the settlers had emerged victorious in the tripartite struggle.

Conflict Following the Colonial Era

Beginning in 1825 and continuing for much of the nineteenth century, a succession of Indian wars nearly tore Sonora apart. The state's boundaries now included the former province of Ostimuri, home to Yaquis and Mayos. Yaquis led most of the unrest of the nineteenth century, but Mayos, Opatans, Apaches, and occasionally Seris also played a role. Religious orders had been exiled and replaced by secular priests, those who reported to bishops and church hierarchy rather than superiors in their orders. The clergy per se had retreated from or disavowed significant roles in these often-violent encounters that might better be described as wars between indigenous peoples on the one hand and those who sought to supplant them and acquire their land (usually with the support of the Sonoran and Mexican governments) on the other.

A legal case from Moctezuma in 1836 illustrates well just how drastically the alignments in the struggle among Indians, priests, and settlers had been altered. The local priest, one Padre Moreno, claimed lands formerly part of the Oposura Mission and began tilling them and grazing his cows on them. The Indians objected and complained to authorities. The local justice of the peace and the state governor both sided with the priest, arguing that he had the law on his side and that the Indians were simply ignorant.[56] The Indians protested and occupied land they claimed to be theirs. The governor sent in troops to evict and arrest the protestors and was apparently forced to kill some of the Indians.

By the beginning of the twentieth century, with the exception of a few Yaqui and Mayo skirmishes, Indians had been militarily subdued, vastly outnumbered by vecinos and mestizos, and for all practical purposes marginalized from the events that shaped the state of Sonora.

A symbol of the ongoing clashes remains in the municipio of Cajeme in southern Sonora, the site of which lay beyond Sonora's boundaries until after independence. Cajeme's seat of government is Ciudad Obregón, Sonora's second largest city and the locus of its greatest family fortunes, mostly derived from the immensely productive farmlands that formerly belonged to Yaquis. The municipio is named after the Yaqui military genius who nearly managed to set up an independent Yaqui state in the 1880s. Cajeme fought to keep Yaqui lands out of the control of the very forces that today dominate Sonoran ruling circles and politics. Sonorans named the municipio in honor of the man whose lofty goals their leaders repudiated with violence and whose people they strove to destroy.[57]

CHAPTER ONE

Pedro de Perea, His Heirs, and the Colonization of Sonora

☙ EUROPEANS, BOTH PRIESTS AND SETTLERS, STOLE LAND FROM INDIANS. Whether they coveted Indians' lands for settlement, agriculture, mining, creating Christian utopias, or for mere imperial demonstration, the settlers routinely pushed Indians from places they found to their liking.¹ Priests carved the land into missions over which they exercised complete control, reducing formerly free-roaming Indians to serfdom or peonage and forcing them to live in towns. Both European groups typically justified their expansionism by claiming that Indian lands were not put to good use or that pagan and barbarian Indians required the presence of Christian guidance and influence. When Indians resisted, the Europeans applied military force. In a few cases during the colonial period, however, Indians fought back by taking advantage of Spanish legal proceedings. At times the missionaries aided the Indian cause against settlers, as in the following example.

In 1658 a small band of Sonoran Indians appeared before Governor Enrique Dávila y Pacheco in Parral, the capital of Nueva Vizcaya, now located in the state of Chihuahua. Their leader and spokesman was one Damian Sidaycavit, the traditional governor of the tiny pueblo of Tuape on the Río San Miguel in Sonora. For more than two weeks they had journeyed on foot southeastward, crossing the punishing mountains and canyons of the Sierra Madre to present their case before Governor Dávila y Pacheco. In their petition they requested that the governor order the restitution of lands they claimed had been wrongfully taken from them by Captain Pedro de Perea.[2] We do not know the nature of the governor's decision, but the Indians' appearance before him marked the culmination of nearly two decades of struggle to reclaim their land. Part of that story includes the founding of Sonora and the man most historians credit with its original colonization, Pedro de Perea. While Pedro is the named defendant in the lawsuit, he dies early in the conflict and fades as a player. The archival documents refer to him only as *difunto*—deceased. They pit the persistent Indians of Tuape against Pedro's heirs. In the background, Jesuit missionaries watch the proceedings.

Around 1637 the first nonclerical Spaniards settled in Sonora on land that was part of the ancestral holdings of Native Americans.[3] In so doing, they stirred up this conflict over land rights that lasted until it was resolved in Parral in 1658. Early in the conflict, Jesuit missionaries advised the Indians to take legal action against the settlers. Documents from the historical archives of Parral portray the strategy the Indians and their advisors employed to reclaim lands that Spaniards had taken from them. The documents also underscore the accused Spaniards' refusal to turn over the purloined lands and the response of Spanish courts to the strategies of both sides.

Pedro de Perea, a military captain, led the first contingent of Spanish soldiers and settlers (the two often played the same role) into what is now Sonora. He was not seeking a military conquest but rather was intent on establishing a colony. The foray had the full backing of the Crown, and the Spaniards considered their mission a license to civilize the region, which for them meant to establish an enclave of Spanish culture, institute European customs and norms to guide the "barbarian" Native peoples, and, even more important, extract wealth from the land. If Indians stood in the way of convenient development of human and natural resources, so much the worse for them. The Crown hoped to see Spanish colonizers populate the far-flung regions of New Spain, thus securing it under the control of the king. Colonizers would provide more permanent expansion of the kingdom than soldiers.[4] In the remote north they would plant the Spanish flag, asserting the king's presence in areas where settlers from other kingdoms, especially England, might be tempted to establish new outposts.

In this case, the nondescript Eudeve settlement of Tuape on the Río San Miguel, a minor, ephemeral stream in central Sonora, became the location of a struggle that would be repeated numerous times in northwest New Spain in the following one hundred fifty years. It would also symbolize the conflicting currents in Spanish expansionism: evangelizing and pacifying Native peoples versus expanding the royal treasury and establishing Spanish colonies in lands claimed by the king. The conflict would set the stage for Sonora's colonization and outsiders' eventual appropriation of Indian lands and Indian water. The clash of forces would continue through the expulsion of the Jesuits in 1767, and on through Mexican independence. It continues today in Mexico in the form of the neoliberal drive against cooperatively and communally owned lands.[5] The Tuape saga delineates the dynamics among the three interested groups struggling over control of the land: Indians, priests, and settlers.

In the Tuape case, the facts presented before Governor Dávila y Pacheco clearly favored the Indians, as all parties acknowledged, yet subordinate authorities had been reluctant to rule in the Natives' favor. A Jesuit priest who ministered to the Indians provided testimony on their behalf, describing their agriculture and their lands. His deposition supported Indians' ancient land tenure in Tuape, their use of the land for their crops, and their intimate knowledge of the terrain. The Indians' stubborn persistence through endless delays and continuances, along with the demonstrable improbability of the Spaniards' land claims, forced the Spanish courts to recognize the validity of the Indians' petition. Still, these courts, as far as the documentary record demonstrates, did not rule against the settlers. Instead, they brought pressure on the Spanish settlers to relinquish their holdings and settle the case without the magistrates having to issue a formal ruling against them.

Prior to Pedro's arrival in 1637, the only Europeans to be found in Sonora, apart from a smattering of prospectors in search of precious metals, were priests—a couple dozen Jesuits and a small handful of Franciscans.[6] These resided in newly created mission communities, not on landed estates under private ownership. Indeed, the Crown entrusted Jesuits with "pacifying" the Natives, converting them to Catholicism, and shaping them into a new breed of peasantry freed from their "savage" past, humbly, quietly, and piously tilling the land, reaping harvests, and laboring to maintain the mission communities. Implicit in this charge was the creation of missions, which, the priests soon learned, would occupy Sonora's most appealing land, making it off-limits to settlers.

Native uprisings had frustrated the Crown's earlier attempts at colonization in what would come to be called the Opatería, roughly corresponding with northeastern Sonora. In 1540 Coronado attempted to found a settlement at Corazones, probably on the Río Sonora. He left forty soldiers in charge when he departed for the north. After blatant mistreatment at the hands of the Spaniards, the Natives, probably Teguimas, revolted and obliterated the colony, killing all but four of its Spanish settlers.[7] Following the Corazones debacle, indigenous Sonorans—Teguimas, Eudeves, Nébomes, Pimas, and Seris (as Spaniards came to call them)—seemed to have resisted settlement by outsiders. Teguimas and Eudeves became so renowned for the deadly accuracy with which they shot volleys of poisoned arrows at intruders (and perhaps each other) that most expeditions left Sonorans to their own devices.[8]

By the early seventeenth century, a more systematic Spanish campaign of pacification and conversion of Indians had reached Ostimuri, the land of the Yaquis and Mayos that now makes up southern Sonora south and east of the Río Yaqui. Between 1618 and 1619 Captain Martínez de Hurdaide, based at the presidio at El Fuerte on Sinaloa's Río Fuerte, led a military and pacification expedition to central and eastern Sonora. This major foray was intended to soften the region for Jesuit evangelists rather than to establish encomiendas (grants of land and people paying taxes to the absentee owners) or colonies of Spanish yeomen and emerging landed gentry. The goal of the missionaries was to convert the Natives to Christianity and to the ethic of individual peasant farming. The Crown granted the Black Robes virtual free rein in the new territory but gave them only ten years to complete the conversions. When that time had expired, Indians would become normal subjects of the Crown, obligated to pay tithes and taxes.[9] Those goals—creation of a peasant class and collection of tithes—were never fulfilled in the one hundred fifty years of Jesuit activity in the Northwest, nor were any tithes collected under the Franciscans, who succeeded the Jesuits. Indians had nothing taxable or titheable.[10]

When Hurdaide withdrew his troops and their numerous Indian allies, only the Jesuit priests remained behind, though military assistance was never far away.[11] Their vision involved founding communally based, self-sufficient mission enterprises centered first on spiritual, second on economic goals. The development of land and resources for private or even royal enrichment was not a stated part of the Jesuit program. In pursuit of the utopian goal, missionaries began active evangelization in Sonora in the 1620s, arriving in Mátape in 1629. By 1638 (perhaps slightly earlier) they had begun the slow process of converting the Indians of the Río Sonora. Northward progress was slow, however, and no Jesuit priest resided in Arizpe, in the northern portion of the valley, until around 1650. Formal evangelization on the Río

San Miguel, the next major drainage to the west of the Río Sonora, did not commence until the late 1640s.[12]

At that time, New Spain east of the Sierra Madre, the province called Nueva Vizcaya, was already well populated by nonindigenous people and was the site of considerable mining activity.[13] The governor of Nueva Vizcaya ruled over the lands to the west of the Sierras as well. Although Durango, in the Guadiana Valley, was the official seat of the province's government, the discovery in the early 1630s of rich silver deposits near San José de Parral, several hundred kilometers to the north, resulted in a silver rush and the rise of a boomtown. While other deposits waned, those of Parral seemed to yield a steady return and Parral became the largest town in the province. During the late 1630s its importance surpassed that of Durango and Parral became the de facto seat of the government of Nueva Vizcaya.[14]

Much of what is now Sonora, the Northwest of New Spain—including what would come to be called the Opatería and the Pimería Alta—was still unknown and undescribed territory for Spaniards. Those lands, which lay to the west of the rugged Sierra Madre, were the last to be colonized in what is now Mexico. Some of the earliest observers compared the lands favorably to parts of Spain in climate and topography. These same lands would prove receptive to European crops and livestock. The Opatería in particular contained well-watered valleys with fertile soils and an ancient history of cultivation.

The Arrival of Pedro de Perea

Sonora remained devoid of private property until the arrival of Pedro de Perea.[15] Pedro was a small-time conquistador and government-sponsored Andalusian who obtained the backing of Spanish authorities to help pacify the Northwest and open it up for economic development.[16] In 1626 he succeeded Martínez de Hurdaide, a devout Catholic and very tough soldier, as captain of the presidio of Sinaloa.[17] Perea, perhaps even tougher but, as far as Jesuits were concerned, clearly lacking in piety, took his job seriously and by 1634 had made forays deep into Sonora, battling Indians along the Río Bavispe. Accompanying him were Jesuits who offered baptism and absolution for those who surrendered to Spanish authority. The priests tagged along not because of the piety of the conquistadores but because in 1573 the Spanish Crown had issued royal orders that prohibited Spaniards from attacking or abusing Indians for any reason whatsoever.[18] And they were required to bring priests along with them on conquering expeditions. The orders were stern and specific but often only casually enforced. Along the way, Perea developed a reputation for ruthlessness and a willingness to depose any Natives who resisted Spanish entradas or his whims. Jesuits early on noted his penchant for excessive violence and found him less than enthusiastic about defending priests who were under attack from apostate Indians.[19]

Perea was too ambitious to remain a mere captain of a presidio. With the blessing of the governor of Nueva Vizcaya, he journeyed to Mexico City and in 1637 secured from the viceroy of New Spain the authorization to colonize Sonora, which, the viceroy agreed, would be called Nueva Andalucía after Pedro's home province. Returning to the Northwest and Parral, he convinced the governor to name him *alcalde mayor de Sonora*, an imposing but rather empty title for a territory devoid of Spaniards, but one which would endow him with almost unlimited authority. He would become the Crown's chief officer—administrator, commander in chief of the militia, chief justice, budget director, and planning czar.[20] The governor authorized him to muster forty soldiers, twenty-five of whom would travel with him to Sonora at his own expense.[21] The twenty-five original soldiers were on loan and not permanently attached to him. Recruiting the remaining fifteen would be at Pedro's own expense as well, and these soldiers would have to agree to become colonists of the unknown place called Sonora.

In return for endorsing Perea's commission, Governor Cadereita of Nueva Vizcaya instructed him to found a villa (town), construct appropriate fortifications, introduce European agriculture, open mines and refineries, and provide for the propagation of Spanish culture, all in the space of four years. The governor may have granted a two-year extension when Perea had not completed the requirements by 1641 or 1642, but Pedro never fulfilled the terms of his commission.[22] His subsequent designs on Sonora were somewhat dampened by the restrictions imposed by the viceroy and the governor, who must have sensed that in Pedro they had an intrepid soul, but perhaps a loose cannon as well. Furthermore, Pedro was subject to the proscriptions on the behavior of conquistadores imposed by the Laws of the Indies: He was not to inflict arbitrary violence on Indians. He was to respect their property and women. His expeditions were to be accompanied by priests.

In spite of these limitations, Pedro believed that he had pretty much free rein, apart from gratuitous violence. With his charter in hand, he led his band west across the Sierra Madre. He may have ordered his men to the Río San Miguel as early as late 1637 and may even have accompanied them on the initial entrada. He almost certainly relied on geographical reports of the Jesuits, who had been in the region for several years and perhaps had suggested that he locate in Tuape (rather than a better location, which they reserved for themselves). At any rate, he visited the San Miguel Valley and must have soon departed, leaving his men in charge. By 1640, while his soldiers were encamped along the Río San Miguel and prospecting for precious metals in the nearby hills, he was busy in New Mexico recruiting men and their families to settle permanently around Tuape and replace the temporary soldiers.[23] In addition to colonizing the unconquered province of Sonora, the men thus recruited were to serve as a local militia and work as miners and farmers. The New Mexican authorities viewed settlers as lowlifes and undesirables and the governor and his administration probably viewed their departure for distant parts favorably.[24]

Once again in Tuape, Pedro selected a ranch site to his liking and named it Nombre de Diós. In whirlwind fashion he relocated his family, servants, and livestock to Tuape from Basiroa, three hundred kilometers to the south in the Río Fuerte drainage. By 1641, probably earlier, Perea had enticed twelve New Mexicans and at least some of their families to Tuape to be permanent *colonos*, or settlers. (Twelve was the minimum number of married vecinos required to establish a villa under the Laws of the Indies.) These would become the original nonindigenous Sonorans, part of the foundation of Sonoran society, traceable to New Mexico, where more than three thousand Spaniards and their offspring were already to be found. Nombre de Diós was the first secular Spanish settlement in Sonora, and while Pedro de Perea is usually credited with the founding of Sonora, Sonorans seldom mention the genetic descent of the state's founding families from Spanish or mestizo New Mexicans.

Pedro de Perea may have regretted his precipitate action in selecting Tuape as his first settlement, for it was not long before he found the narrow valley at Tuape inadequate for his designs for a villa, and before two years had passed he had transferred his headquarters to the Río Sonora, settling on a location near Banámichi. Based on the testimony of several witnesses in the archival documents, he appears never to have viewed the Tuape settlement as anything other than a temporary place to house his family while he constructed a villa—a permanent town—elsewhere.

While the legal arguments presented in the archives do not mention the formal requirements of a villa, they are assumed in the depositions. Creation of a villa brought with it a grant of land from the Crown four leagues (roughly ten miles or sixteen kilometers) on a side. This was to be measured and divided among the twelve original settlers, so each would have received a handsome tract of land. In addition, a certain area of ejido, or common land, would surround the villa and provide extra resources for wood gathering, grazing animals, foraging for wild plants, and such things.[25] The founding of a villa was no simple act—one needed men, families, and a goodly swath of land. The land would have to be appropriated from its current inhabitants, who might object.

An additional requirement the governor of Nueva Vizcaya had imposed on Alcalde Mayor Perea was that a priest accompany him. The Jesuit Gerónimo Figueroa joined the Perea party. Father Gerónimo, a Native-born priest with Indian ancestry, had experienced many challenges as a missionary among the Tarahumaras. The padre quickly discovered to his dismay that Pedro had little patience for the obstacles created by the presence of Natives and tended simply to push them out of the way and take over their lands, grabbing by force what he could not obtain by peaceful accord. Padre Gerónimo, viewed by his Jesuit contemporaries as a gentle, saintly sort, could not stomach Pedro's barbarian treatment of Indians and withdrew from the entourage.[26] Perea was unfazed by the Jesuit's resignation. He foresaw nothing but obstacles and frustration from the Jesuit presence and turned instead to Franciscans to fill the mandated position in his retinue. He had become acquainted with the Brown Robes during his recruiting drive in New Mexico and calculated that as missionaries the friars would be more understanding and accommodating of the necessities involved in settling the lands over which he had designs.

The Franciscans seemed quite willing to accept appointments in what had generally been acknowledged as Jesuit territory. Five of them showed up on the Río Sonora in 1644 (Franciscans had already been present on the eastern reaches of the Río Bavispe, probably since 1636)[27] and quickly established a Franciscan missionary presence on all four of the Opatería's rivers—the western Bavispe, the Moctezuma, the Sonora, and the San Miguel. Perea's bold move in thrusting Franciscans directly into the heart of Jesuit territory set off a territorial conflict between the Brown Robes and the Black Robes that gave rise to unpriestly antagonisms until an accord was reached in Arizpe in 1651 and the Franciscans retreated eastward.[28]

Pedro took sick in 1644, perhaps suffering from wounds or from a stroke he experienced as a result of a rash attack he mounted against the Pimans of Magdalena, in which his forces were roundly defeated.[29] He returned to

Tuape to recuperate, appeared to be improving, but then died suddenly in October 1645, apparently from the same wounds or stroke.[30] He may have expired in Banámichi, and, according to a *relación* of the events of the time, he was honored in death far more than in life.[31] Even though the Jesuits provided Pedro with a solemn and dignified burial, they do not appear to have shed many tears at his demise. The Crown had already ceded Sonora to them, and without Pedro de Perea's sponsorship the Franciscans had no one to explain or defend their presence in the province. Pedro's expansionist dreams ended unrealized with his death, and while the name *Nueva Andalucía* appears occasionally in documents (including the documents in the appendix),[32] it barely took hold officially. (Father Pedro de Pantoja was briefly named *padre visitador* to Nueva Andalucía in 1644.[33]) And though his men remained and multiplied in the region, he never completed construction and population of his required villa.

As the narratives in the documents reveal, Pedro de Perea appropriated lands around Tuape for himself, his family, his retinue of servants and slaves, and his men but was stymied by legal requirements for demonstrating that the property was his. He became furious when Indians rejected his offer to purchase their lands outright, but, controlling his violent urges, he (according to them and their priest) offered them sacks of grain, coarse cloth, trinkets, and crude tools in return for permission to lease the best agricultural lands and springs around Tuape. Unstated in these negotiations was the threat of military action should they refuse. Pedro had a force of twenty or so soldiers and settlers who possessed arms and horses, as the Indians were well aware.

Once the Spaniards occupied the most desirable lands, they fenced off natural artesian wells, all the while allowing their cattle to run free. They ran a canal from the springs directly to Pedro's new house, apparently for his family's convenience and to water an orchard he planted outside his door. (Europeans appear to have viewed the presence of orchards with trees of European origin—especially quinces and pomegranates—as a clear symbol of conquest.) Much to the consternation and anger of the Indians, the loss of free-flowing irrigation water they had formerly diverted from the springs dried up their crops, while the Spaniards' free-range livestock destroyed many corn and bean fields. (A single cow can destroy an entire milpa [cornfield] in only a few minutes.) The Spaniards' new dams, canals, and cows undermined the Natives' ability to derive their sustenance from the soil.[34]

Even in Pedro's absence, his men had been active at prospecting, and by

1640 he or they had announced the first discoveries of silver in Sonora. By the mid-1640s, they had founded two important mines in the rough hill country between the Río San Miguel and the Río Sonora. The strikes were large enough that the Crown recognized the Real de Santiago in 1647 and the Real de San Pedro de los Reyes somewhat later. Miners abandoned both sites after a few years of production, but in 1649 the Real de Santiago had become the political center of Sonora and the headquarters of Captain Simón Lazo de la Vega, alcalde mayor of Sonora. By the 1650s the governmental center had shifted to nearby San Pedro de los Reyes, where it remained for at least six years. By 1657 the capital had moved east to the more important strike and the new real at San Juan Bautista in the mountains southwest of Cumpas, on the Río Moctezuma.[35] Even with the decline of the mines near Tuape, Pedro's wife, María de Ibarra, as well as her offspring and the men who colonized Sonora with Pedro remained in the region and came to form the earliest elements of Sonoran colonial society.

After perhaps two years at his (apparently temporary) residence in Tuape, Perea may have moved his family east to the vicinity of Banámichi on the Río Sonora. Attempting to fulfill his orders from the governor, he appears to have begun construction on an ersatz fort at a location on the Río Sonora near Banámichi, where he remained until he took sick in 1644. Whether or not María de Ibarra moved to the Río Sonora to be with her husband, and whether she accompanied him back to Nombre de Diós for his hoped-for convalescence is not clear, nor are her whereabouts after his death.[36] The narrative in the documents makes it appear as though she continued to live in Tuape until her death and never abandoned the place. As of 1658, Perea's son Pedro Junior was still in residence there.

The decision to relocate from Tuape to the Río Sonora makes sense, but Perea's original choice of Tuape is puzzling—unless, that is, he was following the recommendations of the Jesuits. The present site of Tuape, while quite scenic, lies some distance from any farmable acreage. Except for a few quite limited terraces in the floodplain of the Río San Miguel, the land is rolling to mountainous. What appears to have made the site desirable was the presence of one or more *manantiales*, or artesian water sources. The descriptions of water sources in the following narrative are vague. The manantial may have been a *nacimiento*, a spring that is located in the riverbed itself (and that often disappears in the sands of the channel during the dry season), or it could have been a spring in a side drainage, which would have made it easier to control for irrigation. The latter was probably the case. At any rate, the manantial, which lay less than a league to the north of Tuape, was presumably reliable and thus permitted permanent irrigation of bean and cornfields, even in years when summer rains failed. Such a water source would constitute the sole basis for permanent residence in the area. Annual rainfall in the San Miguel drainage is usually insufficient for reliable crop production. In years of heavy summer rainfall, one rainfall-fed crop is possible, but the timing of the rain is critical: if the arrival of the rains is delayed from the normal onset, which is the first week in July, until late July or early August, the corn crop may have insufficient time to mature before the fall drought and the arrival of late fall frosts. In some years the rains fail partially or entirely. Still, the Indians of the region practiced plantings by both means—*de aguas* (irrigated) and *de verano* (rain fed)—and thus produced a reliable harvest.

Jesuits and Indians on the Río San Miguel

As the documents explain, when the Jesuit Lorenzo de Cárdenas arrived in the San Miguel Valley, he appears to have ordered the Indians to drain cienegas and swamps in the area and to plant wheat in the former marshland. The destruction of the wetlands may have caused the springs to dry up, thus endangering the Indians' crops, results that the Indians (or the priest) appear to have blamed on Pedro de Perea and his men, perhaps unjustly. The missionaries demanded their wheat, dismissing corn as an inferior grain, just as the Indians probably wondered why the priests put them through so much work to raise an alien grain with yields significantly lower (as little as one-fifth that of corn) than harvests from milpas and that required more intense labor and irrigation.[37]

Father Cárdenas also revealed that Jesuits created missions with vague boundaries, such as the lands he mentions near Banachari, a site perhaps located well to the southeast. (Cárdenas recalls that it lay a "long league" downstream from Tuape, in other words, more than four kilometers.) Banachari was included within the mission of Mátape but lay at some distance, perhaps the same as a contemporary ranch by that name southeast of Ures, some fifteen kilometers north of Mátape. The priest oversaw planting wheat there, which could only mean that the mission claimed jurisdiction over the land. When settlers allowed their cattle to graze free on mission lands, they were intruding on what the Jesuits viewed as *their* property. How the Black Robes kept their cattle (which they raised in considerable numbers) in check is not apparent. Father Marras, Cárdenas's successor at Mátape, did train many Eudeves to be cowboys, however, and priests may have controlled the herds by ordering the Indians to watch them constantly and to maintain them well away from crops.[38]

Pedro de Perea appropriated the best farmlands at Tuape and a nearby *ranchería* (now disappeared) called Uparo (or Úparo). As a result, the Natives were no longer able to farm. Rather than accept starvation, they migrated, apparently en masse, to the prosperous but distant mission at Mátape or to some lands under the mission's jurisdiction, at least for the growing season. There, the Jesuit mission priest Daniel Ángelo Marras (referred to as "Daniel Ángelo" in the narrative)[39] or his predecessor, perhaps Padre Cárdenas himself, provided them with land and even some water for irrigation both there and at the intermediate location of Banachari. The Tuapeños proved themselves successful farmers, drawing the admiration and envy of many local Indian farmers. Still, at least some of the Tuapeños returned to Tuape each year to plant corn during the rainy season in side canyons and valleys that lay beyond the choice lands that Pedro de Perea had appropriated and that did not require irrigation. Some of the Indians may have chosen to live at Tuape in the off-season (winter months). They hauled their harvest of corn and beans back and forth with them between Mátape and Tuape with what must have been enormous physical effort.

The Tuapeños' choice of emigration to Mátape, over one hundred kilometers distant from Tuape, is puzzling. Several missions on the Río Sonora lay within fifty kilometers and undoubtedly offered arable land for farming and, equally important, mountains for hunting and gathering. The narrative makes no mention of additional factors involved in the relocation, but the Indians of Mátape spoke the Eudeve language, not Teguima, the language of the missions on the Río Sonora, and the comfort of speaking with people in one's own language would have been most appealing to the Tuapeños.[40] Spaniards later lumped Eudeve and Teguima under the general linguistic classification of Ópata, but they were different languages, for the most part mutually unintelligible.[41] For whatever reasons, the Eudeves of Tuape must have found living among the Eudeves of distant Mátape preferable to life among the Teguimas of the Río Sonora. The possibility also remains that the priests ordered the Indians to move, with the threat of punitive action if they refused. The Laws of the Indies mandated the reduction or congregation of Indians into mission communities, and punishment awaited those who resisted or preferred to continue living beyond the reach of the priests.[42]

A further possibility is that the mission lands of Mátape were vast and the Tuapeños were allocated lands within the mission but at a point closer to Tuape than to Mátape itself.

In the complaint outlined in the narrative, the Natives of Tuape, now residing in Mátape Mission, demanded the restitution of the lands they formerly inhabited. Their principal point of contention was that they had agreed with Captain Pedro de Perea that he could use their lands for a short time in return for a payment of trinkets and an amount of corn and beans equal to what they would lose by ceding to him the use of the lands. The Indians were adamant, however, that the agreement was temporary. Pedro had demanded initially that the Indians sell him the land, but such transactions were unknown among Indians and one especially brave Native had demurred. He informed Pedro that although he himself was old, he had children and grandchildren who would need the land. An angry Perea then offered food as rent and a few trinkets to sweeten the deal. And, according to several witnesses, he assured them that Nombre de Diós would be his temporary home only. His permanent residence would be on the Río Sonora; hence he would require the lands for two years only. After that he would not attempt to control lands within two leagues (probably about eight kilometers) of Tuape or Uparo.

In 1652, perhaps fifteen years after Perea had appropriated the Tuape lands and seven or eight years after his death, the Indians reminded the settlers at Tuape, notably Pedro's widow, daughter, son, and son-in-law, and perhaps other heirs and settlers, of the agreement. Perea's widow, María de Ibarra, acknowledged that Pedro had agreed to those terms. She promised to turn the land back over to the Indians and remove all livestock, but only at the end of an additional two-year period beginning in 1652, not in 1637 or thereabouts, when Pedro had first seized the land. Pedro had perhaps moved his wife and family east to Banámichi, but at least some of his heirs, and maybe even María herself, chose to remain at Tuape or returned there when Pedro was dying. Especially active in the proceedings were Pedro's son Pedro Junior and his son-in-law, Captain Juan Munguía de Villela, who appear to have viewed Tuape as their private fiefdom and refused to recognize the two-year limitation, even though María de Ibarra, their mother and mother-in-law, had agreed to it.

By 1658, the time of the final documents in the folio translated in the appendix, at least sixteen years, perhaps as many as twenty-one, have transpired since the arrival of Pedro de Perea at Tuape. Cattle have significantly multiplied and the Indians are cut off from the water they depend on for irrigation. Through several spokesmen, the Tuapeños have requested the magistrate (and future alcalde mayor) Francisco Coto to enforce the original agreement and expel the Spaniards from Tuape. A decade earlier, Indians had enlisted Father Cárdenas as an advocate. Cárdenas had arrived at Batuc in 1629 and had served as the first resident priest in Sonora. In addition, he had served at various missions in Sonora and by all accounts was intimately familiar with the geography of the area and with the circumstances under which Pedro de Perea and his entourage came to occupy Tuape.

Father Cárdenas seemed more than willing to verify the legitimacy of the Indians' claim. Throughout his testimony one can detect Jesuit distaste for Perea and his estate. The priest, for example, questioned why Pedro would have given the name Nombre de Diós to a hacienda he knew to be only rented from its rightful owners. He underscored the way the settlers trampled Indian crops and allowed their cattle to lay waste to milpas. He emphasized the legitimacy of the Indians' claim to Tuape, suggesting that their residence at Mátape constituted an exile forced upon them by the machinations of Pedro de Perea. Father Cárdenas apparently died a year before the final proceedings reflected in the documents. However, the document he signed, signifying the truth of his deposition, was dated July 1647, more than ten years prior to the final disposition of the case and the filing of the present document. His deposition apparently took place in Movas, a Pima Bajo town on the Río Chico, about 140 kilometers southeast of Mátape. Clearly, Father Cárdenas's testimony relied heavily on impressions and memories from several years earlier, describing as he did the human and natural landscape around Tuape prior to the arrival of the Spaniards. The fact that the Indians sought his testimony establishes that they were actively pursuing the return of their lands by that time and were willing to travel to Movas to obtain his testimony, but implicit in his testimony are the Jesuits' support and even the promotion of the Indians' campaign for justice.

After the death of Padre Cárdenas, the padre provincial (Jesuit supervisor) designated Father Daniel Ángelo Marras to replace him as Jesuit advocate for the Indians. In addition, the magistrate Francisco Coto, apparently with the consent of the Indians, appointed one Juan Franco Maldonado, of unknown origin, but known to be one of Coto's lieutenants, to be the Indians' legal advocate.[43] On paper, at least, Maldonado delivered a spirited case for the Indians. What transpired behind the scenes or whether his activities were all for show is, of course, not possible to determine. Navarro García describes him as "a good person, very devout, and who prays a good deal, a simple and uncomplicated man who never diverges one iota from the party line of the Company of Jesus... and says what Father Daniel Angelo Marras tells him to."[44] Franco Maldonado operated a mercantile shop in Mátape, an enterprise that relied entirely upon the approval and permission of the resident Jesuit priest. A careful reading of the documents in the context of Sonora in the 1650s suggests that Franco Maldonado, however eloquent his defense of the Tuapeños, was acting as a proxy for the Jesuits and their economic interests.

Legal and Economic Complications for the Indians

In defending themselves against the petition, Pedro's heirs, notably his son Pedro Junior, his son-in-law, Captain Juan Munguía de Villela, and his daughter Josefa, seem to have claimed that the lands where Spaniards had settled were unoccupied at the time of their arrival. (Their pleadings have not turned up in the Parral archives.) According to them, the Indians had abandoned (or never used) the fields and had thus turned them into *terrenos baldíos* (unoccupied lands), which, under Spanish law, were up for grabs. Father Cárdenas, however, contests their claim. He had routinely visited parishes in the region prior to Perea's arrival and recounts seeing numerous milpas and frijolares that the Indians regularly maintained, extending from the Río San Miguel across the crest of the intervening mountains to the east, well into the drainages of the Río Sonora, and to the west as well. For at least six years prior to the Spaniards' appropriation of the lands, the Indians had been farming these marginal plots. The same fields, along with those nearer to Tuape and in valleys and canyons to the west of the Río San Miguel, were now abandoned due to the Spaniards' appropriation of land and water. Father Cárdenas reiterates the suffering the Tuapeños experienced when they were no longer able to farm and when their supplies of firewood were exhausted due to the presence of Pedro de Perea's family, servants, slaves, livestock, and the accompanying settlers. In vain they struggled to plant their corn along with some wheat for the mission priests. Their efforts were to no avail, as irrigation water was diverted for the Spaniards' use, and livestock invaded the milpas and fields and destroyed their crops. Pedro de Perea and other settlers ordered cowboys to watch the cattle herds, but their best efforts came to naught. The cattle always sneaked into the fields and undid the work of the farmers. Now, Father Cárdenas asserted, even though the Tuapeños had become successful farmers in Mátape, they longed for their ancestral lands and had a perfect right to have them returned to them free of others' cattle.

We must bear in mind that only a smattering of Spaniards had visited the Río San Miguel. The mission of Mátape was only founded in 1629 and the Río San Miguel lay well to the uncharted northwest, so it is doubtful that any of the Indians, whose ethnic identity is not mentioned in the narrative but who were probably Eudeves, spoke Spanish. In that case, Native testimony had to be translated for the scribe through an interpreter. While it is not clear that Padre Cárdenas spoke the Eudeve language, Jesuits of that day were expected to gain fluency in the language of their charges, so we can assume that he had some degree of facility in the language, though it may have been minimal.[45]

Whoever the authorities were who stepped forward to assist the Indians in filing their petition, they had to have been aware that Pedro de Perea, in accepting the office of alcalde mayor, was bound by specific duties and subject to severe penalties for violating his contract. He was also under scrutiny by royal authorities. The Laws of the Indies ordered conquistadores and their like to respect Indians' property and women and avoid abusing them physically.[46] So, instead of simply seizing the Tuape lands for his use, Pedro was forced to offer goods in return for leasing the lands and to limit his tenure to two years. He probably calculated that once he had abandoned the homestead around Tuape and moved on to the Río Sonora, he would have washed his hands of any further complications wreaked by other Spaniards, including his heirs, who might choose to hang on to the hacienda. On the other hand, the priests, also knowledgeable of the Crown's policy toward Indians, probably noted several violations of regulations and urged the Indians on, guiding them through the process of filing a *demanda*, a legal challenge to the presence of the Spaniards. The priests would have relished their role as advocates for the Indians out of sympathy with the Tuapeños' plight, but they also would almost certainly have recalled Pedro's earlier abuse of the Company (as the Jesuits were sometimes known) and his importation of the Franciscans as replacements, and they might have hoped to gain some degree of revenge by helping to dislodge Pedro's heirs from lands they were wrongfully occupying. In addition, as priests, they must have been aware of numerous gentile Indians on the Río San Miguel and with evangelists' zeal envisioned establishing missions there in the near future. The presence of *colono* Spaniards in the area would make their missionizing more difficult, but better to have them there than in the more heavily populated Río Sonora. As far as the Jesuits were concerned, the fewer non-Jesuit outsiders in the region, the better.

Even more important, the Jesuits were gradually becoming an economic force in the region. By controlling the regional economy through the marketing of commodities, they could control the development of Sonora and ensure that the region could become a Jesuit empire. Under the regime of Daniel Ángelo Marras, this nearly became a reality. During Padre Marras's watch, and well into the 1670s, Mátape became Sonora's leading commercial center, marketing grains and other foodstuffs, hides, meat, tallow, and cloth. The mission also owned mines and smelters worked by African slaves.[47]

In his testimony, Father Cárdenas revealed his staunch adherence to the Company of Jesus and its role in pacifying the Indians of northwestern New Spain. While he clearly argued for the legitimacy of the Indians' claim to Tuape, he took pains to point out that the Indians needed the technology and industry of the Jesuits merely to survive. It was their priest (apparently Cárdenas himself) who ordered swamps and ponds to be drained and canals and ditches to be constructed in order to increase agricultural production. Prior to the arrival of the Jesuits, he implied, the Indians were primitive, unsophisticated farmers languishing in the absence of European technology. It turns out, however, that much of that increased production went to planting wheat and orchard trees for the enjoyment of Europeans.[48]

The Indians' case faced another huge impediment: Juan de Munguía, son-in-law of Pedro de Perea and a principal defendant in the case, had served as alcalde mayor, the chief judge and authority for Sonora, in 1652 and 1653. He was succeeded by Francisco Coto, with perhaps one alcalde intervening. Whether or not the succession was friendly or hostile would make a huge difference in the lawsuit's outcome. Alcaldes investigated the actions of their immediate predecessors and submitted a formal *residencia*, or evaluation of the term of office, based upon extensive reviews of finances and interviews.[49] From time to time they pronounced their predecessors guilty of egregious violations. Successors also appear at times to have had some personal grudges to settle with previous alcaldes. All Spaniards in the region would have known each other. Nearly all may have been related through marriage as well. In the case of Pedro de Perea, however, it would have been common knowledge that he had been booted from office and ordered out of the province, and only his death saved him from great embarrassment or a tense confrontation with his superiors in Parral and Mexico City. Former alcaldes routinely bribed their successors to gain better grades, but Pedro was dead and most dead men offer no bribes. For Juan de Munguía, revealing unsavory information against one who had fallen into disfavor with the Crown, even his ex-father-in-law, might have gained points.

By the time of the final determination in Parral, María de Ibarra had died and willed her estate to her daughter Josefa de Ibarra, who apparently vigorously defends her claim to ownership of Nombre de Diós. Why María chose to bestow her goods on Josefa, rather than on her sons, Pedro Junior and Tomás de Perea, and her other daughter, Andrea de Ibarra, is not made clear, but María must have been a resentful individual indeed to have reneged on her agreement with the Indians and to have cut her other children out of her will. She resented Pedro de Perea's dissipation of her dowry, as we learn in the documents, and may have disliked her son-in-law, Juan de Munguía, as well. She considered Pedro's waste of her goods disrespectful and irresponsible—he hocked her jewels to raise money for his escapades.

The documents are lengthy and repetitive and extend over a decade, so I have chosen to present roughly half of the pages in the folio in the appendix. The scribe (equivalent to a notary public) from San Pedro de los Reyes, Ignacio de Barraiersa, who recorded much of the first half of the folio, had decent handwriting. In keeping with customary Spanish writing, however, he did not incorporate punctuation into his transcriptions. The beginning of one sentence and the end of the previous one are usually only implied and only context can help establish where one thought ends and the next begins. Nor are thoughts organized into paragraphs. The reader must often guess where one thought ends and a completely different one begins. The written text often consists of one sentence many pages long. In the translated narrative, periods are of my insertion and are not found in the original document.

Although the folio dates from 1658, many of the documents are not the originals. In some cases they are a copy transcribed over the years from earlier written testimony, but the copying apparently was always carried out in the presence of witnesses willing to verify the accuracy of the reproductions. The original scribe recorded the testimony of several different witnesses from a variety of locations in Sonora, including Parral in Chihuahua, the mine at Real San Pedro de los Reyes, Mátape, Movas (on the Río Chico, a tributary of the lower Río Yaqui that enters the Yaqui at Ónavas), and Tónichi, a (probable) Eudeve village on the east bank of the Río Yaqui some twenty kilometers upstream from Ónavas. We can only assume that the scribe either traveled to these distant locations and gathered testimony as part of the ongoing investigation and then made a single copy for Francisco Coto's review, or else he gathered the material and made copies for presentation to the provincial governor in Parral. The change in the geographical setting of the deposition is not reflected by a concomitant change of sentence, paragraph, paper, ink, or handwriting in the document. The testimony ranges over eleven years, from 1647 to 1658; the period covered is from roughly 1637 to 1658.

The documents provide an intriguing insight into the geography of the Tuape region. Natives quite naturally set boundaries by landmarks, especially prominent hills, mountains, arroyos, and springs, but locaters in this document also include a grove of cottonwoods, a mesquite bosque, a palm grove, a thick growth of reed grass, and a hot spring, all of which Padre Cárdenas took pains to enumerate. Unfortunately for us, the topographical landmarks have undergone name changes and the groves and stands of trees, bosques, thickets, and bushes have long since been eradicated or have otherwise vanished. Still, the witnesses' familiarity with these landmarks is critically important in establishing their aboriginal ownership of the lands in question.

Three factors, then, seem to be central to the Indians' apparently successful argument: the Tuapeños have a continuous history of planting corn and beans that extends over many generations; they possess an intimate geographical familiarity with the lands in question, a proof of their long possession of the land; and a variety of witnesses agree that Pedro de Perea obtained a contract with them for two years or for at most a temporary use of their land, and when he moved to the Río Sonora, he abandoned any claims to the Tuape estate. The Indians' court-appointed lawyer, Juan Franco Maldonado, further argues that any agreement was null and void because Pedro de Perea never fulfilled the requirements stipulated by the Crown for establishing a villa and thus had no authority to claim the lands at Tuape or anywhere else under his grant from the governor or viceroy. His license to colonize Sonora was a contract. Contracts bestowed privileges but contained correlative responsibilities, and Pedro had failed to live up to the responsibilities, thus voiding the contract.[50] Maldonado's argument was a strong one.

Also noteworthy is the absence of testimony from Indians themselves. Most documents from northern New Spain during the colonial period reflect the voices of only Spaniards and other Europeans. The Indians themselves seem invisible or nondescript background players. A careful reading of the document, however, reveals that it is they who brought the action against Pedro de Perea's estate (though urged on by the Jesuits); they who educated

Padre Lorenzo Cárdenas in the history and geography of the Tuape region and persevered in pushing their claims for more than a decade. Hardly passive, hand-wringing bystanders, they stubbornly persisted in their demand for justice and the restitution of their traditional lands. They stoically made the arduous journey to distant Parral in pursuit of their patrimony. The depth of the Jesuits' intervention is, of course, an object of speculation.

Although Francisco Coto, the government magistrate, possessed unequivocal arguments for finding in favor of the Tuapeños, he chose rather to wash his hands of the matter and forward the case to the provincial governor in Parral. The details of the final decision of Governor Enrique Dávila y Pacheco have not emerged in the documentary record and we have no reason to believe that the governor ultimately found in favor of the Tuapeños, for we have no record of an *auto*, or court finding. Instead, the court and the lawyers brought pressure on Pedro Junior, Josefa de Ibarra, and Juan de Munguía to agree to a final *concordia* ceding the lands back to the Indians and to agree to remove their cattle. Furthermore, they agreed to leave the house and other buildings at the headquarters of Nombre de Diós to the Indians, asking only that the Indians help them construct new buildings at a different (undisclosed) location, to which the Indians heartily agreed. The Perea heirs caved in, according to their words, because legal costs were high, the case had dragged on too long, and they hoped to achieve a friendly compromise with the Indians. In reality, the Pereas had no defense, as several officials reminded them. Better to agree to a noble-sounding concordia than to suffer the indignity of a written court order. The defendants and the courts had strung the case out for the better part of two decades and something had to give.

Whether or not Captain Pedro de Perea's heirs actually fulfilled the provisions of the new concordia is not clear, especially since it was not accompanied by a formal court decree. The continuous history of the settlement, however, suggests that the displaced Tuapeños returned and in one way or another reclaimed their ancestral lands after a prolonged exile. Nicolas de La Fora, an engineer and inspector, visited Tuape in 1766 and referred to it as a "little pueblo of Indians" whose residents at the time were suffering from a powerful epidemic of typhus.[51] In 1818 the indigenous people of Tuape (presumably Opatans) accused those of Opodepe of treason, claiming that they were amassing bows and arrows to supply an uprising. Opodepans responded that they were merely helping their *protector* (benefactor and, it turns out, exploiter) Juan Gándara prepare to defend his estate against

Seri attacks. The real dispute was over which pueblo controlled the irrigated lands of Meresichi, which Gándara coveted for his own ends. The protector of Indians ruled in Opodepe's favor, but the ruling came to nothing since the office was abolished following independence. The conflict demonstrates that Tuape was a viable town of (apparently) Ópatas who claimed the lands had been theirs since time immemorial. This lends further credibility to the notion that Tuapeños in fact reoccupied their lands after 1658 and the concordia (agreement) with Pedro de Perea Jr.[52]

Finally, in 1902, nearly two and a half centuries after the concordia, anthropologist Aleš Hrdlička made a brief ethnographic study of Tuape and found that most of the indigenous residents still spoke the "Ópata" language.[53] Had the legal complaint filed by the Tuapeños in the 1640s been completely unsuccessful, it is doubtful that Tuape would have perpetuated its indigenous tradition.

And so the Tuapeños' arguments for restitution of their lands appear to have been successful. As the documents demonstrate, nearly two decades passed before they obtained a ruling on whether they could reclaim what was rightfully theirs, and even then no formal ruling emerged, no court document officially finding in favor of the Indians and against the Perea family. The Spanish courts and litigants for the defense dragged the case out as long as they were able. Pedro de Perea founded his initial colony in Tuape somewhat before 1640, and the proceedings presented here were not completed until 1658.

In the end, we must conclude that the Spanish justice system forged a just solution to the conflict. Still, even in the face of overwhelming proof of gross injustice, the court attempted to nudge the Spaniards rather than rule against them. This served to deflect an official record wherein a small band of Indians would be revealed as victorious over a powerful contingent of Spaniards. In the documents available to us, no one contests the Indians' petition. No one denies that the Spaniards broke promises and treated the Indians' land claims with disrespect. The political pressure exerted behind the scenes on and by the magistrates was sufficient to goad the Perea family into signing a third concordia, but in the larger picture it seems to me that the same pressure turned out be too overwhelming to permit the court to issue a formal finding that would allow "illiterate savages" to triumph over loyal Catholics and men born subjects of the king. Added to the pressure was undoubtedly the Spanish fondness for litigation, or as Nancy Farriss described the tactic, "whenever the case appears to be going in favor of the other party, obstruct the proceedings."⁵⁴ To whatever extent this deep-seated tendency toward litigiousness prolonged the proceedings, in the end the Indians seem to have gotten back their land. Quite possibly, the Jesuits could manipulate the system just as well as colonial Spaniards.

In the meantime, Pedro de Perea's family and his associated settlers began the settlement of Sonora in the Río Sonora Valley. The Spaniards present in northwest Mexico during the 1640s and 1650s were principally miners or merchants dependent upon mining. The gold and silver strikes from mines founded in the 1640s at Santiago and San Pedro de los Reyes had been exhausted by the mid-1650s. However, by 1657 a major strike to the east led to the founding of San Juan Bautista, which then became the regional capital of Sonora.⁵⁵

As miners, the settlers had the ear of the Crown, which claimed one-fifth of all precious metals. Other Spaniards learned of the mines and arrived in central Sonora in increasing numbers. They brought additional livestock, claimed "unclaimed" lands, and forcibly recruited Indians to labor in the mines. While no records have come to light detailing the settlers' claims and homesteads, they became farmers, ranchers, and miners, all with increasingly large estates made up of lands formerly belonging to Indians. It seems safe to assume that any productive agricultural land they controlled was obtained at the expense of Indians. From the Indians' standpoint, the mines proved a most destabilizing institution.

The Jesuits discovered to their dismay that mines proved to be a powerful counterforce to their evangelization efforts as well. Jesuits themselves had introduced cattle, claiming they would be a boon to the Indians, but appear to have controlled their flocks and taught the Indians to be cowboys and keep watch over the herds. Settlers invariably brought their livestock with them and gave them free range. They loosed their cattle onto Indian lands, thus unleashing an ecological firestorm the Indians and the priests had no tools to counter, as they point out in the narrative. Furthermore, the mine workers who flocked to the area from elsewhere were often a morally loose bunch with low regard for the clergy, the missions, and religion in general. At the same time, the arrival of entrepreneurial miners and their mining claims stimulated the demand for private property among new arrivals, who often brought with them what we might call the "American Dream"—the hope of acquiring a landed estate or the title of hidalgo.⁵⁶ Spaniards thus imposed the notion of land as a commodity to be bought and sold, an idea contrary to Native land tenure and to the communitarian ideals of the Jesuit missions. The clash between these desperately competing ideologies would only be settled to the detriment of the Indians.

In spite of mining's dismal influence, the Jesuits were of two minds concerning the industry. They clearly profited from sales of grain, cloth, beef, tallow, and hides to the mines and became notorious for undercutting the prices charged by traveling merchants. In this way the missions, especially that of Mátape, accumulated profits and sent shipments of silver off to Mexico City.[57] On the other hand, the mines were magnets to a class of people generally unwelcome within the cloistered confines of the missions. The priests loathed them and deplored their negative influence.

Finally, the Indians suffered from the depredations of epidemic diseases, at least some of which can be attributed to the working conditions at the mines and to so many people living in close proximity in unsanitary conditions. Decimation of their numbers as a result of waves of pathogens left Indians far more vulnerable to Spanish expansionism and left the priests with dramatically fewer converts than they had anticipated. While the mortality of Native populations in the Opatería was vast, the losses were seldom clearly spelled out in the seventeenth century and do not receive prominent consideration in extant documents from that period. Daniel Reff estimates that in the first two centuries after the first contact with Europeans, the aboriginal population of the Opatería (the land of the Ópatas, including both Mátape and Tuape) fell from about sixty thousand to just over six thousand, with the most dramatic declines occurring during the first century of occupation.[58]

From Tuape, Pedro de Perea's men spread out, mostly to the east and north, where the richest mines and the most fertile and well-watered agricultural land lay, and not to the west, where the desert becomes drier and hotter and lacking in reliable water sources for irrigation. Mineralization is also spottier west of the Río San Miguel. By the time the Tuapeños filed their complaint, the mine at Santiago, to the east of Tuape, had already become home to numerous Spaniards, so many that the magistrate and alcalde mayor Simón Lazo de la Vega was able to fashion an effective militia from the settlers. These he mobilized into a fighting force. With the recruitment of several hundred Indian allies, he easily suppressed a 1648 rebellion of peoples to the north of Arizpe who were actively resisting the evangelizing of Jesuits, notably the Jesuit priest Gerónimo de la Canal[59] (see chapter 2).

Included among Lazo de la Vega's Spanish militia was Juan de Oliva, one of Pedro de Perea's original recruits from New Mexico, also mentioned as an exemplary Spaniard in the document (see appendix). Perea left Oliva in charge of constructing his new house in Tuape while he returned to Basiroa to transport his family and estate northward. Under Juan de Oliva's direction, the house was finished in three months. By the time of the 1648 rebellion, Oliva had apparently become a successful rancher, combining the careers of cattleman, miner, and soldier. He and other Spaniards were prepared to put down any Indian rebellion, especially those opposing the entradas of the Spaniards.[60] By all appearances, Oliva had become a permanent resident of the valley of the Río Sonora, along with at least forty additional settlers who also had become militiamen. These frontiersmen were built of stern stuff and were resolved to brook no insolence from Indians.

Pedro's Legacy

Pedro de Perea did not survive to see the fulfillment of the personal fiefdom he hoped to forge out of a territory previously inhabited only by Indians. The orders from Mexico City brought by Father Gerónimo de la Canal included a specific order that Pedro and all his family be expelled from Sonora.[61] With his death, however, official displeasure with Pedro diminished and those instructions were never followed. Following the signing of the third (and apparently final) Tuape concordia, however, Pedro's son-in-law, Juan de Munguía de Villela, appears to have been ordered out of the Río San Miguel. Even so, he must have done well in the Río Sonora, where his descendents propagated and flourished and Munguía himself became alcalde mayor of Sonora. Munguía weathered the review of his period of service and went on to found the town of Santa Cruz near the Sonora and Arizona border.[62] One hundred years later, the Indian population of the Río Sonora had drastically decreased, while the number of vecinos (settlers of Spanish origin) had vastly increased. Shortly thereafter, vecinos would outnumber Indians.[63] The stage was set for the gradual privatization of much of the land of eastern Sonora and the disappearance of the Opatan peoples.

I suggest that the dispute over control of the lands at Tuape reflects the more basic dispute between Jesuits and settlers over communal, church-controlled lands versus private property. To that extent, the Jesuits were using the Indians to achieve their corporate agenda. The priests' eagerness to endorse the Indians' petition, which they in all probability originated, may well reflect the Jesuits' megalomania and their justifiable concern that settlers might undermine their control of the region.

The Tuape dispute was but one of many that occurred in the Northwest.

Technically, all lands there were owned by indigenous groups or the king of Spain, and in the absence of established procedures, no one else could claim title to them. The Jesuits in their missionizing paid little heed to the legal status of the lands and did not bother with surveys. Since the Crown had authorized the Order to missionize the Northwest, the clerics proceeded aggressively in attaching boundaries as broadly as possible to their missions, assuming their right to assimilate lands to their jurisdictions that had traditionally been part of indigenous communities, and expanding at will the boundaries of the missions to engulf all potentially valuable real estate and everything in between.[64] Father Cárdenas seems to have been involved in such expansion of boundaries when he oversaw the draining of swamps at Tuape and Banachari, as he recalls in the documents. He felt free to order the Indians to plant wheat on land that "belonged to no one."

At the same time, settlers seemed to have had no qualms about homesteading when and where they pleased and viewed Indian occupation as a nuisance and the Jesuits as an impediment to economic development. They frequently complained that the Jesuits were too powerful, that they tied up the best agricultural land for themselves, and that they used the Indians as personal slaves. Francisco Coto, alcalde mayor in 1660, complained that "in Sonora the only king was the Jesuits."[65] At the same time, however, settlers, especially miners, could hardly survive without provisions of food, fiber, hides, and tallow from the Jesuit stores, a fact the Jesuits, especially Father Marras of Mátape, took great pains to emphasize. Whenever the Jesuits saw the settlers becoming too vocal in protesting the Jesuits' power, they would threaten to cut off their supplies. Settlers, though they benefited from the low prices the priests charged, came to resent the priests' dominance of local trade, especially given their observation that unpaid Indian labor produced most of the commodities sold by the missions.

The settlers often counted among their supporters against the Jesuits the various alcaldes mayores of Sonora, who often had ties to mercantile interests undercut by Jesuit commerce. One of the alcaldes, Gregorio López Dicastillo, dispatched an investigator to enumerate the commercial dealings carried on by the missions. In 1674, based on an investigators' report, Alcalde Dicastillo lodged a formal complaint against the Jesuits with the Audiencia in Guadalajara.

But Dicastillo was not alone. Other conflicts between Indians and settlers and complaints about Jesuits, land holdings, and the rights of Indians also reached royal authorities, and the resulting confusion forced the Crown to propose sending out investigators. By 1674 the Audiencia of Guadalajara found so many land disputes in Sinaloa and Sonora that it ordered José García de Salcedo, a Knight of Santiago, to investigate the situation and "share and divide among Spaniards and Indians the lands that shall seem necessary to each party according to their merits, always giving consideration to providing the natives with all the [lands] they may justly need."[66] The Audiencia hoped also to determine whether both miners and Jesuit missionaries were exploiting Indians and treating them cruelly. Part of their interest was perked by the charges that Dicastillo had filed against the Jesuits. If land allocation proposed by the Audiencia were to take place, it would directly affect the plans of the Jesuits, who still hoped to control all the lands and peoples in their realm.

The intent of the Audiencia seems to have been noble enough but failed to consider the power and designs of the Jesuits. An advisor to the Audiencia pointed out that the Jesuit Order in fact controlled *all* the lands in question and that neither Indians nor settlers exercised real control. Under the Jesuit mission system, no private lands were up for grabs. The Jesuits piously protested that allegation and voiced vehement opposition to the proposed allocation of land, maintaining that they owned no lands whatsoever and that they were in fact protectors of the Indians against the acquisitive settlers. That claim was true, as far as it went. At the same time they launched a vigorous lobbying campaign with the Audiencia. They portrayed themselves as selfless messengers of God's word with no interest in earthly holdings. Padre Daniel Ángelo Marras wrote in a tone of deeply offended indignation that he and the Jesuits were the object of "false and malicious reports" lodged by vicious plotters against "my sacred religion and my person in particular." He labeled the list of charges filed by Alcalde Dicastillo as "infamous libel" and "false slanders."[67] The Jesuits could foresee only mischief arising from such a pointless investigation.

Bowing to Jesuit pressure from many quarters, the Audiencia cancelled the fact-finding mission and scuttled the project to allocate land based on need. As a result, the tension between Indians and settlers was never formally addressed.[68] Such was the influence the Jesuits wielded in the late seventeenth century that they could bring powerful political bodies to their collective knees. Even those settlers bearing mercedes (land grants) from the governor were shunted aside at the whim of the priests. The resentments against the missionaries' high-handed tactics produced a lingering desire for vengeance that persisted through the expulsion of the Black Robes in 1767.

In spite of the Jesuits' success in quashing a land survey, they could not conceal the ever-heightening confrontations surrounding land claims. What the saga of the Tuapeños presents in vivid terms is that Spanish settlement of northwest New Spain, whether by missionaries, farmers, or miners, always involved the displacement of Native peoples to their ultimate detriment. Notions that Spaniards settled empty or unused lands were a distortion of the demographic realities of the pre-Columbian region, as Father Cárdenas takes great pains to emphasize. What he failed to add was that whenever the priests ordered the Indians to cultivate wheat and raise cattle, whenever they forced Indians to labor in mission-owned fields, they were removing potential arable or useful lands from Indian use. The forcible relocation of Indians into reductions—as exemplified in the transference of the Tuape Eudeves to Mátape—did violence to their traditions and their legal ability to maintain aboriginal land claims. It also left them increasingly vulnerable to infection with epidemic diseases. Spaniards, Jesuits and settlers alike, settled Sonora—and everywhere else in New Spain—only through the use of military force and, ultimately, the eviction of Native peoples from their ancestral lands. Certainly the conquest was complex: some indigenous groups (including Opatans) allied themselves with Spaniards in attacking other groups, their ancient foes. Still, with the notable exception of most of Yaqui country, by the end of the seventeenth century settlers could be found in all territory previously controlled by Sonoran indigenous peoples.

The real power players in the Tuape case, then, are the Jesuits and the settlers, and their struggle concerns the strategy for Hispanicizing the Northwest of New Spain. Would it be along the lines of individual property, laissez faire capitalism, and private investment (with an adequate return to the royal treasury), or along the lines of corporatist, highly centralized religious theocracy? The Indians are the ostensible lead actors in the drama of this document. In reality they are but shadow forces, proxy fighters in a larger war. The Jesuits clearly and vigorously supported the Tuapeños in their legal claim against the Perea family. They may have won the Tuape battle, at least as far as we know. But it was clear to settlers that Jesuits coveted dominion over the lands and Native peoples of the Northwest and possessed a grim determination not to be outdone by their secular rivals. The secular forces ultimately triumphed. The Jesuits were ousted in 1767. The Franciscans who replaced them watched, more or less helplessly, as the mission system was dismantled under orders from the Crown. For all practical purposes, by the early nineteenth century, missions no longer existed. All land previously bound up in missions had gone up for grabs.[69]

In the case of Tuape, then, Indians and priests combined to combat the land grabs of settlers. It would be a mistake, however, to view this cooperation as a pattern followed throughout the colonial period. In other cases, the settlers sided with the priests against Indians.

CHAPTER TWO

Father Canal Calls in the Troops

Jesuit Entradas on the Río Sonora

☩ AROUND THE TIME THAT PEDRO DE PEREA WAS ATTEMPTING TO SETTLE AT Tuape, Jesuit missionaries had become active on the upper Río Sonora, in that portion of the basin east and north of the canyon now known as Puerta del Sol. A decade earlier, in the late 1620s, they had founded missions in the southern and eastern reaches of the Opatería. In 1638 they arrived for good at the Río Sonora but had sent advance missionaries well prior to making settlements. It seems likely that they directed Pedro to Tuape on the Río San Miguel, perhaps hoping he would stay away from the Río Sonora.

The advance missionaries faced terrifying prospects. They usually embarked alone or in the company of a small number of supposed Native converts of untested loyalty. The priests spoke only stammering bits of Native speech, facing alien peoples of unknown disposition and distinctly barbarian (from the European viewpoint) customs. The clerics preached a blatantly incomprehensible message that relied on untranslatable metaphors and arcane mysteries delivered with dubious translations laced with irrational threats. From their headquarters or advance stations, the Jesuits armed themselves with faith, reinforced and exhorted each other repeatedly, then shoved their intrepid brethren from the protection of the nest into a perilous sea of gentility.

Their first missionary on the Río Sonora was the Portuguese priest

Bartolomé Castaño, an apparently charismatic preacher and accomplished linguist. Other Jesuits reported that Father Castaño lived in dire poverty, and he seems to have achieved a positive reputation among the Indians of the region, due especially to his use of music. Father Pedro Pantoja, a skilled organizer, joined him in 1639, and the two founded missions at Baviácora, Aconchi, and Banámichi along the Río Sonora.[1] According to Pantoja's claims, they were rapidly successful in establishing the missions, baptizing several thousand Indians, generally pacifying the Natives, and inculcating the Catholic faith. Or so he reported.

By 1640, however, the Jesuits could claim little progress in evangelizing north of Banámichi, in the upper portions of the valley of the Río Sonora. Pedro de Perea may have sent an expeditionary force north around that time, probably to clear the way for the Franciscans he had invited to administer to the Indians, but surely not to assist the evangelizing Jesuits. Whether Padre Castaño met with the Franciscans is a matter of speculation. Apparently he was a bit too strange even for his superiors. He was transferred to work elsewhere, and Father Gerónimo de la Canal was drafted to replace him and carry out the difficult task of overcoming Native resistance to the north of Banámichi and nudging the Franciscans out of territory that the Jesuits viewed as rightfully theirs.

Father Canal was installed on the Río Sonora in the mid-1640s and may have run into conflicts with Franciscans. At any rate, the Jesuits dispatched him in 1643 or thereabouts to Mexico City to protest Pedro de Perea's importation of Franciscan priests into Jesuit territory, a mission that placed him in direct opposition to Pedro and his men. Much to the Jesuits' satisfaction, in 1644 Father Canal was successful in extracting from the viceroy an edict ordering the Franciscans out of Sonora and Pedro de Perea out of the alcalde mayor's office—a triumph for the Jesuits, but perhaps a stumbling point for later relations with Pedro's security forces.

While Father Gerónimo was representing the Jesuits in the capital, he received new orders, directing him to evangelize the northern reaches of the Río Sonora. Departing Mexico City, he arrived at Sinoquipe in June 1646, in the company of several Native assistants, presumably interpreters and guides (to whom he referred as "mis muchachos,"—"my lads").[2] He had been charged with the pacification of Sinoquipe, Arizpe, and the lesser-known village of Cucubazunuchi (or Cucubazunichi).[3]

Father Canal's writings give us no sense of his linguistic abilities. The peoples of the central Río Sonora probably spoke Teguima, an Opatan language. The Hímeris, who lived to the northeast and who may have also lived in northern villages, spoke Pima. The two languages are about as close as Spanish and French, so fluency in one does not bestow fluency in the other. Father Castaño may have been an accomplished polyglot, but we have no indication that Father Canal spoke any language other than Spanish. Our understanding of the language distribution picture for the northern Río Sonora in the mid-seventeenth century is confused. Pima speakers abounded to the north and west, but Sumas, of unknown ethnic and linguistic persuasion, and Chihuahuan peoples such as Janos and Jocomes, also linguistically unidentified, frequented the area as well, especially mining camps, perhaps entire villages. Apaches were beginning to appear in the region at the time. Padre Cristóbal Cañas, mission priest of Aconchi, writing eighty years later, in 1730, noted, "The languages vary considerably, so mixed in villages that in some cases the village priests must understand two [languages in addition to Spanish]. It is notable that when four or five Indians of various tongues get together, they hold forth for some time in their language and everyone understands them."[4] Whether or not any priests were fluent in local languages is difficult to establish, though some claimed the ability.

At the very time that the saga of the Tuape Indians was working its way into the courts, Padre Canal was making his first stop at Sinoquipe, some twenty miles south of Arizpe. He wrote that he began by preaching with a slow delivery, warning the Natives that baptism was necessary to avoid eternal punishment in hell.[5] No one came forth to be baptized, but he continued to preach to no one in particular. And so he continued for twenty-three days without a convert. He was not comforted when the chieftain of the village informed him that the people there "would prefer to die like dogs than be baptized." This was not fertile ground for the evangel. However, Padre Canal did not lose heart from his failure or the harsh response; he found consolation by "considering the diminished capacity of [those] people." Instead of capitulating, he moved his tent north to Arizpe.

His proselyting fared no better at Arizpe. He thundered to the Indians there the inevitability of the tortures and fires of hell facing those who failed to submit to baptism. But after twenty-five days only he and his "muchachos" gathered at his ramada. Faced with such dismal results, he was prepared to depart a complete failure when to his amazement the village governor (chieftain) approached him and informed the priest that on the following day he wished to be baptized and put on a "new body and soul."[6] Thus the chieftain opened the door and Father Canal claimed to have baptized over two hundred Indians. He was greatly assisted, he recalled, by a fortuitous incident. A young man had been hunting birds with a bow and arrow and accidentally hit a woman in the chest with an arrow. When the priest heard the news he rushed to the injured woman's side and beseeched her to accept baptism, which she did, according to his version of the story. He fully expected the woman to die, assuming that the arrow had been poisoned, as was the custom among those people. To his astonishment, the next morning the woman was up and around as if nothing had happened. This incident, Father Canal believed, helped convince the Natives that baptism did not kill the victim, as was widely preached by Native healers.

If Padre Canal thought that the Indian woman's apparent miraculous recovery from the arrow wound in Arizpe would make things easier for him in Cucubazunuchi, he was gravely mistaken. His assistants and interpreters warned him that sorcerers had threatened them with death and intended to kill the priest as well. An Indian woman allowed him to set up his encampment in a ramada, but men came forth and scattered all his religious adornments and trappings. When he summoned up his courage and entered the village, most of the inhabitants hid themselves to prevent him from seeing them. He distributed some trinkets among the children, but this had little effect on the older people. Throughout the long night he heard sounds of his things being stolen and in the morning fully armed men approached his miserable dwelling and warned him to leave. His hopes were slightly elevated when he managed to baptize "four or six" children and two Indians from farther north. However, his despair reached its nadir when one of the local Indians engaged him in a debate. The Indian adversary refused to accept Father Canal's theological pronouncements. They were all lies, the Indian asserted, and it was the priests, not the Indians, who were deceiving people with their falsehoods. It was the Indians' god, not the priests' god, who had created the earth, the rivers, and the valleys, "and he added so many and such things with so much pointedness and in such abundance and with such quickness in the telling, that one had to assume that the Devil himself was dictating the stories and I was astonished to hear such audacity, to hear such arguments, being contrary to the style of the Indians." Father Canal had been defeated in debate by a savage.

This discouraging exchange convinced Father de la Canal that the Indians there in fact intended to kill him, recalling as he did that although the pueblo appeared almost empty, all the while he was aware that hostile and well-armed Indians were hiding in preparation. He made a few feeble attempts at conversions, but his muchachos (who, he noted, were of the same nation as the local people) were uneasy, to say the least, and could recommend to him no location in which to hide. In spite of their words of encouragement and assurances to him that he was bringing the light of the Gospel to the region, they appear to have counseled a retreat at top speed. Heeding their nervous counsel, he hastened south to Sinoquipe, where at least no one had threatened him. There he managed a few baptisms, "although with great difficulty and very few."

Opposition to Evangelization on the Upper Río Sonora

The documents available make no mention of any further proselyting activity in the Río Sonora valley by Father Canal. He later wrote an extensive commentary on missionary activity farther east, mostly on the Río Fronteras and the Río Bavispe, where he reported the widespread practices of cohabitation, tranvestism, and, perhaps, sodomy, noting with satisfaction that stern measures had diminished the popularity of such vices.[7] He makes no apparent references to his missionizing in 1646 in those documents, however.

Still, Padre Canal was not finished trying his luck. By summer of 1649, he had returned and participated in urgent discussions with other priests, Father Ignacio Molarja of Arizpe and padre visitador Pedro Pantoja of Baviácora (who had been promoted to the office of visitador in 1644). The three decided they had reached the limit of Christian patience and tranquility. The Indians north of Arizpe were obdurate and threatening, especially those in the two villages named Cucuribasca and Buchibacuachi (probably present-day Bacoachi).[8] These insolent Natives were not merely resisting conversion but did so with arrogance and open defiance. Padre Pedro Pantoja claimed that Pedro de Perea had previously "pacified" the pueblos some five years earlier, and at least some of the Natives and children had been baptized. He may have been referring to evangelizing by his Franciscan predecessors, whom Pedro had sponsored. But, if that claim was correct, the pacification was superficial and brief, indeed.[9] Since that time, neither Jesuit priest nor military captain had maintained the discipline and spiritual power necessary to inculcate the obedience and catechistic drilling satisfactory to the priests and soldiers alike. Baptisms had ceased and backsliding was evident.

Father Pantoja attributed the deterioration to lack of funding for a priest. The five-year vacuum of priestly endeavors had resulted in the spreading apostasy that now racked the pueblos. If Franciscans had been missionizing in the villages earlier, they were obvious failures as well. By now the rebel Indians were refusing to submit to demands from Spaniards that they acknowledge the sovereignty of His Majesty and submit to the authority of the priests. The indignation of the priests was evident.

In an attempt to reestablish Spanish control, Jesuits requested military backup in the form of small squadrons of troops from the presidio in El Fuerte, Sinaloa. In response (and rather surprisingly, given the modest scale of the Native resistance), Captain Alonzo Ramírez del Prado led military expeditions against the "rebels" three times, but all three campaigns proved unsuccessful and the troops were forced to turn back in the face of potent resistance and without the real might of Spanish armaments being demonstrated. The priests viewed the military response as woefully inadequate. The token expeditions resulted in the Indians being "victorious and even more warlike."[10] The soldiers, on the other hand, grumbled that they had not been permitted to engage the troublemakers in battle, according to Father Pantoja, because they had not been issued the proper orders. The lack of physical punishment to the perpetrators left the pueblos "infested with demons, sons of Satan, and sorcerers, the likes of which you have never seen."[11]

By the time Father Canal reestablished contact along with Father Ignacio Molarja, the missionary now stationed at Arizpe, and Padre Pantoja, the Natives were in open defiance. The previous year Canal had returned with Father Molarja and claimed that in their *tlátoles*, the Indians had called upon the Natives to kill the priests.[12] Father Molarja also believed his life was in danger and that when he had visited the pueblos, the rebels had held arrows to his chest and pushed him out of the village, following him with bows flexed. Father Pantoja characterized the incident as "they thrusted the arrows against his chest with tlátoles of death." Father Gerónimo had already made known his anger and fears to Padre Pantoja, and the padre visitador had complained to the governor in Parral and the viceroy himself in Mexico City. The Indians wanted nothing less than to drive all priests and settlers from their country and would kill them if necessary.

This was not an acceptable state of affairs to the Jesuits. The three priests agreed that the velvet glove of Christian charity had been ineffective. In spite of a few conversions, they were no closer to stamping out the taint of paganism than they had been a decade earlier. Simple preaching would have to be replaced with measures that the Indians would clearly understand and that would demonstrate the Spaniards' unflagging determination to make them subjects of the king and faithful to the Church. Conversion of pagans through the teachings of love and salvation was fine, if it worked. Here on the Río Sonora it was clear that that strategy was not working. It was time for the iron fist. Christian charity could go only so far.

The Military Solution and the Campaign

And thus the three priests approached officials in the Real de Santiago, a mine (now lost) that had been founded by Pedro de Perea or his men, located somewhere in the hilly country between Aconchi on the Río Sonora and Tuape on the Río San Miguel and home at the time to the alcaldes mayores of Sonora. The current chief magistrate there was Captain Simón Lazo de la Vega, who occupied the office that Pedro de Perea had created for himself but never managed to fill. And it is his extensive report on the proceedings that provides the description for the events that transpired.[13] The priests presented the chief magistrate with a spirited case for military intervention in the two pueblos and even beyond, if necessary. In addition to the urging from the priests, Captain Lazo may also have received instructions from the provincial government. Those peoples to the north were unnamed by language or ethnicity, but their lands bordered those of the fierce Hímeris, a Pima-speaking people considered the most warlike and dangerous in the region, and the belligerents appear to have been frequently allied with them. Now these unpenitent pagans had rejected the evangel. They had refuted the priests' most cogent arguments. And now they had threatened the very lives of the priests. Almost, but not quite equally ominous, the pagan savages would bring down their malevolent influence, including witchcraft and putative death threats, on the few converts to Christianity that the padres could point to as their meager success in the region. A convert who strays back into paganism may be worse than an untamed pagan. Better dead Indians than apostates.

We must keep in mind that tensions between the missionaries and the settlers were probably still simmering. If the missionaries had experienced strained relations with Pedro de Perea, all was now forgiven, at least under the dire circumstances they faced and until the next confrontation. Father Pantoja claimed to have treated a dying Pedro de Perea with magnanimity, glossing over his earlier insults to the Company of Jesus. Still, the military arm of the Crown frequently viewed the priests with dimmed enthusiasm and vice versa. The priests needed to demonstrate that armed intervention was a necessity, not merely a convenient assist to their evangelization. They were forced to grit their teeth and request armed backup. Apparently at their suggestion, Captain Lazo interviewed witnesses to assess the gravity of the threat independent of the priests' pronouncements. He must have been inwardly smiling.

Battlefield-hardened Spaniards were quite willing to corroborate the priests' dire descriptions. The priests first called on Miguel de Casanova y Ami, who had served proudly with Pedro de Perea. Don Miguel, who identified himself as a resident and miner of the Real de Santiago, cited his military experience serving under Pedro and the conflicts he had seen and participated in with the Indians beyond Arizpe,[14] warning that unless they were quickly brought under control, His Majesty's coffers would be drained and the limited military forces stretched to their limit. This was no time for delay and wavering.

The second, an equally effective witness, was Juan de Oliva, one of Pedro's recruits (apparently from New Mexico). He had served as Pedro's lieutenant and was his right-hand man in dealing with the Indians of Tuape. He testified that the rebels of the two towns and their allies constituted "the most bellicose Indians found in these parts in my twelve years of experience and I have witnessed them on various occasions."[15] The Natives had offered stout defense of their lands against the entrada of the Spaniards, and their arrogance since defeating the Europeans could well lead to increased aggression and the loss of the provinces unless the Spaniards quickly revealed their armed strength.

Captain Simón Lazo de la Vega needed little more incentive, justifying a military campaign against the two pueblos as essential to their "reduction and pacification." He had, however, witnessed the failure of the three understaffed campaigns against the two pueblos, and perhaps a fourth, and wished to take no chances of a similar defeat. Before taking any action, however, Spanish military policy required that he present the rebel Indians with a *requerimiento*—a formal warning that they must surrender to the representatives of the Crown. He dispatched a delegation that read aloud the order that the dissident pueblos immediately surrender and appear before him in the plaza of Santiago announcing their subjugation to His Majesty. It is not clear in what language the ultimatum was read.

Captain Lazo knew full well that any Indians who understood the requerimiento would sneer at it. Not content to wait for the inevitable rejection of his demand, he methodically began to organize a huge army and set about detailing a military expedition that would leave no possibility for defeat and would teach the unruly Natives a clear lesson. He began by issuing a general proclamation by town crier to all "vecinos and miners" of the Real de Santiago, ordering them to muster in the plaza and to be prepared to contribute to the military campaign. Anyone who failed to do so would be fined. When the group had assembled, he asked of each person what they would contribute to the effort. Many men volunteered not only arms, supplies, and beasts of burden, but their persons as well. Others unable to serve, perhaps women or men too old to fight, sent servants as proxies. And thus, using the tactic of peer pressure, he received pledges of about fifty mules, twenty-six horses, ten assistants, and ten harquebuses. The extent of what he himself possessed and brought to the battle is not clear, but Santiago was a real de minas, not a presidio, and hence the magistrate would not have been equipped with a stout supply of arms and beasts of burden. Those men who volunteered their services, about twenty of them, did not constitute a trained militia but were more like a ragtag group of volunteers, many without any formal training, but most with experience in some sort of military fighting. It was the captain's job to shape them into an ordered fighting force posthaste—not an easy task.[16]

Captain Lazo by no means confined his requisitions to the Real de Santiago. He sent a messenger to officials of the nearby Real de Nacatóbari, dictating that they provide ten Spaniards to guard the Real de Santiago in the absence of most of its men in the campaign against the Indians. Furthermore, he issued orders for each mission and real in the region to provide a certain number of "friendly Indians"—two hundred from Sahuaripa and one hundred from the Valley of Sonora. Most intriguing of all, he presented Pedro de Perea Ibarra, son of the former alcalde and original colonist of Sonora, with an order for the immediate shipment of "three hundred arrobas of necessities [including perhaps vizcocho, or hardtack]" and one hundred cows as food for the army, to be delivered by Perea's cowboys within three days from receipt of the order. The hapless Pedro de Perea must have cursed the existence of the rebellious Indians, especially given that he and his mother were facing a legal battle of their own against the Indians of Tuape. As the heir to his father's fortune, he was considered a wealthy man. And he must have known that don Simón was not one to trifle with niceties. The captain's order was terse and unequivocal.

Meanwhile, Father Molarja, sensing, I suspect, that the time to strike was nigh, wrote once again to Captain Lazo from his mission at Arizpe. Again he underscored the lethal threat to the priests from the villages and the Indians' apostasy. Buchibacuachi (he referred to it as "Bacobachi") was overrun with drunkenness and tlátoles, and, he had heard, one of the unconverted Indians had shot a newly baptized lad from Chinapa with an arrow. Please, he wrote, do punish these terrible pagans soon or worse things will happen. (Not that he was fearful for his own life, he added, but he was deeply concerned for the safety of the neophytes.) The three priests sweetened their entreaty with donations to the military expedition: fifty head of cattle, ten quintales of corn flour, four quintales of hardtack, eight mules, and two servants.[17]

Shortly thereafter, as the army mustered in Arizpe, Captain Lazo de la Vega received a most curious document. The traditional governor of Baviácora requested (undoubtedly via the mission priest, none other than the padre provincial, Pantoja) that his pueblo be allowed to send Indian troops to join the forces attacking the two rebellious pueblos. They resented the treatment the priests were receiving in those pagan settlements and wanted nothing more than to punish the evildoers for their foul behavior. Or so the letter stated. It was composed, of course, in Spanish. It is doubtful that any Indian was literate or spoke the tongue of the Castilians. Captain Lazo was more than happy to accommodate.

The mustering was lengthy and complex. The captain issued a formal justification, a proclamation defending the use of military force. The Indians of Cucuribasca and Buchibacuachi had prevented baptized Indians and padres alike from practicing their faith. (Freedom of religion can be a useful doctrine.) They had threatened the priests with violence or death. They had laid their hands on one priest. They had spread malicious tlátoles among neighboring settlements. They had failed to obey Captain Lazo's orders. And thus they would have to be punished. Lazo rather cleverly asked the priests to review the justification and sign a document to the effect that the charges were true and the need for punishment clear. They agreed, however reluctantly, and signed such a document. Sensing a potential pitfall, however, they added a disclaimer that decried any "mutilation of members or spilling of blood." Their consciences thus cleared, the priests viewed themselves as righteously off the hook if violence flared up. And Captain Lazo could, if necessary, wave the document containing the priests' authorizing signature to any who might question the need for the military foray.

And the army took shape. Twenty-five additional Spaniards appeared. Most remarkable, 882 Indian fighters appeared, each representing a mission. Three hundred arrived from Oposura and Cumpas alone, and most other missions sent fifty or one hundred. All Indians were armed, an unusual and clearly temporary situation (Spaniards typically viewed with a jaundiced eye the practice of arming Indians). The arms would have consisted of little more than bows and arrows, shields, and lances, and the Indians would have arrived on foot, but it was still a formidable gathering of fighting men, many of whom had trained since early youth in warrior skills. The logistics of organizing, feeding, and directing this massive force presented a major challenge to Captain Lazo. This was the largest military expedition ever seen in the region, larger in military terms than Coronado's expedition a century earlier. More than one thousand soldiers would advance on two small towns in order to teach the inhabitants a lesson. Food alone would be a challenge. Live cattle would probably accompany the force and would be sacrificed as needed.

Providing food and accommodations was not the only logistical challenge. Included among the Indian troops was a contingent of one hundred from Batuc, a Eudeve mission, and fifty each from Nacámeri and Ures, both Pima Bajo missions. The others—Aconchi, Arizpe, Banámichi, Baviácora, Cumpas, Opodepe, Oposura, and Sinoquipe—were probably Teguima-speaking missions. None of these languages (Eudeve, Pima, or Teguima) was intelligible to speakers of the other two and in general Indians of that era did not speak Spanish. Just how Captain Lazo, who probably spoke only Spanish, dealt with the polyglot nature—four languages—of his forces is not addressed in the documents. It seems doubtful that he had received significant training in military operations, especially ones dealing with large numbers of troops with little in common, no training in modern military procedures, and ambiguous motivation. The captain had his work cut out for him.

The horde proceeded north from Arizpe about fifteen miles and pitched camp near Chinapa, already a Franciscan mission town of Teguima speakers.[18] From there Captain Lazo dispatched two Indian governors and some Indian fighters to Cucuribasca, or, as the captain noted with greater accuracy, "the rancherías of Cucuribasca." This meant that rather than constituting a pueblo, Cucuribasca was a collection of smaller settlements. The Indian emissaries returned with a report that the rancherías were empty. Not a soul was to be seen.

The scouts may have been relieved at finding Cucuribasca completely evacuated. When they proceeded northward to Buchibacuachi, however, they found it teeming with warriors, its resident population considerably swelled by the presence of Hímeri allies and Indians from other settlements ever farther to the north. With what must have been considerable uneasiness (and, we might speculate, in small and nervous voices), the two governors delivered the requerimientos (the manuscript refers to their delivery as tlátoles) as instructed by Captain Lazo, ordering the immediate submission of the people of the two pueblos. Receiving no response, the emissaries returned (relieved, it must seem) to Chinapa.

Captain Lazo surely expected his orders to the two pueblos to be ignored. He shrugged and sent a message to the villages that they were in rebellion and since they were disobedient to his orders and those of His Majesty, they left him no choice but to declare them "rebel enemies" and bring down "fire and blood" upon them to punish them for their crimes.

Early the following morning (September 26, 1649), the captain ordered a flanking operation to take the pueblo of Buchibacuachi (there was no point in invading Cucuribasca, since it had been abandoned): two divisions of four hundred Indian archers on each side would join a large force of Spaniards and "friendly Indians," all in a formation shaped like "a bat." Lazo left a contingent of two hundred Indians to guard the rear and support his supply lines, while a smaller contingent of Spaniards, presumably from Nacatóbari and Batuc, stood guard in the Real de Santiago, just in case the rebels attacked the real while the soldiers were away fighting.

The captain fired two warning shots from a harquebus and the massive body moved on toward the village. The flanking hordes proceeded with great haste to high points on either side of Buchibacuachi, while the main armed force of Spaniards overran the village. They met with no resistance. Many villagers attempted to flee, but the flanking forces had encircled the pueblo and watched from above, making it a simple matter to intercept four hundred of the rebels. Captain Lazo issued an immediate order for the captives to lay down their arms, and it was done. The town was taken without a fight.

The allied forces remained in Buchibacuachi for several days. On September 28 Captain Lazo ordered the prisoners to be brought before him and their leaders interrogated as to the reasons for their resistance to the priests and Crown. According to the story that emerged, Dimare, the principal Indian leader of the pueblo of Buchibacuachi, had urged the other leaders of the pueblo to kill the priest and enlist the aid of the neophyte Christians to overthrow the Spaniards. Dimare taught that the priests were liars and preached falsehoods while hoping to conquer all the Indians and make them their slaves, just as had happened with other Indians who became Christians. Dimare's confederate, named Ecocore, held the same influence in Cucuribasca. Ecocore had sent out a piece of cloth as a signal to a confederate in the Valley of Sonora (Arizpe?) as a sign that the recipient should assassinate Padre Ignacio Molarja. This cloth would also serve as a signal that the Christianized Indians should rise up against the Spaniards. Dimare would communicate the same message to the neighboring Indians ("otras naciones") and those to the north, thus provoking a general uprising. The busy activity in Buchibacuachi as described by the scouts was a result of Dimare's (apparently successful) attempt to recruit other peoples to attack the Spaniards and drive them out of the region, according to the testimony that Captain Lazo heard. Even more Indians arrived as the captives were rounded up, possibly from settlements of differing ethnicity. Finally, Ecocore confessed to having ordered the killings of Christianized Indians and to having been behind several robberies that had occurred in recent times. Father Molarja had escaped the assassination plot only because two old men argued against it, reminding the Indian followers of Ecocore that were the padre to be killed, the Spaniards would return in even greater numbers to kill all the Indians. Their words were effective and thus the padre was spared, at least according to the Spanish report. The perpetrators probably confessed under torture and interpreters translated their confessions for the Spaniards.[19]

Captain Lazo sentenced the two leaders to be hanged, and we must assume that his orders were quickly carried out. He ordered all the Indians' weapons to be burnt in the center of the pueblo of Buchibacuachi and instructed his men to erect a pole claiming the town for His Majesty, warning all that no one was to touch the pole without his (Lazo's) permission under the penalty of death for treason to the king. Unsheathing his sword, the captain gave three blows to the pole. The infantry echoed his action. The three priests who had acted as chaplains for the army—Father Gerónimo, Father Molarja, and Father Ejidio de Montefrío, the priest from Cumpas, stepped forth and proclaimed the town for the king and for God and erected a cross.

Captain Lazo issued several commands, demonstrating to all that he was in charge. Among these were instructions that a priest was to remain in the pueblos, bringing the "holy evangel" to the gentiles and in so doing pacifying them. But the priests replied, embarrassed, it appears, that they already had their assignments in other missions and could not leave them without orders from their higher-ups. They were members of a highly organized religious society and received orders from their superiors, not from mere captains. To assuage Captain Lazo, who clearly was not accustomed to receiving no for an answer, the three promised that within two weeks a priest by the name of Juan de Huter would be assigned.[20] Thus reassured, Lazo named an Indian leader from the crowd as governor and bestowed on him the cane of office. Next he named seven Indians as topiles, installed them with canes of office, and abruptly ordered all of them to return to their rancherías. He then renamed the pueblo, christening it as Our Lady of La Paz. That name has disappeared, so either it did not stick or the pueblo was abandoned and lost.

The following day the captain ordered all the Indians of Cucuribasca to relocate to Chinapa, renaming it La Aldea de Santa María de los Angeles. He appointed an Indian governor and ten topiles, charging them to rule wisely and justly. He ordered the pueblo of Cucuribasca and all its rancherías burned to the ground. Today, Chinapa is still Chinapa and Cucuribasca is known only through ancient manuscripts.

Several days later Captain Lazo, who must have been slightly skeptical of the Jesuits' ultimate intentions and unwilling to rely on their collective memories, presented to the four priests involved a document containing a brief description of the military campaign. In the document the captain emphasized that the troublesome pueblos had been pacified at no expense to the Crown and without any bloodshed, certainly both important considerations when higher-ups and his successor would evaluate Captain Lazo's achievements in an official inquiry called a residencia. After the priests had read the document, he asked them to sign it as witnesses to its truth. Their signatures appear clearly enough, but, I should add, in uncharacteristically small handwriting. On one hand, the priests' complaint had provided the captain with an easy victory in the Spaniards' relentless march to the north. On the other hand, Lazo knew that the priests were aware that he, the captain, had done them an enormous favor, wiping out with only minor difficulty a most inconvenient and embarrassing pocket of resistance to their evangelizing. Perhaps one should draw no conclusions from such subtle details.

The Aftermath

As if to underscore the priests' political sensitivity, Father Juan de Huter was in fact reassigned from Oposura to the upper Río Sonora Valley. On October 24, 1649, Father Huter sent a letter of gratitude to Captain Lazo, acknowledging his assistance and not only promising the priests' ongoing support but dedicating three Masses to be said in his name as well.

A curious epigram to the saga of the rebellious Sonorans is attached to Father Huter's letter, though it has been crossed out with a large *X* in the manuscript. In it Father Huter reports that he had been informed through the Franciscan priest Father Juan Suárez, who preceded him in the upper Río Sonora region at the request of Pedro de Perea, that the Indians of his (Father Suárez's) congregation viewed the Indians of Father Huter's congregation as enemies. Father Huter informed Captain Lazo of this situation and counseled caution and prudence. This jives with the comment of the author of the relación (perhaps Padre Pantoja himself), who recalled that Jesuit padre Cristóbal García, an early evangelist in the upper Río Sonora, "baptized over four hundred and fifty children, catechized the adults, and instructed them that the Indians should not permit other religious to take possession of the missions."[21] The "other religious" can refer only to Franciscans. The conclusion can be drawn (but must remain conjecture at the present), at the risk of igniting volatile emotions in certain circles, that at least some of the hostility that faced the Jesuits was derived from the influence of their predecessors and competitors, the Franciscans. The relación putatively written by Father Pantoja portrays relations between the two orders as cordial and spiritually elevated. The reality was probably otherwise and the tantalizing possibility remains that one order was not above sabotaging the political aspirations (and bragging rights) of the other.

And who were these rebellious peoples that brought such trouble to the Jesuits? Father Canal, although ambiguous about ethnic matters, noted that one of his goals was "baptizar todas las rancherías de la lengua común de sonora [christen all the settlements of the common tongue of Sonora]." That common language was probably Opatan, and in the valley of Sonora, Teguima, one of the two known Opatan languages. In the pueblo of Bacobatzi (not identified, but perhaps the same as Buchibacuachi), he noted a "number of baptized Hímeris." This remark suggests that the pueblo was itself not a Hímeri town, but one in which some Hímeris could be found. These appear to have been Pima-speaking peoples. In his description of the events in the three towns, however, Father Canal makes no mention of differences in language. Sinoquipe and Arizpe were both Opatan-speaking locations, according to Padre Zapata in 1678.[22] Charles Polzer believed that "the fact that Jesuit missionaries immediately preached and baptized in the Native dialects at the pueblos previously controlled by the Franciscans demonstrates that the Indians there were of the same linguistic group as the Ópatas of the central Sonoran missions."[23] Indeed, when Captain Simón Lazo de la Vega dispatched a small troop of Indian emissaries north to the offending pueblos, they mentioned no difficulty in delivering the captain's message to the assembled group, indicating that they spoke the same language, which would probably have been Teguima. Captain Lazo did discover, according to his records, that the Natives of the offending pueblos were in close contact, perhaps even conspiracy, with peoples farther south on the Río Sonora, which suggests that no insurmountable linguistic differences separated the two groups.

Finally, we have the unusual situation of Captain Lazo de la Vega ordering the residents of Cucuribasca relocated to Chinapa, which was probably an Ópata (Teguima)-speaking town. In 1678, when Padre Juan Ortiz Zapata conducted a survey of the missions of Nueva Vizcaya, he noted that Chinapa was an "Ore" (Teguima) town, as was Arizpe, based, ostensibly, on the language(s) spoken there.[24] If a substantial number of speakers of a different tongue had settled in the town, per the captain's orders, they would surely have been sufficiently represented three decades later and Zapata would have mentioned them.

Without any further information, then, we must assume that the two offending pueblos were Opatan. We will probably never discover the truth of the matter but cannot reasonably ascribe any other ethnicity to them.

However, one intriguing and disturbing question remains: how was it possible for Captain Lazo to muster such a huge army, composed mostly of Opatans, but including Pimans as well, to attack other villages that were also Opatan? Several answers are possible. Opatans and Pimans were both known for their warrior tendencies and loved a good fight. The prospect of going on a long trip for a battle may have appealed to large numbers of young men who would have an opportunity to demonstrate their prowess. Another possibility is that most of them had no idea just what sort of battle they had been ordered to take on. They may simply have responded to an order to muster forces for a fight or have obeyed orders from their priests. Or they may have felt the same as the Indians of Baviácora, who seemed to have harbored a long-standing grudge against the people of the two pueblos, as least according to their priest, Padre Pantoja.

During the conquest of Mexico and during the first century of Spanish occupation of New Spain, Spaniards became adept at forming alliances with Native groups. This enabled them to recruit large numbers of Indian soldiers to take the battle to unconquered and hostile peoples. Cortés's forces conquered Tenochtitlán only with the intervention of large armies of Tlaxcalans, who entertained ancient grudges against the Aztecs.[25] Tlaxcalans further assisted Spaniards in the conquest of other peoples as well and served as colonists under Spain's imperial policy for populating the north of New Spain with Spaniards. Martínez de Hurdaide's expeditionary forces against the Yaquis and Nébomes and into the Opatería one hundred years later were composed primarily of indigenous armies. Spaniards understood well the dynamics of recruiting local indigenous people to suppress the rebellions to the north and took full advantage of their willingness to fight.

Just what the thousand or so Natives learned from the campaign against the rebellious towns is hard to fathom, but the quick submission of the rebels may well have presented a clear lesson to any of the troops who might have entertained thoughts of defying the Spaniards. They may also have gleaned some understanding of European military tactics, though they had little opportunity to put them to use. In military campaigns in the Opatería Spaniards seldom used Indians as more than scouts and cannon fodder until much later.

We can understand why Gerónimo de la Canal omitted any reference in his reports to the military operations that achieved what evangelizing had failed to accomplish. Equally interesting is the description of Father Canal's work by the author of the manuscript presented by Charles Polzer, S.J., who attributes the manuscript to Father Pedro Pantoja.

> Father Provincial persuaded Padre Gerónimo de la Canal his companion, to baptize in the pueblo of Sinoquipe. Canal entered all the remaining parts of the valley to catechize the people, thus extending and spreading the Holy Gospel everywhere. In less than three years, the Fathers visited the province again for the catalog [a triennial listing of all Jesuits in New Spain] and reported to the visitor that over 20,000 adult Indians had been baptized. This was over and above all the children who had been baptized in the new and older missions.[26]

Since Father Canal and Father Pantoja were intimately involved in the military incursion, they cannot have been ignorant of its results. Still, their histories make no reference to the iron fist that accomplished in a couple of days what the velvet glove had not accomplished in years—the "pacification" and at least partial elimination of the unruly Indians of Cucuribasca and Buchibacuachi and the assassination of their leaders.

The so-called pacification of the towns north of Arizpe was perhaps not as complete as the captain and the priests might have hoped. In 1681 much of the anti-Spanish currents already visible would become more focused and result in major worries for the Spaniards. Chinapa became one of the hotbeds of subversion, as we shall soon see.

Finally, we must suppose that the entire episode provoked sensations of uneasiness among the more sensitive Jesuits, who must have fretted that the military operation might have sent the message to other Indians that the priests were warmongers. Fathers Canal and Molarja had been quick to invoke the armed forces to soften Indian resistance. How, then, to convince other Indians that the priests were emissaries of God and peace and not puppets for the king's soldiers? It seems doubtful that the conquest of the two defiant villages assisted the Jesuits in evangelizing the region. The Indians may have become more docile out of fear, but the heavy-handed approach probably did not produce more devoutly Christian converts. We must also suppose that the settlers would long remember how the Jesuits needed their military assistance to accomplish their goals.

CHAPTER THREE

The Conspiracies of 1681

Sonora and the Great Pueblo Rebellion

✣ BY THE LATE 1650S THE JESUITS IN SONORA, BUOYED BY THE SUCCESS OF THE military campaign against resistant villages, seemed confident that they had overcome general resistance from Natives of the valleys. Other less settled groups from the north and east—Conchos, Janos, Jocomes, and Sumas—continued sporadic raiding, however, though not on a scale sufficient to disrupt the Jesuit evangelical master plan. Sumas appeared in significant numbers in the northeastern Opatería in the 1650s.[1] By that time the missions extended to the northern limits of the Opatería and possibly onto ground that was contested among peoples from Nueva Vizcaya, east of the Sierras.

During the following two decades, mines proliferated in the region along with an influx of Spanish settlers who developed both mines and ranches. The largest settlements in the Opatería at the time were at Nacozari and, some fifty kilometers to the south, San Juan Bautista. Mining towns also grew at Bacoachi, Chinapa, and Tepache. Families of Spaniards slowly became established settlers, all of them dependent to varying degrees on Indian labor to work the mines, construct buildings, herd cattle, and tend to the Spaniards' personal needs. From 1650 through 1680, Spaniards encountered no resistance worthy of mention from the Natives of the Opatería. The Jesuits seemed to have accomplished their goal of pacification rather well.

The Pueblo Rebellion of 1680 in New Mexico shattered the Sonorans' complacency.² The rebellion traumatized the Spanish Establishment of New Spain more than any other event of the previous century. While the causes were complex and Indian uprisings against Spanish rule were widespread during the seventeenth century, the August 10 revolt represented the greatest military defeat ever imposed on Spaniards in North America. Allied indigenous forces drove all Spaniards from the northern Río Grande Valley and obliterated every possible trace of the previous Spanish occupation. Never again, the insurgent Indians vowed, would they accept abuse and repression from priest, captain, or vecino, be subjected to arbitrary Spanish cultural impositions, have their lands and labor appropriated for outsiders' benefit, or be forced to adhere to the White Man's way of life.

Spaniards lost twenty-one (or twenty-two) Franciscan missionaries, nineteen (or twenty) of them priests, half of the total Franciscans in New Mexico. At least 375 settlers (perhaps more than 380), including many women and children, lost their lives in the attacks.³ In addition to the assassinations, the insurgents put to the torch the Spaniards' churches, homes, and government buildings. In destroying the churches they took particular care to profane the Catholics' sacred objects and despoil the images of saints—a clear message of their scorn for the religion the Spaniards had forced on them and an ironic payback for the destruction of their own religious symbols (especially kachinas) ordered by Catholic priests. In all, the insurgents laid waste to thirty-four pueblos and many associated ranches and haciendas. One Indian was quoted as stating that "God and Saint Mary had died, but their [the Indians'] god, the one they obeyed, would not die."⁴

Spaniards discovered the plot a full day before its Indian conspirators intended to initiate it. Governor Antonio de Otermín had sent out dispatches from Santa Fe to all Spanish outposts advising of the imminent uprising, but the warnings came too late. The Indians' plans were already in place and their leaders ordered the beginning of the revolt one day earlier than they had intended. Most of the Spaniards were caught off guard and though they were well armed, they had no time to coordinate their responses to the attacks. Still, Governor Antonio de Otermín managed to herd a multitude of terrified vecinos into the fortified government complex in Santa Fe. There they held out for nine days against the freedom fighters until the Indians cut off their water supply. Thereupon the governor called a meeting of his top remaining aides. Summoning all his remaining firepower, he orchestrated a desperate move and the huge company broke through the siege. One soldier was killed, two injured in the fighting, which, Spaniards claimed, resulted in over three hundred Indians dead. The governor suffered two wounds to his face and a gunshot in the chest. The victorious Pueblo Indians appear not to have given extended chase and were content to allow the survivors to depart in panic. The horde of refugees managed to retreat—carts, cattle, and all—apparently assisted by the Spaniards and Christianized Indians of Isleta Pueblo, who remained loyal to them.

The fleeing mass of Europeans, along with their Indian allies and various servants, plus carts and pack animals, staggered the 140 leagues (roughly five hundred kilometers) to El Paso, where they found refuge, food, and shelter provided by Fray Francisco de Ayeta, who met them and was determined to address their needs.[5] They arrived with 1,946 persons of all ages, but only 150 capable of bearing arms. Their food and possessions were borne on the backs of 471 pack animals of various kinds.[6]

Perhaps most disturbing for the Spaniards, apart from the loss of life and property, was the depth of the Native patriots' planning and their precision of execution. Some Spaniards had an inkling prior to the eruption that all was not tranquil among the Pueblo Indians, and officials intercepted two of the plotters, who divulged some details of the plot, thus probably saving the lives of hundreds more Spaniards. But for the most part, Spaniards had no warning that many (but not all) of the northern Río Grande peoples had united, with impressive fury, to drive the widely hated foreigners out of New Mexico. While perceptive observers might well have concluded that no peoples take kindly to being invaded, publicly humiliated, tortured, and executed, mostly for practicing a religion that had stood by them for many centuries, no one had committed such suggestions to the public record. The effective secrecy of the plotters was unnerving to the previously complacent Spaniards.

The Spanish survivors in El Paso faced grave danger from starvation but were fortunate to have the services of Fray Ayeta, who, in spite of having just lost more than half of his brethren, a majority of the Franciscans of the north, mobilized all possible aid in the Chihuahua region to supply the refugees through the winter of 1680. By September 18, Father Ayeta had calculated the logistics of supplies and had garnered sufficient food from Casas Grandes to the south in the form of corn and cattle.[7] From Parral, other Spaniards requisitioned enough wool and enlisted sufficient women to weave it to provide clothing for the refugees. Spanish authorities, hoping for a quick rally and recapture of the lost territory, mustered fifty-five men as a counterrevolutionary task force. They were unable to provide them with arms, however, and even worse, the mounts needed for military action were sickly, thin, and overworked. No logistical support existed for the prompt reconquest.

Fray Ayeta, the real hero of the survivors of the Pueblo Rebellion, could not have slept much in the first month. By Governor Otermín's own description, carts were departing and arriving day and night to supply the displaced multitudes.[8] No starvation was mentioned, and the refugees received ample corn and meat throughout the crisis months. By October the priest had requisitioned and paid for 1,640 cattle and 600 *fanegas* of corn (much of it from Casas Grandes), all without the normal quartermaster documentation the Spanish bureaucracy required.[9] It seems clear that Ayeta's ministrations amounted to the difference between wholesale starvation and survival of the refugee colony at El Paso.

From Mexico City, Viceroy Conde de Paredes called for an immediate reconnoitering of forces, an inventory of resources—personnel, food, and arms—assuming that a counterattack against the apostate Indians would ensue in short order. He feared that unless mobilization took place immediately, the winds of rebellion would resound well beyond New Mexico and affect Sonora and Parral as well.

Sonora in 1680 was especially vulnerable to Indian uprisings, according to Spaniards, since it was plagued with "barbarous peoples."[10] Apaches had acted as spies and coconspirators for the Pueblo Indians and were now present in Sonora as well, presenting a new and formidable threat. The viceroy joined other leaders in exhorting Sonorans to assist in the reconquest of New Mexico and contribute to the aid and protection of the survivors in El Paso. It would be costly (even though the dead priests' salaries would no longer be paid), but the costs of failing to act would be far greater. Conde de Paredes set a date of January 17, 1681, for a council of war and revenge.

If that great meeting did take place, it resulted in very little of consequence. Well before that time the Spaniards realized that it would take far longer to regroup, rearm, and overcome the psychological disarray resulting from the devastating defeat. In the fall of 1681, Governor Otermín managed to organize a small expeditionary force to reconquer the lost lands, but it fell apart well before arriving at the northern Río Grande, part of the problem stemming from disillusioned loyalist Indians abandoning the offensive.[11] Twelve more years would pass before the Spanish flag once again rose over Santa Fe and priests once again held Mass in northern chapels.

The reconquest would be easier than they feared. The aspiration of some of the Pueblo Indian leaders of the rebellion to live once more in their Native autonomy was admirable, but naïve. The pueblos were not unified in their resistance to Spanish occupation, nor could they agree on or unite for a common defense against the inevitable counterattack. It might take Spaniards some time to regroup, but they were not given to suffer such defeats lightly, and with proper planning they could summon vastly superior military resources. They chipped away at the pueblo strongholds, aided by the deep divisions that appeared among the pueblos, differences that ultimately allowed the Spaniards to reconquer the area with only modest effort and without significant losses, and with the assistance of many Pueblo Indians.[12] With the reconquest, by 1696 Spaniards had reestablished their presence even more solidly than before.

The News Arrives in Sonora

The revolt and its consequences had profound repercussions, not merely for the expansionist plans of the Crown, but for the psyches of Spaniards and Natives as well. News of the successful expulsion of Spaniards from New Mexico spread as rapidly as the state of communications would permit. Spaniards of the mining town of San Juan Bautista,[13] the political center of Sonoran Hispanics, learned of the events by a letter to Alcalde Mayor Lázaro Verdugo on September 15, 1680.

The date when the news of the rebellion arrived in Sonora is mentioned in two letters that Governor Otermín received from Sonorans and copied as part of a very long report.[14] He forwarded the original letters to the viceroy in Mexico City to be included in the official archives. Francisco Agramont y Arce, former governor of Nueva Vizcaya and resident of Sonora, had written one of the letters at the time from the Real de San Juan Bautista. The other letter came from Sergeant Major Juan Bautista Escorza, who lived at and may have owned the mine at Nacatóbari, a defunct location near Tepache. He had perhaps served as alcalde mayor of Sonora.

Agramont wrote that he had received written notice describing the disaster in New Mexico and the ensuing retreat of the Spaniards. The notice may have come from Governor Otermín, but more probably it was from Fray Ayeta.[15] Otermín and Ayeta both seem to have been friends of Agramont. Otermín described him as one with much experience in the region and much familiarity with its peoples and places, especially its Indians.

Former governor Agramont reported to Otermín that on the afternoon of September 15, news arrived in San Juan Bautista of the uprising in New

Mexico. On the sixteenth, he dispatched a letter to Otermín in which he sought to console him for the calamity and to thank God that he had escaped, even though wounded, and to assure him Fray Francisco de Ayeta was worthy of tending to the Spaniards' needs. Agramont commended Otermín for the salvage of eighty harquebuses and even more for successfully spearheading the miraculous escape from Santa Fe and all the ambushes and blockades that must have been planned by the insurgents along the way. Perhaps Agramont was unaware that many Christianized Indians from Isleta Pueblo had aided the escape and prolonged retreat down the Río Grande Valley to El Paso and that the insurgent Pueblo Indians seem to have lost interest in the Spaniards once they disappeared south of Albuquerque.

Agramont acknowledged the perils that had been created in the northern frontier by the Pueblo Rebellion and the complicated logistics of supplying the horde of displaced persons, praising all the while the excellent discipline Otermín had exercised to save the New Mexican Spaniards in the arduous journey down the Río Grande to El Paso. He also underscored the now ominous threat of Indian uprisings in San Juan Bautista and all of Sonora. He had warned Otermín not only that the Pueblo Rebellion had endangered New Mexico, but that Spaniards were also on the verge of losing "all of this province of Nueva Vizcaya, because the Janos and Sumas and other nations from here whose territory borders on theirs are of different dispositions, even worse [than the Pueblo Indians], and with the success of the Indians of New Mexico ... [there is] ... no doubt that they will try the same here, especially since we have even less defense here than there [in Santa Fe]."[16]

The Janos and Sumas feared by Agramont were seminomadic peoples from northwestern Chihuahua and north of the Opatería whose ethnic affiliations and languages are obscure.[17] Their homelands lacked any clear geographic boundaries. They had already established a reputation for roaming and for raiding Spanish settlements, as had been the case in Teuricachi in 1651. Worse, as was common among nomadic peoples, they had for the most part resisted the evangelizing efforts of the Catholic priests. In Spanish eyes, they compared unfavorably to the settled agriculturalist Pueblo Indians and would naturally be more inclined toward inflicting violence and allying themselves with other peoples who might wish to drive the Spaniards back to Mexico City or even out of the hemisphere altogether.

Agramont went on to offer platitudes and religious reassurances, but nothing more, saying only "Let me know if I can help in any way."[18] As for himself, he had grown weary of the turbulence of life in the warlike provinces and planned to return to Mexico City and find himself a "quiet corner" in which to live out the remainder of his days. News of the Pueblo uprising had perhaps hastened his departure from such savage and unpredictable realms.

Sergeant Major Juan Bautista Escorza probably heard the news from Agramont or from Lázaro Verdugo, the alcalde mayor of Sonora. Escorza also wrote to Governor Otermín, whom he appears to have met previously. Escorza was apparently the second in command in Sonora, sergeant major to Alcalde Mayor Lázaro Verdugo, so his official status in regard to Agramont is unclear. He had also been interim alcalde mayor in the late 1670s.[19] He would soon become deeply involved in the counterinsurgency campaign against the reputed conspirators in Sonora. In his letter of September 17, he offered the governor sympathy, labeling the Pueblo revolt "an event without precedent in New Spain that could easily spread to another province."[20] It had been led, he wrote, by infidel Indians.[21]

So much for Escorza's platitudes. He had known something dreadful had happened, he wrote, when on September 10, 1681, he had received a letter at his residence in Nacatóbari. The contents of the note, which he did not divulge, so alarmed him that he immediately mounted his horse and galloped all the way to San Juan Bautista, several hours distant. He made inquiries there but all appeared tranquil and no one expressed any inkling of unusual occurrences. Not content with the appearance of normality, Escorza dispatched messengers to Huásabas and Teuricachi, each many hours distant, asking for information about any unusual occurrences in these distant towns. Nothing. Finally, on September 15 (or 16), Agramont received word of the uprising via Fray Ayeta and immediately notified all the vecinos in the region.

Thus Escorza claimed he had been forewarned or given a premonition of disaster. This was not all. In his letter to Otermín he expressed deep and powerful emotion at Otermín's escape, viewing it as part of divine providence, and reminded the governor that God works in mysterious ways. (Apparently the twenty-one dead Franciscans and three hundred some slain Spaniards were not included in the divine providence.) Meanwhile, Escorza invited Otermín to visit him at his house near the mine at Nacatóbari. The mine and smelter were not in operation at the time, due to a shortage of wood (possibly timbers that cost him one peso in silver each). Times were hard. In four months he had not sold four pesos' worth of silver and he now found himself up to his ears in debt, having spent twenty-five thousand pesos on his mine in the previous year. He had a neighbor named don Pedro, who lived with his wife in a house with an orchard that Escorza owned some six leagues away. Escorza cheerfully informed Governor Otermín, whose political future was cloudy indeed and who had just experienced the horrors of a virtual holocaust, the violent loss of many friends, and a terrifyingly narrow escape with his own life, that he looked forward with anticipation to that day when Otermín would pay him a visit (and perhaps spot him a modest loan).

Escorza appears to have anticipated the arrival of a squadron of soldiers from Governor Ysidro Atondo of Sinaloa to assist in the defense of Sonora. According to his information, the promised troop would pass through Teuricachi (irrationally, according to the region's geography) on its way to San Juan Bautista. Despite Atondo's assurance, the squadron never materialized.[22] Atondo was far too busy preparing for the evangelization of California to be concerned about nervous settlers in Sonora.[23]

And thus the vecinos of Sonora came to learn of the might of united Indians—that they were indeed capable of smashing the previously unassailable power of the Spaniards and their priests. The message sent shudders through every Spanish spine in the region. Jesuit priests in Sonora may have shaken their heads in sorrow but inwardly added that the Spaniards should have known that putting Franciscans in charge of Indians was a mistake. The friars, decent enough fellows, spurned all attempts at learning Indian languages and were widely known to have taken a hard line with pagan Indians. All this would lead to no good.[24]

On October 6, 1680, Governor Otermín wrote from El Paso that having evaluated the situation, including the two letters from Sonora (which offered nothing at all), and seeing that the refugees still lacked cooking facilities and *jacales* (huts) for the upcoming winter and had little in the way of fighting power, he had abandoned consideration of a quick sortie to retake the lands and places lost to the insurgents. He delayed until January any consideration of reconquest. The postponement would become rather protracted.

We can safely assume that well before September 15, 1680, many Indians in northwestern Nueva Vizcaya had learned of the struggle and victory of Native peoples. Some may even have been planning a similar movement in Sonora prior to the New Mexican revolt: as we shall see, subsequent events revealed that some Opatans were aware of the rebellion in New Mexico and were developing plans of their own to drive the European scourge from their lands.

When Alcalde Mayor Lázaro Verdugo informed settlers of San Juan Bautista and other towns in Sonora of the New Mexico violence, they rightfully feared that the same uprising could happen to them. Even those who had never experienced anything other than subservience from the seemingly placid Opatans and other Indians of the region now began to interpret every Native movement with suspicion. Sonora was without a presidio—a staffed garrison. Any of Ysidro Atondo's troops that might protect the settlers and their possessions were stationed far to the south in Sinaloa, so the settlers' fright was compounded with the knowledge of their vulnerability to attack. If a similar uprising were to take place in Sonora, the vecinos, who probably numbered fewer than one hundred as opposed to more than one thousand in New Mexico, would be even less prepared than their New Mexican counterparts to resist any organized rebellion. Sonora and extreme western Chihuahua already suffered from intermittent raids by groups of Apaches, Conchos, Janos, and Sumas, and a coordinated attack against the largely defenseless settlers would have catastrophic results for the Spaniards of the Northwest.[25]

For the next several months the vecinos remained nervous but continued their more or less normal lives, while casting ever-suspicious eyes on Indians. Indians built the vecinos' houses, watched over their children, cooked their meals, herded their cattle, tended their crops, broke rock in their mines, and fired their smelters. Without Native labor the Spaniards could not continue to develop the region in accordance with European standards. The Spaniards living near mining towns were probably even more uneasy because of the variety of peoples who gravitated toward these towns—Chinarras, Conchos, Eudeves, Janos, Jocomes, Necuas,[26] Pimas, Sumas, and, more recently, Apaches, all of alien appearance and speaking foreign tongues, many of them far rougher cut and less impressed with Spanish power and customs than the settled Opatans, and, for all the vecinos knew, all plotting to kill them. They recalled that the governor of Nueva Vizcaya, as soon as he received word of the Pueblo uprising, had promised Verdugo the squadron of General Atondo's troops from Sinaloa.[27] Though the number of troops to be dispatched was not large, they would have provided some measure of physical and psychological security for Sonora, at least for the mining *reales*. As we have seen, the troops never arrived. Instead the vecinos lived under an ever-increasing cloud of fear.

A Conspiracy Revealed: Lázaro Verdugo in Action

Thus it came as no surprise when Alcalde Mayor Verdugo summoned all vecinos to an emergency council on July 2, 1681, in San Juan Bautista. There he announced that he had it on excellent authority—from one Javiel (or Javier), a loyal *ladino*, or Spanish-speaking servant, of a land- and mine-owning vecino named Lorenzo Quintero[28]—that Natives and other nearby peoples were planning an uprising to kill all non-Indians or drive them from Sonora and the neighboring province of Ostimuri, just as the Pueblo Indians had driven the Spaniards from New Mexico.[29] This news confirmed the vecinos' greatest fear.

The details of the investigation and counterinsurgency in the weeks following Verdugo's announcement are derived almost solely from his dictated documents and those of his subordinates and of his successor, Francisco Cuervo y Valdez, who later assembled the documents in a folio. While Spanish authorities took great pains to have witnesses sign statements, testify to the veracity of accounts, and have depositions taken under oath, we must keep in mind that Alcalde Mayor Verdugo was nearing the end of his term, and the evaluation of his term and his ensuing pension depended on positive findings from an investigation of his tenure, conducted by his successor. He required the strong approval of the investigators. Thus it was in his personal interest to inflate his own importance in the events, exaggerate the potential menace of the so-called conspiracy, and interpret his actions and the dangers they averted as favorably as possible. While he was careful always to have his reports attested to by appropriate witnesses, it was still only natural that he would describe the events in the most positive light possible.

Javier, a sometime resident of Chinapa, probably a Spanish-speaking Indian, had mentioned the rumors of conspiracy to Lorenzo Quintero. At first Quintero had dismissed his servant's warnings as insignificant rubbish, but when Javier persisted, Quintero took heed—and promptly locked him up in the town prison, not as a criminal but as a protected witness, to keep him from fleeing the pueblo out of fear of reprisal from the conspirators. Learning from Quintero of Javier's report, Alcalde Verdugo ordered him released from jail so that he could tell his story to an emergency meeting of the vecinos of San Juan Bautista. Once Javier began to spell out details, Verdugo and the vecinos appear to have taken his story seriously. Verdugo ordered him to remain in Quintero's custody to provide more information as the case developed.

According to the story Javier related, Indians had been holding *convocos* (clandestine meetings) and delivering *tlátoles* (insurrectionary speeches) in Chinapa, where the rebellion was to begin. Chinapa sits on the banks of the Río Sonora north of Arizpe in the vicinity of several mines and was a frequent gathering place of Indians of various ethnicity from throughout the region (it had supposedly absorbed the displaced Indians of Cucuribasca as ordered by Captain Simón Lazo de la Vega). Javier also implicated not only Indians of Chinapa but also Natives from several other towns of the Opatería, including nearby Bacoachi and missions from all over the Opatería: Cuquiárichi, Tebidéguachi (now abandoned), Cuchuta, Teuricachi, San Juan Guachinera, San Miguel Bavispe, and Santa María de Bacerac, these last three on the eastern arm of the Río Bavispe. The conspirators were not limited to Opatans: Javier implicated Christianized Sumas and Janos and gentile Jocomes and other unchristianized pagans, including Indians from Cananea and Quiburi as well.[30] These last two were villages of Sobaípuris, a Pima Alto group. Later witnesses would mention Terrenate and Bamocho, also Piman towns. Perhaps even worse, Apaches, whose reputation as unrepentant savages with a penchant for violence against vecinos was now well established, were also reportedly involved in the planning. Just how reliable a person Javier was is not made clear in the record. Since Quintero himself was no respecter of Indians, one might question his motives in announcing his discovery of a plot to overthrow Spaniards. Still, all authorities seemed to accept Javier's account at face value, assuming his report to be true, and subsequent testimony, though derived largely through torture, corroborated most of what he warned. Spaniards had suspected something was up ever since they received the news of the Pueblo uprising.

Alcalde Verdugo, though his term of office was about to expire, seemed determined to showcase himself as a resolute fellow who would brook no insolence from Indians. He took action immediately, realizing he had no time to request governmental authorization and funding from distant Parral for his counterterrorism operations, including any hangings that might be necessary. As he wrote afterward, this was an Indian uprising that had to be squelched.[31] To get to the root of the rebellion he hastily recruited and deputized miners, most of whom lacked formal military training and possessed little in the way of weaponry. Indeed, San Juan, Nacozari, and Tepache were the only towns with more than a handful of Spaniards.

Within hours of hearing Javier's testimony, Verdugo dispatched to Bacoachi a contingent of these deputies led by Lorenzo Quintero, Javier's master, to arrest an Indian suspect named Diego Suri. Verdugo ordered a separate contingent to an adjacent pueblo in search of one Pablo Dimara. Javier had named each as a principal conspirator. Verdugo then organized a patrol of ten men of his own and the tiny squadron departed for Chinapa on

July 2 at 8:00 p.m., having to cross a rugged mountain range in the dark of night. Hardly stopping, even in the rugged terrain, Verdugo and his troops arrived in Chinapa on July 4 at sunset to interrogate the perpetrators and determine the depth and extent of the planned rebellion. Verdugo hoped his arrival with soldiers would produce a display of shock and awe to the conspirators, making it easier to round them up and proceed with prosecution. By the time of his arrival, Lorenzo Quintero had apparently already captured Diego Suri and had him en route to Chinapa as a prisoner.

Prior to his departure, Verdugo posted a letter ordering Pedro de Peralta, the captain of the mining town of Nacozari, to enlist a squadron of ten soldiers and head directly to Cuquiárichi, some forty kilometers to the northwest (and near the site of the presidio that would be constructed ten years later at Fronteras). Verdugo instructed Peralta to arrest the governor of that pueblo and several Indians close to him, including his topiles, and transfer them posthaste back to Nacozari, where there was a secure prison in which they were to be incarcerated. He ordered Peralta to depart without fail, accepting no excuses from recruits, and to arrive unannounced the better to surprise the conspirators and make their arrest and interrogation simpler.

Alcalde Verdugo had Diego Suri in custody. He also exhibited a special interest in interrogating Pablo Dimara, one of the principal conspirators fingered by Javier. Dimara was not in the town but was visiting in a pueblo a couple of hours away. Verdugo feared word of his imminent arrest would cause Dimara to flee, a most reasonable assumption. To entrap the accused conspirator, Verdugo ordered a messenger to find him and inform him that the alcalde had named him the new governor of Chinapa. Dimara took the bait and arrived in the pueblo with his selected topiles and was thus immediately arrested and clapped in the prison.[32]

Meanwhile, apparently with the help of Javier, Verdugo called before the Chinapa village council of vecinos another Indian (of unnamed ethnicity), Antonio Demigra, who was supposedly knowledgeable in the social undercurrents of the region. Demigra appears to have spoken no Spanish, so Verdugo appointed an interpreter, swore Demigra in, and asked him what he knew about the alleged conspiracy. Apparently without hesitation, Demigra named Pablo Dimara as the chief conspirator (the *motor* or *moctor*), the principal source of the tlátoles, and the primary fomenter of agitation and planned insurrection. (As skittish as the vecinos were at that time, the delivery of tlátoles was itself a crime. Spaniards began to refer to tlátoles as objects that could be transferred as readily as harquebuses.) At various meetings in

Chinapa and Bacoachi, Dimara had delivered tlátoles, pointing out that baptism seemed to be a Spanish way of forcing Indians to do all the Spaniards' work. Baptism itself was a bad institution and should be abandoned, he had argued. Spaniards must also be eliminated. When Demigra was asked by the accusers if the Indians had stashed arms in the towns, he noted that no, they had no arms. Pablo Dimara had warned that any attacks must be guerrilla style, since the Spaniards had vastly greater fighting resources. The battles must be in the mountains, not in the plains, where Spanish cavalry would of course have an overwhelming advantage because the Indians had no horses. So it was in the mountains that he had called for stashing arms. Dimara could not predict whether the Indians would defeat the Spaniards or vice versa, but whatever the outcome, it could be no worse than things at present.

Demigra, whom Verdugo described as being about thirty-five years old, went on to describe the tlátoles. They had taken place in houses and in the fields belonging to the mission, where the padre would never notice anything going on.[33] The Christian Indians seemed to be resistant to the call to arms, especially those from the Río Sonora, but gentiles from other places were more receptive, as were old men. As for Demigra himself, he had not attended the tlátoles. He wanted no part of them. He was merely reporting what had been told to him as having taken place in the tlátoles. He spent all of his time at home or in the church with the padre. Or so he said.

When Alcalde Verdugo summoned Pablo Dimara before him and interrogated him, the Indian did not deny the charges. He was an old man, probably sixty years of age, Verdugo estimated, a *topile* of Chinapa. He had recently lost his older brother, a coconspirator. Dimara seemed both proud and sheepish about his subversive activities. Yes, he had carried tlátoles to various villages with the help of his brothers and Diego Suri. Yes, he had met in the house of his brother, the governor of Chinapa, with ten or so other Indians, both Christians and gentiles, and discussed an uprising. Yes, he was the principal leader in the conspiracy. Yes, he had called on Indians to plan the killings of Spaniards (apparently in general, not any named individuals). Why did he do and say such things? The devil had deceived him, Dimara replied. The origin of the conspiracy, he said, was Cuquiárichi, one of several places that implicated Indians would point to as sources of the unrest.

Verdugo summoned more Indian witnesses, all of whom had previously confessed, or, more probably, had been forced to confess under torture, as we shall see. Another witness attributed the conspiracy to Pablo Dimara, his brother Ignacio, and a third brother, now dead, who had been the traditional governor of Chinapa. They had recruited gentile Indians to the cause and had partaken in discussions of the necessity of killing the Spaniards. They had smoked together (*chuparon*) in their secret meetings where they delivered their tlátoles. (Communal smoking was a regular part of Native deliberations and important occasions.) They had asked the gentile Indians to carry the message to Tebidéguachi, but the witness knew nothing of the success of these envoys. Another witness could add little to what Antonio Demigra had said. He had heard that the Dimara brothers were the instigators but had never attended any tlátoles himself, since the brothers appear to have been his enemies.

The alcalde summoned witness after witness. He found most troubling the testimony provided by the elderly traditional governor of Bacoachi, Ignacio Turoque, a conspirator of nearly equal standing with Pablo Dimara. Turoque offered testimony without being asked, volunteering in his testimony the information that he and his two brothers had actively recruited rebels to join them. He testified that at least fifty Indians from all over the region were involved in tlátoles. They were actively recruiting other Indians to join in the effort, but with mixed success. He attributed the origin of the conspiracy to Sumas and Janos.

Turoque also testified that Diego Suri had visited towns on the Río Sonora but had found his efforts spurned. In that well-watered valley, the crops were abundant, the Indians well fed. They professed to be uninterested in driving the Spaniards out. They had reached accommodation with the invaders and were comparatively well-off. They wanted only to plant their crops in peace, not live like the Apaches and Sumas, who were constantly on the move, were often hungry, and lacked necessities. Elsewhere, Turoque's approaches were also rejected when Indians argued that the Spaniards were tolerable, since they provided them with grain and blankets.

The next witness was a younger man named Francisco Quigue. He had overheard numerous conversations among the insurrectionists and provided some of the most detailed testimony of all those interrogated. For example, Diego Suri had invited Apaches into the conspiracy, hoping that the Apaches would become "their comrades and with them kill the priests who had them whipped and the captain who would hang Indians, and from the Spaniards take away their horses and cattle, and the merchants to relieve them of their shirts and trousers and clothing."[34] Suri and the other conspirators, according to Quigue, had agreement from Apaches that in the first cold snap at the beginning of the new year (apparently January 1682, but perhaps earlier), they would join in killing and driving out the Spaniards. This they would do with the additional help of Sumas, Janos, and Jocomes from the east. Principal in the planning of the revolt along with Diego Suri was the governor of Cuquiárichi, Ignacio Jojói. The Apaches would be potent allies, for they routinely filtered in and out of towns like Cumpas and Nacozari, especially at night. They had penetrated the walls of San Juan Bautista and were familiar with the town's weaknesses.[35] Quigue had also heard Diego Suri guarantee that Cuquiárichi itself was primed for rebellion. Ready as well were Teuricachi and Guachinera. From his testimony, the conspirators' intelligence appeared to have been well coordinated.

And so the details emerged. The conspirators, concerned that any meetings in the town might draw attention, often gathered in the mission fields, where they pretended to be working, or they assembled after dark. There they would smoke and plot. They would organize secret convocos, according to Spaniards—in combination with the tlátoles—without authorization from Spanish administrators, the meetings themselves apparently a crime. Tlátoles, convocos, and *chupando* (smoking) all constituted clear evidence of widespread sedition and conspiracy. In addition to their plotting, some of the conspirators had been involved in the murder of a young servant of a Spaniard. He had learned of the conspiracy and threatened to report it. As a result of his apparent blackmail, he was murdered—stoned to death at the outskirts of Chinapa at eight o'clock in the morning—broad daylight.

In those first three days in Chinapa, Alcalde Verdugo claimed to have listened to eighteen hours of testimony from conspirators and insiders.[36] He had grown impatient with the litany of descriptions of Indian sedition. In addition to warning of the clear and present danger of a rebellion, he had proclaimed that the murder of the servant posed a threat to every Spaniard. What he had heard contained sufficient evidence for him to bring criminal charges against three Indians from Chinapa and three from Bacoachi and impose the death sentence on all. Chief among the accused were Pablo Dimara, Ignacio Juras, and Ignacio Turoque, the traditional governor of Bacoachi. It was time to punish the prisoners for their crimes against individuals, the Spaniards, and the king. Verdugo ordered the scribe to proclaim the charges against the conspirators and encouraged vecinos from Chinapa to add their names in support of the alcalde's action. The Spaniards crowded around the alcalde, eager to add their signatures, however crude, as witnesses to his findings and endorsers of his fateful decision over the lives of the accused conspirators. Twenty-eight vecinos signed the document.

The next day Alcalde Verdugo arrested Javier, the original informant, without explanation and placed his name along with those of the other conspirators in the documentary record. Javier's fate is unknown.

And so the judicial proceedings moved from Chinapa to Bacoachi, some twenty kilometers to the north. It, along with Cuquiárichi, seems to have been the center of the conspiracy. In keeping with Spanish legal practice, Alcalde Verdugo appointed a public defender for the incarcerated Indians accused of conspiracy. His name was Pedro de Montoya and he had only a few hours in which to concoct the defense of his charges. Whether he was arguing aggressively in his pleadings as their advocate or merely going through the required motions is impossible to determine from the written documentary record. At any rate, Montoya argued that the incarcerated Indians should be released from prison. After all, their confessions had been delivered through an interpreter of dubious qualifications. The accused had no real understanding of the workings of the courts, and their confessions were gathered under the terror they experienced when the heavily armed militia arrived and (we must assume) manhandled them and, quite possibly, tortured them. They had no comprehension of the deadly serious nature of the accusations. As Indians they were of *poca capacidad*, best translated as "diminished capacity." Furthermore, one of the accused (Francisco Quigue) was a mere lad, unjustly arrested and imprisoned for crimes he did not commit and for reasons he could not understand. Others were clearly innocent of all charges, having had the misfortune of being gathered up during the mass arrests.

Montoya also presented more than thirty petitions (absent from the documentary record) requesting that the accused (or at least some of them) not be executed. Alcalde Verdugo responded by ordering his assistants to add Montoya's memorandum and the petitions to the official record.

That same day the wives of two of the accused came forth to plead with the alcalde. One of them, the wife of Francisco Quigue, argued that he was under twenty years old, too young to have been involved in such gravely conspiratorial matters. He spent much of his time in the mission church. He also was of diminished capacity and had no idea what he had become involved in. He did not understand the charges against him, some of which, she claimed, were lies concocted by his enemies. If he had brought tlátoles to Chinapa, it was through ignorance or fear of reprisal if he refused, not through willing participation in any conspiracy. She pleaded with Verdugo to reduce the sentence of death for her husband and the father of her son.

The wife of Juan Caiso, a man advanced in years, argued that he was too old to have been involved in such goings on. Indeed, she said, he spent all of his time either at home, in his milpa, or in the church. If he had been actively bringing tlátoles, why would he spend so much time in the church helping the priest? She pleaded with Verdugo not to take away her husband and the father of her children.

Pedro de Montoya, the public defender, followed with his final plea. Whatever the charges, no one was guilty of a capital crime. If guilt seemed evident, the accused should be subjected to some lashes, say twenty, and assigned to work for the priest. For the older man, Juan Caiso, Montoya argued that he would be more valuable to the priest alive and teaching in the mission than dead and hung from a tree.

Verdugo gave no indication that he had heard any of Montoya's pleadings. However, it does appear that the pleas from the two wives struck a sympathetic note, and Verdugo decided the crimes of Juan Caiso and Francisco Quigue were of lesser severity. He reduced their sentences from death by harquebus or hanging to ten years of hard labor on the estate of a Spaniard. But for the perpetrators, the *motores*, the *principales*, Verdugo would not be moved. He had been convinced of their guilt from the moment that Javier made his first warnings of the impending uprising.

On July 8, less than four days after arriving in Chinapa, Verdugo ordered those with the most egregious involvement to be put to death. They were to be taken forcibly from jail, bound with ropes around their necks and paraded through the streets while a town crier boomed to all the citizenry the nature of their crimes. They were to be beaten as they walked. Then they were to be marched to an execution site, have hoods placed over their heads, then be executed by firing squad. When dead, their bodies were to be dangled from a public scaffold as a clear example to other Indians of the fate of those who dared challenge Spanish rule.

And thus Pablo Dimara, Ignacio Juras, and Ignacio Turoque, the governor of Bacoachi, met their death. The remaining two prisoners with serious charges, Juan Caiso and Francisco Quigue, were sent to toil in the mine at Nacozari. A soldier duly reported the executions had been carried out in keeping with Verdugo's instructions: two executed in Bacoachi, one in Chinapa. The fate of Diego Suri is unclear, but one reference suggests that he died during the proceedings, another, that he was living among wilder peoples to the north.[37]

The following day, July 9, Verdugo produced another conspirator, one

Javier Jaure, about twenty-five years of age.[38] How or when he was captured is not stated. His testimony was apparently recorded after he had been softened up, probably tortured, until he expressed his willingness to confess. According to Verdugo's report, Jaure stated that Indians of the region, led perhaps by Pablo Dimara and Diego Suri, had been plotting for three years to kill and expel all Spaniards from the Opatería. If this was correct, their conspiracy predated the Pueblo Rebellion. (Jaure was the only one of the accused to establish such a date, however.) The inspiration for the Sonora uprising had originated with an old man from Chinapa named Senotero, about whom we have no further information. He had aroused the passions of the Natives by harping on a now familiar theme: the Spaniards had brought Indians nothing but suffering and pain. They enslaved the Indians, forced them into a new and false religion, and made their lives worse. It was time for the Indians to drive them from the land. Only then would their lives improve.

Javier Jaure appears to have taken the old man's message to various pueblos on orders from Pablo Dimara. He journeyed to Arizpe, south of Chinapa on the Río Sonora. There he held convocos and found his words were welcomed. He claimed to have recruited several Indians willing to carry tlátoles elsewhere, but whether they actually did so is not mentioned in the record. One Indian from Arizpe named Lorenzo had urged quick action, suggesting launching attacks on the Spaniards before they had opportunities to load their harquebuses. Thus Arizpe, too, seemed ripe for rebellion, the southernmost pueblo on the Río Sonora to be implicated. Farther south, the Indians were not interested in any uprising whatsoever. Through all the ferment in the pueblos of the northeast Opatería, they would remain uninvolved.

Javier Jaure revealed himself as a spirited revolutionary. He had traveled throughout the Opatería, carrying the tlátoles to numerous pueblos to the east and north. At Guásavas he had visited a ranchería where he ran into an old man who seemed especially receptive to the tlátoles. Jaure could not recall the man's name, but he had convinced the old fellow to carry the tlátole to Guásavas itself and report back to him what he found. In other rancherías and pueblos he had made similar successful contacts. He reported recruiting enthusiastic young volunteers, all eager to get rid of Spaniards. One of them urged Jaure on, assuring him and others that the Spaniards' harquebuses were clumsy and difficult to load, that in the time it took the Spaniards to load and reload they could fling four arrows.[39] In Guásavas Jaure may have recruited Gerónimo Jumari, who was later arrested in Tepache.

After his testimony was complete, Jaure remained proudly unrepentant. With all his heart, he wanted to see Spaniards killed or driven from the land. That was all he had to say.

Pedro de Montoya pleaded meekly for his client to be released from jail. In spite of his confessions, the young man did not know what he was doing. His confession had been forced by torture and could not be taken at face value. He also was of "diminished capacity" and could not possibly be of danger to Spaniards. Yes, he had named names and provided details, but he was not himself a conspirator, even though he had admitted bringing tlátoles and arguing for the killing of Spaniards, and yes, he believed in all his heart that the Spaniards must be killed.

Verdugo would have no part of Montoya's tepid plea. Javier Jaure was a menace and must be done away with. He sentenced him that very day to be removed from jail, tied up, and dragged through the streets and beaten while a public crier called out his crimes. This punishment was to continue until he was dead, after which his body was to be raised on a gallows and left untouched for eight days as an example to other Indians who might pretend to rise up against Spaniards. No one was to offer any sacraments or to pay for burial expenses. And so ended the life of Javier Jaure.

Now that things in Chinapa and Bacoachi had been mostly cleaned up, the alcalde mayor turned his attention to other parts of the province and took charge of the investigations and purges there. In less than a week he had extracted confessions, prepared indictments, pronounced sentences, and ordered executions. He departed Chinapa and Bacoachi for Cuquiárichi.

The Conspiracy in the East: Escorza and Verdugo Hold Court

At the time of the first meeting with the vecinos of San Juan Bautista on July 2, Verdugo had issued orders for Captain Pedro de Peralta of Nacozari to organize and lead another hastily conscripted militia composed of miners and ranchers to Cuquiárichi, arrest their governors and topiles, and incarcerate them in Nacozari. Peralta departed with ten soldiers on July 3 and arrived at Cuquiárichi on July 4. As ordered, he proceeded to arrest the governor and topiles of the town and transported them back to Nacozari, roughly fifty kilometers to the south. He also sent out a dragnet to other villages as well, arresting an unspecified number of Indians, but at least one representative topile from Guásavas, to the southeast.

During the subsequent interrogations, Captain Peralta learned that the proposed rebellion may have originated from Sumas in Casas Grandes (in Chihuahua). Other testimony stated that the unrest might have been inspired by Indians of New Mexico the previous year.

Over the next several days, Peralta interrogated a host of Indians. In doing so he unearthed chilling information from the young Indian from Guásavas who had been imprisoned along with the other suspects from Cuquiárichi. He claimed that conspirators from a host of pueblos had gathered together in Cuquiárichi several months earlier and, while smoking (chupando), agreed to a scheme whereby they would bide their time until late winter. At a preordained moment they would stage several fake attacks by Indians masquerading as Apaches. The rebels would carry out these diversionary attacks far from the larger pueblos, especially San Juan Bautista, and would thus lure the militia away from where most of the vecinos lived. The Indians would then launch strikes at the defenseless pueblos and at the soldiers, who would have been divided into smaller squadrons to respond to the multiple attacks. The participating pueblos named included Cucurpe, far to the west of San Juan Bautista, and never before mentioned in connection with conspiracy.[40] This bit of information was especially troubling, since it brought the Indians of the Río San Miguel into the conspiracy.

On the eighth or ninth of October, Captain Peralta transferred his tribunal back north to Cuquiárichi, eager to extract further information. He discovered almost nothing. Subsequent prisoners professed themselves disturbingly ignorant of any events or plots beyond the most general rumors. One prisoner, Ignacio Jojói, governor of Cuquiárichi, refused to swear by God and the sign of the cross that he would tell the truth—an unprecedented obstinacy. Nor would he answer questions. Captain Peralta seemed frustrated or puzzled, perhaps not aware that the youthful Francisco Quigue in Chinapa had already mentioned Jojói as a prime conspirator. Whether the captain was an inept extractor of information or the Indians simply dug in their heels and refused to divulge information is difficult to determine. Witness after witness professed ignorance of any conspiracy or convocos or tlátoles. Through July 10, Peralta had amassed an impressive collection of statements and conjectures but had little other than a long list of "know nothings" to show for his efforts.

On July 11, Lázaro Verdugo with his contingent of soldiers arrived in Cuquiárichi from Bacoachi. He was undoubtedly nervous from what he had learned from his interrogations in Chinapa and Bacoachi, believing now that without a doubt the conspiracy was widespread. Upon arrival he received a letter from Juan Bautista de Escorza of Tepache, who one year ago had expressed to Governor Otermín of New Mexico his fear about unrest in the region following the Pueblo uprising. In his letter, Escorza warned Verdugo that Indians around Tepache were in constant convocos. He had information from an important Spaniard, Captain Pedro de Valencia, that suspicious activity was everywhere. This could mean only that an additional pueblo was in rebellion.

Once again Verdugo wasted no time. He reviewed the testimony Pedro de Peralta had accumulated, then brushed the captain aside impatiently and assumed control of the interrogations. Verdugo revealed himself as a deft and merciless inquisitor by comparison, perhaps because he was vested with the authority to use whatever means necessary to get at the basis of the unrest. Unlike Peralta, he would not hesitate to torture recalcitrant witnesses to make them reveal what they knew. At the same time we must keep in mind that Verdugo was in charge of the documentary record of his activities and was facing the closing days of his term as alcalde mayor. Thus he had a strong motivation for portraying himself as an efficient and focused champion of Spanish authority and domination. He had already seen to the execution of at least four alleged conspirators and he seemed hell-bent to execute more. The conspiratorial ferment in the Opatería left him in no mood to trifle with petty details.

As his first act, Verdugo had Ignacio Jojói dragged from his prison cell to appear before the tribunal once again, and then he commenced with his interrogation. Jojói had appeared before Pedro de Peralta two days earlier and had refused to take the customary oath. Furthermore, he had refused to name names and point fingers at other conspirators. He remained obdurate in his refusal to provide information to Peralta, replying to all questions that he did not know the answer. A frustrated Peralta had dismissed him, knowing full well that Jojói would be back at a later time.

Who, Verdugo asked, were the principal coconspirators cooperating with Jojói? Jojói would mention only Diego Suri, who had apparently died or disappeared. What was Suri's message? the alcalde demanded. Jojói replied that Suri argued that they should use the revolt in New Mexico as an example. The Spaniards were their mortal enemies. If they could get rid of the foreigners, they could return to their old pagan ways, living at their ease, just as they pleased. And who besides Diego Suri had held convocos and carried tlátoles? Jojói remained aloof and refused to answer. Through an interpreter, Verdugo warned the Indian that he would be forced to torture him unless he coughed up the information the alcalde sought. Jojói would not budge. Verdugo, surely well versed in the highly developed Spanish art of using applied pain to extract information, ordered his "minister" to bind Jojói by the upper arms with ropes and to twist the ropes (apparently with a pole for leverage) until they obtained the desired results. Jojói remained silent. All right, Verdugo told him through the interpreter: If we have to tear your body apart, the loss of blood will be your fault, not ours. We have to get at the truth.[41] Verdugo ordered another twist, without results. He ordered a third twist, still with no response from Jojói. Finally, after the fourth twist, responding to what must have been excruciating pain and on the verge of having his shoulders dislocated, Jojói began to talk. Seeing that the prisoner was now cooperating, Verdugo ordered the torturer to slacken Jojói's bonds.[42]

According to Jojói's forced testimony, his principal contact for bringing tlátoles to various pueblos was an Indian named Basuso, who had died three months earlier. Jojói owned that he had sent the tlátole to Bacerac through another Indian named Banasuri, a Native *fiscal* of the pueblo (probably Cuquiárichi). Jojói had also placed Banasuri in charge of contacting Lucas Canari, governor of Bavispe, with the information and plot. Canari himself had attempted to make an anti-Spaniard pact with Sumas to the east but had not been successful because the Sumas were angry with the Bavispans. They claimed someone from Bavispe had killed one of their number. They had not refused outright to join, however, and Canari seemed to imply that any day they could expect the Sumas to become a party to an uprising.

Jojói's testimony continued. From Bavispe another resident Native named Uriouri had carried the conspiracy to the governor of Bacobichi,[43] who in turn made contact with the gentile Sobaípuris of Quiburi, in present-day Arizona. Those Pima speakers appeared to be more tractable than the Sumas, who seemed sullen in their willingness to participate in the rebellion. At that point, then, Cuquiárichi, Bavispe, Bacobichi, and Bacerac were clearly in collusion with the conspirators. Jojói mentioned further that Guachinera had been recruited as well. He believed that Chinapa was also ready but was uncertain about the state of readiness of the Chinapans. To what extent the Sobaípuris and other Pimans were willing participants was unclear, but they had accepted tlátoles, and that was usually a dead giveaway to conspiratorial inclinations.

By now Jojói had Verdugo's undivided attention. That the conspiracy was widespread he now had no doubt. Jojói confirmed the rumors of conspiracy that Verdugo had heard in Chinapa and corroborated the testimony of

Pablo Dimara, whose body was probably still dangling from a scaffold back in Bacoachi. Francisco Quigue, now breaking rocks as part of a chain gang in the mines, had also reported the vast extent of the conspiracy. Verdugo questioned Jojói as to when the uprising had been planned. Jojói replied that all were agreed that October was a good time (after the harvesting of corn) to kill the Spaniards, but no more precise date was forthcoming. (Other prisoners mentioned the cold of winter as a date; even others suggested that the following spring had been the appointed date.)

Verdugo was done with Jojói. He would be executed, of course. He had yet to reinterrogate Francisco Baduqui, a topile of Cuquiárichi, whom he now believed to be a principal accomplice in the conspiracy along with Jojói. Baduqui had been interrogated by Captain Peralta but denied knowing anything about a conspiracy. He assumed he was being held prisoner because he was supposed to have been weeding the mission wheat field and had been loitering instead. This was a flippant answer, sure to arouse Verdugo's wrath when he read it in the transcription. Verdugo ordered Baduqui brought before him and demanded of the Indian that he answer his questions and tell the truth or be subjected to the same torture that had made Jojói talk.

Apparently Baduqui needed no more prompting. He named the principal conspirators as Jojói, the late Diego Suri, and himself. He echoed Jojói's statement that the planned uprising was to occur in October, probably in Bacoachi or Bacobichi,[44] where the Indians would kill all Spaniards, their relatives, and their associates. When the attacks against the Spaniards were complete, the perpetrators would flee to the mountains to hide. Verdugo asked Baduqui about Bavispe's participation in the uprising. He replied that virtually the entire town was prepared to join in. Verdugo asked Baduqui if, in fact, he had hoped to kill all the Spaniards. Baduqui, with little to lose, replied that yes, indeed, with all his heart he wanted to kill the Spaniards.

A string of marginally involved prisoners, mostly topiles, followed Baduqui, none of them of interest to Alcalde Verdugo. After grilling them, he released a half dozen from jail, exhorting them to be responsible officials, obey the authorities and priests, and report any unusual incidents to Spaniards.

By now the testimony had confirmed Verdugo's fears. He rushed a letter to Pedro de Montoya, reappointing him as public defender and giving him an hour to make his case. It appears that Montoya immediately set off from San Juan to join Verdugo in Cuquiárichi or was already present with Verdugo's entourage. His defense pleadings, however, were lame and brief, a feeble rehash of the same limp arguments he had offered in defense of the now deceased defendants of Chinapa and Bacoachi. Montoya made one novel point, however: Don't you think, he asked Verdugo, that the execution of the rebels in Chinapa and Bacoachi would serve to deter Jojói and Baduqui from any further mischief? Is there really any need to torture the prisoners, who will confess to anything at all to escape the excruciating pain the "minister" inflicts?

Verdugo was not interested in Montoya's pleas. He stuffed the effete defense brief in with the other documents and sentenced both Jojói and Baduqui to death. Pedro de Montoya was underestimating the threat from these Indians, and torture was the only way to extract vitally important information. Some of the alcalde's top men had departed stealthily for other pueblos, where they conducted secret investigations of their own into the conspiracy. Everywhere they inquired they found the seeds of sedition—plots; furtive communications with Sumas, Janos, Jocomes, and Apaches; envoys bringing tlátoles to every part of the province; clandestine convocos; Indians chupando in council circles. Pedro de Montoya was either naïve or blind to the depth of the conspiracy and the urgency facing Alcalde Verdugo. It was July 14, and from the confessions of the convicted rebels, Bavispe was seething with sedition. A revolt was scheduled for October.

Verdugo chose not even to witness the execution. He departed posthaste from Cuquiárichi to Bavispe, a trip of many hours, leaving the details of the death sentence and the execution in the hands of an underling by the name of Juan de Santa Cruz, who reported shortly thereafter that he had carried out the executions of the two motores. Six traitors down.

In his instructions for the executions, Verdugo noted the report from Juan Bautista Escorza of rebellious stirrings in Tepache. In response to Escorza's warning, Verdugo ordered that pueblo and the region around it placed under martial law and furthermore placed Escorza in charge of scouring the eastern Opatería for conspirators. The Indians of Tepache should be warned that any hint of uprising from them would be dealt with ruthlessly. Escorza's star was on the rise. The pedantic miner from Nacatóbari had been promoted and placed in charge of the investigation in the east. He had become Verdugo's lieutenant general of the war.[45]

Lázaro Verdugo's next report was written in Bavispe on July 17. The trip to the river town had taken more than two days and must have been undertaken as a more or less forced march. His advance soldiers had rounded up six Indian *fiscales* and placed them under arrest in a holding tank. One by one, Verdugo interrogated them but found little to pique his interest. After releasing four of those being held after the sweep, he finally called Lucas Canari, traditional governor of Bavispe, before his tribunal.

Verdugo's questioning of Canari was characteristically tough. The alcalde had reviewed previous testimony from confessed rebels, several of whom, including Ignacio Jojói, had fingered Canari as one of the prime conspirators. Canari stood out as the point man in Bavispe and the one who had made overtures to Sumas in hopes they would join in the mutiny. It seems rather surprising that Canari denied knowing any of the others involved in the conspiracy and claimed never to have attended any convocos or to have carried tlátoles. His denials seem a bit thin and Verdugo pounced on them like a cat after a trapped mouse. Canari was forced to backtrack on his ignorance of convocos and tlátoles but ended his first testimony maintaining he was ignorant of any uprising and unaware of the conspiracy. When his testimony was complete, Verdugo turned him over to his torturer, who asked the alcalde if he should apply the "usual tortures." Canari's defender, Pedro de Montoya, pointed out, however, that his accusers were notoriously untruthful men and that local Indians and the priest held Canari in high respect. If Verdugo were to look around at the pueblo of Bavispe, he would find it a model of tranquility and well-imbued Catholicism, not a seething pit of sedition. His men also pointed out that if Canari were tortured, word would leak out and perhaps dry up some of their sources of information. They had no doubt that he was lying, hiding behind vague denials, half-truths, and equivocations. At that point, however, torture would be counterproductive.

Verdugo considered the situation and advice and remanded Lucas Canari back to prison, leaving for the time being the question of whether or not to torture him for further information. His forbearance was not procrastination. He had ordered some of his soldiers to other parts of the region to gather information on the extent of the conspiracy, especially concerning the Sumas of Carretas (in Chihuahua) and the Janos and Jocomes.

So, while his men continued their investigations—judicial and extrajudicial—Verdugo continued to interview the adult males of Bavispe, relentlessly pursuing the track of the potential subversive. He interrogated all available governors, topiles, and fiscales but, apart from Lucas Canari, found only blank, uncomprehending faces. Questioning and requestioning the witnesses, all of whom had been rounded up and sequestered in jail, produced no further information. Forced to set most of them free, the best Verdugo could do was to threaten the people of Bavispe: if any of them learned of subversion or Indians bearing tlátoles or convocos in the town or from elsewhere and failed to report them to Spanish authorities, he would kill every young man in the town, without exception. Verdugo appears to have been of a mood to carry out his threat.

The documents now shift the focus to events in Bacadéhuachi, well to the southeast of Bavispe. Juan Bautista de Escorza had acknowledged receipt of his commission from Verdugo on July 20 in Tepache. As far as he was concerned, he had been appointed to the post in the nick of time. He had received a dispatch from a vecino named Pedro de Valencia reporting murmurs of unrest or insurrection at the hamlet of Tepache. Furthermore, a bilingual mestizo named José Ramos reported, much to Escorza's satisfaction,[46] that Indians of varying nationalities had come and gone and that that village and numerous others were rife with suspected convocos and tlátoles. Several reports cited Bacadéhuachi and Nácori Chico as the sources of the ferment. Following orders from Verdugo, Escorza assembled a troop of fourteen men armed with harquebuses and four without and departed forthwith for the Sierras.

The following day the Escorza squadron arrived at Bacadéhuachi after a forced march through the night. Escorza probably envisioned arriving to an atmosphere of hostility, of impending rebellion punctuated by suspicious glances and muffled conspiratorial sounds. He cannot have been pleased when instead he found the town celebrating the fiesta of Santiago, with mock battles between Moors and Christians taking place in a general spirit of levity. This was not Escorza's image of an apparent hotbed of subversion. Not to be dissuaded from his orders, however, he apparently waited a short while, hiding his true intent, appearing to be interested in the pageantry, but in reality he and his men were discerning who the real players on the plaza were and on whom he should serve warrants—namely, the governor and his topiles. After a short wait, he got down to the business of ferreting out the conspirators, even if he had to interrupt the festival (which would have been arranged by the mission priest) to conduct his inquisitions.[47]

Without preliminaries, he arrested the village governor and his topiles and their associates. Since none of the Indians spoke Spanish, he selected an interpreter, the same José Ramos who had supplied him in Tepache with tales of rebellion and treachery. In an earlier interview, Ramos had informed Escorza that Bacadéhuachi was alive with sedition, mostly brought in by other Indians: Jovas, Jocomes, Janos, and Sumas. The Indians would meet at the Río Bavispe, some five leagues away, to plot. Since Ramos was an informer, one must question his neutrality as an interpreter. Indeed, the narratives containing his translations are confused, often meandering, and at times, incoherent. What is clear, though, is that Escorza promised Juan Sagori, the governor of Bacadéhuachi, that if he came clean in his testimony, he would have nothing to fear and would not be punished. The appointed public defender would later remind Escorza of that promise.

The Indian governor told Escorza and his tribunal that an individual named Miguel had come through the pueblo bearing tlátoles and proclaiming the success of the Pueblo uprising in New Mexico. The message had fallen on deaf ears. But Sagori recalled having heard someone say that an uprising had been planned for the following April. He had little more to report.

Escorza set to his task and lined up the suspects, grilling them. He showed himself willing to use torture at any sign of recalcitrant testimony. His preferred method involved crushing the fingers with wooden rods lashed around the digits and tightened at his order. It was effective. Several Indians testified, along with the governor, of their knowledge of an uprising planned for the following April, not October, as Indians from Cuquiárichi and Chinapa had maintained. The *tlátolero* Miguel had assured them that in spite of their misgivings (those who rejected the tlátoles argued that at least with the Spaniards they had supplies), following any uprising they could take refuge in the sierras. Yes, they affirmed, the governor Sagori had full knowledge of the plan. Included in two reports was the figure named Banichuri (or Buchaurini), identified as the intellectual source of the impending uprising.[48] Although he was identified as such only in Bacadéhuachi, Banichuri represents an intriguing figure. He claimed he was God, that he had created all the earth, that the Spaniards were destroying it with their cattle and other livestock, and that they were the reason why the earth no longer yielded its fruits and why the springs and watercourses had dried up. The Indians should no longer sell corn to the Spaniards, he preached, but rather should let the occupiers be consumed by fire. Then the earth would return to its former fecundity, with ample rain and no more chilling cold. It seems a shame that we have no further information about this apparently charismatic man.

Other testimony was equally revealing. Ysidro Juduri testified that Javier, the servant of Lorenzo Quintero, had informed him that all the Natives of the region hoped to rise up and overthrow the Spaniards, further complicating Javier's role.[49] Another witness, after being tortured, confessed that the Indians had stockpiled weapons in the home of a certain Indian of the pueblo, a disclosure of great interest to the Spaniards. A quick check revealed nothing more than men normally kept in their homes. Another suspect implicated a shadowy character named Cristóbal Cocoba. Escorza was sufficiently worried that he sent soldiers to Cocoba's milpa, where he was working, and had him arrested, bound, and brought before him summarily.

Cocoba turned out to be a prosecutor's dream. Angry at his relatives and neighbors and feeling shunned and neglected, he testified readily. He volunteered that he had departed from his home in Guachinera, where his relatives refused him food, and moved closer to Bacadéhuachi, where he was still a bit of an outcast. He was eager to name the leaders of the convocos and the movers of tlátoles, all from Guachinera. One leader even had a cache of arms in his house, he said. All of them were bent on eliminating the Spanish presence from the region.

By this time Sergeant Escorza was angry enough at what he heard to hang several of the Indians. He believed Cocoba. In preparation for executions, he sent soldiers to summon the mission priest, Padre Luis Dávila, to administer last rites, but the curate was nowhere to be found and was said to be visiting other villages of the mission. Disgruntled, Escorza dispatched a request to the priest at Guásavas, Padre Joseph de Covarrubias, requesting him to hie himself forthwith to Bacadéhuachi, since the sergeant was about to execute some Indians whose crimes were so grave as to warrant the death penalty and he needed a cleric to administer the appropriate death rites. He posted the letter on Wednesday and gave the priest until Friday to get to Bacadéhuachi and attend to the souls of the Indians about to be hanged or shot. Meanwhile, Escorza took more testimony, hoping, it seems, to add to the lineup of those capitally condemned.

Finally, on July 27, Sergeant Escorza had finished with his judicial inquiries. He gave the Indians' public defender a chance to be heard. Juan de Lira, whom Escorza had appointed defender, pointed out that the sergeant had promised immunity to the governor if he would talk. The rest of the condemned should be set free, he said, since all their confessions amounted to nothing more than talk among the Indians about an uprising and had produced no action. Furthermore, some of the defendants had no idea what was going on. Escorza had condemned the Indians for (among other things) not notifying the Spaniards of the seditious currents running through Bacadéhuachi. Lira responded that they could not have warned the Spaniards, since they spoke no Spanish. They were not guilty of any crime.

Escorza added Lira's written comments to the file, ignoring them completely. He plowed into the sentencing: two of the accused, Juan Maiboca and Joseph Duqui, were to be executed by a firing squad, and Juan Maiboca was ordered beheaded afterward, with his head impaled on a post for all to behold, a testament to the folly of convening convocos and transporting tlátoles. Furthermore, he ordered the houses of the two to be razed to the ground, leaving no trace of their former presence. As to the governor of Bacadéhuachi, Juan Sagori, Escorza judged him also deserving of execution, but recalling the public defender's reminder that he had promised to let the governor off if he told the truth, he commuted the death penalty and instead sentenced him to be sold into hard labor in a mine for ten years and his house razed. Another Indian was to be sold into hard labor for four years. Three others he let off easily, judging them to have been less blameworthy. Their sentences: two hundred lashes each. The accuser Cocoba, a real snitch, he freed from jail, finding him a simple victim of circumstance. Whether or not the priest from Guásavas arrived in time to salvage their sinful souls we do not know, but the sentences were carried out that day or one day later.

That same day, Escorza ordered all the Indians of Bacadéhuachi gathered into the plaza. He instructed them to bring every bow and arrow they owned and add them to a pile in the plaza. While the villagers watched, he had his soldiers set fire to the lot. He barked warnings to the crowd. No one in that town was to keep such arms in their house for the space of one year under the pain of two hundred lashes and hard labor, and after that period, never more than one bow and six arrows per house. For two weeks not a soul was to depart from the village. Violators would be roundly punished.

Escorza observed that all the Indians indicated that they would obey the orders.

The captain's timing was fortunate for him. He had acted boldly in rounding up suspects, executing the most likely offenders and punishing all other likely perpetrators. All that time he had known that his superior, Lázaro Verdugo, would meet up with him shortly. Verdugo had been occupied in ferreting out rebels in Bavispe, some five hours' journey to the north. From Bavispe he moved his tribunal south to Guachinera, eager to pounce on the leaders of that supposed nest of rebellious intrigue. To his dismay, we must assume, in Guachinera he found orders awaiting, notifying him that Francisco Cuervo y Valdez had replaced him as alcalde mayor. Cuervo had ordered Verdugo to return posthaste to San Juan Bautista to turn over the reins and the power. That meant that Escorza would be operating on his own until Cuervo could join him and take over command of all operations. Escorza was free to do as he pleased.

Verdugo's departure for San Juan Bautista coincided well with Escorza's desire to move his inquisition to Guachinera, several hours' journey northwest of Bacadéhuachi and supposedly the home of several influential rebels. He ordered his squadron to that pueblo and transferred his tribunal with them. To his great good fortune, the troops encountered a small party of Indians not far from Guachinera, apparently on their way to pay homage to the new alcalde mayor Cuervo. That hapless group included nearly all the supposed subversives of Guachinera who had been mentioned in the confessions recorded in Bacadéhuachi. Escorza ordered the lot taken prisoner and brought before his tribunal.

The information Escorza gathered in Guachinera, added to that already accrued from the repeated questioning of Indians in Chinapa, Bacoachi, Cuquiárichi, and Bacadéhuachi was disquieting. Leadership of the conspiracy appears to have rested primarily with the traditional governors and their topiles.[50] These Native officials were usually the most influential and respected men of a mission community. Priests made the actual appointments. They retained the power to appoint and unseat the leaders. By creating a shadow government of Natives in each mission, the priests relieved themselves (and the Crown) of detail work and could appear to be above petty resentments, disagreements, and gossip, while retaining the power to rule in all important matters. Now it looked as though the priests had appointed a network of traitors and had allowed much of the province to fall into the hands of rebels. Military officials seldom viewed the Jesuits with admiration, and the conspiratorial reality made the clergy appear so much more inept or disloyal. The revelations from Guachinera may help explain the remarkable absence of clergy in the proceedings against putative conspirators.

The interrogators must also have been dismayed to hear prisoner after prisoner state that the Indians disliked the Spaniards enough that they hoped to see them killed or evicted from lands that had formerly been their own. The Indians resented the *tapisque*, the mandatory recruitment for working for Spaniards; being forced to endure long hours of arduous labor and unhealthful and dangerous conditions in the mines; having to work as servants for the indolent Spaniards; and being subjected to the Spaniards' whims, their whips, and their punishments.

In spite of these growing concerns, Escorza's tribunal in Guachinera yielded satisfying results. Escorza called as a witness another informer, one Juan Juridaca, who provided a long and meandering account of how the governors and their topiles demonstrated antagonism toward priests and Spaniards, and how Juan Uro, governor of Guachinera, had invited the other conspirators to his house to meet with him and a group of Conchos (from Chihuahua) to plot an uprising.

Escorza, at least for the time operating without supervision, once again resorted to torture, using wooden rods to twist and crush fingers. From his victims he learned that a core of four or five rebels was the source of much of the unrest. They included the governor of Guachinera, Juan Uro; one Pedro Tasay (both of whom he tortured); Christóbal Chiguari; Francisco Sodora; and an elusive figure often reported as Sodora's brother, one Francisco Sivacome Muchica. All had been previously mentioned in testimony gathered in Bacadéhuachi. Some witnesses also pointed to Bavispe (some three hours' journey to the north of Guachinera) as the real source of the plotting. (In Bavispe Verdugo had heard a litany of witnesses pointing to Guachinera as the center of foment.) Pedro Tasay, after being tortured, confirmed the revelations of a previous witness that governor Juan Uro had met with a core group of conspirators, that some Conchos from the east were involved, and that a network of plots moved back and forth among the pueblos. Tasay also revealed that a ritual dance had taken place at the governor's house, at which a live eagle had been presented by one party to another. At the same time that this damning testimony was implicating more suspects, Escorza received a dispatch from Father Covarrubias from Guásavas disclaiming any authority over Juan Maiboca, Pedro Tasay, or Francisco Sivacome Muchica, three prime conspirators. They were not sheep of his flock.

By now Escorza was convinced that in addition to the prisoners he held in Guachinera, the governor of Bavispe, Lucas Canari, and his topiles were key figures. Verdugo had already questioned Canari but had released him pending more interrogations. Eager to expand his inquisition, Escorza assembled a troop of soldiers and set out posthaste for Bavispe, but when they reached the Río Bavispe they found their way impeded by the river's high current. Escorza returned to Guachinera but ordered the soldiers to cross when the waters subsided and arrest the governor of Bavispe and his entourage and deliver them to him in Guachinera. By the next day the governor Canari had been arrested and transported to Guachinera, where the soldiers brought him before Escorza and his court.

Cuervo Takes Over

All was ready for another round of executions when Escorza was abruptly upstaged by the arrival of his new superior, Francisco Cuervo y Valdez.

Cuervo had written from San Juan that he was about to depart for Guachinera in the company of ten soldiers. He requested that the offending governors and topiles all be arrested and kept securely under guard so that he might interrogate them forthwith on his arrival.

Escorza must have cursed his luck. All this work to ferret out conspirators, and Cuervo would receive the credit! And Escorza might well have worried about the rashness of some of his executions, uneasy that he could face court-martial if Cuervo chose to conduct any sort of investigation into his handling of the accusations. His fears were quickly allayed, however, when on his arrival Cuervo issued a blanket endorsement of the executions and sentences, adding only that any miners to whom the sentenced Indians had been sold would be required to post a bond with the royal treasury for the otherwise free labor they would receive for the next decade.

From here on, though, Cuervo took charge of the proceedings, inquisition, investigation, arrests, tortures, and executions. He ordered any new prisoners be kept under guard apart from those imprisoned by Escorza. The sergeant major was left to act as an observer at Cuervo's proceedings, until he was dispatched somewhat later back to Bacadéhuachi and Nácori Chico.

Cuervo proved himself to be an even sterner inquisitor than Escorza, and a true zealot when compared with Peralta. He carefully studied previous testimony and when suspects appeared before him he peppered them with questions. If an Indian demonstrated any tendency to avoid answering questions straightforwardly, he did not hesitate to apply devices for extracting information. He applied rope and poles to the upper arms of Francisco Sodora of Guachinera. With other prisoners he freely ordered rods to crush fingers. In the case of governor Juan Uro of Guachinera, the finger crushing failed to force the Indian to answer, so Cuervo ordered his arms bound with cords and the cords tightened until the prisoner talked.[51] He still refused. Cuervo ordered cords bound around his legs, without further description of the technique. This seemed to work, and Juan Uro coughed up a mountain of information implicating himself and other leaders in the pueblos and verifying previous accusations. Cuervo also threatened Uro with *genuine* torture if the leg "treatment" failed to produce cooperation on his part. When the questioning reached Francisco Sivacome Muchica, the record indicates that he chose to divulge all he knew, including testimony damaging to himself and his close friends.

The description of the testimony and procedures reveals Cuervo to have been a thorough and seasoned veteran of inquisitions. He followed protocols scrupulously, making sure that each Indian's interpreter verified the accuracy of his interpretation and that the public defender (in this case one Juan Gutiérrez de la Cruz) observed all the proceedings, explained to the Indians what was transpiring, and concurred in the accuracy of the written content of the testimony. Furthermore, once the transcription of the testimony was complete, he ordered each of the accused back into the courtroom, where he would have his testimony read back to him and, in the presence of the defender and the interpreter, verify its accuracy. In that way, no one could claim that Cuervo (perhaps unlike Escorza) was arbitrarily or capriciously executing or punishing.

Public defender Gutiérrez was allotted six hours to prepare and present his defense to the inquisitors. He dwelled on three points. In the first place, he argued, none of the Indians had been accused of any actual acts against Spaniards, only words. No uprising had taken place. He acknowledged that the defendants had discussed an uprising, but conspiring and acting were two different things. As his second point, he argued that all the inflammatory talk—the tlátoles and convocos—had originated in Cuquiárichi and others had transported them to Bacerac, Bavispe, and Guachinera. Hence the local leaders were less guilty than their compatriots to the west, if they were guilty at all. Finally, he claimed, the defendants were Indians, not people of reason, and as such were *incapazes*, not really capable of rational decisions, and thus should not be subject to capital punishment. They lacked the natural light of reason. On these grounds, the men should be set free.

Cuervo, as was the case with Verdugo and Escorza, ordered Gutiérrez's plea filed among the other papers of the archive. He was not about to be dissuaded by the mere formality of the defender's arguments. Gutiérrez, after all, was one of Cuervo's party.

An unusual twist to the defense arrived in Cuervo's hands at the last minute, however. Padre Antonio Estrella, priest of the mission of Bacerac (which included Bavispe and probably Guachinera), submitted a two-page letter addressed to the alcalde in which he vehemently and articulately opposed the execution of the defendants. He argued, as did Gutiérrez, that the guilt for any real plot lay with the Indians from Cuquiárichi, who had already been executed, not those of *his* mission. Furthermore, the accused included men who were the pillars of his congregation, men who had repeatedly demonstrated their piety. If they were to be executed, the example to the rest of the Indian congregation, whose adherence to the *doctrina* was always tenuous anyway, would undermine the efforts of the Jesuits to evangelize them.

Estrella pleaded for a lightening of the sentences. Such intervention from the clergy in criminal matters was rare and a daring move for the priest. He was sticking his neck out and risking criticism of the Jesuits at the same time.

Padre Estrella's pleas did not dent in the slightest Cuervo's clear intent to eliminate all plotters from the face of the earth. Priests were notorious mollycoddlers. He pronounced the death sentence on Juan Uro, Juan Bagueri, Lucas Canari, governors; Pedro Tasay and Andres Sarina, topiles; and Christóbal Chiguari, Pablo Sino, Francisco Sodora, Francisco Sivacome Muchica, and one Juanillo, simply described as an "Indian." All three governors and some of their topiles were to be executed for their crimes against the "Royal Crown." There would be no mercy. For Juan Uro, Juan Bagueri, and Lucas Canari, the governors of the three pueblos, Cuervo dictated:

> I order that they be removed from prison where they are being held and each be led through their village under full guard and custody, with the voice of a town crier proclaiming their crimes, and then taken to the gallows and bound to a stake and that they be shot[52] until they die naturally and then hung from that same gallows for a period of four hours and then their heads impaled on the said gallows.[53]

As to Pedro Tasay and Andrés Sarina, topiles; and Christóbal Chiguari, Pablo Sino, Francisco Sodora, and Francisco Sivacome Muchica, they were likewise to be removed from the prison and taken to the place of execution, the gallows, where they were to be beaten, blindfolded, and hung from the scaffold until dead, then drawn and quartered and their dismembered remains placed on the roadways leading into the towns. The lesser conspirators were condemned to one hundred lashes and all were to be stripped of their canes of office.

The executions were to be carried out to the letter in the three pueblos, each of the condemned to be executed in full view of those who knew him. At the last minute Padre Antonio Estrella of Bacerac appeared and made a special appeal for clemency for Andrés Sarina and the Indian Juanillo, arguing that they were vital to his community and in no way deserving of the death penalty. Cuervo ignored the plea for Sarina, but the intervention of the priest may have spared the life of Juanillo, the Indian. Since he was quite young and not quite responsible, his punishment would be one hundred lashes and imprisonment, with the public reminder that he would still be put to death if he further offended the Royal Crown. All the others were summarily executed, some on August 6 in Guachinera, the remainder on August 8 in Bacerac, except for Lucas Canari of Bavispe. He was to be transported to his hometown to be executed in public. When the military transport reached the Río Bavispe, however, they once again found it in high flood and were unable to cross. Cuervo instead ordered a gallows erected then and there and summoned all local people to attend the execution (from across the river?), which was carried out on August 10.[54] Among the spectators in the audience to the executions in Guachinera and on the banks of the Río Bavispe were Sergeant Major Juan Bautista de Escorza and Captain Pedro de Peralta. Townspeople were also present, on Cuervo's orders.

Cuervo had finished his work in the Bavispe region but sent Escorza back to the sierras to finish his investigations in Nácori Chico and other pueblos.[55] Cuervo himself returned to San Juan Bautista, hoping he had eradicated the conspiracy.

Escorza arrived in Nácori Chico on August 10, hoping to track down any remnants of "venomous treason."[56] His findings were mixed but sparse. He summoned before him an Indian leader who was reputed to be an admirer of Spaniards and loyal to them. This witness explained that the villages there were small and scattered and subject to infighting, and that communications with Bacadéhuachi and other mission towns were minimal. He had learned of the supposed conspiracy only because he had been in attendance at the fiesta in Bacadéhuachi the day that Escorza had originally arrived and he had watched while Escorza's men arrested the governor and his topiles. Escorza found this witness unproductive, but probably truthful.

Next he interrogated the governor of Nácori Chico, who had also attended the fiesta in Bacadéhuachi and had witnessed the two executions and the exile of the two whose sentences had been commuted. He also admitted that his compadre, the governor of Bacadéhuachi (now serving ten years of hard labor), had led him to believe that he had heard tell that the Natives of Bavispe were being armed and prepared for a general uprising based on some tlátoles from a *Chichimec* (a general term Spaniards applied to hunters and gatherers in the region north of the settled areas of central Mexico) who was wandering about the region deceiving people, but this was all secondhand knowledge. He could not verify rumors of Sahuaripan and Concho hatemongers in the vicinity. Yes, he had heard rumors of rumblings of discontent but had paid no attention to them, considering them of no moment. The governor was vehement that no one in Nácori Chico had carried or accepted tlátoles. He knew nothing more but would assuredly inform the Spaniards if they did hear something. And so it went. This might well have been a classic case of Native resistance in the form of foot-dragging and denial, combined with the secrecy for which Opatans were notorious.

Escorza had little cause for torturing or inflicting severe punishment on the governor, but in order to teach him and others the importance of keeping Spaniards better informed, he revoked the governor's cane of office in the presence of all townspeople and bestowed it on the previous witness, who spoke some Spanish and had acted as an informant and demonstrated his loyalty to Spaniards. Escorza also appointed as local alcalde and topiles other Indians who were known to hold Spaniards in high esteem. That would teach the Natives a lesson.

Although he had uncovered nothing in the way of treason in Nácori Chico, Escorza ordered erected a scaffold for hanging "traitors." It does not appear that his men actually used it in that pueblo, for they had no legitimate suspects, but it stood as a warning of what would happen to those who conspired with rebels. He also saw to the rectifying of some unspecified problems in Nácori having to do with pagan practices.

Traveling on to Santo Tomás de Serva, a part Jova village now lost, Escorza made the same inquiries, with the same inconclusive results. However, the village governor confirmed that a few months earlier the governor of Bacadéhuachi had arrived with the news that Indians from Bavispe were hoping to rise up against the Spaniards. However, no one in Santo Tomás had any interest in participating. No one. He, the governor, had not advised Spaniards of this treachery because his heart was peaceful and his town would have nothing to do with such nonsense.

Escorza seemed frustrated at not discovering more seditious currents. He revoked the governor's cane of office as punishment for not having informed Spaniards of the rumors of rebellion; rewarded it to another, more sympathetic fellow; and appointed a new gang of topiles and alcaldes. He ordered a gallows erected at the highest point in the village and pointed it out clearly to the gathered residents, reminding them that in Bacadéhuachi the Spaniards had erected a similar scaffold and had hanged two accused perpetrators. Escorza calculated that all the Indians of the district would understand that symbolism. He also ordered the Indians to construct a hostelry wherein visiting Spaniards could be comfortably lodged, thus symbolizing the loyalty of Santo Tomás to His Majesty.

Escorza hoped for more pueblos to exorcise but could find none. He had intended to investigate Guásavas and the hamlet of Uchacari, said to be home to some conspirators, but the Río Bavispe was in high flood, making it impossible for him and his soldiers to cross there. He decided that enough was enough. He had served His Majesty's ends well. He ordered his men southward and led them across a ford in the Bavispe and back to Tepache, where they arrived on August 15, 1681. From there he notified Cuervo of his activities, adding that he had devoted one month of his life to carrying out orders from his superiors, in the most faithful fashion.

The Second Conspiracy of 1681

Back home in San Juan Bautista, Cuervo, an impressive list of executions in his portfolio, hoped that he had eradicated all traces of the conspiracy (and, according to later accusations, he hoped to get back to his real work of extorting money from hapless mine owners).[57] His work was by no means finished, however. By the first week of October, rumors had reached him that new conspiracies were appearing in the vicinity of Teuricachi and Nacozari. Stirrings were occurring again in Cuquiárichi as well. As he would soon discover, tlátoles were moving back and forth to Chinapa, Arizpe, Bacobichi, Bavispe, Bacerac, Guachinera, and other pueblos as well. Even worse, the wilder, nomadic peoples from the north and east were increasingly implicated in rebel plots. Sumas, Janos, Jocomes, and Pimans were routinely mentioned as part of the convocos. Sonoran Indians were exchanging tlátoles with Sumas of Carretas, a frontier town in the plains at the base of the Sierra Madre east of Bavispe. Apaches were not only mentioned by those interrogated but were showing up in villages in the Opatería and were offering support to the rebels. Ten Apaches had appeared in Carretas, wanting to join the Sumas in a regional uprising.[58] Several Indians still maintained that the rebels had arms stored in a mountain cave known as Tosocomache, supposedly ten leagues from Cuquiárichi.

Cuervo referred to the current situation as the "second conspiracy."[59] To combat the insurgents, he would have to begin another round of imprisonments and interrogations and then figure out how to take on the foreign nations, especially Sumas, as well.[60] He suspected that a network of firebrand rebels was still at large, inciting discontented Indians and warlike peoples. He vowed to track down every possible lead and weed out the insurgents. His men would rough up any suspects and subject them to limitless interrogation. He set up his new tribunal in Teuricachi and dispatched Matheo

Verdugo de Chávez, son of his predecessor, to the far points of the Opatería. Under Matheo's military reign, being an adult male Indian in any of the towns named in the conspiracy soon became a crime.

In early October, however, a Jesuit priest slowed down the hysterical pursuit of Indians. Padre Antonio Leal, priest of Cuchuta, Cuquiárichi, and Teuricachi, fired off a letter to Alcalde Mayor Cuervo from his sickbed. In an angry tone he wrote that in spite of his repeated reminders and protests that Indians within his community were bestowed with immunity from arrest by government officials, soldiers continued to violate the sanctuary. One of his charges, named Manuel Tazina, had been violently seized inside the mission by one Nícolas Verdugo (perhaps Matheo Verdugo, son of the alcalde mayor). As a result of this gross violation of Indian rights, the priest announced he was excommunicating all the men involved in the illegal seizure. This may have included Cuervo himself. Father Leal maintained that the soldiers had no authority to make the arrest because the Indian was in and of the *comunidad* of Cuchuta and inside the church there and thus received "ecclesiastical immunity."[61] Furthermore, Father Leal appears to have demanded that Indians be provided with something like due process. Thereafter, Marcos de Alesa, Cuervo's lieutenant, noted, "Since none of the Indians understand the Spanish language, it is only appropriate to appoint interpreters who understand the Ópata language, according to royal regulations."[62] And so Padre Leal saw to it that the Indians had interpreters even before they were arrested and that they were not lynched, at least when they were within his jurisdiction. The exasperated investigator, Marcos de Alesa, grudgingly noted that at least in that jurisdiction (perhaps just those three towns), the ad hoc prosecutors would have to follow that procedure. He appointed one Juan Pascual de la Cruz as interpreter, noting that he was a mulatto, and a Spaniard named Juan Pablo de Salazar to the same post, apparently to keep Juan Pascual honest. We can almost hear the grumbling of the settlers that priests were once again mollycoddling the savages and thus protecting terrorists.

With the matter of interpreters settled, Cuervo began his inquiries in Teuricachi. Marcos de Alesa brought in the prisoner, one Francisco Banasuri of Cuchuta or Teuricachi, whom others back in July had pointed to as having transported tlátoles around the region. Banasuri had been a wanted man for some time. Just how he came to be captured is not revealed in the documents. Under initial questioning he claimed he knew nothing of such things and had heard nothing about any uprising. The inquisitors were sure he was lying. Cuervo reminded Banasuri that the late Ignacio Jojói of Chinapa had provided many names and facts, as had the governors in Bacerac, Bavispe, and Guachinera. All had already pointed the finger at him. Banasuri still denied any knowledge, so they loosened Banasuri's tongue with the skillful application of a few cords and rods, the customary tortures. The captive then "confessed" that as of four months earlier, he had brought tlátoles to governors all over the region, that he was under the orders of Ignacio Jojói of Chinapa, and that even after Alcalde Lázaro Verdugo had passed through Teuricachi (in July) arresting those complicit in the conspiracy, he (Banasuri) had resumed giving tlátoles to other sympathizers, including one Simón Segua, the fiscal of Cuquiárichi.[63] Yes, he had joined other leaders, plotting at night while chupando, all the while planning and delivering more tlátoles. Another Indian involved in plotting and giving tlátoles was one Diego, from a pueblo called Muguaqui (location now unknown). When asked why he initially denied his participation in the conspiracy, Banasuri replied that the fiscal Simón Segua had advised him not to tell anyone of the plans. When asked where the conspirators were stashing their arms, meaning their supply of arrows, Banasuri answered that they were in a cave named Tosocomache, about ten leagues from Cuquiárichi. He added that Simón Segua had been his *noragua* (compadre).[64] Banasuri confessed that Simón had also passed on information to Sumas and Jocomes, who were still unruly discontents. When the inquisitors inquired of Banasuri what he thought the proper punishment would be for traitors to His Majesty and to the Spaniards, he replied, "lashes, hanging." Banasuri was questioned further and requestioned. He swore that all he had told was the truth.

Cuervo proceeded to interrogate each of the captives, especially those he had tortured (at least five of them). Some admitted that an uprising was still planned for the full moon of that very month, with plans even more specific than those of the first, failed conspiracy. Of each prisoner Cuervo demanded to know if they understood the penalty for lying under oath and conspiring against the Crown. Most acknowledged that they knew the penalty was hanging or the lash or both. When asked why they wanted to harm the Spaniards, their universal response was, to avenge the death of their relatives at the hands of the Spaniards.

From his questioning, Cuervo had accumulated a long list of conspirators, all of whom were now in the Teuricachi jail: Francisco Banasuri, the prize captive; topile Lorenzo Mauche of Cuchuta; fiscal Francisco Topiba; fiscal Pedro Sarina; Lucas Eguara; Capitán de Guerra Juan Tebacasane; Christobal Jorobe; Miguel Basuso; his son Miguel Banasi; Francisco Macasane; and

Francisco Caizo—eleven, all told. He had tortured a least five of them. It is surprising that the jail would hold them all.

All eleven seemed condemned to be executed. It appeared that Cuervo would need to move his tribunal back to Cuquiárichi, then once again to Bavispe and Guachinera, in order to continue the second round of rooting out conspirators.

Cuervo had to have been dismayed that the first wave of summary executions—at least sixteen, including the platoon of Indians he had executed in Guachinera—seemed to have had no effect on the conspiratorial movement among the Indians. Their fanaticism seemed unabated and their hatred of Spaniards undimmed or even intensified. All the interrogated prisoners agreed that the Indians of the region were in a mood to throw out the Spaniards. In each case, the witness traced his animosity to some sort of abuse from Spaniards. The Indians were powerless to respond overtly to the oppression routinely dished out by Spaniards, but they could always dream up more subtle methods of resisting Spanish rule, Cuervo knew. Previously, when interrogated as to why they wanted to overthrow the Spaniards, the Indians gave a variety of answers—they disliked being forced to work, the land was poorer due to Spaniards and their livestock, or the devil deceived them. Some added words to the effect that "the Indians of New Mexico had succeeded. If they could do it, we can."[65] Now the message was univocal: the Indians wanted revenge for having their relatives executed, whipped, or mistreated. The Spaniards' policy of relentlessly hunting down and killing subversives was proving to be counterproductive.

In spite of the Indians' boiling resentment, which had been made worse by the executions, Cuervo was still of a mind to execute all eleven prisoners and, if need be, a lot more. Shrugging, it seems, he issued orders from Teuricachi for his troops to serve more warrants and notices of the upcoming executions and further investigations in Cuchuta, Cuquiárichi, and Tebidéguachi, the suspected hotbeds of sedition for the second conspiracy.

While Cuervo was attending to the turmoil in Teuricachi, his assistant, Francisco Pacheco, who had remained in San Juan Bautista, was dealing with a similar plot that had originated in Tepache, some twelve leagues to the southeast of San Juan. Back in July, Captain Pedro de Valencia had warned then alcalde Verdugo that shenanigans were taking place among the Natives of the Tepache area. Juan Bautista de Escorza had posted the same concern before departing from Tepache for Bacadéhuachi the same month. Now, it seemed, the alarm had been sounded and a real threat was in the making.[66]

The story originated in early October with the wife of Lorenzo Quintero, the same man whose servant, Javier, had tipped the Spaniards off about the conspiracy back in July. She had been strolling near her house earlier in October when she overheard a conversation between two Indians. They spoke of plans to attack Spaniards. Tepache had but two or three roads in and out of the pueblo, and the Indians had said they could easily block the roads and form an ambush, she reported. (She must have been fluent in the Native language, probably Teguima.) She was terrified by what she heard and immediately informed her husband. The following day, Quintero claimed that he saw one of the two conspirators, Juan the topile, sneak into his house and remove two *cañutos* (tubes) of arrow poison (*yerba la flecha*).[67] The Indian then moved furtively from the house. Even worse, Quintero's maid, an Indian, reported that she had gone to the river to fetch water and overheard some Indians there saying that they would kill her master, Lorenzo Quintero.

Quintero took these reports quite seriously and filed a notice with Captain Pedro de Valencia in Tepache on October 8. Captain Valencia duly summoned Quintero to make a formal statement. Based upon Quintero's statements, Valencia then summoned Quintero's maid, Cecilia, to make a statement under oath concerning what she had seen. She testified that one of the Indians was named Juan, the topile. She had overheard him speaking with another Indian with whom she was not familiar at a place called Junta Los Ríos. She had heard Juan the topile state that he wanted to kill Spaniards and that he had a stockpile of poisoned arrows with which to kill them. Furthermore, she had seen Juan carrying the cañutos of arrow poison, and he was holding all-night meetings in his house, where men were chupando and dancing all night. She had overheard Juan say that he and other Indians were angry with Lorenzo Quintero because the Spaniard's cows had invaded and destroyed their milpa, devouring all their peas, squash, and watermelons. (We can assume that they had already harvested the bulk of the corn.) The Spaniards were no good, he had said; they were violent men.

Captain Valencia, an old man but alert to the conspiracies that had rocked other parts of the Opatería, immediately had Juan the topile seized and brought before him. His full name was Juan Juraque and he was a topile of the Tepache mission and servant of Pedro Valencia himself. Valencia asked about the stranger with whom Juan had been seen chatting, who he was and what he had been doing in Tepache. Juraque replied that he did not know the stranger's name, but he had come from Guásavas with tlátoles to set up a convoco because he wanted to kill the Spaniards to avenge the death of some relatives. The stranger from Guásavas worked as an ore crusher at a smelter owned by one Captain Andrés de Almagro. To the charges that he had removed cañutos of arrow poison, Juan said no, he was merely picking up a digging stick and a hatchet handle from Quintero's house. He had had meetings, he acknowledged, but they were celebrations and not anything dangerous. He was innocent of anything sinister, he claimed. Juraque grudgingly confirmed under repeated questioning that he had indeed been susceptible to the stranger's tlátoles and had agreed to his request to help spread the conspiracy. The stranger had assured him that once the Spaniards were killed or driven out, the earth would once again be theirs and their lives better. Indeed, the stranger spoke so convincingly that Juan agreed to prepare poisoned arrows to use on the Spaniards.

The tlátolero from Guásavas was in contact with dissident Indians throughout the region, Juan said. His attempts to recruit among the Indians of Tepache had been a failure, however, because in that pueblo they felt as Juan felt in his heart, that the Spaniards weren't all that bad and they got along with them. Sort of.

Pedro de Valencia sensed that Juan was lying or at least vastly understating his role in the conspiracy that was surely being enacted there in Tepache. He promptly notified Sergeant Francisco Pacheco in San Juan Bautista that a stranger was carrying tlátoles and organizing convocos in pueblos. In the meantime, he would keep Juan Juraque incarcerated in Tepache.

Sergeant Pacheco y Zevallos had no time to contact Francisco Cuervo and request authorization to round up the stranger, for Cuervo was off interrogating Indians in Teuricachi. So Pacheco forthwith issued a search and arrest order for Gerónimo Jumari. He was discovered working as a rock breaker in a silver smelter owned by Captain Andrés de Almagro, apparently not far from where Juan Juraque labored making charcoal for the smelter. Jumari was immediately arrested and brought in shackles to Pacheco on the twelfth of October. Pacheco now had in prison the two men who seemed most involved in the unrest at Tepache—Juraque incarcerated in Tepache, Jumari in San Juan Bautista.

Pacheco promptly began interrogating Gerónimo Jumari. The Indian acknowledged that he was from Guásavas. He had met Juan Juraque in Tepache (not far from the mine in which he worked). It was Juan who was the activist, who had urged Gerónimo to join the cause and carry tlátoles to other peoples and towns. Juan had expressed a strong desire to kill Spaniards as vengeance for executions that had taken place in other pueblos. He had urged Jumari on, minimizing the risk to the Indians of an uprising, assuring him that the Spaniards could easily be defeated.

Gerónimo's answers seemed shifty to Pacheco. He probed further. Slowly, Gerónimo appeared willing to accept more responsibility for the subversion, even acknowledging that he had suggested that Juan Juraque produce as many poisoned arrows as possible. He still placed the onus on the topile, however. It was Juan who was the prime mover in the rebellion and was organizing the tlátoleros and convocations in pueblos all over the region.

Pacheco read Juan Juraque's deposition, taken under questioning from Pedro de Valencia, and compared it with the account Gerónimo had made to his inquiries. The comparison of the two "confessions" revealed too many discrepancies for his liking. Each accused the other of being the motor. The only way to resolve the question of ultimate responsibility was to have the two appear side by side.

Transporting Juan Juraque from Tepache to San Juan Bautista took a week. Under Pacheco's careful questioning, Juraque's testimony wavered. He finally acknowledged that he had joined with Gerónimo Jumari and had agreed to the latter's demand that he produce poisoned arrows—that was the reason he had lifted the two tubes of arrow poison from Lorenzo Quintero's house. But Gerónimo also seemed reluctant to answer honestly. Pacheco saw no alternative but to apply torture—in this case, to Jumari's thumbs. This method seemed to work rather quickly and Jumari soon acknowledged that he was the principal activist, that he had recruited Juan Juraque, that Juan's account was true, and that he, Gerónimo, hoped to kill Spaniards in revenge for their killing of his kinsmen.

The two interrogations left little doubt in Pacheco's mind that both were insurrectionists. Jumari may have been the instigator and a missionary of conspiracy to Indians, Christian and gentile alike, seeking recruits for rebellion. But Juan was a menace as well. Anyone who would undertake the manufacture of poisoned arrows with their deadly effect (and the excruciating pain they produced) would be a menace to the Spaniards. Pacheco appears to have decided to have the two put to death. First, however, he appointed a public defender as required by royal mandate, and prepared the proper *autos* and *diligencias*. It looked as though two more Indians would face the firing squad or scaffold. That decision, though, would have to be left to Alcalde Cuervo, who at the moment was facing major difficulties in Teuricachi.

The defendants' appointed defender, Felizardo Bérnave Moreno, gave Pacheco further reason to act with deliberation. He submitted his written pleas on October 21. He pointed to the "dissonance" of the confessions. Lorenzo Quintero's complaint was based purely on suspicion, nothing verifiable. Cecilia, the young Indian witness, was not credible. She had an axe to grind with Juan Juraque and was eager to secure her employer's favor. Other testimony, available to Pacheco and Moreno, but not to us, was equally suspect. It wasn't a crime for men to smoke together or have dances. These were ancient Indian customs. The supposed conversations reported by Lorenzo Quintero's wife and her maid Cecilia could not possibly have been overheard in the detail that the witnesses reported. The confessions, extracted under torture, were not themselves reliable. The charges should be thrown out and the two defendants set free. If Pacheco were to have the prisoners executed, it would be on flimsy evidence.

Pacheco appears to have taken the defender's argument seriously.

Meanwhile, sixty-five kilometers to the north, Cuervo had seemed bent on executing the Teuricachi Eleven and additional conspirators wherever he found them. These perpetrators of the "second conspiracy" were a threat to His Majesty. At that point, however, events took a strange twist. On October 20, during his deliberations about how to proceed, Cuervo's soldiers returned from the neighboring towns reporting, rather breathlessly, it seems, that the pueblos of Cuchuta, Cuquiárichi, and Tebidéguachi had been completely depopulated. Not a soul was to be seen in them. The Indians had fled en masse—seven hundred of them—into the sierras. The three towns were no more.[68]

The news shook Cuervo. This was unheard of, a case of mass civil disobedience. Laws of the Indies forbade Indians to leave their pueblos without the permission of the priest, but that prohibition had not inhibited the Indians from fleeing the regime of terror.

Cuervo considered the alternatives. He could pursue the mass of fugitives and try to force their return to the pueblos, but he had no more than thirty soldiers available and the Indians would be highly motivated to resist in rough terrain, perhaps arming themselves at the very cave where they had stashed their supply of bows and arrows. A throng of Indians in mountain country with bows and arrows could easily defeat soldiers on horseback armed only with clumsy and slow-loading harquebuses. And even supposing he defeated them, once they were forcibly returned to their pueblos, he would have to use soldiers to enforce his orders.

On the other hand, he could wait them out, knowing that sooner or later they would run out of food and shelter—there were seven hundred of them—but that might take a long time, and the complications could prove even more embarrassing. These were serious problems, but he faced even larger worries. Among the three of them, Verdugo, Escorza, and Cuervo had executed at least sixteen Indians and had another eleven awaiting sentencing, most of them due to be executed. The wave of killings had apparently succeeded only in arousing the hatred of the entire population of several pueblos. Furthermore, the preemptive strikes and the spate of executions had already made a dent in the workforce and now with the arrests in Teuricachi more workers would be unavailable. At least three of the eleven current prisoners had been servants of a widow named María de Ávila, a landowner influential in local circles. One of the prisoners had overseen care of her fruit orchards, and a replacement would require some degree of training. Good servants were hard to come by, and Cuervo had deprived her of their help. Now the entire workforce, the manpower for mining activity in the northeastern Opatería and the women who kept the labor force alive, had vanished, leaving settlers and miners with no reserve of labor. Mining would grind to a halt. Lázaro Verdugo, the previous alcalde and prosecutor, had early been warned of this consequence in a sheaf of letters he received protesting the first round of executions, but in the exhilaration of capital punishment he had paid no heed. Now the reality was closing around the Spaniards.

Discouraging news arrived as well from San Juan Bautista and Nacozari on October 21. The vecinos there had learned of the arrests connected to the second conspiracy and had worked themselves into a state of panic. They were crowding their churches, saying special rosaries, holding novenas, and beseeching the Virgin Mary and anyone else within hearing to have mercy on them. The terror their New Mexico compatriots had experienced a year earlier was about to be bestowed on them. Now the news of the depopulation of the Indian towns had reached them as well and only increased their terror. (Imagine a force of seven hundred Indians overwhelming a town of fewer than one hundred Spaniards, including women and children!) They had no troops, few weapons, and no hope for defense. The promise of the small squadron from the presidio at El Fuerte, Sinaloa, supposedly promised by Captain Ysidro Atondo, was a chimera. The vecinos wrote to Cuervo, voicing their desperation, pleading with him to assist them in procuring more security. Thirty or so of them signed the letter.

Confused and worried, Cuervo summoned a council of war. The situation presented no simple solution. He could foresee no end to the bloodbath, but if he let up in his prosecution, he could easily be tagged as soft on Indian criminals and failing to protect the vecinos of Sonora.

The alcalde finally settled on a simple course of action. He would release two of the least guilty prisoners of the eleven in custody with the condition that they immediately journey to the mountains and confer with the refugees. They were to instruct the displaced villagers that if they would return to their homes, there would be no further punishments. They had only to return and agree to obey their priests, attend to their crops, and show respect for royal laws. Cuervo would declare a general amnesty and would ban any further reprisals. If the Indians agreed, they would each bear a carved cross in their hand as a sign of peace. If they did not agree to those terms within six days, Cuervo would amass his soldiers and pursue them relentlessly, punishing them with all the wrath the Spaniards could muster. And the Indians would have no illusions about the Spaniards' seriousness.

And so Alcalde Cuervo released Juan Tebocasne and Lorenzo Mauche, whose putative crimes were the least egregious of all the prisoners. Each departed bearing as a show of faith a cross in his hand and a ribbon around his neck. The two left the prison with great joy, eager, Cuervo reported, to carry the good news to their relatives and townspeople now gathered in the wild and distant mountains. The remaining prisoners would be detained in the Teuricachi jail as hostages.

To Cuervo's apparent relief, the former prisoners returned in two days, reporting that the fugitives had agreed to Cuervo's terms. The Indians descended from the mountains to the plaza of Teuricachi on October 24, carrying crosses in their hands as a sign of peace.[69] There they joined the people of Teuricachi itself. Cuervo welcomed them, through an interpreter, then delivered a stern message (he referred to it as a tlátole), warning that they must never again engage in tlátoles and convocos against his royal majesty, and that they must obey their priests and dedicate themselves to raising their crops and learning the doctrines of the Church. Lest anyone present miss the message due to faulty translators, he repeated it, emphasizing the sternness of the message and the solemnity of the occasion. Then, with a flourish, he released the remaining prisoners with the same admonition to them, and further warning that they would be watched. Cuervo reported that the Indians greeted the occasion and the release of prisoners with a show of pageantry and joy, raising their voices as one to show their agreement.

During the triumphant ceremony, a contingent of soldiers from San Juan Bautista arrived at Teuricachi led by Sergeant Major José Romo de

Vivar, who offered whatever support Cuervo might require.[70] Since he found himself woefully shorthanded, Cuervo requested that Romo take his twenty-five soldiers and deliver his message of reconciliation to Bacobichi, Chinapa, and Arizpe. Romo de Vivar departed that same day. Arriving in the towns, he reported that he announced the general asylum and issued the same tlátole that Cuervo had delivered in Teuricachi, with the same apparent results.

The pueblos implicated in the second conspiracy appeared to be effectively pacified. Cuervo had yielded to their civil disobedience but in return won what he took to be an enduring peace. Romo de Vivar, however, had two missions yet to fulfill. On October 29, after the celebrations in Cuquiárichi had died down, he retained an Indian guide and led a squadron of soldiers to the mountains north of the pueblo. They followed the guide to a cave high in the mountains, the place the Indians called Tosocomache. Several reports from interrogated Indians had pointed to that cave as the place where rebels had cached arms—primarily bows and arrows to be used in the uprising.

The cave was empty. Romo could detect no sign of recent use. He asked the guide if the cache could possibly be located in a different cave in a different place. The Indian replied that no, this was the only cave for many miles around. The existence of the cache was a false rumor.

Late that same afternoon Romo de Vivar and his men returned to Bacobichi. There they were met by the mission priest, Padre Carlos Celeste, who led them to the mission chapel. Inside the church Romo de Vivar found two refugees, Juan Caiso and Francisco Quigue, the old man and youth whom Lázaro Verdugo had sold into hard labor for twenty years for their role in the intrigue in Bacoachi and Chinapa. Inside the church they were immune from arrest or punishment. Romo de Vivar solemnly informed them that due to His Majesty's generosity, their crimes were forgiven and they were free to leave without punishment. He warned them, however, that if either of them deviated in the slightest from the true path, that prescribed by the mandates of the royal justices and the orders from their padre, they would be punished with full severity.

The conspiracies of 1681 were finished.[71]

The "Conspiracies" Reconsidered and the Aftermath

Cuervo was satisfied with his results, since peace seems to have been established. In assessing the realities of the claims, however, we must ask two questions: Was the conspiracy real? If so, had it constituted a genuine threat?

It seems likely, given the widespread testimony (though much of it was obtained through torture) that many Indians of the Opatería and elsewhere were inspired by the Pueblo Rebellion. Their communication was widespread, and activists among them would indeed have striven to construct a united front against the Spaniards. That much seems unassailable. Some were plotting, hoping to organize a group for armed struggle. The Spaniards could have expected no less, since they were by any measure invaders who had taken over Native peoples' lands and forced them to adopt alien customs and accept foreigners as lords and masters. Nearly all the testimony used to establish the conspiracy's reality, however, was gathered under torture and filtered through interpreters, who may well have had their own political agendas. A threat, perhaps, but only perhaps.

Was the threat serious? It seems doubtful that the lives of any Spaniards were endangered by any clandestine organizing that was taking place. The Indians appear to have lacked any systematic organization and any plan that might have enabled them to pull off an attack similar to that achieved by the Pueblo Indians. The frequent use of the term *uprising* by Spaniards was an exaggeration at best and a downright distortion at worst. Labeling the widespread and naïve discussions among the Indians an uprising was a self-serving artifice perhaps skillfully employed by Verdugo, Escorza, and Cuervo.

If the Indians were planning an attack, it was far off, indeed. The prisoners provided three different dates for the supposed uprising—October 1681, winter of 1681, and spring of 1682. Spaniards could not produce a single example of specific planning. The one bit of concrete evidence the interrogators had compiled was that several Indians admitted that arms were stashed in the cave called Tosocomache. But when José Romo de Vivar searched the remote mountain, he found the cave not only empty but also unused for an extended period of time. If that persistent story of the arms cache turned out to be wishful thinking on the Indians' part, how much of the remainder of their stories were similarly hopeful expressions of an unachievable reality? I suspect that most of the Indians' confessions of complicity with other peoples were wild exaggerations, perhaps meant to create consternation among the Spaniards or, even more likely, they were an indigenous manner of delivering hoped-for outcomes. It seems inconceivable that the scattered pueblos could unite and arm themselves to the degree necessary to drive out the Spaniards. None of the interrogators—Verdugo, Peralta, Escorza, Cuervo, or Pacheco—had uncovered the slightest evidence of an actual plot that constituted a threat to Spanish control of Sonora.

Throughout the duration of the conspiracy, the so-called uprising, Spaniards suffered not a single casualty. The Indians, on the other hand, suffered sixteen leaders executed, at least.

Who were these conspirators? Luis Navarro García, who first uncovered the documents concerning the conspiracy of 1681, attributed it to Ópatas. However, after I reviewed the manuscripts with tighter scrutiny, it was not clear to me that the planned uprising was primarily Opatan in origin. Indeed, Spaniards did not mention the ethnicity of the most prominent conspirators of July and August 1681, Pablo Dimara, Diego Suri, Ignacio Jojói, and Javier Jaure, nor the ethnic identity of the fallen plotters of Bacadéhuachi, Guachinera, and Bavispe. They referred to nearly all their captives simply as *naturales* and the Natives of their hometowns as naturales as well. In their confessions these men made clear their contact with non-Opatans and frequently identified the alien peoples—Apaches, Conchos, Janos, Jocomes, Pimans, and Sumas. Nowhere, however, do they identify the conspirators as Opatans per se or even imply that their ethnicity was established until October, when Francisco Banasuri—through an interpreter—identified himself as an Ópata. Since the towns involved were all home to peoples of varying indigenous origins, it seems risky to label the putative rebellion as Opatan. Opatan ethnicity was not a given in the 1680s in what would later come to be called the Opatería.[72] Finally, we must remember that the term *Ópata* was not a term Opatans used for themselves. The pueblos involved in the convocos would later come to be identified as Teguima, Eudeve, or both, often with a component of other peoples as well. Referring to them as Ópata in 1681 goes beyond any extant evidence.

Within a year of the uncovering of the supposed conspiracy, all trace of resistance to Spaniards in the Opatería had disappeared, much to the great relief of the Europeans. They remained jittery, with good reason, well aware that the Pueblo Indians of New Mexico were still ruling their own destinies in the absence of Spanish authority. Still, the years 1682 and 1683 passed without significant interruptions to the tranquility of Sonora.

In 1684, however, Sumas, Jocomes, and Pimans rose up in Chihuahua, in Ostimuri, and in far northern Sonora, and Sonorans found themselves compelled to respond, especially to the challenge of the Suma uprising.[73] Lucas Canari, the late governor of Bavispe, had reported the Sumas to be undecided about joining the resistance. Although José Romo de Vivar appeared to have gained the pacification of Sumas in Tebidéguachi, those represented only a small, local population and could not speak for the Sumas in general. In May

1684 eastern Sumas attacked and sacked Carretas, a mission to the east of Bavispe, in present-day Chihuahua. The Franciscan priest Fray Antonio de Aguilar escaped from the attackers and found refuge in Bacerac. Meanwhile the Sumas sacked Janos and killed the priest, burned the town, and profaned the church. Sonoran Hispanics, with good reason, feared the inroads of the nomadic and pagan Sumas, especially when reports reached San Juan Bautista of the presence of Sumas in pueblos associated with previous unrest and of Jocomes in Bacerac.

Alcalde Cuervo immediately ordered his soldiers to keep a close eye on those pueblos known to have been seditious in 1681, but not a single sign of Native unrest came back to him.

In what must be called an astonishing turnaround, Cuervo recruited large numbers of Opatans for the campaign against the Sumas. They acted primarily as scouts but probably were responsible for the ultimate demise of the Sumas as a people. Sumas were reluctant to engage the Opatans, saying that Spaniards, not Indians, were their enemies. But the Opatans fought on. They proved the main force in combating the Jocomes, who were raiding as well. This alliance with Spaniards ultimately worked against the Opatans, however, for Apaches, who soon replaced the Sumas as raiders, became the Opatans' enemies and began attacking Opatan missions and garrisons with their usual ferocity. The attacks would continue for nearly two centuries.

In 1682, former alcalde mayor Lázaro Verdugo wrote in his report of the failed conspiracy that he had personally financed all the campaigns, since he had not had time to receive official permission or authorization. He did not mention that he had systematically inflated the significance of the episode from a conspiracy to an "uprising," thus elevating the significance of his bold intervention. He hoped, of course, to be reimbursed for money he had spent and to receive accolades from those who would soon evaluate his residencia.[74] A year later he had received no payment compensating him for his efforts. His son Matheo petitioned for the reimbursement on his father's behalf, with unspecified success.[75] We may owe the Verdugos many thanks, for it appears that in response to their petition, Alcalde Mayor Cuervo requested his aides to gather up all the documents from the previous year's uprising (as he called it) to bolster the Verdugos' case for reimbursement. And thus we have, more or less intact, extensive accounts of the conspiracies of 1681.

CHAPTER FOUR

Sorcery in Eastern Sonora

Hechiceros

✣ THE POLITICAL UNREST OF THE 1680S SEEMS NOT TO HAVE INVOLVED the missions and missionaries themselves to any great degree, though this omission may be a reflection of a deliberate decision by priests.[1] They may have chosen to accentuate the peaceful nature of their missions and their work as evangelists, rather than risk being portrayed as mollycoddling their Indians. They may have sensed that given the atmosphere of hysteria that prevailed among the settlers, intervention could only bring damage to the Order. They seem to have been preoccupied more with ridding the mission Indians of their pagan practices than investigating their possible subversive bent. In this chapter I examine a case of conflict in 1704—accusations of sorcery—among Indians adjudicated by Spanish authorities. In this unusual case, the priest takes no stand on the question of sorcery. Instead he refers the case to military authorities, making it a *causa criminal* (criminal case). These secular authorities stepped in and assumed command in the case where the clergy feared to tread.

Soldiers appear to have dealt with accused sorcerers on several occasions. One of them in the 1690s involved Father Miguel Guerrero of Bacadéhuachi, who called on Captain Juan Mateo Manje to investigate a spate of murders by sorcerers.[2] Manje did not divulge the details of his investigation.

Such a request from a priest was not uncommon. Jesuit documents from northwestern Mexico frequently portray missionaries obsessed with the workings of *hechiceros*, a term that can be variously translated as shamans, sorcerers, witches, or simply Native (non-Catholic) priests. The early Jesuits found these Native practitioners of the occult to be ubiquitous among indigenous people and diabolically influential and effective in undermining missionaries' goals. Priests often attributed backsliding or failures in conversion to the work of such influential individuals. They also explained rebellions as liaisons between hechiceros and Satan. In some cases, the priests actually feared the hechiceros, believing that they could manipulate unseen powers beyond the cleric's own abilities and inflict bodily harm or death.[3]

Andrés Pérez de Ribas, in his detailed 1645 *History of the Triumphs of Our Holy Faith*, set forth the Jesuits' position. Referring to the indigenous people of what is now northwestern Mexico, he stated that "any worship that was to be found was reduced to barbarous superstitions or sorcery, knowledge of which was acquired by certain persons who had intimate dealings with devils." In Pérez's eyes, "this knowledge was a heritage passed on from their elders. The latter taught it to others at the hour of their death, charging them to practice some of the ceremonies of sorcery and superstition, which they used to cure, kill, and deceive." He went on to explain how "such sorcerers are usually healers, and they are the most sinful and feared people among them, because they know that their sorcery can kill whenever they want." Pérez concluded, "Because these sorcerers deal so much with the devil, it is they who are most opposed to Gospel preaching and most persecute its ministers. They are the instruments most used by Satan to introduce whatever evil he wants among these blind people ... [T]hese sorcerers spread rumors, just as they have often done, that the waters of Baptism kill children."[4]

Pérez was expressing a view of sorcery popular in many clerical circles. In 1484 two Dominican priests had published *Malleus Maleficarum*, a treatise on witchcraft in which they argued that *not* to believe in witches and the devil "manifestly savours of heresy."[5] Dominicans as an order were apparently given to the relentless ferreting out of devilry in all its manifestations. The Sonoran priests of 1700, however, were Jesuits, not all of whom appeared to share the Dominicans' dogmas on sorcery. We must not assume that ecclesiastical pronouncements by one order were binding on or even accepted by other orders.

Still, rooting out sorcery became a passion with many, but not all, clerics during the first century of the Jesuit period (and wherever Christian missionaries first encountered Native Americans). These witch hunts became a powerful tool of social control. By the time of the incident described in this essay, in the early eighteenth century, simply *being* a sorcerer was a prima facie crime in much of Nueva Vizcaya and throughout much of New Spain. In many areas, practicing sorcery was proscribed as a criminal activity. Elsewhere it was not.[6]

While some clerics attempted simply to discredit sorcerers by demonstrating the ineffectiveness of their practices, many others assumed that any sorcerer (i.e., anyone who performed acts involving unexplained power not sanctioned by the Church or the clergy, including curing) was in league with the devil. Such actions were an abomination to the Church. A person accused of sorcery was required to demonstrate that the charge was false. Failure to do so could provoke severe punishment—usually public whipping, or even death. As the defendant in the Bacerac case discussed below would discover to his great consternation, proving one's innocence was not an easy task.

In central and southern Mexico, the Holy Office of the Inquisition dealt with questions of occult manipulations, but the office apparently never operated in the vast, open lands of Nueva Vizcaya. Still, the Church's position on the occult weighed heavily in the minds of evangelizing Jesuits, who realized that Indians generally were exempt from the Inquisition's jurisdictions. As one scholar explains, the inquisitors had to deal with both Indian and Spanish superstition and wizardry, and, as the process of cultural diffusion continued, a fusion of the two. Witchcraft was a different crime from sorcery. The inquisitors were convinced that the "witch has abandoned Christianity . . . has worshipped Satan as God . . . and exists only to be his instrument." Practitioners of black magic were judged to have derived their powers by entering into a pact with the devil, and in doing so they were accused of inferential heresy. By the late sixteenth century, the task of dealing with sorcery and witchcraft among indigenous people of central Mexico was relegated to bishops. This was not the case in the Northwest.

Ópatas were well known as healers, called curanderos by Spaniards. But the ability to heal, when it transcended empirical observations of practical medicine, could easily be interpreted as the possession of supernatural power, especially when it was practiced outside authorized liturgical circles. There was little doubt in many Jesuit minds that hechiceros could tap supernatural powers. Since the clerics themselves, as representatives of the true faith, seemed unable to evoke cures as readily as the Native healers, and since these Native powers were not channeled through the Catholic Church, they must be evil. Hence, the sorcerers must be rooted out. In this context, the 1704 case of an accused hechicero from the mission town of Bacerac, in present-day eastern Sonora, affords insight into how the obsession with sorcerers conflicted with the Crown's desire to carry out due process of law.[7] In this case, where one might assume the clergy to have played an active role, the priest's presence is notable for his unwillingness to intervene.

I argue that this incident is important for understanding colonial Sonora not so much for the charges of sorcery leveled at a traditional governor as for the way the Spaniards and Jesuits chose to address it (or, in the case of the priest, not to address it).

The Bacerac case was not the first in which Spanish civilian authorities charged an Indian accused of sorcery with a criminal offense. The previous year (1703), an Indian named Mateo de la Cruz, of the "nación de Sonora" (probably an Ópata, since contemporary Spaniards considered the towns of Sonora, namely the Río Sonora, to be Teguima or Ópata),[8] had been charged with sorcery for causing the illness of a resident of San Diego de las Minas, a mining town near Parral, Chihuahua. This case is worth considering in some detail, since it casts light on the Bacerac case and its ultimate outcome was dictated from the same jurisdiction.[9]

Juan Achero, a New Mexican with a "Sonoran" Indian wife, swore under oath that Mateo had caused his illness and threatened him with death. Achero had taken ill and was confined to his home. Mateo had arrived at his home, not knowing that Achero was ill and without being summoned, and had produced a handkerchief in which two cane tubes (cañutos) were wrapped. Under oath Achero claimed that Mateo assured him that evil was trapped inside the tubes. According to his testimony, Mateo blew with all his might into the tubes, then used them to blow air all over the sick man's body. He wrapped the tubes in a handkerchief, then, using fantastic gestures, placed them beneath a shrine in the sick man's room. Mateo, the sick man claimed, then warned him not to unplug the tubes or evil would flow out from them. Some of Mateo's gestures included parodies of the Conception, the holy crucifix, and a prayer to San Antonio. (These actions were apparently themselves illegal, or, as the investigator put it, "contrary to the law of God.") By all accounts, Mateo cured the sick man.

Apparently, the former patient did something to violate Mateo's instructions, however, for, according to him and to Mateo, several days after he had regained his health, he fell and suffered injuries. Mateo came once again to Achero's house and warned that he was about to die. The former patient blamed Mateo for the accident and accused him of sorcery.

When the investigator in the case questioned Mateo, he did not deny visiting the sick man and hoping to cure him. When the investigator asked what was in the cañutos, Mateo said there was nothing. (Undoubtedly a perfectly true response!) He also denied making claims about the powers of the tubes and using them to blow over the body of the sick man. He did not make diabolical gestures or invoke sacred items for evil reason. The investigator was not satisfied with Mateo's answers. He interviewed everyone possible near the case, probing to see if anyone had caught Mateo committing other acts of sorcery (*cosas contra la ley de diós*). None had.

The investigator referred the case to the captain general of the jurisdiction, whose offices were in San Francisco de Conchos, a long distance from San Diego de las Minas. Mateo had been transferred there as a prisoner. When questioned about what his methods of curing consisted of, Mateo replied (rather humbly) that all he did was make an altar and pray on his knees to God, as priests had instructed him, and that the tubes were only images and part of his prayer to God. An Apache had given them to him and he used them to try to help the sick man. Mateo believed the accusations were part of an attempt by Achero and others to steal Mateo's livestock, of which they were envious.

The case wound up more than a year later in the hands of Juan Fernández de Córdoba, governor of Nueva Vizcaya and the same governor who would decide the outcome of the case in Bacerac. The governor found that Mateo had acted scandalously and sacrilegiously, using occult methods for curing, and fomenting superstition and general evil. The smoking gun turned out to be the two cañutos, sufficient evidence to convince the governor of Mateo's guilt. Mateo was a bad example to all, even though he had supposedly cured a sick man.

Córdoba sentenced Mateo to two hundred lashes, two years in prison (reduced by time already spent), and two years of hard labor, ordered him to refrain from further bad acts, and mandated him to the town of Atotonilco, Chihuahua, where he would remain in the custody of the priest, who would educate him in true religion and demonstrate the evil of his previous ways. Apparently, Governor Córdoba believed Mateo was capable of inflicting harm in an occult fashion.[10]

Mateo's identity as a Sonoran suggests that Ópatas were known throughout the region for their ability to cure, usually incorporating a mixture of medicine and spiritual manipulation to heal. The ferocious severity of the sentence tells us Spaniards feared the influence of such curanderos, especially Indian curanderos, and that Governor Córdoba himself must have been fearful of the spiritual powers of the Indians as well to have imposed such a brutal sentence. It is also significant that no clergy were overtly involved in the case. Mateo faced *criminal* charges and was investigated by civilian authorities, not by the Inquisition or religious experts. These considerations make Mateo's case relevant to what occurred in Bacerac in 1704.

The Bacerac Incident

Bacerac was the political seat for the district that included the towns of Bavispe to the north and Guachinera to the south, as well as the settlement of Tamichopa, some fifteen kilometers south of Bacerac. The town came under the military jurisdiction of the presidio at Fronteras (Corodéhuachi), a rigorous three-day journey to the northwest and some fifty kilometers south of present-day Douglas, Arizona. Bacerac had close ties with the missions of Bacadéhuachi, also in Ópata country some sixty kilometers to the south, and Cumpas, some ninety kilometers to the southwest. The villages of the Bacerac district were isolated, cut off by steep, rugged mountain ranges and narrow canyons from the remainder of the Opatería, which included villages on the western Río Bavispe and on the Río Moctezuma, Río Mátape, Río Sonora, and Río San Miguel. Bacerac seems to have been the name originally given by indigenous people to the entire valley stretching roughly fifty kilometers north to south and ten to twenty kilometers east to west. In colonial documents the name came to refer only to the settlement, while the valley has come to be known as the Bavispe Valley. At the upper (southern) end of the valley, the Río Bavispe disappears into deep and convoluted *cajones* (narrow canyons) of high mountain ranges. At the lower (northern) end, the waterway is constricted into a narrow valley and enters once again into deep canyons. There is little agricultural land along the river downstream from the valley until it opens at Guásavas, nearly 140 kilometers below. Due to the tremendous distances to other settlements and its rugged topography, the Bavispe Valley is physically and psychologically isolated even today.[11]

In 1704, all of the Opatería lay under the judicial administration of Parral (present-day Hidalgo del Parral, Chihuahua), situated in the eastern foothills of the Sierra Madre Occidental, some five hundred kilometers and a two-week journey southeast of Bacerac. Documents in the Parral archives refer to all the immediate accusers and the defendants in the Bacerac case as naturales (Natives), not as Ópatas, a name that came into general use at roughly that time.[12] These Natives spoke a language that was originally labeled *Teguima* by the Jesuits and by the nineteenth century was included in the catchall term *Ópata*. The language is related to Cáhita, the language of the Mayos, Yaquis, Pimans, and Tarahumaras.[13]

Catholic missionaries may have been active in the Bavispe Valley as early as 1610, when the Franciscan (not Jesuit!) priest Fray Marcos Duro supposedly baptized numerous Indians, a claim Jesuits tended to view with skepticism.[14] This was at least ten years before the first Jesuits arrived in the Opatería. By 1632, documents clearly establish that Fray Tomás Manso had established or at least occupied a mission at Bacerac. He had arrived from New Mexico as part of a Franciscan plan for the evangelization of Sonora. The inevitable turf war that erupted in the following decade between Franciscans and Jesuits as Pedro de Perea recruited additional Franciscans (see chapter 1) to evangelize Jesuit territory resulted in the withdrawal of Franciscans from the valley by roughly 1651. By 1653 a Jesuit had been installed at the mission and was actively evangelizing among the Indians. In spite of the apparent arrival of Jesuits, no extant records name a resident Jesuit until roughly 1678, when a Jesuit arrived to minister to the Indians. What transpired in the mission during the twenty-five-year period of documentary silence is a matter of conjecture, but it constitutes a long priestly vacuum in the life of any mission and the mystery period could have permitted the development of a strong culture of *curandismo*. Padre Horacio Polici arrived at Bacerac in 1697 or thereabouts.

The Bacerac case centered on fifty-year-old Marcos Humuta (variously spelled Umuta or Sumata, and frequently Vmuta), the traditional (appointed) Ópata governor of the Jesuit mission of Bacerac. Marcos had been governor for some time, perhaps as many as eighteen years, in August 1704, when he was accused of practicing sorcery. The fact that he had held the canes of office for so many years suggests that he was widely respected in the community. His accusers, however, alleged that Marcos's evil spells had killed several people and caused illness in other victims. They also accused Marcos of abusing his power as governor. Based upon their accusations, he was arrested on charges of sorcery and incarcerated by early October 1704. In that year government officials removed him as traditional governor of the Bacerac district.

Marcos's principal accuser was María Seguida, from the nearby village of Guachinera, where Marcos had grown up. María was illiterate, about fifty-five years of age, and also an Ópata. Miguel Baduqui (or Baduque), a secondary accuser, was identified as a *macehual* (man of the town). Roughly fifty-five years old, Miguel was likewise an illiterate Ópata from Guachinera. Both María and Miguel were curanderos who claimed to have known Marcos Humuta from their early years.[15]

It is notable that neither of the accusers, nor those naturales who later joined in denouncing Marcos, spoke Spanish. Marcos could sign his name and was at least marginally literate, which probably was a requirement for the office of *gobernador*. He apparently understood Spanish but must have spoken it poorly, for an interpreter signed the transcript of his testimony.[16]

The case came under the jurisdiction of Miguel de Abajo, captain general of the Fronteras presidio. De Abajo dispatched Lieutenant Captain Pascual Picundo to investigate the allegations, which he must have considered serious. The captain general instructed that all testimony be set down by a scribe and translated (the language at Bacerac at the time was Teguima) by an interpreter named Juan Moreno, whom de Abajo also appointed. We will never know whether Moreno was a competent and faithful interpreter, but his signature appears on all summaries of testimony that required translation.[17]

The investigation began with the deposition of María Seguida in November 1704. María's testimony is remarkable for its ferocity. She testified under oath that she had known Marcos and that he was a sorcerer. God had given her this knowledge. She claimed that Marcos's spells had killed several people and that his *hechizos* (spells and incantations) had produced a wave of sickness throughout the region during the previous summer. She mentioned the names of many of Marcos's victims, including his own wife, who had recently died from an illness. She claimed that his evil tools consisted of *palos* (sticks), with which he transmitted his spells; *piedras* (stones or large pebbles), which were imbued with unspecified power; and *carrizos* (hollow reeds), which also produced evil results. According to María, Marcos brought the sticks to Bacerac from Bavispe and Guachinera. He would leave them on the ground or bury them along pathways. Smoke would arise when his victims, or innocent passersby, stepped on the sticks, and the person would soon die. When waved like wands, the sticks could transmit curses or hexes.

María described how she discovered where Marcos had buried the sticks. She claimed she had dug them up herself and carried them to the church, where she asked the Jesuit priest, Horacio Polici, to deal with them. According to many witnesses, the padre ordered the offending sticks burned in front of the church and in the presence of the entire pueblo. María interpreted this as the priest's tacit acknowledgment that Marcos was an hechicero. To support her testimony, she produced some of the stones she had also dug up and that she claimed Marcos had enchanted. María went on to relate that Marcos had accused one of her female patients of being an hechicera and demanded that she confess to the parish priest. When the woman refused, Marcos bound her arms with leather straps and tightened them until she thought she would die. He then warned the miserable creature never to tell anyone that he was a sorcerer. Nonetheless, the woman had revealed the terrible secret to María and promptly died. María claimed that Marcos had inflicted the same treatment on another Indian named Miguel, whose last name she could not recall.

María Seguida further testified that after she had exposed Marcos as a sorcerer, he borrowed two *bestias* (burros or mules) from the parish priest and fled through Carretas Pass to Chihuahua. She swore that she had observed Marcos removing his clothing and flying through the air, as any sorcerer could easily do. Finally, María described how she had once attended to Marcos's wife, also named María, when she was ill. The curandera noticed in front of Marcos's house a tree trunk decorated with carved figurines, obviously possessed of evil power. The wife warned Seguida that Marcos inflicted spells on anyone who revealed his secret. The fact that the wife died shortly thereafter suggested that Marcos had taken his revenge on her.

Spanish authorities scarcely took María Seguida's charges at face value. Under questioning from Lieutenant Captain Picundo, she acknowledged that she could not produce a witness to Marcos's evil actions. Nevertheless, she insisted that God had given her knowledge of his wicked power and that the Virgin Mary had guided her to the place where Marcos had buried the sticks.

Miguel Baduqui backed up María's testimony. According to Miguel, he and María were the only curanderos in the region (María would later claim there were others). She had told him that Marcos had been a bad man from birth and had killed many people through his sorcery. Miguel believed her because God had told him it was true. Moreover, he had used herbs, principally *hierba buena* (peppermint), to cure many people of Marcos's spells. Unfortunately, others, who failed to call on him to undo Marcos's hexes, had died.[18]

Miguel also accused Marcos of having buried his malevolent sticks in numerous places, including near the church door. Their dark power came from the devil, with whom Marcos had made a pact. But, Miguel added, María had exposed Marcos and his treachery. Knowing that he was up to no good, she had followed him around and dug up the sticks. Finally, she took them to the church, where Padre Polici ordered them burned in front of the townspeople. Miguel claimed that the traditional governor of Bacadéhuachi would verify his testimony.

Shortly thereafter, Lieutenant Captain Picundo interviewed Marcos Humuta himself, using an unidentified scribe to record the conversation. Marcos had sent off a letter to Miguel de Abajo from the Bacerac jail protesting his innocence and pleading that the captain general come to Bacerac and bring the investigation to a just conclusion.[19] Marcos acknowledged that several people from Bacerac and Guachinera were making accusations against him and professed that he understood the seriousness of the charges. Nonetheless, he was bewildered by what could have prompted them. After all, he was a Christian who believed in God and Jesus. He suggested that perhaps the widespread belief that he was a sorcerer originated from his lifelong fondness for performing tricks and stunts. For example, he would take a strip of cloth, fold it, and conceal part of it up his sleeve, thereby fooling his audience into thinking that he had actually shrunk the cloth. On other occasions, he would "place a lighted candle in his mouth, close his mouth, and pull the candle out still lit." Acquaintances who were unaware that he practiced these sorts of tricks may have thought he possessed supernatural powers.

As to the accusations against him, Marcos claimed that María Seguida had invented her stories. In fact, she and Miguel Baduqui were the real sorcerers, attempting to blame him for the evil they were doing. Marcos's defense seems both touching and persuasive. He appears to find perplexing the widespread animosity against him.

Picundo interviewed twelve additional Native witnesses, most of whom agreed that Marcos Humuta was an hechicero. Some of them claimed that Marcos had been a sorcerer all his life. Others had once admired him and thought he was a good governor but now were convinced that he possessed evil powers. All the witnesses against Marcos reiterated María Seguida's allegations. One witness testified that he had gotten out of bed during the night to attend to "the necessities of the body" and had observed Marcos lurking in the street at midnight. Other witnesses said that they had known for a long time that Marcos was an hechicero but could provide no evidence that would support their belief other than the fact that people believed that Marcos was a sorcerer because of María's accusations. The governor of Bacadéhuachi, who María had indicated would attest to Marcos's evil acts, traveled to Bacerac but only swore that he was aware that people had accused Marcos of witchcraft. Seemingly unwilling to be caught up in the dispute, he claimed to have no immediate knowledge of any evil that Marcos had caused.

After interviewing other witnesses, Lieutenant Captain Picundo ordered María Seguida and Miguel Baduqui to submit to his questioning once again to clear up numerous inconsistencies in their testimony. He asked María to explain how it was that she had first attributed the magic stones to Miguel Baduqui and only later claimed that they were part of Marcos Humuta's evil arsenal. He then called on Miguel to explain why he had initially attributed some of the artifacts in evidence (the carrizos) to María Seguida and then changed his testimony to attribute them to Marcos Humuta. Both accusers replied that they had distorted the truth because they feared Marcos's great power as gobernador of the district. Miguel claimed that Marcos had threatened to strangle (*ahorcar*) him if he made his accusations public.[20]

Captain Francisco Pacheco y Zavallos, Picundo's immediate superior and former alcalde mayor of Sonora, appointed as a fiscal (inspector) a Spaniard or *criollo* named Nicolas de la Torre. Although de la Torre purported to be an advocate for the defense, he immediately pronounced Marcos Humuta guilty as charged and urged Captain General de Abajo to punish him to the full extent of the law. "If Marcos Humuta is not punished, all these Indians will think it is no crime at all to be an hechicero and the whole province will become infested with witchcraft," de la Torre wrote. "And the Prince of Darkness will succeed in propagating his false sects." If de la Torre was speaking sincerely, we must conclude that belief in witchcraft had penetrated into the vecino population as well as among Natives. Whatever his beliefs, it is clear he believed Marcos could no longer be an effective governor. Or perhaps he had a personal grudge against Marcos.

An impressive vecino (and an apparently good-natured skeptic) named Antonio Morales neatly countered de la Torre's hasty (or biased) conclusion, however. Morales testified to Marcos's good character and described the accusations against him as falsehoods. According to Morales, Marcos was an exemplary governor, a stalwart Christian, and a good and courageous man who had learned to read and write. He pointed to the many inconsistencies in María Seguida's testimony and accused her and Miguel Baduqui of blasphemy in falsely invoking God, the Virgin Mary, and various angels. The deaths in Bacerac, while unfortunate, were normal occurrences. Many people regularly died of "*bubas* [perhaps bubonic plague], tumors, and swellings," not to mention childbirth. It was no different from anywhere else. Marcos had been falsely accused.

In an apparent attempt to judge the general mood of the people of Bacerac, Pascual Picundo called a town meeting in front of the church. Based on the response, he concluded that the residents generally believed that Marcos Humuta was an hechicero. Therefore, in the interest of public tranquility, he should be punished (at least for the sake of appearance). But Picundo also believed that both María Seguida and Miguel Baduqui had lied. Consequently, he recommended that all three parties to the proceedings be exiled "at a minimum forty leagues" (160 kilometers) distance from the district. Curanderos and curanderas must cease their practices "under penalty of death." Anyone who henceforth consulted a curer would be subject to two hundred lashes, the same penalty that was applied to Mateo de la Cruz in Chihuahua.[21] He could think of no other remedy to the public discord raised by the accusations against Marcos Humuta. Whether or not Picundo believed in witchcraft, he saw it as a divisive practice and, perhaps, a distraction for military authorities who had many more important functions to carry out.

At this point the file of documents from the investigation was apparently forwarded to General Miguel de Abajo in Fronteras, who in turn forwarded it to Juan Fernández de Córdoba, the governor general in Parral. Had Marcos been aware of Governor Córdoba's sentence imposed in Mateo's case the previous year, he would have winced, noting the draconian terms of the governor's decision. However, on June 1, 1705, roughly six months after Marcos Humuta had been incarcerated and the first testimony taken in the case, Governor Córdoba's provincial justice remanded the files to Captain Francisco Pacheco, whom Miguel de Abajo had originally charged with overseeing the case. In his cover letter, the justice scolded Pacheco and Bacerac officials for conducting an inadequate investigation. He ordered Pacheco to review the record and return a finding "within eighty days." In the meantime, he instructed the captain to spirit Marcos away from Bacerac and hold him in protective custody at either Oposura (Moctezuma) or Cumpas until the case could be resolved. In acknowledging receipt of the packet on August 20, 1705, Pacheco made the additional notation that María Seguida and Miguel Baduqui were also under arrest.

Captain Pacheco, who appears to have been the right man for the job, suddenly took an active interest in the case. He resummoned many of the witnesses and subjected their testimony to thorough scrutiny. Pacheco also appears to have asked Padre Polici to render his opinion in the matter. In mid-November, the priest wrote a lame, hand-washing sort of letter, stating that the case was volatile. He verified that María Seguida had brought him some sticks and that he had ordered them burned. Although charges of sorcery against Marcos Humuta were widespread, they had not been proven. (How could they be?) In the priest's estimation, Marcos seemed a good enough fellow. But there was so much sentiment against him that Padre Polici had lent Marcos a couple of bestias (donkeys) and encouraged him to move far away—perhaps to Papagóchic, in a distant Chihuahuan valley. Nowhere in the written record does Polici offer his opinion on the truth or falsity of the charges against Marcos.[22]

After reinterviewing the witnesses and reviewing the documents, Pacheco announced his findings in late December 1705, more than a year after the investigation had commenced. The captain, who seems to have viewed talk of sorcery with a jaundiced eye, absolved Marcos of all charges. He characterized the accusations as unproven "calumnies" and restored Marcos to the governorship of Bacerac. Even so, the currents of controversy and dissension in Bacerac were powerful enough that Pacheco ordered Marcos not to come within thirty leagues (130 kilometers) of the town, or he would suffer severe consequences. Pacheco came down hard on María Seguida and Miguel Baduqui, whose testimony he described as false and vicious. He sentenced Miguel to one hundred lashes to be administered while the man was seated on a burro and led around the village, with a *pregón* (town crier) calling out the reasons for his punishment. Thereafter, Miguel would perform four years of forced labor. Pacheco sentenced María Seguida to fifty lashes administered in the same fashion as Miguel's punishment. She was also sentenced to four years of incarceration, during which time she would be indoctrinated in the "mysteries of the Catholic faith."[23]

Pacheco issued one additional order: María and Miguel would henceforth obey Marcos Humuta. How they could obey him when he was stationed in a distant valley is left unstated. At any rate, Pacheco then forwarded his recommendations to the governor in Parral. On May 28, 1706, nearly two years after the first accusations were leveled against Marcos Humuta, Juan Fernández de Córdoba signed and sealed the order affirming Pacheco's findings. The case was closed. The files contain no record of what subsequently happened to any of the protagonists in the controversy. It was Marcos's great fortune that the principal investigator turned out to be a skeptic concerning sorcery; had he been a believer in witchcraft, he might have viewed the case much differently and Marcos could have faced a severe physical punishment, not just exile.

We have only indirect information about how the Ópatas looked upon the powers of their shamans or healers. Early Jesuits reported that shamans were often powerful, prominent, and influential individuals, and shamanism appears to have been an important social force in the Opatería.[24] Although the Ópatas appear to have had no strong beliefs in gods, they nonetheless possessed a vigorous mythology and firm beliefs about an afterlife.[25] Within the first few decades of Jesuit occupation, the Spanish missionaries stamped out most of the Ópatas' religious ceremonies. Eliminating beliefs about sorcery and the influence of shamans proved more difficult. After three-quarters of a century of Jesuit evangelism, the Ópatas retained their belief in sorcery but had become aware of the priests' aversion to or fear of sorcerers' power. They must have learned quickly that denouncing someone as a sorcerer—either by rumor or by invoking God, angels, and the Virgin Mary—could produce a vigorous reaction among many of the clergy such that the accused individual might never escape the charges. In the decades following the Bacerac case, other priests in the Opatería lamented the power of curanderos. One notable Jesuit, Padre Cristóbal Cañas of Aconchi, warned that as of 1730 curanderos still abounded "whom the devil talks to in the form of a jaguar, puma, dog, or, most commonly, in the form of a snake."[26] Other priests concurred, accusing hechiceros of murdering several of their brethren.[27]

Whatever María Seguida and Miguel Baduqui hoped to gain, they effectively destroyed Marcos's standing in the pueblo. They may simply have been up to no good and leveled accusations against Marcos Humuta in order to cover their own intrigues or, more probably, to settle old hostilities. They may have decided Marcos was abusing his powers as governor and this was the most effective way to get him removed from office. They may have reflected a mission-wide disillusionment with the way Marcos discharged the duties of his office. Regardless, the indigenous community wanted him gone, and so it happened. Certainly, Marcos could not be an effective governor as long as he faced widespread suspicion and hostility among those he was expected to preside over, nor could he function as a governor while in exile. Others must have filled the vacuum created by his absence,[28] but his replacement would also face a divided community and would probably have been forced to take sides in the question of Marcos's culpability. Marcos's legitimacy as governor had been undermined, quite probably for reasons that the inspectors did not uncover and perhaps did not care to uncover.

On the other hand, widespread accusations by indigenous residents against a Native governor invariably weakened the imposed system of civilian semi-self-government that Spaniards and Jesuits alike found most useful for maintaining social control. The office of traditional governor was a Jesuit and Spanish institution created and widely implemented for maintaining a liaison between Spanish authorities, including priests, and aboriginal inhabitants.[29] That office and others (fiscales, topiles, and *alguaciles*, or Native magistrates) served to reward loyal individuals but also to divide and conquer the Native population. Priests usually controlled the appointments, but, as we saw in the case of the conspiracies of 1681, military authorities felt free to remove and appoint governors at will without consulting priests or Indians.

The traditional governor was usually a man both respected by the people and acceptable to the priest and military authorities. To put it another way, the governors had to satisfy three constituencies: their community, their priest, and the military. Governors were expected to administer numerous details, settle disputes, arrange for social events, and ensure proper compliance with Catholic practices—a wealth of activities that would have proved bothersome for priests or soldiers. Priests relied heavily on them for maintaining the tranquility of the mission pueblos. Any time a governor ran afoul of the indigenous community, the clerics faced a difficult choice—whether to support the unpopular governor and risk facing a hostile populace, which could delay progress in Christianizing the pueblos, or to remove the governor and potentially commit an injustice to an innocent man. The institution of governorship could not help but lose some of its prestige and power under these conditions.

More than 160 pages of documents testify that the Crown's representatives took the Bacerac case very seriously. The fact that a simple accusation of sorcery in an isolated valley of northwestern New Spain attracted such minute attention is itself revealing. The accusation did not originate with the clergy. Indeed, the local priest seems to have considered Marcos Humuta innocent of the charges brought against him but either harbored lingering doubts or hoped to avoid public controversy. However, fear of hechiceros appears to have reached a fever pitch in Bacerac, much as it had in Salem, Massachusetts, twelve years earlier.[30] Caught in the middle, the priest may well have requested the investigation, judging it too hot to handle, perhaps a reflection of the tenuous control he maintained over his Indian congregation and his mission. On the other hand, it is possible that his neutral position plus the invocation of military authorities defused a potentially violent confrontation between the opposing community factions. If the Crown had invested Jesuits with a mission to pacify Indians without military intervention, priests could jolly well invoke the Crown's representative to resolve socially divisive problems that would force a priest to make a decision in a socially inflammatory case.

What is not at all clear is how the situation, the clash between Marcos and his accusers, would have evolved prior to the occupation of the Opatería by priests and the armed forces that supported their entradas—how the Opatans would have resolved such conflicts among themselves. Marcos held his office only at the pleasure of Spanish and Jesuit authorities; his term and tenure depended on their ongoing stamp of approval. Pre-Columbian social leveling mechanisms no longer functioned in the mission communities, and in this case at least, accusations of sorcery had to suffice. We can speculate that prior to the arrival of Europeans, respected leaders would have adjudicated the charges or seen to it that they never arose in the first place.

But charges of sorcery were hardly unusual in that age. The Bacerac case stands out for the fact that the religious authority (or authorities, since Padre Polici would probably have consulted other Jesuits about the incident) seemed eager to turn the entire matter over to civil authorities, as was the case with Mateo de la Cruz. Normally, the clergy were prosecutors, judge, and jury in matters involving sorcery. Captain Pacheco's no-nonsense approach appears at odds with investigations of sorcery elsewhere in New Spain. And his decisive resolution of the matter casts Father Polici in a rather negative light. The reader is left with the uneasy suspicion that Father Polici was himself a believer in sorcery.

In contrast, the captain sensed that Marcos's accusers were attempting to settle old scores. Regardless, Pacheco dismissed the talk of sorcery out of hand, while Father Polici refused to do so. The prompt and (ultimately) efficient intervention of civil authorities in this instance may have been due to their sense that the matter was causing discontent and dissension in Bacerac that might spread to other regions. Territory lost to Spaniards in the 1680 Pueblo Rebellion had finally been retaken in 1693, scarcely a decade earlier. That huge setback taught the Spaniards to react quickly to the slightest hint of Native unrest and dictated that authorities give greater consideration to Indian institutions and sense of justice. Pacheco's decisive action, though it required Marcos to wait two years, seems to have been a triumph of justice for which European critics rarely gave credit to Spanish authorities.[31]

Here was a case, perhaps rare, in which nonreligious Spaniards delivered justice to an Indian who had been denied that justice by the clergy.

As the colonial period drew to a close in the Opatería, accusations of sorcery slowly fell out of fashion and dwindled. Flare-ups occurred, however. In 1744 Carlos de Roxas, priest at Arizpe, declared that at least ten Jesuit missionaries had been killed by hechiceros.[32] Claims such as these became fewer, however. Ignaz Pfefferkorn, a crusty and somewhat cynical Jesuit of German extraction assigned to the Opatería for several years and expelled along with all his colleagues in 1767, observed in 1795 that

> the Sonoran sorcerers persuade the ignorant folk that they have received from muhaptura [the devil] the power to make everybody sick or well, to plague people with all kinds of misfortune, and even to kill them in the most horrible manner at will. To give weight to their bragging they show the people different kinds of pebbles, sand, herbs, the bark of trees, pieces of wood marked with different figures, hair, feathers, coals, and more such stuff, all of which they generally keep in an earthen pot. This trash they extol with proud and arrogant bearing as mysterious objects and make the gullible people believe that in this pot are kept the implements with which they can kill men and animals. Hence, the sorcerers are not only terribly feared by the Sonorans, but there are many even among the Spaniards who are heartily afraid of this rabble.

Pfefferkorn concluded by pointing out that "these sorcerers have never seen one claw of the devil, nor have they alliance or communion with him. They are nothing but imposters who use the innocence and gullibility of their countrymen to their own advantage."[33]

By the mid-nineteenth century, the Ópatas had been converted to Christianity and pacified. Spanish-born Franciscans had been expelled from Mexico and control of what was left of the missions had been turned over to secular priests, who were appointed to parishes by bishops, not religious orders. By law, former mission lands had become privatized. Ópata culture was in rapid decline.[34] Few if any disturbances, conflicts, or uprisings for which sorcery could be invoked as a cause have come to light. Then, too, at least some Enlightenment ideas had finally reached the distant province of

Sonora. The possibility of seeing criminal charges lodged against individuals for practicing sorcery seemed more and more remote.

Still, belief in sorcerers and curanderos and their power to do evil has persisted and retains considerable popularity in Mexico today. Vestiges continue among the clergy as well.[35] While popular religious movements at times challenge scientific principles, it seems impossible that any law enforcement authority would invoke criminal law to deal with the supposed perpetrators of occult mischief.

CHAPTER FIVE

Father Guerrero Nails Simón García

✝ PRIESTS RESPONDED TO RUMORS AND ACCUSATIONS OF WITCHCRAFT in ways as varied as their personalities. While some were stern purifiers of the faith, others paid little attention to curandismo, perhaps because shamanism involved beliefs in the supernatural and a vaguely delimited region of Catholicism they could choose to ignore.

The physical activities of Indians were a different matter. How a priest managed the mission Indian populations was a clear reflection of his effectiveness. The isolation and separation of missions often made communications among priests difficult, but they managed to maintain a healthy chain of gossip and discussions of their brethren. Each must have looked to the loyalty of his congregation, the attendance at Mass, and the maintenance of the mission buildings as clear symbols of his worth as a missionary. These manifestations could not escape the notice of their brethren of the cloth.

Father Guerrero of Bacadéhuachi must have lacked charisma, charity, or warmth. In 1707 his congregation of Indians abandoned the mission of Bacadéhuachi in numbers large enough to fill a long list. Some of them were repeat runaways. The ever-increasing number of absentees and recidivists convinced him that only military force could stanch the flow of wayward Indians from his parish. He invoked Spanish law to get the Indians—*his* recalcitrant Indians—back in church. His strategy for dealing with the potential embarrassment of multiple runaways ignited a storm of controversy. It also provoked deep divisions among the Jesuits and underscored the tenuous nature of their relationship with settlers and the military.

Jesuits, Reduction, Runaways, and the Laws of the Indies

Priests and settlers made their entradas into northwestern New Spain in the middle third of the seventeenth century only with authorization from the Spanish Crown. Royal authorities monitored their presence, and their activities were subject to the provisions of the Laws of the Indies. These were ordinances originally promulgated in 1573 during the reign of Spanish king Phillip II in response to reports of anarchy in urban developments in the Americas and of Spaniards' gross abuses of Indians. The specific proposals were the result of the work of the Council of the Indies, the Crown's administrative arm in Havana. The original regulations were expanded and recodified in 1680 and thereafter.[1]

The laws are best known for their provisions dictating with great specificity how new towns in conquered (newly discovered) lands were to be founded, designed, and constructed. They regulated the location, size, and arrangement of the plaza, the location of the church and government buildings, the arrangement and orientation of streets, and so on. More or less faithful application of the laws accounts for the predictability of design in many Latin American urban settings, far more so than in the Iberian Peninsula itself.

In addition to establishing standards for founding and developing urban spaces, however, the Laws of the Indies also dictated how Indians were to be treated and absorbed into the Spanish empire. The many provisions of the Laws of the Indies subjected Indians to both protections and restrictions. The Indians themselves had no say in the laws' formulation. The regulations were supposedly designed to protect them from abuse and exploitation. At the same time, the laws required that as pagans they would receive proper—and forced—education in Catholicism and in European cultural norms. Each would receive a Spanish given name and would be expected to become conversant in the Spanish language. With guidance strictly and properly applied, over time the Indians would become loyal subjects of the king and devout agrarian Catholics, or so the laws' promulgators hoped.

Of greatest importance from the Indians' standpoint was the enforcement of reduccion, or reduction, the policy of requiring—sometimes forcing—Indians to dwell in the immediate vicinity of mission towns and their priests. The Laws of the Indies mandated reduction.[2] Apart from larger settlements (perhaps towns) on the Río Sonora, most Indian communities of the Opatería were dispersed over a broad area in small hamlets called rancherías, so reduccion often entailed the forced resettlement of indigenous people to the vicinity of the mission centers—herding them in—where the clergy could constantly monitor their activities with a fatherly, knowing, and wary eye.[3] Reduccion also reflected a Jesuit and Iberian assumption that only urbanized folk were civilized, and those who dwelt beyond the pale of the town and the reach of its priests would live as barbarians and pagans. Required attendance at Mass was one means of building proper urban habits. Another was the rigorous requirement that Indians work on a European schedule.[4]

While the laws required the Jesuits to gather the Indians into missions, the missions enjoyed a ten-year period during which the Indians would not be subject to tithes, taxation, or other exactions from the Crown. During that decade the priests would convert and indoctrinate the Indians. When the ten-year period was up, the Indians would revert to the status of tax- and tithe-paying subjects.[5] That provision had technically expired nearly sixty years prior to the documents discussed here. Indians were still confined to the missions and undergoing indoctrination. Their conversion was taking far longer than the lawmakers foresaw and hoped.

Some priests believed the message of Christian Spain was so transparently superior and overpowering to naïve Natives that they would naturally cleave to the new missions and their emissaries and reject the old practices and beliefs, viewing reduction as a boon. Many of the clergy, however, appear to have suspected that only more or less rigid enforcement of civilizing policies would lead the Natives from their religious, cultural, social, and political backwardness and nomadic tendencies into the light of settled European modes of behavior. Nomads and wanderers do not constitute a fertile ground for conversion or for catechism. Nomadic peoples routinely resisted reduction and Christian education.

Whether a given priest preferred a gentle and tolerant approach to a stricter enforcement of the new code of conduct depended on the individual missionary. In general, however, the priests found it necessary to impose strictly enforced codes of behavior on their new charges. They had no patience for polygamy, idolatry, Native curing, or pagan ceremonies and immediately sought their extirpation. They sought out and neutralized or killed witches, sorcerers, and shamans. They railed against casual sexuality. They rooted out the consumption of alcoholic beverages—Laws of the Indies specifically forbade the selling or trading of wine to Natives, on the grounds that it makes them "ill and torpid, and easily kills them. They become alienated, commit idolatries, perform heathen ceremonies and sacrifices, and in anger they engage in quarrels, lose their lives, and commit many carnal, vile and incestuous vices."[6]

A practical corollary to the new round of mores dictated by Spanish authorities, especially the requirement of reduction, was a strictly enforced prohibition against wandering, leaving the mission, or visiting other sites without the permission of the priest. The missionaries feared that Indians who were absent from the fold would easily be seduced back into the grasp of pagan forces. Furthermore, these Indians were heavily recruited by mine owners desperate for laborers to extract ore from the ground. Once the Indians were put to work, the mine owners were loath to surrender them to authorities, especially given the scarcity of free labor in the Northwest. Mining camps were spiritual wastelands, sources of vice where lowlifes, libertines, folk lacking in Spanish bloodlines, and dangerous ideas freely circulated. And the work itself was dangerous.

Following a bitter struggle over the use of Indian labor, the missionaries and miners were forced to accept a government-ordered compromise, an agreement that satisfied neither side, called the *repartimiento*, whereby only a limited number of Indians from any one mission might be recruited for outside work. Under this provision Indian governors (appointed by the priests) might be required to provide labor recruiters from the mines with a certain number of workers for a specific, defined period.[7]

The battle for control of Indian labor (in which the Indians had no say) had been fierce. Life outside the missions might tempt Indians to stray from catechism, but even more significant, the priests relied on forced Indian labor on mission lands—two to three days a week—to produce the crops and other products that supported the mission and constituted its source of exchange. Without the crops and whatever crafts the Indians might make that could be bartered outside the mission, granaries, kitchens, and coffers could easily be jeopardized. Indian labor also constructed and maintained the mission buildings and Indians acted as servants for the priests. They performed irreplaceable functions in church rituals as well. In their absence mission activities would suffer and the priests would be left to their own resources. Even worse, Indians who circulated beyond the influence of the priests (especially in mining towns) could come under the sway of rebellious or insurrectionary leaders and ideas conveyed by firebrand Natives who delivered tlátoles, inciting Indians to reject the yoke of the white men (as Indians often referred to Spaniards) and return to life as they had enjoyed it prior to the arrival of Europeans. In light of these dangers, it should come as no surprise that the Laws of the Indies of 1680 prescribed a penalty of twenty lashes for Indians who moved from one town to another without authorization.[8]

And so the priests took roll at religious rites, especially Mass. While they may have been too occupied personally to maintain records of who was present and who was absent, they appointed Indian converts to offices called alguaciles, fiscales, and topiles to take on those tasks. In addition, they relied on a network of informants to advise them about personnel matters within the communities. If Indians were to go missing, the priest would soon know about it. Some priests routinely administered lashes for those who missed Mass, a punishment authorized by Spanish authorities (see chapter 6). While the absence of one or two parishioners might not be sufficient cause for concern, if several were to go unaccounted for the priest would surely notice and contemplate what sort of action he could take. The larger the number of truants became, the greater the priest's worry.

Father Guerrero Calls for Help

What, then, was a priest to do when Indians came up missing from the mission communities? This is apparently the situation that Father Miguel Guerrero Villaseca of Bacadéhuachi found in his parish in 1707.[9] Just how he came to note the absence of a number of Indian parishioners is not clear from the documents. Some of the wayward Indians may have been from Nácori Chico, which was a *partido*, or district, of the Bacadéhuachi mission. Because the smaller town was only a *visita* (outlying village) of the larger mission town, the priest visited there only occasionally and absences might have gone unnoticed for some time. On the other hand, the priest may have noted the absences early and tried unsuccessfully to round up the wayward Indians and return them to the fold. From the description in the documents, Padre Guerrero was successful at arranging the forced return of some recalcitrant Indians, but some of the returnees simply ran away again once they had been brought back to the fold.

An incident described by Captain Juan Matheo Manje, who is also involved in this saga, lends some insight into Father Guerrero.

> I could not go with them [Eusebio Francisco Kino and Father Manuel González to the Colorado River] because it was my duty

as Lieutenant Governor and military Captain to answer the call of Father Miguel Guerrero. I had to go out and punish some witches who, with mean and diabolical operations, were killing people in the towns of Nácori and Vacadéhuachi.[10]

Manje did not specify the nature of the "operations" or the nature of the punishment he applied to the witches. However, the episode does demonstrate that Father Guerrero was not at all averse to invoking the assistance of the military when his spiritual influence failed to elicit the desired response. The request to Manje does not speak well for his abilities as a priest.

When his informal roundups yielded disappointing results in repatriotizing the restless Indians, Father Guerrero sought help from civil authorities. He apparently began by contacting the alcalde mayor at San Juan Bautista first and supplying the lists of the missing parishioners. When that appeal produced only limited success, the padre contacted the governor in Parral, who seems to have ordered the Indians back to their mission. That order is not included in the documents. Even after the governor's order, however, several of the Bacadéhuachi truants failed to return within the required time, so Father Guerrero fired off another complaint. This time the governor took stern measures. The actions he took constitute the bulk of this file in the Parral archives, but the unfolding of the events is seen mostly through the reports of two men, Captain Asencio Domínguez and the alcalde mayor of the province of Ostimuri, Blás Ezquerr.[11] The provincial governor appears to have been somewhat out of sorts that his first order had not been fully complied with. He would tolerate no further disobedience or insolence.

Padre Guerrero cannot have undertaken his appeal to civil authorities lightly. Relations between Jesuits and military or civilian men fluctuated between polite and hostile, and for priests to rely on military solutions to administrative problems was tantamount to acknowledging impotence and being forced to call for help. No priest could have enjoyed invoking the use of force to quell Native uprising or punish dissidents. The priest may have derived temporary satisfaction at seeing his orders enforced, but the policy of invoking military assistance reflected badly on the missionary's ability to oversee his flock. We have already seen how Gerónimo de la Canal requested military assistance but failed to mention the armed intervention in his written reports. Father Guerrero cannot have felt much more enthusiastic than Padre Canal about being known as the priest who needed soldiers to force wandering or uncooperative subjects to return to the mission, especially since the accomplishments of Father Eusebio Kino were familiar to most priests, for better or worse. Father Kino was wildly popular among the Pimans of his missions, so much so that Indians flocked *to* his missions, not away from them. Father Guerrero cannot but have resented Kino's natural rapport with the Natives.

Padre Guerrero must also have known that runaways tend toward recidivism. If the risks entailed in running away were preferable to the burden of remaining under the priest's authority, invoking force to gain the Indians' return would be unlikely to alter their inclinations. Applying too drastic a punishment to the runaways would be an incentive for repeated violations and any Indians inclined to wander would plan their absences in greater detail so as to avoid capture. However, the priest could hardly allow the absences to go unnoted and unpunished. He would lose respect among his Indians and, as he knew well, they would take advantage of his weakness in every possible way. And he would be unfavorably discussed by his Jesuit brethren and would become the object of uncharitable gossip by settlers. He had no other recourse but to demand the forced repatriation of his absent charges. In doing so he joined a wide array of border clergy who arrived at the same conclusion: only brute force would change the pagan Indians into decent Catholics.[12]

It appears that he calculated poorly. Padre Miguel would discover, probably to his dismay, that invoking force to curb runaways could have most undesirable consequences. He issued the complaint in anger and desperation, it appears, and the authorities took him at his word. It seems odd that he did not communicate with other priests serving missions close to the mining camps. He could have requested that they post discreet inquiries about Indians working the mines, where he had good reason to believe that all the truants had wound up. Perhaps Father Guerrero had so attempted, or perhaps he was angry enough that he craved certain punishment for the violators, and not some feeble hand slapping that a less vigorous priest from a neighboring mission might administer.

Governor Juan Fernández de Córdoba in Parral responded to Father Guerrero's request by ordering the distinguished captain inspector Antonio Bezerra Nieto (or Becerra Nieto) to arrange a posse of sorts. Bezerra Nieto had already established an illustrious career in the region, much of it spent at the presidio of Janos, where he was routinely engaged in making fact-finding sorties, enforcing mining regulations, suppressing Indian uprisings, relocating obdurate parties of Natives, and tracking down and capturing raiding parties. The captain was apparently not in a position to undertake another strenuous campaign into Sonora merely to round up a few recalcitrant Indians (who, after all, did not appear to be causing any problems at all) just to satisfy the vengeful sentiments of a resentful priest. Instead, on September 27, 1707, at the governor's urging, he appointed a trusted officer named Asencio Domínguez to head the disciplinary mission along with four soldiers, hardly a stalwart military enterprise. Domínguez was no stranger to special assignments. For unknown reasons, he seems to have responded with enthusiasm to this mission, perhaps because he was looking forward to visiting the warm, picturesque valleys of Sonora after facing the bleak prospect of being stationed for the winter in chilly, isolated, and treeless Janos on the high, windswept plains of Chihuahua. Domínguez seems to have relished these sorts of missions. He would be involved in quelling Indian protests for at least another decade. While on this mission to retrieve wayward mission Indians, he received special supplemental orders from Governor Fernández de Córdoba to arrest Father Eusebio Kino's friend Juan Matheo Manje at his home in Bacanuchi on the Río Sonora. The charges? He had slandered Jesuits.[13] We must keep this in mind with Captain Domínguez's later exchange with Padre Visitador Francisco María Pícolo.

By October 20, 1707, Domínguez had accepted the orders and by November 1 he and his squadron had passed muster and arrived in Sonora. His assignment involved visiting all the likely spots where fugitive Indians might be hiding out. Most likely they would be working at newly opened Sonoran mines. Extracting minerals from rock was labor intensive, and the owners, even small-time operators, were in constant and often desperate search for laborers, of which Sonora still had a chronic shortage in the early eighteenth century. Indians not only bored their way into the rock to extract the ore, they also carried the ore to the surface, made charcoal, fired the smelters, and reduced the ores to precious metal. The owners also valued Indians, male and female, both young and old, as personal servants for their households, as concubines, and as wives.

The first stop for Captain Domínguez was the mining town of Quimbunazorra, now abandoned, located not far from Arivechi on the Arroyo Sahuaripa and close enough to Sahuaripa that residents attended Mass in the chapel there.[14] On his arrival, Domínguez announced "determinedly" the nature of his mission to the leading official, Captain Simón García, about thirty-eight years of age, who informed him sadly that he had a mostly Indian *quadrilla*, a work gang assigned to a mine or smelter. Of late, however, the quadrilla was not functioning since an Indian named Alejo had warned the other Indians about the previously issued orders requiring them to return to their missions, and he and some of them had fled. Alejo, apparently from Bacadéhuachi, had been seen in Sahuaripa, but no more information was available. Domínguez read the orders (diligencias) aloud so that all, including Captain García, would be aware of the severity of failing to obey them and moved on.

The next stop for Domínguez and his men was in a mine called Tonibabi, in the vicinity of present-day Moctezuma. Here he once again announced his purpose—rounding up "fugitive" Indians—and found an Indian named Felipe who was from Bacadéhuachi and who had heard and disregarded the first order. When Domínguez inquired why he had disobeyed the order, Felipe responded that upon hearing the order he had journeyed to San Juan Bautista, where the alcalde mayor of Sonora, Manuel Hoguez y San Martín, had told him that because he was in the company of his master, one Juan Moreno, he was not a slave and could live where he pleased. And so the alcalde had given him permission to remain. Captain Domínguez left no written comment on this but merely noted it for the record and moved on. Juan Moreno, Felipe's master, signed the statement along with Domínguez.

At Pibipa, a mine whose location is now lost but is known also to be in the vicinity of Moctezuma, the conditions were more complicated. Domínguez carried with him a list or lists of the missing Indians from Bacadéhuachi, which Padre Guerrero had compiled for his previous complaint to the governor (and had probably brought up to date for the present foray). Captain Juan Antonio Ortiz de Cortés, the officer in charge of Pibipa, simply told the captain the names of all Indians in the mining town.[15] One Indian at Pibipa, a woman named María, was from Guásavas, not Bacadéhuachi. Another fellow, named Ignacio, whom everyone called "The Bishop" and who possibly hailed from Bacadéhuachi, was a servant on the mining hacienda of a Spaniard.[16] Two others named on the list of truants were also present. They were arrested and handed over to Captain Domínguez and, we must assume, turned over to someone who led them, bound and on foot, back to Bacadéhuachi to the waiting application of justice by the priest. We do not know the severity of punishment that awaited the runaways, but it was a severe offense. The Laws of the Indies mention twenty lashes, and failing to attend Mass, a relatively trivial misdemeanor, was punishable with five lashes. The penalty for repeat runaways must have been far harsher.

Domínguez noted some important details that Captain Antonio Ortiz de Cortés brought to his attention. The Indian they called "The Bishop" was married to an Indian woman who lived at the smelter and María of Guásavas was married to another man. Both men worked at the smelter, which was the only operation within fourteen leagues (about fifty kilometers) of San Juan Bautista. The quadrilla (work gang) of which they were a part could hardly function in their absence. If the orders to return Indians to their mission towns were carried out, the mines and smelters would have to close. As if to show good faith, Captain Ortiz de Cortés turned over to Captain Domínguez his servant, a boy about eleven years old. The lad owed Ortiz de Cortés a few pesos that the captain had advanced to him, as was the case with most servants in the region.[17] Two other Indians, apparently from Bacadéhuachi, were also working as servants of Spaniards. They, too, appear to have been turned over to Domínguez to his satisfaction. Ortiz warned Domínguez that the Spaniards needed the labor of the Indians to be able to continue to maintain their enterprises (and maintain the flow of taxes to His Majesty). Apparently resigned to losing his only help, he turned the Indians over to Domínguez's men to be forcibly repatriated to Bacadéhuachi and its angry priest. With these names checked off the list, Captain Domínguez seemed at least temporarily satisfied with Antonio Ortiz's explanation but was not entirely convinced. Once again we have no record of what became of the captives when they arrived, bound and exhausted, at the priest's home in Bacadéhuachi.

In Cumpas, an ancient Indian town about thirty kilometers north of Moctezuma, Captain Domínguez located two more Bacadéhuachan Indians and turned them over to the local (Indian) governor to be transported to their proper place. Alcalde Mayor Manuel de Hoguez was present (his home in San Juan Bautista was but a few kilometers to the west), but he offered no apparent objection whatsoever to the capture of the wayward Indians, pledging instead his full cooperation with the governor's orders. He could hardly do otherwise, since he was an appointee of the governor and any insubordination would result in his being removed as alcalde and losing his pension.

By early December, Domínguez had arrived at the remote mine of Aguaje to the south of Hermosillo, now abandoned, but then the site of a prosperous mine and wild boomtown. The official in charge was Joseph de Subiate (Zubiate), an ambitious entrepreneur of doubtful principles and checkered reputation (see chapter 6) who had already served as alcalde mayor of Ostimuri. Just how aggressively Domínguez might have questioned Subiate is a matter of speculation, but Subiate was already an influential politician and successful miner who would not easily be intimidated or forced to alter a course of action. He heartily accepted the governor's orders and offered Domínguez an inspection of the mining quadrilla. Domínguez found only an Indian woman, whom he turned over to be returned to Bacadéhuachi. There had been three other Indians in the town, but when the previous orders had arrived, they had fled in the direction of Parral, Subiate said. If Captain Domínguez was satisfied with Subiate's report, he did not say so. Aguaje was a rather large mining town, with probably several hundred inhabitants, many of them Indians—Mayos, Ópatas, Pimans, Seris, and Yaquis—and most of the remainder were mestizos and others of various mixed-blood origin. In such places, few people asked others for personal information.[18]

Circling north, Asencio Domínguez arrived next at Pópulo, an agricultural site on the Río San Miguel, some fifty kilometers north of Hermosillo. There he learned that a woman from Bacadéhuachi along with two children and a nephew were living in the house of the local official, Captain Domingo García de la Serna, who was absent. When Captain Domínguez attempted to capture the woman, she fled with her children and nephew. His soldiers went searching for her and, after following her trail, rounded her and the children up and brought them to the captain. When he asked why she had hidden herself, she replied that the mayordomo had told her to do so. Domínguez read her the orders and, we must assume, sent her off, with or without the children, to face Father Guerrero at Bacadéhuachi, some two hundred kilometers to the northeast.

Captain García de la Serna was a miner from the farming and mining town of Opodepe, some fifty kilometers north of Pópulo on the Río San Miguel. Domínguez arrived in that town and confronted García with the list of missing Indians. The latter reported that several Indians on the list had been there but had departed, some fleeing the retribution from Governor Córdoba's first order, others to search for better work, another to search for a lost brother in Parral, others to Arivechi or Quimbunazorra, and so on. Domínguez may not have located any more Bacadéhuachans working in mines, but the captain did mention disapprovingly that he had sent García de la Serna's concubine off to her hometown. One senses that Captain Domínguez did not believe Captain García de la Serna's stories. We can also sense that the loss of his concubine did not sit well with García de la Serna.

Remaining only a short time longer in Opodepe, Captain Domínguez tracked down another Indian from Bacadéhuachi. In this case an Indian woman working as a servant in the house of a Spaniard had married an

Indian outsider (probably an Indian from the south) who had suffered a ghastly wound from an axe. He lay near death in their house and the woman explained that she had not obeyed the previous order to return to Bacadéhuachi due to her desire to tend to her wounded husband. She pleaded that she be allowed to remain with him through his convalescence. Domínguez did not note whether or not he honored her request.

The next stop was at the mine called Sonora, a place not now identified. There Captain Domínguez found one Indian, whom he turned over to the resident officer with a stern order to see that he was sent off to Bacadéhuachi.

Finally, on December 20, 1707, Captain Domínguez returned to Sahuaripa, not far from Quimbunazorra. He discovered to his extreme anger that a captive runaway (presumably one he had ordered sent back to Bacadéhuachi) had escaped. He had previously (date uncertain) remanded the runaway to the custody of the Indian governor of Sahuaripa, a Jova. The Indian governor's explanation for the escape must have been unacceptable to Captain Domínguez, because he went into a diatribe against the hapless fellow. In a rage, Domínguez had the governor arrested, ordered him stripped of his canes of office and, invoking the concurrence of Governor Fernández de Córdoba, sentenced him to be bound with his hands lashed around a tree and given fifty lashes.[19] That sentence, seemingly brutal, would prove wildly controversial.

The Campaign Against Simón García

At this point the roundup circuit became anything but routine for Asencio Domínguez. He returned to the mine at San Juan de la Cueva de Quimbunazorra to ask additional questions of Captain Simón García. He found the captain in a most uncooperative mood. According to Domínguez, García railed at Domínguez's soldiers, asking if they had nothing better to do than conduct raids at dawn, seizing free Indians as if they had no rights, abusing them even if they were legitimately working the mines.[20] Warming to the sport, García refused to cooperate with the captain, denouncing his mission and threatening to put him under arrest for trespass. García went so far as to look to the priest from Sahuaripa, Padre Pícolo, for help, but to no avail, at least initially. Domínguez ordered his men to seize the two Indians who worked for García and take them to Bacadéhuachi. Both of the fugitives fled, however, and Domínguez resignedly read the orders to García and made his way back to Sahuaripa, seething at García's lack of cooperation and preparing a request that he be arrested.

Simón García's resistance was an insult to Captain Domínguez, but nearly as bad was the situation in Pibipa. When the captain returned, he learned that Captain Antonio Ortiz de Cortés had allowed two Indians from Bacadéhuachi to flee, in spite of his having promised faithfully to turn over any runaways. Incensed at this disobedience, Domínguez issued an immediate order to seize Ortiz's real property. Ortiz was both a farmer and a miner and owned a goodly supply of grain as well as mining equipment. His herd of livestock included twenty-eight mares, a stud donkey, and five yokes of oxen—clear proof of the extent of his farming activity. In addition, Ortiz's employees pointed out that he owned a modest mine and smelter. Domínguez took note and seized all these goods, placing them under the trusteeship of two supposedly trustworthy residents of Pibipa.[21]

Meanwhile in Sahuaripa, Father Francisco Pícolo had intervened by sequestering the accused Jova governor in a safe place. When Captain Domínguez arrived to administer the fifty lashes, the Indian was not to be found and Domínguez assumed he had fled. Clearly seething at the insubordination of the locals, Domínguez ordered a house-to-house search of the Spaniards. He was unsuccessful in producing the runaways but in the house of the priest he discovered two letters protesting the Jova governor's treatment, one written by Padre Pícolo (who was the current Jesuit visitador), addressed to Father Guerrero at Bacadéhuachi, the other from Father Juan San Martín, priest from Batuc. Both letters reflected unfavorably on Domínguez's tactics. The captain was also surprised to learn that Antonio Ortiz of Pibipa had taken sanctuary within the church at Sahuaripa, where, according to Spanish law, he could not be seized. Domínguez entered the church and spoke with Ortiz, trying, he claimed, to convince him that he would be better off departing peacefully with the captain than resisting arrest. Ortiz replied that he would go quietly, but only when he received a reply from Governor Fernández de Córdoba in Parral to a letter he had dispatched through the helpful services of Padre Pícolo.

Captain Domínguez was now in a showdown with Father Pícolo on at least two fronts: dealing with a Spanish fugitive from the law on one hand, and the punishment of an Indian subject of the Jesuits on the other.[22] Domínguez assumed an air of wounded pride at the description of his actions he discovered in the letter from Pícolo to Guerrero. He was just doing his job, he reminded Pícolo. What went on in Quimbunazorra was between Governor Córdoba and him and was beyond Pícolo's jurisdiction. He acknowledged that he had acted precipitously in not informing Pícolo of the action, but nevertheless, he could not justly be accused of behaving scandalously. He was merely carrying out written orders from Governor Córdoba, which were (he reminded Pícolo) a result of a complaint filed by a member of the Company of Jesus, the very recipient of one of Pícolo's letters. Domínguez maintained that he had attempted to notify several of the priests and apologize for any excesses by him or his men, but they had all been absent from their missions or, even worse, had refused to speak with him. The Jesuits were the problem, not he.

Even more intriguing is the exchange that ensued between the padre visitador in Sahuaripa and Padre Miguel Guerrero of Bacadéhuachi, who had originated the complaint against the runaway Indians. Pícolo by all descriptions was a strict and stern Jesuit administrator but was appalled at the mistreatment of Indians, especially the Jova governor, as a result of Father Guerrero's complaint. He wrote an angry and sarcastic letter to Father Guerrero, scolding him for not informing him of the situation: "[the arrival of the soldiers] is the first news I have of the Governor's order, and I do not know if these soldiers have come here at the Governor's order and I do not know if he has issued orders for Indians from all pueblos or just this mission."[23] He slammed Father Guerrero's inflexibility. Some Indians could readily move around and be productive members of missions. There was no need for all Indians to be anchored permanently to one place. Continuing in this line, he *ordered* Father Guerrero to return immediately to Sahuaripa an Indian from Nácori Chico named Juan Tánori and his family in the company of the courier who delivered the letter. A census of Nácori Chico at the end of the documents indicates that the Tánoris may have numbered around thirty people. They were among those who had been forcibly repatriated to Bacadéhuachi through the actions of Captain Domínguez. Father Pícolo noted that Juan Tánori was old and had become a successful miner and farmer in the Sahuaripa area and had every right to remain there, regardless of what Father Guerrero might order. Father Guerrero might have been pleased with Captain Domínguez's military action, viewing his harsh treatment of the runaways as their just deserts. He might have been somewhat taken aback at the excessively rough treatment the runaways received at the hands of Asencio Domínguez and his troops, but perhaps he had remained righteously indignant concerning the Indians' unauthorized sojourns. Or, we might hope, he may have regretted the vehemence with which he pursued the absences, especially when he learned of the death of Alejo on the return trip to Bacadéhuachi. But he must have cringed at the vehemence of

Father Pícolo's remonstrance, for the visitador made it abundantly clear that his subordinate had committed a major error, potentially disastrous both for its consequences and for Guerrero's failure to consult first with his superiors. The Jesuits ran a tight hierarchical ship and Padre Guerrero had violated its chain of command, demanding military action that involved other priests' missions. It also seems likely that Father Pícolo would continue to take Father Guerrero to task for unnecessarily inflicting punishment and running the risk of letting his personal frustrations undermine many years of evangelizing activity. His peremptory order to return Juan Tánori to Sahuaripa was a clear dressing down. The scolding Father Guerrero received at the hands of his superior had to have cut deep. By 1709 he had departed from Bacadéhuachi and subsequently disappears from the record in Sonoran Jesuitry.

Padre Pícolo also pleaded with Asencio Domínguez and with Governor Córdoba by courier letter[24] not to carry out the sentence on the Jova governor, as it would cause deep resentment among the Jovas and undo much missionary work the Jesuits had invested among them. Reducing the Jovas from seminomadic peoples of the sierras dwelling under primitive conditions in widely scattered hamlets into townspeople had been an arduous task, and the wanton administration of lashes, especially those applied for an infraction the Indians did not understand, would probably cause them to flee as a people and resume their barbarian ways well beyond the reach of the padres. Meanwhile, three other priests wrote to Domínguez from Bacanora, a town some thirty kilometers to the west with a sizeable Jova population. The three pleaded with Domínguez to delay carrying out the sentence against the governor, warning that if he went forward with the punishment, a general uprising of the Jovas would probably ensue. The Jova governor was a poor, lowly Indian who loved his priest and was beloved by him and by the Jovas in Sahuaripa and Bacanora (and perhaps by other Indians as well), and they would surely become irate if he were mistreated for an act that was beyond his control or comprehension.[25]

Captain Asencio Domínguez apparently agreed and seems to have backed off at least for the moment on the application of lashes to the careless Jova governor. It was a moot point: the Jova governor was in hiding. Domínguez reminded the priests, however, that he was merely carrying out his commission from the governor in Parral, which was his bounden duty, and his was not to question the appropriateness of the lashes. He bridled at what he considered the insults and false charges that had been hurled at him by the priests, especially Padre Pícolo, when he was only carrying out orders.

He saw the hand of the priests in the sanctuary offered to Antonio Ortiz and in the disappearance of the Jova governor and his inability to locate him, even with house-to-house searches. He was offended, wounded by the misrepresentation of his actions when he was but a lowly military man, admittedly lacking in the refinements of the more cultured priests.

Returning to Bacadéhuachi, Domínguez appeared satisfied with his work in spite of Padre Pícolo's obstructionism and his order to return the Indian Tánori and his relatives from Nácori Chico to Sahuaripa. He had been issued orders by Governor Fernández de Córdoba and (he believed) had largely fulfilled them. In his closing remarks Domínguez wrote that most of the missing Indians had been returned there and to Nácori Chico as had been ordered by Governor Fernández de Córdoba. In departing, he had urged the Indians to become the sort of loyal peasants the Crown hoped to produce:

> I counseled them to live in peace in their pueblos, caring for their women and planting their crops of wheat and corn and other crops that His Majesty might order for their yearly nourishment, listening to and respecting their governors and other justices, obeying their priests and fastidiously attending mass and other Christian educational events.

Even as he bestowed this fatherly advice, Domínguez appears to have left one major concern unaddressed: a known sorcerer and his family had fled Bacadéhuachi for parts unknown and was certain to wreak evil wherever he went. Parral had not yet provided instructions as to how to proceed, whether or not to pursue the truant and arrest him on charges of sorcery. For Domínguez this boded a disquieting prospect after a mostly successful campaign.

Back in San José de Parral, Governor Fernández de Córdoba heard Domínguez's report and, on the basis of what he read, appears to have been angered by Simón García's refusal to cooperate, his intransigence, and his withholding of information. Equally offensive was Antonio Ortiz's resisting arrest in Pibipa. Fernández was an autocratic sort, not given to quibbling with his subjects. In a contest of wills with Father Kino's friend, Juan Matheo Manje, Córdoba freed Manje from prison when the Jesuits withdrew the charges against him (he was accused of slandering the Jesuit Order and its priests), but he immediately tossed Manje back in jail when Manje criticized the governor's handling of the case. The governor thought it perverse that Indians should wander outside their pueblos "without knowing the [Holy] doctrine"[26] and had thus been sympathetic to the complaint lodged by Father Guerrero of Bacadéhuachi.

On the other hand, it is not clear that Governor Córdoba had become aware of the controversy surrounding the rough treatment of the Jova governor in Sahuaripa, though the priests had supposedly intervened by posting letters to him. If he was aware of it, he chose to ignore it. He praised Asencio Domínguez's success in "populating" Bacadéhuachi by returning wayward Indians to the custody of the priest.

Córdoba would tolerate no insolence from the likes of the officers from Ostimuri who were slow or reluctant to obey his orders. He concluded from Asencio Domínguez's report that García and Ortiz were in outright defiance. He drew up warrants for their immediate arrest on the grounds of failure to obey his commands. To carry out his wishes he instructed Blás Ezquerr, alcalde mayor of Ostimuri,[27] to bring the two miscreants into Parral as prisoners and seize all their belongings.

Blás Ezquerr received his marching orders at his office in the now defunct mining town of Baroyeca, the territorial seat of Ostimuri, which lies near the Río Mayo in southern Sonora. With all due pomp Ezquerr organized a military escort and arrived after several days' marches at Quimbunazorra, where he put Simón García under house arrest, pending the confiscation of his goods, and did the same to Antonio Ortiz, supposedly in Pibipa. Apparently Ortiz's defiance of Domínguez's orders was sufficiently egregious that Ezquerr ordered Ortiz immediately sent off to stand trial in Parral. All of his property—mine, farm, equipment, and livestock—had already been seized. All that remained were Ortiz's saddle and trappings and some personal effects. The list of Ortiz's clothing and bedding provides a glimpse of the material life of a Spanish civil or military functionary of the early eighteenth century:

> two sheets made of Rouen cloth (from Rouen, France)
> one *acerico* (small pillow)
> a used shirt of Rouen cloth and some undershorts
> one lace tie and one *valona* (high collar)
> some silk socks and stockings
> some new white shoes
> one cotton mattress
> two *varas* of blue silk cloth and two dozen buttons

six Munich medallions made of cloth
a large serge blanket in which the preceding items were wrapped

Ezquerr reported that the bundle was deposited with an overseer in Quimbunazorra. Meanwhile, during his transfer to prison in Parral, Ortiz escaped from his captors near Tónichi on the Río Yaqui. Ezquerr sent out a notice to all mining towns but was unsuccessful in recapturing the fugitive. No further information about the lieutenant has surfaced. Since Ortiz's goods were now forfeit, someone unknown probably wound up more nattily dressed than before. What became of his real property and livestock is unclear.

Alcalde Ezquerr arrived at Simón García's house in Quimbunazorra on June 4, 1708. Formally arresting García, Ezquerr ordered his lieutenant, in the presence of other residents as witnesses, to prominently display at the captain's house the royal seal that he carried. He solemnly informed the captain that he was taking him prisoner and asked García if he knew why. García responded that he did not know the reason. Ezquerr then read the orders for his detention as dictated by Governor Córdoba. Because Quimbunazorra had no jail, Ezquerr placed García under house arrest. The captain appears to have offered no resistance and submitted to the confinement.

As part of Simón García's arrest procedures, Alcalde Ezquerr ordered an inventory of the captain's possessions, just as he had ordered for Captain Antonio Ortiz in Pibipa. Captain García was a wealthy man by comparison. He owned a small silver mine in Quimbunazorra plus all the equipment necessary to carry on a smelting operation and concentrate the metal. García had made a considerable investment in mining equipment, especially in light of the high cost of shipping pig iron and iron stock by mule across the mountains from Chihuahua or from Guaymas on the coast.[28] The mining tools included a smelting oven, a large iron crucible, and iron flues for the smelter's chimney. All these large items probably could not have been manufactured at the scene. Also included were bellows (parts of which could have been locally fabricated), pokers, grappling hooks, axes, and other metal tools, most of which could have been forged on site from iron stock carried in by cart or mule. In addition, García owned sixteen mules and four breeding mares as part of his mining operation. He owned several buildings, including his own adobe residence and its furnishings, plus various outbuildings and sheds, most of them also constructed of adobe. He also owned an additional mine, located a league (four kilometers) from Quimbunazorra at a place called San Antonio. It was well worked, managed by a foreman, with six different excavations, each large enough to be supported by mine timbers to prevent cave-ins. The mine also had a forge for fabricating the necessary tools.

In the process of carrying out an inventory of Simón García's possessions, Blás Ezquerr's men came upon his account ledger, more than fifty pages long. Here they discovered that in addition to his mine holdings, García owned a ranch with a herd of cattle and horses. The alcalde ordered all the properties and possessions to be seized and placed under the receivership of two trusted local residents. Before he could begin the job himself, however, Ezquerr took sick and was unable to carry out the inventory (a responsibility that he may well have looked forward to). Instead, he turned over the task to one of his minions, Juan Joseph López de Trujillo, ordering him to round up García's livestock in a place where he could personally inspect them. López dutifully complied, driving the cattle and horses into a corral in the presence of witnesses (so that he could not be accused of misappropriating Captain García's property). The results were impressive: García's herd consisted of at least 107 branded cattle, 22 saddle horses, and two herds of breeding mares of about 25 each. López turned over all the possessions Captain García was known to have in the town to a resident who was charged with guarding them. The mine at San Antonio and the buildings there (including a house built from poles) were placed in the hands of a different trustee, known to be a man "of confidence." Alcalde Ezquerr must have been relieved to discover the long list of the captain's material holdings, especially the ranch. Men of such means are far less prone to flee prosecution and leave behind their earthly goods than are those of fewer and lesser possessions. And thus was Captain Simón García bound over for transport to the distant center of Parral, some five hundred fifty mountainous kilometers away, where he was to be tried for the crime of disobedience.[29]

On June 9, Blás Ezquerr, apparently recovered from his illness, ordered all the servants in Captain García's house to appear before them. He hoped this method of public intimidation would allow him to document which of the servants working for García was fugitive from Bacadéhuachi. Any such would be bound and forcibly returned to Padre Guerrero's authority. Ezquerr discovered not a single violator, however. Following this failure to turn up evidence, all references by Alcalde Ezquerr to the Bacadéhuachi priest and his complaint ceased. Whether or not Indians from Bacadéhuachi were still at large was no longer part of the case against Simón García.

From this point onward, communications move back and forth between Quimbunazorra, Ostimuri (later Sonora); and Parral, Chihuahua (then

Nueva Vizcaya). Simón García had been incarcerated in his home, but Blás Ezquerr seems to have suggested a transfer to the prison in Parral, which would be logical given the perceived severity of García's transgression. García argued against the transfer, however, noting that it would require accompaniment by guards whose services would be far better directed toward warding off the damages inflicted by "barbarous Indian enemies" thereabouts. Furthermore, Parral could be reached only after an arduous journey through mountains and high passes infested with "Indian enemies." The captain requested that he be released on his own recognizance. Blás Ezquerr apparently agreed with the captain's reasoning, describing the difficulties and dangers of crossing the mountains. He wrote to Governor Córdoba proposing that he appoint two men of good standing from Quimbunazorra to act as advocates for García and present his case in absentia in court.

For reasons not apparent in the documents, however, Ezquerr soon proceeded with the extradition anyway and ordered Simón García transferred to prison in Parral. He assigned a trustworthy Native of Quimbunazorra named Sebastián Féliz to be in charge of his passage through the mountains and safe arrival at the prison. In addition, Féliz would carry with him and turn over to the governor the pile of court documents that had accumulated concerning the case. We have no description of the journey except that it was long and difficult and that four guards were assigned to the captain. We must assume that he traveled with his hands bound, making for a most uncomfortable ride. The fact that the other accused, Antonio Ortiz, had escaped undoubtedly meant that García's escort would exercise increased vigilance over him, eyeing him more closely than usual, and would make sure that his bonds were especially secure. The succeeding documents have been logged into the archives in Parral and contain copies of the lengthy depositions taken by Alcalde Blás Ezquerr.

If the governor had thought his case against García would be simple, the documents he received from Blás Ezquerr in Quimbunazorra would quickly have disabused him. The captain proved himself to be a resourceful defender of his position and, the governor would probably discover later, seemed to have garnered the support of at least some priests. Furthermore, García made a very good case for having truth on his side. He repeated his request to be released on his own bond, given that he had a reputation as a good and honest man (which no one appears to have contested). On June 28 the governor agreed and ordered him freed from prison on the condition that he remain within the limits the real of San José de Parral.

In his initial testimony presented before Governor Córdoba, García professed to understand the charges Captain Asencio Domínguez had brought against him. When asked if he understood the consequences of disobeying the governor's orders, García responded that he understood that the disobedient deserved to be punished for any act of disobedience. When asked why he had refused to return the Indians of Bacadéhuachi to their pueblo as ordered by Captain Domínguez, he answered that he had not disobeyed any order to return Indians to Bacadéhuachi. When asked why he used disrespectful language and inappropriate words with Captain Domínguez, who was following the governor's orders, he responded that he had obeyed all the original orders and that the captain was exceeding his authority by continuing to question and requestion him, which provoked his (García's) outburst. In other words, he pleaded not guilty to all the charges.

Governor Córdoba did not find García's responses convincing and apparently ordered him to stand trial, requiring him to face further procedures. The remaining documents available, however, are limited to the depositions and testimony gathered by Alcalde Blás Ezquerr. These documents had been recorded in Quimbunazorra in early June and Sebastián Féliz had carried them along with him during the transfer of Captain García to prison in Parral. The order of the documents in the folio suggests that since the proceedings against Captain García would continue, he may have requested them to be introduced as part of his defense in July 1708. Once the governor released him from prison on his own recognizance, he could effectively represent himself in court. We have no documentation of any further court proceedings.

In his responses to Alcalde Ezquerr while being questioned in Quimbunazorra, Simón García argued that he had acted in an exemplary fashion as the leading officer in the mining town of San Juan de la Cueva de Quimbunazorra, and his actions in contesting the demands of Captain Asencio Domínguez should be interpreted in that light. He established his credentials as a proper leader by citing incidents in his favor, those times when he acted to the great credit of the king, the governor, his townspeople, and the Church. He presented ten responses to the order for his arrest, instances of his leadership, loyalty, and piety, knowing that his contemporaries in Quimbunazorra, who could not have been many, would corroborate his claims. He could not have had many enemies there, as we shall see.

The captain took credit for maintaining the peace and tranquility of the district, which included Tacupeto and towns high in the mountains. He cited examples: When Natives complained about unrest occurring in Yécora and Maicoba (among Mountain Pimas) in the mountainous country to the southeast and in Tepache to the north, he forthwith mustered a squadron of militia at his own expense and quelled the disturbances, restoring peace and tranquility without inflicting harm on anyone. He took special pride in pointing out that when in 1690 the district of Tacupeto was sacked and burned by "Indian enemies" (Pimas Bajos and perhaps Sumas),[30] it was he who immediately took steps to rebuild and redevelop the towns, including Quimbunazorra, attracting residents and assisting them in relocating. He had taken special care to invite priests, hosting them in his own lodgings at his own expense in order, he said, to ensure that residents of the Tacupeto district might attend Mass and experience "spiritual pastures." The list of his accomplishments and virtues continued. When a previous alcalde mayor had called for donations to the king, he, García, had been the first on the list, with a gift of fifty pesos.[31]

García's most important reply to the charges was embedded among the lists of his accomplishments and virtues, however. He took strong issue with Captain Domínguez's description of the events that led to his arrest. According to García, Captain Domínguez and his troops had rampaged through Sahuaripa, bursting into houses and threatening residents as they searched for fugitive Indians. All of this frenzy occurred before Domínguez had presented the governor's warrants to Captain García, who, as the ranking officer, should have been served with the papers prior to any punitive actions taking place. After terrorizing Sahuaripa and finding no Bacadéhuachans, Domínguez and his men had conducted a dawn raid at Quimbunazorra, rampaging into the town just as they had in Sahuaripa, breaking unannounced into homes and terrorizing the citizenry, hoping to find fugitives among the gangs of mine laborers. García had heard the commotion, and, as the top official responsible for the public health and safety of the mining town, he had considered it his duty to confront Domínguez and demand of him an explanation for so disturbing the peace and violating the security of the inhabitants. When so confronted, Captain Domínguez did not take García's challenge lightly. He whipped out the governor's signed warrants for the Indians' arrest. Examining them, García claimed that he had recognized them as official documents and immediately offered to assist Captain Domínguez in the search, at the same time reminding him that all the noise and brutality were not necessary and only served to stir up resentment and cause the Indians to flee and hide in terror.

Simón García maintained that after Domínguez had produced the warrants, he informed the captain that two men who were working for him, named Alejo and Simón, were indeed from Bacadéhuachi. They had not turned themselves in on the previous visit because they had hidden out of fear when they heard the uproar caused by Domínguez and his men. After Domínguez departed, García located the two supposed fugitives and turned them over to Padre Francisco Pícolo, the priest and visitador in Sahuaripa, so that they would not receive excessive punishment at the hands of their own priest, Father Guerrero. This was a clever move on García's part, because Father Pícolo had superior status to Father Guerrero in Bacadéhuachi (Pícolo was, in a sense, Guerrero's boss), and the latter could hardly lodge a protest against García's actions. (He was, after all, arranging for the return of fugitive Indians to Bacadéhuachi and thus complying with the governor's orders.) Asencio Domínguez, however, must have been enraged by García's adroit move, his animosity toward the captain further elevated. At any rate, Father Pícolo appears to have arranged for the captive named Alejo to be taken back to Bacadéhuachi, presumably while shackled and bound. Unnamed Indians killed Alejo during the transfer. If he was bound and shackled during the forced march, he would have had no chance to escape the marauders.

As if to underscore his compliance with the governor's orders, Simón García also added that prior to Captain Domínguez's arrival he had turned over to a military officer three additional Indians from the list of Bacadéhuachi, even though the three owed him a total of more than 150 pesos. On another occasion he had turned over another three Indians to a different officer. In a third incident he had discovered seven Indians from Bacadéhuachi in his work gang and had remanded them to an officer of the governor. Instead they had fled. The officer followed them and captured them forty kilometers away, tied them up, and threw them in jail awaiting transfer back to Bacadéhuachi. Clearly, Father Guerrero had a long list of absentee Indians, and Captain García, if he was telling the truth, had aided the padre's cause in repatriating them and could not be justly accused of disobeying Governor Fernández de Córdoba's orders.

Captain García had presented Alcalde Ezquerr with a list of nine witnesses who might corroborate his testimony. Indeed they did, and with results most damaging to Captain Domínguez. Some of the witnesses were by their own admission relatives or near relatives of García (one was a compadre—García was his son's godfather). Some were not able to testify on certain points, since they had not witnessed the relevant episodes. While it might be argued that some of the witnesses had been pressured into giving favorable testimony, all of them seem at some point to have presented descriptions of the captain's conduct in considerable detail, invariably in terms favorable to García. All the witnesses supported the captain's testimony in one form or another and not one presented a conflicting report. All agreed that Simón García had been an effective leader, protecting the peace and prosperity of Quimbunazorra and Sahuaripa and other outlying towns in the district of Tacupeto. Several noted that he had a special way with Indians and was fluent in some Indian languages, the only non-Indian in the region with that linguistic facility. All agreed that he went out of his way to encourage priests to stay and minister to the spiritual needs of the populace. Several testified to García's generosity in raising funds for the king. In general they painted a picture of a competent and admired leader, an exemplary Spanish settler.

A Conflict of All Against All

Even more important, though, nearly all witnesses testified that Asencio Domínguez and his troops had acted in a brazen and violent manner. They had stormed through Quimbunazorra and Sahuaripa, breaking into houses and causing a general uproar in their search for the Indians, without any pretense of justification, rogue soldiers behaving like roving brigands and thugs in their search for illegals. They especially mistreated Indians, including the Jova governor from Sahuaripa, whom they attacked and beat when he did not provide the fugitives they sought. It was only when Simón García confronted them, demanding that they provide some sort of evidence for their raids, that they calmed down. García was justifiably irate, but the witnesses verified that as soon as he saw the proper papers he offered to assist the soldiers as his office required. Even so, he scolded them for using unnecessary terrorist tactics.

The testimony of the witnesses also painted a picture of gratuitous and racist cruelty to Indians. The first witness had been present with Simón García at his mine early one morning and observed that "about four or five soldiers arrived and in their middle they were pulling three Indians tied together at the neck, one behind the other, and were flogging one of them." García, incensed, demanded to know what gave them the right to treat the Indians so. In response, the soldiers produced the governor's warrants. After seeing that document, by all testimony, García cooperated.

Another witness testified that

he had gone to hear mass in the pueblo of Sahuaripa and while he was there he saw two soldiers enter the town bringing behind them two bound Indians. There they put them in stocks [a pit?]. Then they turned over the responsibility for them to the [Indian] governor of the pueblo. And afterward Capt. Gerónimo de Zambrano arrived, one of the most respected vecinos of this jurisdiction, with his wife and children who also were on their way to hear mass. He [Zambrano] related . . . how a little before arriving in town he had run into the two soldiers who were bringing an Indian interpreter and who knew the Indians they were searching for, and he told the soldiers that some Indians who were accompanying Capt. Zambrano and caring for his children, were [among] the ones they had been searching for. Then the soldiers attacked the Indians, beating them cruelly, grabbing the children away from them and tying the Indians up, without paying any attention to the tears of the children or the fact that Capt. Zambrano was an old man. As a result of the soldiers' actions, one of the Indians escaped and went to warn the wives of those whom the soldiers had tied up. His voice carried through the whole town and its labor gangs. Since this witness was in the town it happened that one of the Indian prisoners managed to flee from the stocks and so one of the soldiers blamed the [Jova] governor, denounced and beat him. On the next day, the village priest [Francisco Pícolo], having heard of the mistreatment of the Indians, paid a visit to the soldiers and reprimanded them, asking what right they had to treat the Indians that way, that he himself was there by order of the governor [of Nueva Vizcaya] to deal with unruly Indians. The leader of the soldiers replied that they were still just following the orders they were carrying from your grace. The priest said to them, "Return to your presidio. I will deal with the Indians and I will deal with Father Guerrero." And saying this the priest turned his back on them and returned to his home.[32]

And so all the witnesses agreed that Domínguez's troops treated the Indians and residents cruelly and inflicted unnecessary destruction on their homes and harm on their persons all in the pretext of carrying out the governor's order. They treated the Indians as though they were vicious savages, and only the intervention of Simón García and the priest from Sahuaripa kept the brutality against the Indians from escalating even more. One of the witnesses seemed quite pleased that when Domínguez ordered García to produce his labor gangs at his mine he found not a single Indian from Bacadéhuachi, which must have further infuriated Domínguez.

Another resident testified that Simón García could not have been too disrespectful toward Captain Domínguez and his troops, for he had returned to the village after a short absence and found them drinking chocolate together at García's house, all seeming in a tranquil mood. All the witnesses agreed the Captain García was cooperative with Captain Domínguez in rounding up the runaway Indians, and that García even seemed to bend over backward to assist in the operation, remarking to one vecino that he would cooperate with Governor Córdoba's order even though it would put an end to his work gangs and thus kill his production of precious metals.

In general, then, the witnesses described Captain Simón García as a popular and conscientious leader, a more or less prosperous and generous mine owner and one considerate of human rights. He was at least conversant in some Indian languages, notably in the language of the Mountain Pimas of Yécora and Maicoba, but probably in Opatan languages and perhaps even in Jova, which was widely spoken in Sahuaripa. By all their descriptions, he got along well with the clergy, which must have come as unwelcome news to Padre Guerrero in Bacadéhuachi. The testimony was unanimous that he was a good man. The clergy, including Father Pícolo of Sahuaripa, as well as the witnesses providing depositions shared García's indignation at the mistreatment of the Indians. The witnesses seemed to believe that the Indians had a right to work in the mine if they so desired, but that they would never oppose an order from a higher authority sending them back to their pueblos.

An underlying current in the witnesses' testimony was that the Indians preferred working in García's labor gangs to working the fields of the mission of Bacadéhuachi under the supervision of Father Guerrero. That did not speak well of the padre. The long list of unauthorized absentees from his parish constitutes prima facie evidence of his failure as a priest. The picture of Simón García described by the documents contrasts strongly with that of Asencio Domínguez. The military man from Janos seems to have had a strong streak of cruelty and enjoyed carrying out orders in the most efficient and quickest way possible, using gratuitous brutality without any consideration of further repercussions. He and his soldiers acted as a rogue military force, trampling with impunity on the rights of citizens when it suited them, ever willing to brandish the orders from the governor to justify their arrogant and apparently sadistic practices. They seemed quite willing to beat up defenseless Indians, to tie them together at the neck, and to arrest a woman who was tending her dying husband. Juan Matheo Manje's description of his arrest by the captain further underscores the latter's lack of civility. Governor Córdoba must have known of Domínguez's tendency toward brash and reckless behavior. He appears to have condoned it.

The folder of documents ends with the testimony of the last witness. The cumulative depositions were certainly damning to the reputation of Captain Domínguez. Whether or not he submitted a rebuttal to Governor Fernández de Córdoba may never be known. Nor has any document surfaced indicating the governor's disposition of the case. We may never find out whether or not Simón García was exonerated, as the documents suggest he should have been. All we know is that the governor continued to call upon Captain Asencio Domínguez to enforce his orders, however poorly conceived.

As to the fifty lashes to be applied to the back of the Jova governor of Sahuaripa, the record is likewise silent.

What these documents also demonstrate is that in the European conquest of New Spain's Northwest, conflict was not limited to the battleground between Indians and European settlers. Priests argued and skirmished among themselves, mounted vigorous campaigns aimed at settlers and soldiers, and imposed their power onto Indians. Settlers fought among themselves, jousted with priests, and hoped to conquer and disperse Indians. Indians postured and squabbled among themselves, alternately cooperated with and resisted priests and, of course, retaliated in any way they could against intrusive settlers.

Both priests and settlers, however, had strong institutional support in their confrontations with each other. Each could appeal to the alcalde mayor in Sonora, the provincial governor in Parral, the viceroy in Mexico City, the Audiencia in Guadalajara or Havana, or, theoretically, the king himself. Indians had no recourse or support other than what the conquerors chose to afford them. That support usually turned out to be minimal. For all practical purposes, they were slaves of the priests, wholly dependent on the clerics' benevolence or lack thereof. Settlers were acutely aware of the priests' power over the Indians, which was often exercised to their detriment and to the detriment of the mines and thus the king's revenues. They would not forgive the Jesuits for the power they wielded.

As for Indian justice, only with advocates from one side or the other could they make their case in the courts. Failing to receive support from the Jesuits (or settlers), they could only resort to rebellion. In the Opatería, however, the lone notable resistance occurred in 1696 when a brief regional rebellion led by the Opatan Quihui was sufficiently noteworthy to draw the attention of priests. Quihui proclaimed that the Indians' lives and lands had been on a downward spiral since the arrival of the Spaniards. The only solution was to kill and evict all of them. A company from the newly created presidio at Fronteras quickly quelled that skirmish and executed its leaders. Quihui was killed in a lightning strike.[33]

A puzzling aspect of this conflict among priests, settlers, and Indians is the lack of reference to the repartimiento, which had been in effect for more than thirty years. Elsewhere in the region, mine owners invoked the regulations, forcing mission communities to provide a certain number of workers. In the several towns mentioned in the Simón García case, no mention of *tequíos* (labor gangs authorized by the repartimiento) occurs. For reasons not apparent in the documents, the mine owners did not take advantage of the obvious source of labor. Instead, they chose to employ fugitive Indians, thus guaranteeing further conflict with the clergy.

CHAPTER SIX

Father Januske and the Indians Take On the Vecinos and Their Livestock

1715

☥ THE ADVENT OF SETTLERS AND MINERS—SPANIARDS, PEOPLE OF MIXED ancestry, and Indians from other regions—into the northwest of New Spain presented Jesuits with a host of unending headaches. The priests struggled to keep non-Natives out of the missions, where they could easily undo the arduous task of evangelizing the Natives. Indians always seemed slow to internalize the Catholic doctrines and quick to adopt the vices of outsiders with relaxed moral standards or to revert to their pagan ways. Statutes forbade non-Natives from taking up residence in the missions without permission from the priests, but enforcement of the prohibition lay low on the scale of governmental officials' priorities.[1] Still, a priest could, if he wished, present a legal challenge to any vecino or outsider dwelling in the mission without authorization.

The problem of dealing with non-Native newcomers also extended to the livestock they imported. Jesuits viewed the introduction of livestock (burros, cattle, horses, goats, mules, pigs, and sheep), wheat, and orchard crops as an unmixed blessing to the region. The Jesuit scholar John Bannon summed up neatly the prevailing opinion: "The Indians of the missions [of the Opatería] regularly enjoyed a more secure existence than their pagan fellows.... [T]he padres taught them new and better methods of agriculture, and established stock ranches among them. Mission Indians rarely went hungry."[2] Bannon, however, provides no evidence for this view. Indeed, as we saw in chapter 1, the introduction of wheat could lead to a loss of Indian agricultural productivity, and, as we also saw in chapter 1 and will see in this chapter, the arrival of livestock jeopardized the food security for many hundreds, if not thousands, of Indians. What cattle wreaked for the Indians of the Opatería places Bannon's pronouncement in the realm of fantasy.

If some priests, such as Father Guerrero, were preoccupied with punishing uncooperative Indians, others felt the need to protect them from outside influences. Priests occasionally became outspoken in defending what they saw as interference with Indians' rights (such as they were) or undermining the missionaries' task of Christianizing them. This chapter presents a case where a priest invoked the intervention of civil authorities, not to punish wayward Indians, but to protect them from the onslaughts of vecinos' takeover of Indian lands. In this case, outsiders without a legitimate claim lived within the mission and claimed the right to run cows and beasts of burden on mission lands. The problem only grew worse. After years of abuses, a priest assumed a vocal and aggressive role in defending Indians against several powerful Spanish settlers.

The circumstances resemble those of the Indians of Tuape (see chapter 1), who struggled against Pedro de Perea and his heirs when they illegally took over the Indians' lands and allowed their herds to run wild over Indian fields and springs. In that case, however, the Jesuits remained largely in the background, though they were willing to testify on behalf of the Indians. In this case, a priest stepped forth and boldly challenged the right of settlers to live in mission communities and to run their cattle at will on Indian (mission) lands. He led the charge against the intruders.

In March 1715, Father Daniel Januske, Jesuit priest at the mission of Oposura (later Moctezuma) in eastern Sonora, journeyed to hear confessions at Cumpas, a visita about twenty-five kilometers north of the mission.[3] Padre Januske relates that during his visit to the pueblo, he stopped by the dwelling of some Indians whose presence had been notably lacking from his congregations of late (many priests were fastidious about taking roll). He admonished them for their repeated absences at Mass and proceeded to administer to one (or perhaps both) of them the customary five lashes for failure to attend Mass.[4] Just how vigorously the padre applied the whip is unclear, but Januske appears from his written correspondence a rigid, unsympathetic sort, not at all convinced of the innate goodness of his Opatan subjects.[5]

When Januske was finished flogging his backsliding charge, the chastened Indian(s) departed in haste, but the priest found himself confronted by the victim's irate son-in-law, a vecino (non-Indian, probably a Spaniard) named Juan Grijalva (also known as Juan de Grijalva). Januske claimed that Grijalva shouted disrespectfully at him, showering him with insults and threatening retaliation for the whipping his father-in-law had received. Juan's brother Bernardo Grijalva soon joined in the growing fray. According to Januske, Juan Grijalva, in addition to dealing shouts and insults, challenged the priest to apply the lash to him next, something akin to saying, "You are tough when it comes to whipping powerless Indians. How about taking on someone your own size?"

The priest had experienced repeated run-ins with Grijalva in the previous several years and was uneasily aware that Grijalva was a vecino, not an Indian, and thus not subject to priestly authority to punish. Priests were usually above participation in melees, and he was clearly frightened. Januske maintained that he tried to remain calm but shot back at Grijalva, calling him an impudent rascal, stepped past his tormenter, and hastened to his temporary quarters, presumably the *casa cural* (parsonage) attached to the chapel at Cumpas. Januske claimed that Juan Grijalva followed close behind him, shouting and threatening him, barging into his very home, whereupon the priest ordered him out and barred the door. Juan continued his verbal assault and carried on outside the locked door. According to the priest, he did so in the full presence of several Indians, who, Januske feared, would be highly impressed with Grijalva's boldness and, probably, the content of his accusations. It must be remembered that few, if any, of the Indians understood Spanish and would have had difficulty in understanding the nature of the discussion. That the argument was heated required no interpreter.

Juan's brother Bernardo had provoked a similar scene in Cumpas a month earlier. At that time (according to Januske) he had accused the priest of all manner of indecent behavior, of being a drunkard, monopolizing scarce farmlands for his own benefit, forcing the Indians to work without compensation, and not allowing them to work their own fields.[6] Bernardo topped off his tirade by threatening to expose Januske to his father superior (padre provincial) as well as to the Audiencia in Guadalajara and authorities in Mexico City, to which the priest retorted that he was welcome to do so, beginning right then. (The mere fact that Bernardo could cite the list of Januske's hierarchical superiors demonstrates that he was at least a somewhat educated vecino.) Grijalva shouted back that he had known many other priests, and all of them were fine except for Father Daniel. The priest in turn accused Bernardo of approaching him while carrying a club in his belt.

Bernardo's behavior was so threatening and offensive to Padre Januske that he forbade him henceforth to set foot in the pueblo of Cumpas—authority the priest possessed at the time.[7] Januske realized that he had no means of enforcing the expulsion from the mission town and should Bernardo choose to ignore it, the priest would have to rely on civil authorities to carry out his edict. Priests were by precept forbidden to bear arms.

Padre Januske entertained a low opinion of vecinos and other wandering non-Indians. Most of them worked at least part-time as miners, and as far as the clergy were concerned, miners constituted a broad collection of greedy, hardscrabble lowlifes and undesirables, most of mixed blood, some of them mestizos without the European genetic makeup that priests might hope for, of questionable background and breeding and of dubious moral comportment. In Father Januske's Bohemian eyes, ranchers and mine owners, even though they might be Spaniards, were little better.

Juan Grijalva apparently was a Spaniard who had impregnated an Indian woman from Cumpas and then pronounced her to be his wife. He took advantage of his wife's status as a member of the indigenous community to elbow his way into the mission and claim land rights therein.[8] His residential status there was thus questionable. At that time the clergy deplored and condemned such marital arrangements, for the bond joining the couple was merely casual, lacking formal sanctioning by the priest. (It is clear that Father Januske did not perform any such ceremony for the couple!) In short, the two were apparently a common-law couple, demonstrating the sort of blasé approach toward marriage that the clergy abhorred. Januske intimated that Juan used his pseudomarriage as a pretext for seizing control of land and moving his herds of cattle onto communally owned Indian lands.

When confronted with his trespass, Grijalva invariably asserted (much to Father Januske's distaste) that his activities were all carried out with the permission of his father-in-law, an Indian who was the legitimate owner of the land and an Indian member of the mission community. We can further assume that Juan encouraged his in-laws to defy the priests' supposed autocratic powers by flagrantly refusing to attend Mass and, quite probably, by slacking on the mandatory two or three days' work each week in mission fields and buildings. Perhaps Father Januske had eased off on the lashes, fearing that more forceful application of the whip might raise the dander of other unruly vecinos and recalcitrant Indians.

In light of the Grijalvas' challenges to his priestly authority and to save face among the impressionable Indians who observed the scenes, Father

Januske fired off a written complaint to Captain Francisco Pacheco y Zevallos, alcalde mayor of Sonora, who resided in the nearby mining town of San Juan Bautista and had done duty during the conspiracies of 1681. Januske called upon the alcalde to punish the Grijalvas by lodging criminal charges against them. He also requested that the alcalde have the Grijalvas physically removed from their so-called ranches, which, he claimed, illegally impinged on mission lands. Januske had ordered them out of the mission but had no means of enforcing his order.

An irascible sort, Januske hoped for drastic measures to curtail the degrading influence of such ranchers and miners. From his experience as missionary at Tubutama in the Pimería Alta, where he had been lucky to escape with his life during a Piman uprising, he harbored few illusions about the mischief renegade Indians could stir up. They required the constant supervision of priests to prevent them from rapid—and potentially lethal—backslides. A decade after his clash with the Grijalvas, he called for expulsion of all "mulattos, castas, vagabonds, and miners" from the missions.[9] That would have taken care of vermin like the Grijalvas (and, he must have mused, the powerful general José Subiate as well, as we shall see). He also proposed making it a crime to harbor fugitives from the missions and urged severe punishments for those Indians who left the pueblos without authorization. He recommended the creation of a father protector of the Indians whose job included the authority to regulate their travel and to punish violators of his suggested statutes. Indians were like children to him (and to most missionaries) and required the firm guiding and disciplining hand of the clergy.

The fact that Januske felt compelled to write to Alcalde Mayor Pacheco y Zevallos suggests that events were unfolding much to the displeasure of the priest. Such clerics hated to have their authority challenged, especially within the limits of their mission lands. Januske undoubtedly possessed the legal right to eject insubordinate vecinos, but the power of enforcement usually lay far away in a mining town or off in the provincial capital of Parral in distant Chihuahua. At the same time, Januske's letter must have sat uneasily with Pacheco y Zevallos, since relations between civilian or military authorities and priests of the Jesuit Order were often strained. Friction between the two power factions from time to time boiled over into outright hostility, each trying to undercut the authority of the other. Both sides must have recalled the attempt by Alcalde Mayor Gregorio López Dicastillo in 1674 to curtail the power of the Jesuits and investigate their use of Indian labor. Though the

Jesuits prevailed at that time, largely through political chicanery, the animosity that settlers felt toward them only increased (see chapter 1).

Father Januske had to have been painfully aware that under the best of circumstances petitioning the alcalde mayor was thus a risky business, for he had surely burned some bridges when in letters he wrote in 1713 he had denounced the alcaldes' "defamatory and malicious harangues."[10]

Most alcaldes considered the Jesuits to be sanctimonious opportunists obstructing the economic development of the region and using the Indians for their own selfish purposes. They would have preferred to see the mission priests kicked out of Sonora and the fertile and handsome valleys their missions occupied made available to nonclerical settlers and miners. Januske had lodged previous complaints with alcaldes, including Pacheco y Zevallos, documenting the series of abuses against Indians and against the missions, but the alcaldes either tut-tutted his complaint or issued vague and meaningless orders that only encouraged the Grijalvas and others to perpetuate their mistreatment of the Indians. In his 1713 correspondence, Januske had petitioned Pacheco y Zavallos to curtail the depredations of livestock in the milpas of the mission of Oposura, but at that time the alcalde mayor had ignored his impassioned letters and even returned one or several of them unopened.

As crass as the alcalde's actions toward the priest seemed, Januske had reason to believe that he had recently come to entertain a more charitable stance toward the priests. In 1707 Pacheco y Zavallos, acting in the capacity of chief magistrate of Sonora, had issued an order for the arrest of Juan Matheo Manje, former alcalde mayor of Sonora and traveling companion of Padre Eusebio Kino. Manje had originated a complaint against the Jesuits, arguing that they were interfering in civil matters rather than confining their attention to the spiritual betterment of their congregations. Pacheco y Zevallos, acting under the Parral governor's instructions, had ordered Manje arrested and hauled off to Parral. Captain Asencio Domínguez carried out the orders. In Parral Manje was tried and convicted of slander, which brought satisfaction to the Jesuits. Though he was later exonerated, he understood the message that he should avoid trifling with the Jesuits' reputation. Now, several years later, from a Jesuit's optimistic perspective, any alcalde mayor who possessed the determination to arrest Manje might just be a good bet after all to side with a priest in a dispute.

Later events would reveal Pacheco y Zevallos to be a simple moneygrubber who probably did not object to the padre's letter but who had no intention of taking any steps that might cut into his personal earnings. He owned one of two stores in San Juan Bautista and was a major cattle baron himself, his brand registered with the Crown.[11] He was part of a coterie of public officials that included General José Subiate,[12] one of the worst violators of Indian rights in Sonora, as we shall see below, and he would no more have attempted to punish the general than he would sue the king. He had arrested Juan Matheo Manje on orders from the governor of Nueva Vizcaya in Parral, not because he wished to do so but because he had been so ordered.

Father Januske knew all of this but harbored enough hope that he still petitioned the alcalde mayor. He had experienced great disappointment in Pacheco y Zevallos's predecessor, Domingo Picado Pacheco. He had shot off letters to Picado Pacheco by courier, noting the devastation the herds of cattle were inflicting. They were returned to him unopened. The priest even tried having a petition delivered to the alcalde by a sympathetic vecino, but to no avail. Other priests, especially Father Nícolas de Oro of Bacadéhuachi, tried to intervene on Januske's and the Indians' behalf with the alcalde and the chief military officer in Sinoquipe, but without success. Padre Oro described General Subiate, the principal offender and owner of the huge herds of cattle that were inflicting the bulk of the damage, as "powerful and violent," given to abusing Indians physically and verbally.[13] Father Oro had been present in Oposura in June 1713 when a group of Indians captured and corralled two hundred cows that had been savaging their milpas. The priest added that the cattle had become so comfortable in the Indians' fields that they seemed to have been born and grown up there. Alcalde Domingo Picado Pacheco turned up to view the scene firsthand, lamenting the events but refusing to take any steps to curb the grazing.[14]

Picado Pacheco was every bit as reluctant to rein in the invading cattle as every other alcalde mayor. Rather than respond to Father Januske's pleas to stop the depredation of the Indians' milpas, he issued a stern order in which he accused Januske of allowing Indians to work outside the missions, which was against the mission rules derived from the Laws of the Indies. When he ordered vecinos to return the Indians to the missions, one of the landowners, named Valenzuela, protested that the Indians had become indebted to him (a common practice to ensure perpetual service from indentured Indians), and before he would release them, he wanted the money they owed him. Picado Pacheco then ordered Father Januske to pay the rancher the debts of those Indians who rightfully belonged in Januske's mission, and those of any other Indians who were indebted to their masters. It was Januske's responsibility to ensure that "his Indians" (as he often referred to them) did not depart from the mission and wind up indentured servants. And thus did Picado Pacheco respond to Januske's intervention on behalf of the Indians. He was no admirer of the clergy.

Father Januske appears to have been despondent about the punitive retaliation taken by Picado Pacheco. (It is not clear that the alcalde could force collection of the debt.) However, the alcalde absented his post for reasons not stated in the documentary record.[15] He seems to have fled south under a cloud of scandal and with a possible indictment looming, taking his lieutenant with him. In doing so he vacated the position of alcalde mayor and perhaps vacated as well the fine imposed on Januske's mission.

When Francisco Pacheco y Zevallos took over from the departed Picado Pacheco, Father Januske had hoped for a better response, but, at least initially, it was even worse: he received the silent treatment, even when he had his letters delivered from the hands of a respected vecino who offered to be Januske's personal courier. The priest was somewhat heartened, however, when he received a note of apology from Pacheco y Zavallos, now advanced in years, explaining that he had been crippled in an accident and had been unable to respond to the official duties that devolved on him during Picado Pacheco's absence but wanted Father Januske to rest assured that he would do all he could to assist the priest once he recovered. In the meantime, however, he would not be able to post the requested injunctions against the cattle ranchers. Pacheco gave no indication as to when he might be able to take some steps to alleviate the suffering the Indians were experiencing due to the callous behavior of the general and the smallholders. His response to the priest's vehement pleas was to agree that the situation was desperate and do nothing.

Still, this response was not as discouraging as a flat-out rejection. At least Picado Pacheco was not around to stonewall his urgent requests for relief to the Indians. Padre Januske had one target specifically in mind, the worst of all violators of Indian rights, General Subiate. Januske had locked horns with Subiate repeatedly in recent years and had accused him of gross mistreatment of Indians.[16] Subiate, who owned several mines and vast ranchlands, had been running huge herds of cattle from the vicinity of Nacozari, in the mountain country north of Cumpas, as far west as Bacoachi on the Río Sonora. The drought of 1713 had been bad and even though Nacozari was home to some of the finest grazing land in all of Mexico's Northwest, situated in the pleasant oak woodlands of northeastern Sonora, Subiate's livestock had stripped the pastures bare. Subiate had looked beyond his vast estates and loosed his herds to wend their way south along the Río Moctezuma to Cumpas, where they invaded many milpas and frijolares and rapidly devoured and trampled them, in addition to nibbling to the bare ground virtually every pasture and mountainside in the region.

The depredations of the vast herds had already destroyed much of the Indians' harvest and jeopardized their water sources. Other vecinos were also founding ranches on Indian lands, so much so that Padre Januske deplored the "invasion" of outsiders around Cumpas. When vecinos founded new ranches on mission lands (always in violation of Spanish laws, he claimed), they brought more herds with them, portending even greater ecological and economic disasters for the already destitute and marginalized Indians. (The missionaries habitually referred to the mission Indians as "los pobres indios" [the poor Indians] or "los pobres naturales," [the poor Natives]). So much for the purported benefits of the introduction of livestock to northwestern New Spain.

The destruction wreaked by livestock was nothing new in the Opatería. The Indians of Tuape had noted their losses in the 1640s (see chapter 1). In a widespread rebellion in 1690, Pima Bajo Indians in the northern Sahuaripa Valley had laid waste to the town of Onapa, the mining town of Tacupeto, and several other towns and settlements in the province of Ostimuri, their wrath a direct outgrowth of the loss of their milpas and fields to uncontrolled grazing by cattle. In spite of more than half a century of wanton destruction of Indians' crops, no Spanish authority had been willing to rein in the settler's imperialistic destruction of the Indians' livelihood. Father Januske saw his chance and he was not one to be denied.

Beginning in 1713, and possibly earlier, Januske had sent petitions and angry letters of protest to everyone he could think of, accusing the general and other vecinos of gross violation of laws limiting the cattle herds and of not respecting the legal rights of the Indians. He pointed out that Spanish statutes prohibited stocking livestock on ranches in numbers greater than the land could support and forbade as well the locating of any ranch within one and one-half leagues (roughly seven kilometers) of any mission pueblo. Subiate and several other vecinos were in violation of these laws and in their crass disregard of Indian rights were endangering the lives of the Indians of the missions and the very existence of the missions themselves. Januske warned that the plight of the Indians was so stark that they faced the prospect of having to depopulate the pueblos of Oposura and Cumpas, leaving him with a vacant mission. Even worse, the Indians would disperse to wild areas, well beyond the influence of the priests, where they would resume the lives of barbarians and savages. He lamented the waste of all the Crown's efforts in attempting to civilize these poor souls.

General Subiate was not the only violator of Indian rights in 1713. The Grijalva brothers and most of the other vecinos joined him in abusing Indians.[17] Still, they were small fry by comparison. Subiate was powerful and arrogant and seemed to enjoy wielding his influence. In responding to Father Januske's accusations, he wrote to Pacheco y Zavallos with wounded pride of his sadness at learning of what he deemed the falsehoods the priest had written about him. He was also dismayed, he said, by reports of complaints against the priest being voiced in the presence of the recent alcaldes mayores and their lieutenants. Subiate sarcastically referred to the seventeen years of friendship he had enjoyed with Januske, and how he had always respected the priest's authority in spiritual matters, how perplexed he felt at receiving the vicious and slanderous attacks against him from a man of the cloth. When it came to the law, however, things were different. How he chose to run his herds was his private business. On such matters Subiate would listen only to civil authorities. And, he reminded Januske and everyone else, he had many friends in powerful places. He needn't have bothered with this scornful comment, however, for Januske had already written to the father visitador Francisco Xavier Mora, his superior, noting that the alcaldes mayores all seemed to fear the general.

General Subiate was not content with merely responding to Padre Januske's accusations. He went directly over Januske's head to the visitador, Father Mora. In a carefully crafted letter he sent his cordial greetings, reminding the visitador that he, the priest, was the godfather of Subiate's children, and that in his, Subiate's, warehouses he had stockpiled stacks and bags of merchandise and food that he had ordered especially for Mora and was about to deliver to him, noting especially that two loads of white flour were included. In the meantime, all of Subiate's considerable retinue of assistants stood ready to help the visitador in any way that he desired. "I am always prompt at providing for your reverence whatever you may request, whether on loan or of my own person, these are always at your service." And, almost as an afterthought, he added that he was saddened by the malicious and false charges against him that were circulating in the region via Father Januske's letters. *Of course* he had proper title to his lands—documents provided by none other than His Majesty's royal ministers! He chided the visitador for allowing Januske to say such infamous things, charges clearly based on utter ignorance and even some degree of malice. It was the visitador's responsibility to rein in the wayward priest.

Besides being a tireless letter writer with an indefatigable intent to make things right for "his" Indians, Januske was not one to be intimidated by authority or worry about Subiate's attempts to curry favor with Father Mora. Mora and other superiors had yet to admonish him, so he continued unrestrained and relentless, undoubtedly familiar with Pacheco y Zevallos's Jesuit-friendly actions in the Manje affair and sensing that he would soon be appointed permanent alcalde mayor to replace the departed (and for Januske, not lamented) Picado Pacheco. Even so, Januske was surely aware as well of Pacheco y Zevallos's dubious leanings and connections and his foot-dragging two years earlier when he had used illness as an excuse for not enforcing the laws against the vecinos' livestock transgressions. He must have gritted his teeth while he was composing—once again—his lengthy complaint to Pacheco y Zevallos, beginning with the assaults, verbal and physical, from the Grijalva brothers. He attempted to be tactful, acknowledging that the document was long—too long. He had put off writing, not wanting to bother the alcalde, but the cumulative insult was too much for any priest to bear. He conceded that the incidents might seem trivial to the alcalde but stressed that the actions of the vecinos were a challenge to decency, Church, and king (the same sort of righteous indignation that led to Manje's arrest). The Grijalvas had attacked his person, his honor, his religion, and the religion of all good Catholic Christians. Januske urged Pacheco y Zevallos to summon as a witness one of the priest's faithful, a fellow named Galindo, who had witnessed the Grijalvas' outbursts and would testify to the same.

By now Father Januske had warmed to the sport in his letter. He railed on in the complaint: the Grijalvas had insinuated themselves into the community. They had turned Juan's in-laws' house into a pit of iniquity, a promiscuous den of card playing and debauchery where loud arguments could be heard, daggers and machetes were unsheathed, and noisy carryings-on were the rule. Surely the alcalde could not permit this licentious behavior in the very shadow of the mission church! Furthermore, Juan had had the gall to construct a corral on his father-in-law's plot and had driven cattle and horses (and apparently goats, sheep, and perhaps pigs as well) willy-nilly onto the mission lands, against every right of the pueblo to be free of them. Bernardo Grijalva had constructed an additional livestock corral, and both of them were in violation of orders from the Indians, who by law were masters of the communal lands. Local Indian authorities had notified the Grijalvas that livestock was not permitted on the lands, but the Grijalvas had scoffed at the warning. Indeed, Juan acted as though he could do whatever he pleased and ignore the rights of the people of the mission and the orders of the padre. And even though Januske had forbidden Bernardo to set foot within the mission town, he brazenly continued to herd his cattle onto the mission lands.

At this point in Father Januske's impassioned plea, his tone and his points take on a decidedly different tack, as if he had been using the Grijalvas' insolence as an excuse to take on a larger issue. It appears that the letter was written over a period of days, and the priest, after reviewing what he had written, decided that the alcalde mayor would be more responsive to a recapitulation of the litany of abuses that had taken place against the Indians than to a diatribe based on personal grievances. Shifting his focus from indignation at the Grijalvas' insubordination and lack of respect for him, he now unleashed a string of accusations against the brothers that they were violating the rights of the Indians. He unloaded a fusillade of charges that resembled a list of human rights violations. And these were not aimed merely at the Grijalvas but at several other vecinos as well, and, we must conclude, at the prime target, General Subiate himself.

The year 1715 brought a drought even worse than that of 1713, when Januske had originally complained, and even intact milpas were producing little or very little corn.[18] Natives had no other crops to fall back on. Beans were planted along with corn but were even more damaged by drought. Squash plants needed the cornstalks to climb during growth—without corn, they were stunted. Settlers had no cowboys to control their flocks and herds, so they loosed the desperate animals to graze wherever their instincts directed them—usually around springs, where water was ample and forage available even during times of drought, and in the nearby milpas, where succulent corn plants suited them well. The results were devastating: savaged crops, dried up springs, fouled water, trampled and densely compacted earth around the springs, and no water for irrigating those lands that Indians relied upon in times of drought. Thus the Indians' basis for survival was jeopardized by the thoughtlessness and greed of the outsiders. Muleteers were bad enough; they, too, loosed their beasts when they arrived in Oposura or Cumpas, and the hungry animals would head directly for the corn and bean fields while the muleteers headed to Juan Grijalva's house of debauchery.[19] At least the muleteers would soon depart. Settlers were always present and the needs of their livestock always preempted those of the Indians.

The settlers demonstrated even less respect for the rights of the Indians than the muleteers. Their cattle would mow down a developing milpa in minutes, leaving the Indians with nothing to eat and no prospect for any help until the following year. In light of the dire circumstances facing the Indians of Cumpas, the least the alcalde could do would be to evict the Grijalvas and other vecinos from the fields they were destroying and turn control of the springs back over to the Indians, and at the same time order the Grijalvas out of Cumpas as undesirables. Father Januske hoped the alcalde would also order the other settlers off mission lands, as right and law required. Perhaps if the Grijalvas could be punished, the civil authorities would also be willing to go after General Subiate. Januske suggested also that the alcalde require the settlers to compensate the Indians for the damage their livestock had caused. This was a stretch, and Subiate himself had laughed over such a suggestion only two years earlier.

Januske's complaint was hardly novel, nor was the battle with ranchers his alone. Several priests had lamented the destruction of crops and springs brought on by livestock, as had Father Cárdenas in his testimony for the Tuapans in the 1640s. Other priests had been equally specific. For example, in 1709 Father Luis Pinelli of Aconchi described in great detail the impoverishment and slow starvation of Indians on the Río Sonora as cattle invaded their lands.

> [The vecinos' livestock] destroy the fields of the Indians—milpas, fruit trees, sugarcane, and even some chiles and orchards. The poor Indians farm with the sweat of their brow. This is their inheritance and patrimony, nothing more.... They have no lands to plant other than along the banks of the rivers and the nearby arroyos around their pueblos and usually no one other than man and wife to labor there. They have no way of making fences to withstand the invasion of burros, pigs, and horses that the vecinos keep in the very same rivers and arroyos of the very pueblos in which they live and plant.[20]

Father Pinelli complained that each year the Indians would lose all or part of their crops. If they dared approach the vecinos to complain, the Spaniards would denounce them as "liars and wild dogs."[21] If as a result of their complaints to officials they were to be awarded any compensation, it would be a skinny colt or some such paltry item, as if, Father Pinelli groused, the Indians could survive for a year on the meat of a colt. In general, he lamented, the vecinos "treat the Indians like dogs."

The priests' frequent complaints against the depredations of cattle were hardly exaggerated. The livestock invasion of the mission Indians' lands resulted, among other things, in the drying up of the mission's springs and the modest stream that fed the fields of Cumpas and Oposura to the south. The effects of these European imports on Indian subsistence were nothing new, as we have seen with the fields of Tuape seventy years earlier. And Father Januske had been complaining repeatedly over the previous five years that settlers were grossly mistreating the Indians. The insidious process of wetland degradation had been going on for some time, perhaps decades. In normal years sufficient water may have remained for emergency irrigation, but prolonged stamping and lounging by cattle compacts the soil around springs, rendering both percolation and seeping more tenuous. Cattle prefer to remain near water (their wild ancestors were streamside herbivores). They graze relentlessly around springs, removing any protective soil covering and vegetation, including roots that aerate the soil. In the absence of large herbivores, dead leaves, stems, and branches decompose slowly in the waterlogged atmosphere, making for a spongy, moist organic soil that retains water and releases it slowly. Livestock, however, remove the replenishing vegetation and trample and compact the soil, increasing its bulk density and squeezing out the water it absorbs. The unrelenting pressure of livestock combined with a series of drought years was bound to result in the gradual disappearance of the springs.

Indians' testimony during the subsequent investigation made it clear that the cattle had been destroying their milpas and springs for at least five years. The cattle were not only damaging the livelihood of the Indians and destroying their water sources but had become a public nuisance in Father Januske's mission as well. He complained that he was roused at all hours of the night by the sound of marauding cattle and barking dogs trying to drive them out. He had discovered to his dismay that the cows had eaten the very fruit trees that he had planted with his own hands. Sleepless nights were aggravating, the loss of European fruits irritating, but starvation of Indians was catastrophic.

Alcalde Pacheco y Zevallos must have been irritated by the letter, which he received on April 12, 1715, since he appears to have preferred spending his time padding his accounts and expanding his economic investments. However, recognizing the realities of the situation—the power of the Jesuits, the dubious legal standing of the settlers' land grab, and the questionable tactics of the Grijalva brothers—he responded quickly. He undoubtedly considered the effect that sustained negative publicity might have on his pension, and though hardly forceful, he initiated a painstakingly thorough investigation.

> I have just received written notice as to how Juan Grijalva and his brother Bernardo Grijalva have had various confrontations with the Reverend Padre Daniel Januske of the Sacred Company of Jesus, missionary of the partido of Oposura and Cumpas, insulting his person with insolent and injurious words, causing to be lost the respect that is due ministers and evangelical workers from all of us who are good Catholic Christians. At the same time [they have] affronted the natives of the said pueblo of Cumpas, inflicting on them repeated troubles and grievances and things scandalous against God our Lord. So that such offenses should be punished according to their severity, I declare that orders shall be drawn up and dispatched so that the abovementioned Bernardo and Juan Grijalva shall appear before me and my tribunal within twenty-four hours.[22]

Pacheco y Zevallos's orders were terse and formal. Father Januske had railed on for many months about General Subiate and his marauding livestock. This was different. Vecinos were threatening and insulting priests, behavior that was as scandalous as it was sacrilegious, and it was likely to incur the wrath of pious officials in Mexico City. If word got back to Parral, Guadalajara, or Mexico City that vecinos could manhandle priests with impunity in Sonora, inspectors would soon arrive and corrective actions would ensue, all reflecting on the abilities of the alcalde mayor. Pacheco y Zevallos wanted none of that. He shipped off a summons to the brothers, warning them that failure to appear before him forthwith would result in a stiff fine. At the same time, he appointed an investigator to get to the bottom of all this, and an interpreter to take testimony from the Natives of Cumpas and Oposura, few of whom spoke Spanish.

The interpreter, one Juan de Villa Vicensio, went right to work, calling before him all the Indians who worked serving the priest—the traditional governor, the fiscal, the mayordomo, the page, the cook, and the muleteer, all of whom the priest had selected as his personal assistants. The interpreter asked each about two things: What had transpired in the exchanges between the Grijalvas and Januske, and what were the damages wreaked by the settlers and their livestock? His transcriptions reduce the testimony to repetitious phrases and sentences. Perhaps his ability as an interpreter was limited.

Regarding the first matter, all witnesses agreed that they had overheard a heated argument between Bernardo and the priest and one between Juan and Januske. Indians were interviewed first. They had heard Bernardo accuse the priest of overworking the Indians. They could understand little more due to their lack of fluency in Spanish. Interviews with vecinos followed. Yes, they had heard raised voices and seen Bernardo Grijalva enter the priest's house, but they were too far away to pick up details of the heated discussion. All seemed to agree that the Grijalvas' voices were angry.

The investigator also interviewed the Grijalvas, both of whom had been taken prisoner pending further proceedings. Each agreed that they had raised their voices to the priest but meant nothing by it other than to discuss their beliefs. They certainly meant no offense to the padre and recognized the importance of demonstrating respect for the clergy. Bernardo acknowledged that he had been carrying a club in his belt but maintained that he always carried one for self-defense in those dangerous regions and had in no way used it to threaten the padre.

On the second matter there was even greater unanimity. The vecinos' livestock had been disastrous for the Indians' milpas and for their springs. Even if they guarded their fields day and night the Indians could not keep the cows from decimating their corn and beans. One Indian testified:

> For more than four years the cattle of Captain Subiate have been invading our fields as well as the cattle of Romero, Ballesteros, and Figueroa. They are doing great damage to our milpas, leaving us and our families with nothing to eat. Since the cattle are now accustomed to living in our milpas, as if they were their own, remaining day and night at our village spring, as Your Grace can see, with so many cattle and horses there trampling the earth around the spring, the water we used to irrigate our milpas is drying up. We have complained to Capt. Subiate many times and to the other owners as well, but they have done nothing about it. The damage reaches all the way to Oposura, but they do nothing and give us nothing to compensate for the damage their livestock inflicts. And so we come to your grace for help and with our padre, who helps us, for we have nowhere else to turn. We plead to Capt. Subiate's mayordomo [foreman] that he get the cattle out of our milpas, leaving us in peace so that it is not necessary for us to run around all night leading the cattle away as if we were cowboys.[23]

Other testimony was the same, a repetition of the damage and suffering wreaked by unrestrained livestock and an indictment of the vecinos who allowed their cattle and horses free access to the Indians' fields and springs. Families were starving, naked, and unable to obtain sustenance. Several of the Indians slyly added that it was not just Indians who suffered from the depredations of livestock. The mission fields were suffering, and the yields that the priests relied on for funds to maintain themselves and the buildings had plummeted. Miners and their families in San Juan Bautista and in Nacozari, a mining town to the north, were also going hungry, since they depended on grain raised in the Moctezuma Valley. As a result of the drought and the abandoned milpas, grain prices had risen sharply and often grain could not be found at any price. Starvation would affect Indian, priest, and vecino alike.

That message would not be lost on Alcalde Mayor Pacheco y Zevallos. Starving Indians might make labor recruiters nervous and cause the wringing of hands in some quarters. Priests would be taken care of by other members of their orders. But starving vecinos would jeopardize all mining and the profits of the owners and of the king of Spain, whose thoughts never strayed far from the royal fifth skimmed off the top of precious metals extracted from the ground. Even the clergy needed to take notice, since starving Indians would abandon their pueblos in search of food elsewhere, in spite of the priests' warnings of the illegality of such wandering. Forsaking their pueblos, the Indians would be abandoning as well the churches that, as they noted, they themselves had built and maintained, a prospect sure to dismay the padres.

The investigator appointed by Alcalde Mayor Pacheco y Zevallos had by now pushed into the background the investigation into the Grijalvas' behavior toward the priest. He now focused solely on the effects of the settlers' cattle on the Indians of Cumpas and Oposura. He summoned more than twenty witnesses, Indians followed by vecinos, including the accused Grijalva brothers and the ranchers named as the worst offenders. Most of the Indians' testimony was repeated word for word from the previous witness, suggesting that the interpreter simply summarized often wandering responses with a verbal formula. Still, the clear picture emerged that the ranchers' cattle had been destroying milpas for at least four years and they had also caused the springs to dry up. Furthermore, Father Januske had complained repeatedly about the problem and the alcaldes mayores had ignored the warnings and pleas.

The investigator himself visited the springs and found them to be "sickly." Not content with his own uninformed impression, he appointed four "respected" vecinos, men knowledgeable in such things, to be observers, view the principal spring, and pronounce on its condition. Oddly enough, three of the four men appointed to observe the condition of the spring were among the very ranchers accused of allowing their livestock to destroy it. Furthermore, the group included Juan Grijalva, who must have been released from custody in order to be a party to the inspection of the springs. As biased as their opinion might have been expected to be, they unanimously agreed that livestock, through incessant grazing and trampling, was destroying the spring on which both Cumpas and Oposura relied for irrigation water.

One probable reason why some violators of the Indians' fields and springs were employed as observers is that they were small-time ranchers (all appear to have been illiterate or only marginally literate). They and several other vecinos, family ranchers all, were vulnerable to the effects of overgrazing wreaked by the huge herds owned by the big-time operators. The major player in the grievances was none other than José Subiate, who by now had become an absentee rancher and was said to be living in Chihuahua, perhaps in search of a more tranquil domain free from the barbs of an antagonistic priest. Subiate, however, retained his ownership of a Sonoran mine from which he had amassed a fortune extracting precious metals from the ground with Indian labor. Subiate had grown wealthy enough to have a spread considered an estancia, large enough that he employed a mayordomo and several vaqueros, a luxury far beyond the means of the other ranchers, who had to manage their herds themselves. General Subiate had also become a very prominent government official. He had served as alcalde mayor of Ostimuri, the province to the south of Sonora, in 1698. Ironically, since he had moved his headquarters to Chihuahua, he had also become the benefactor of a Jesuit college there. Subiate routinely rubbed shoulders with the richest and most powerful men in the Northwest.[24] He may even have been a (perhaps formerly) good friend of Padre Januske's.[25] Taking on the general would be a stout task, indeed, as Pacheco y Zevallos would have known well.

The investigator warned all the ranchers that Alcalde Mayor Pacheco y Zevallos had ordered them henceforth to keep their cattle from damaging the Indians' milpas and harming the springs. All of them, including Subiate's mayordomo, solemnly promised to keep their livestock under control "as much as possible." Those words seemed to leave plenty of wiggle room for an occasional cow or two or five to slip in and nibble at a few milpas and spend a while luxuriating around the spring. Hardly had the ranchers agreed to

Pacheco's order when the traditional governor of Oposura appeared before him and complained that cattle were doing more damage than ever. The Indians were forced to stay awake all night fending off cattle from the milpas, with the result that during the daytime when they needed to be irrigating their fields, they were too exhausted to tend to their work. And the water issuing from the spring was still insufficient to meet their needs. The springs that fed the river (Río Moctezuma) were disappearing, and with them the river itself. Their livelihood was still being systematically destroyed.

Ten days later the Indians (now referring to themselves as Ópatas) submitted another petition, this one more desperate, pleading with the justice to take steps to stop the destruction.

> Thomás Sivacumi and all the pueblo of Cumpas appear before Your Grace with deepest respect and present a petition begging you to help us due to the great harm the vecinos' cattle are causing in our valley and milpas and so that you can appreciate the good reason with which we present another petition. Your Grace can ask Spaniards of San Juan [Bautista] and others of our neighbors and also people of Oposura because the Ópatas there are our relatives. And they also are having their milpas eaten by the vecinos' cattle. Your Grace should ask [the vecinos] if the cattle belonging to Capt. Subiate, Ballesteros, and Figueroa and others are damaging this pueblo and Oposura and if it is not now five years or at least four, maybe more, that we cannot manage our milpas because the livestock are always in our valley and in Oposura and below. Also Your Grace should ask if they know how many cows those vecinos own in their ranches. They should know, more or less, because we do not know how to count, and if their ranches are large enough for so much livestock. And perhaps they know that they do not have enough tanks to water their cattle, and how many vaqueros they have, since they have none. Perhaps they will know that Romero Joseph [Joseph Romero] has a very bad record here, causing damage to our spring, with all his cattle, sheep, and horses as well, there they drink, nowhere else, since there are no other places for them to get water on his ranch. And see if they know that our water source is drying up because of all the trampling by the livestock. Also Your Grace should ask if these vecinos are sad, as we are, and have no corn, just hunger here in the pueblos because the cows will not let

corn grow, for our kinsmen to find grain at a lower price they must go looking for work and food far away, to the lands where Apaches roam. Your Grace should also ask them if we have not pleaded many times for some solution and justice and they refused to help in any way, nor provide any sort of solution. Also they should be asked if we are not poor and suffer great damage in our pueblos as each year more and more cows are born here in the valley and if we have not done more than anyone should be expected as we are left in utter misery.... Here we are left weeping, lacking any food and clothing ... because we are Christians, but we cannot sleep at night because we must labor, even our women and children, herding all the cattle to drive [them out of the milpas]. You should also ask vecinos of San Juan [Bautista] if they know or have heard that *we* have encroached on the lands of those cattle ranchers or have inflicted even the slightest damage to them that they should treat us so shamelessly, as if we were their great enemies or evil pagans?[26]

The investigator took Thomás Sivacumi's rhetorical challenge seriously. Thereafter when he interviewed vecinos, he asked, how many cows did the big ranchers own, what effect were they producing, and did the ranchers possess lands sufficient for the needs of the livestock? According to a vecino named Pedro Fain de Mendizábal:

he knows because he [Mendizábal] had seen that the natives of the pueblos of Oposura and Cumpas receive great harm from the cattle and horses of General Subiate, Pedro de Ballesteros, and Salvador de Figueroa, who live around the referred to pueblos and in his opinion and according to what he has heard, among the three ranchers they have more than ten thousand head of cattle and their lands lack watering holes and forage, so it is not possible for them to maintain such a large herd of cattle and so they produce great damage [on others' lands]. He knows that General Subiate has insufficient vaqueros to care for and keep track of his stock and that Pedro de Ballesteros and Salvador de Figueroa have not a single servant who can assist in herding the cows [away from milpas and water sources] so that they will not inflict damage, and that for around five years the natives have been experiencing damage from the cattle ... and he knows that in that valley the movement of such a number of large livestock is responsible for drying up the water of the stream with which the natives irrigate and which maintains both pueblos.[27]

Fain's estimate of cattle numbers was conservative, according to other vecinos. They estimated the numbers at twelve thousand cows, plus other livestock (figures that Subiate had dismissed as nonsense only two years earlier). Almost equally sad was the dispersion of the Natives to other parts in search of subsistence, which left the maintenance of the church buildings, the proper cleaning and painting of the saints, and all the functions of the mission buildings and trappings without labor for their proper fulfillment. As a result, structures were falling into disrepair in Cumpas and Oposura and all over the province of Sonora as well. Another vecino added that the cattle were also consuming the wheat crop and, at the height of the drought, were denuding the priests' fruit trees. In their testimony the vecinos also attributed the decline and drying up of the stream, the Río Moctezuma, and not simply the spring, to the trampling, drinking, and eating of such vast herds of cattle. (Each cow required about ten gallons of water a day, so ten thousand cows would require one hundred thousand gallons of water, surely a goodly portion of the flow of that modest stream.)

The description of the Indians' struggle to achieve justice is important not only because it increases understanding of the interplay of forces in colonial Sonora but because it clearly presents a dissenting portrait of the advent of cattle culture to lands previously innocent of livestock. As I have already noted, historians of a Eurocentric viewpoint have tended to treat the introduction of cattle into northwest Mexico as a boon to the Natives, providing them with a new and easily accessible form of meat and adding an important source of protein to a previously impoverished diet. Herbert Bolton, in his classic biography of Father Eusebio Kino, commented approvingly on one of Kino's cattle drives:

> He presented a truly patriarchal picture, reminiscent of the fathers of Israel, driving their flocks and herds over the deserts of the Holy Land. As he proceeded on his way he distributed the stock at chosen sites for missions. Some of the cattle he left at the beautiful meadows among the giant cottonwoods of Bacoancos.... In fact this "long drive" of stock by the great Jesuit in January, 1697, was an epoch in the history of the advance of European civilization northward down the Santa Cruz Valley.[28]

We can be nearly certain that those "beautiful meadows" were soon reduced to dust bowls of stubble by the relentless bovine appetites and hooves.

Equally commendatory are the comments of the Jesuit Charles Polzer: "While Kino's critics fussed and fumed, he tirelessly drove herds of cattle and sheep into the San Pedro and Santa Cruz valleys in preparation for a whole new string of missions."[29]

These documents (and those of chapter 1) demonstrate that cattle produced quite the opposite effect. Immense loss of crops, destruction of watersheds, trampling of springs, and fouling of watercourses accompanied the arrival of cattle. The image of vast herds driven by a few cowboys amid clouds of dust must be supplemented by that of terrorized Indians desperately (and often futilely) chasing marauding cows from their milpas, struggling to protect their laboriously constructed irrigation ditches from the mouths and hooves of thousands of cows, and ultimately being reduced to starvation when drought and overpopulation of herds savaged their milpas and dried up their water supplies.

The many pages of testimony of Indian and vecino about the depredations of cattle, especially those of General Subiate, seemed to go nowhere, and for good reason. Alcalde Mayor Francisco Pacheco y Zevallos was a close associate of General Subiate and the two of them seemed intent on doing whatever was necessary to make—or keep—themselves rich.[30]

The documents that recorded the testimony arrived at Pacheco y Zevallos's office and disappeared, only to show up months later in Parral, Chihuahua, in the hands of the governor of Nueva Vizcaya, General Manuel San Juan y Santa Cruz. How the documents were transferred those hundreds of kilometers is unclear. However, the provincial priest, Luis Mancuso, must have been incensed at the inaction of the alcalde mayor and aware of his glaring conflict of interest and thus made an impassioned presentation to the governor, pleading with him to take immediate action to force Pacheco y Zevallos to remove the offending cattle from the valley of the Río Moctezuma.

An additional letter from the traditional governors of Cumpas and Oposura was entered into the record. They complained that the problems were getting worse, not better, and that even more vecinos were placing larger herds in the valley. Alcalde Mayor Pacheco y Zevallos had ordered the vecinos to remove their cattle, but none had responded. Either they had ignored the alcalde mayor's orders, or the orders had been a mere suggestion or polite request. In any case, the miscarriage of justice was appalling.

In response to the vocal and indignant pleas of the father provincial and the Indian governors, Governor San Juan y Santa Cruz issued a terse order to those ranchers who were violating Indian rights, ordering them

> to notify the said cattle and horse raisers that now and without the slightest delay they will remove their livestock from all areas which they do not own to sites for which they possess royal titles issued by His Majesty . . . that they will be fined one thousand pesos plus administrative costs, half of which will go to His Majesty, half to pay for proceedings. In addition, fines will be imposed for damages to milpas and springs both in the past and in the future to satisfy the claims of those injured by the livestock.[31]

He ordered Bernardo Grijalva out of Cumpas in accordance with royal regulations that forbade any Spaniard (or non-Indian) to live in Indian pueblos. The same order applied to Juan, even though he claimed to have been married to an Indian and therefore was entitled to live in the mission and use Indian lands. The governor's order was unequivocal: no matter how legitimate the marriage, no non-Indian would be permitted to reside in the mission. Everyone who was not an Indian (or there by permission of the priest) must leave. This was Governor San Juan y Santa Cruz's policy in 1715.

The governor had to appoint someone local, someone resident in distant Sonora, to enforce his orders. The alcalde mayor Pacheco y Zevallos had been either ineffective or unwilling to take action, apparently hopelessly enmeshed in a conflict of interest, or perhaps too ill to preside. Someone else had to be appointed to take on the ranchers. That task devolved on a man with the title "Captain for Life of the Presidio of Fronteras," one Gregorio Álvarez Tuñón de Quirós, widely known as the most corrupt official in the region, the object of a raft of citizen complaints concerning embezzlement and misappropriation of funds.[32] Álvarez Tuñón had been alcalde mayor prior to the term of Pacheco y Zevallos and would later become an activist in calling for the expulsion of the Jesuits.[33] Governor San Juan y Santa Cruz appears to have been aware of Álvarez Tuñón's reputation for disobeying orders, inventing his own illegal schemes, and enriching himself. However, given the small number of Spaniards capable of carrying out the orders and the motives inspiring Spaniards to remain in those remote northern lands, finding someone not riddled with conflicts of interest would have proved impossible (the governor himself owned many parcels of land and had large investments in mining).[34] To curtail the possibility of corrupt manipulation of his orders, the governor issued stern and explicit orders to Álvarez Tuñón, warning him that any deviation from the strict interpretation and implementation of his orders would have to be cleared with him, the governor, personally. He also lined up two alternative magistrates in case Álvarez Tuñón should refuse or not be available or should flounder in the performance of his duties.

In addition to ordering the ranchers to vacate the Indians' lands, the governor's edicts stated that each cattleman would be ordered to produce the legal documents establishing his right to have cattle on lands in the valley and, in the absence of such documents, would be instructed to remove his livestock forthwith and confine them to lands for which he had legal title. The order specified that the cattle were to be removed without them passing through any pueblo or planted area. Each rancher would be fined in silver or in clothing, according to the measure of the damage he had inflicted on the Indians.

The arrival of the orders from Governor San Juan y Santa Cruz probably left little room for Álvarez Tuñón to turn the events to his economic advantage.[35] As if to underscore the governor's instructions, written orders also arrived from Viceroy Duque de Linares in Mexico City reinforcing the governor's edicts evicting the settlers from the mission community, perhaps also dictating the imposition of fines. Whatever self-enriching manipulations Álvarez Tuñón might have briefly entertained were squelched by the double orders arriving from the mighty powers in distant Parral and Mexico City. This was serious business that reeked of royal disapproval at any hint of malfeasance in carrying out the edicts. One might respond slowly or hardly at all to an order from the governor, but when the governor's wishes were seconded by those of the viceroy, the time for action had arrived. From the tenor of his posturing in the documents, Álvarez Tuñón could be stern and efficient when he wished to be so.

The documents state that Álvarez Tuñón demanded that each rancher with livestock frequenting Indian lands produce a legitimate land title permitting him to own and run livestock, in other words, justifying his presence. None was able to. Each replied vaguely that someone else had the papers, or that they had been filed with a previous alcalde mayor, or that they resided somewhere in Parral, or that they had been filed with a previous governor of Nueva Vizcaya, or that they lay in the hands of don José Subiate (who may well have been the shadowy manipulator of the whole process).

Without proof of their right to be running their cattle on the Indians' lands, however, they could only protest lamely. Álvarez Tuñón, firm in applying the strong hand of justice (and protecting his own career), would not be put off by mumbled assurances that the necessary documents existed. He wanted to see them and until the offending livestock owners could produce the actual documents, he would not budge from the order to evict them and their livestock. Not a single rancher could furnish him with the authentic papers. Álvarez Tuñón pitilessly imposed fines of various amounts, ranging from twenty-five to fifty pesos. Juan Grijalva pleaded that he had married a Native woman from Oposura and was thus entitled to run his cattle on Indian lands. Álvarez Tuñón was unmoved and ordered him to remove his cattle and pay a fine and to pay the Indians of Cumpas twenty-five pesos, warning him that failure to comply with the edicts would result in a fine of a thousand pesos. He imposed a fifty-peso fine on another rancher, Pedro de Ballesteros, who reported that he would soon have the money. Another claimed that the title to his lands was in the hands of General Subiate, who was living in Chihuahua. In that case, the magistrate ordered him to remove his cattle to those lands to which he had putative title but still fined him fifty pesos. Apparently, Álvarez Tuñón was reluctant to trifle with anything having to do with the name Subiate.

The Romero brothers must have irritated the magistrate, for Álvarez Tuñón levied a fine of one hundred pesos on them, affording them but six hours to come up with the fifty pesos each or suffer additional penalty. He declared that their trespass was more egregious than that of most of the others, that they had crassly taken over land knowing well that it belonged to the Natives, and that the presence of their livestock had greatly harmed and continued to harm the Indians. He also warned the brothers that thenceforth if any of their livestock was found causing damage on Indian lands it would be confiscated immediately.

None of the ranchers paid the fine in silver or in clothing. This is understandable, since currency was hard to come by in those regions, as was cloth, another form of exchange. One of them pleaded poverty and offered instead to compensate the Indians with cattle in lieu of paying with money or clothing. The others followed suit.

The Romero brothers failed to produce the money or its equivalent for the fine. Instead, they submitted a letter of protest (indicating that at least one of them was literate and hence of some significant social standing). In their petition they claimed a previous alcalde mayor, Manuel de Hoguez, had granted them the land where they had built a house and where they ran their livestock. They argued that the spring(s) from which they had been evicted belonged to them as much as to the Indians. God had bestowed the provident springs on all and they had never belonged to anyone, much less the Natives. The brothers also hoped to recover the twenty head of cattle that the magistrate had confiscated as a fine in lieu of the one hundred pesos they had failed to pay. Furthermore, they demanded that the Indians pay *them* for the forage that the Indians' livestock had consumed on *their* lands.

Álvarez Tuñón swept the brothers' protest aside, bluntly denouncing it as a "falsification." As things happened, neither they nor any of the other ranchers fined could come up with cash. Instead, each paid the Indians' damages in cattle, at the rate of five pesos a head. Thus the Indians appear to have wound up with some fifty cows. What they would do with those cows and how they would prevent them from destroying their milpas and causing the springs to dry up is not clear. At least we can be sure that fifty cows presented far less of a problem than twelve thousand.

What also remains uncertain in the documents is the disposition of punishment and fines imposed on General José Subiate, the real violator of Indian rights. His foreman, Andrés de Argüelles, listened to the lecture (or harangue) from General Álvarez Tuñón but replied that he could not produce any land titles, since the general had moved to Chihuahua and carried all such documents with him. He, Argüelles, was simply the mayordomo, or foreman, and General Subiate had taken most of his cowboys and moved much of the herd with him. He assured Álvarez Tuñón that he would make every attempt to have his men keep the general's cattle out of the valley but was shorthanded. Thus he remained vague about complete removal of the offending cows and made no mention of paying any fine. In short, Argüelles and his boss seem to have been let off scot-free, which leaves the reader to suspect that fines would never be imposed on Subiate and that any removal of cattle would be at the general's convenience only. This seems especially unjust since, by all testimony, Subiate's herds were by far the largest and the most damaging. His wealth and influence rendered unlikely the imposition of any fine, even one as meaningless as one thousand pesos. How this would sit with Governor San Juan y Santa Cruz, a friend of Subiate's, or Viceroy Duque de Linares in Mexico City is not spelled out in the documents. The desperation of the Indians would likely not faze the powerful Spaniard, who by then was enjoying the good life in far-off Chihuahua. That Subiate seemed immune to punishment would come as no surprise to Padre Januske, who had been railing against the general about his abuses of Indian rights and Spanish law for years and must have understood the considerable power the general exercised.

Father Januske's battles with José Subiate stood the priest in good light with his fellow Jesuits. In 1722 the company named him visitador of Sonora, a post that considerably increased his influence even if only for slightly more than a year. No records have come to light that might indicate that Subiate was ever brought to justice.

In 1718 Manuel de San Juan y Santa Cruz, governor of Nueva Vizcaya, issued an order forbidding "Spaniards, Blacks, Mestizos, Mulattos, Coyotes, and other castes" from entering any Indian pueblos for the purposes of transacting business. He had grown weary of reports, quite probably letters from Jesuit priests or the occasional culturally sensitive military officer, that merchant vecinos would ply Indians with liquor until they were drunk and entice them into gambling away all their seed grains. Left without food for the remainder of the year, the Indians were then reduced to destitution and would be forced to abandon their missions and search for work or sustenance elsewhere. The governor's prohibitions were not new—they were reflected in Spanish colonial laws—but he vowed to be serious about enforcement: the fine for violation would be two hundred pesos, or, if the violator possessed insufficient material resources to pay the fine, two hundred lashes or hard labor in the mines, at the discretion of the governor.[36]

Enforcement of the new order must have been casual or nonexistent, or perhaps it lapsed when Governor San Juan y Santa Cruz left office, for in a few years' time Padre Januske would once again write of the appalling exploitation of Indians by vecinos and call for rigid enforcement of laws and increased restrictions on the mobility and freedoms of Indians.[37]

Father Januske's motives are certainly questionable. He saw his mission labor supply jeopardized, his personal trees savaged, and his evangelizing work undermined. He saw the sanctity of his mission violated and his authority questioned. At the same time, he witnessed firsthand the suffering of the Indians due to the settlers' violation of their rights and he understood, keenly, it appears, that if the trends continued, Indians would be forced to the margins of Sonora and the region would be ruled entirely by settlers while the mission system would languish. He was correct.

CHAPTER SEVEN

Sonora in 1771

Does the Conflict Deepen or Subside?

☩ IN 1715 NUEVA VIZCAYA GOVERNOR SAN JUAN Y SANTA CRUZ ATTEMPTED to resolve the conflict between the settlers who introduced cattle and the Indian farmers whose crops the cattle destroyed.[1] It is doubtful that his solution was more than temporary, for Spanish settlers poured into the Northwest and continued to claim new, expansive ranches with vast herds of cattle.[2] Perhaps priests after Father Januske were less outspoken and less inclined to battle with settlers, but Opatans appear to have remained more or less accepting of Spanish presence for nearly one hundred years thereafter. In spite of the abuse they suffered at the hands of Spaniards, they were drafted, perhaps willingly, into military campaigns and became irreplaceable foot soldiers in defending the Crown's expansion and in fighting off insurgencies from guerrilla fighters of various ethnicity, especially Apaches, Pimans, and Seris.[3] While these groups offered ongoing resistance to European advances, the Opatan communities for the most part seemed reluctant to join any anti-Spanish uprising.

Indians often fought with other Indians, even with groups of the same ethnicity. As we saw in chapter 2, in 1648 the Pimans of Ures willingly joined a military force against peoples of the northern Río Sonora who were either Opatan or Piman (Hímeris). In 1695 Seris joined Spaniards in hunting down rebellious Pimans.[4] Part of the unrest leading to that rebellion stemmed from abuse of Pimans by Opatans whom Spaniards had appointed as their overseers.[5] Pimans acted as auxiliaries for Spaniards in campaigns against Seris in the 1720s and again in 1750, carrying out most of the ground fighting against the Seris without measureable success.[6] Pimans also fought against Apaches, as did Opatans in response to Apache raids on their villages.[7] The decade of the 1760s saw Pimans (Pimas Bajos and Piatos, or Pimans from northwestern Sonora), Seris, and apparently Apaches come together in a more or less united front against settlers, while some "loyal" Piatos joined the fight against rebellious Piatos.[8]

The Indian resistance and raiding of the 1760s was sufficiently widespread and lethal that it rendered life tenuous for settlers. In response, the Crown took drastic steps to curb Indian violence against settlers. By 1771 Spaniards believed they had suppressed the rebellions and made life in Sonora safe for vecinos.

By then the Crown had also expelled the Jesuits from the Americas, along with their ideological vision of closed, utopian communities. In many Sonoran missions Franciscans had replaced them within a year or two. The Indians of Sonora found themselves ruled by different clerical masters with different goals.[9] While Opatans still seemed reluctant to resist the Spanish presence, this was not the case with other Native peoples of Sonora, who continued to attack vecinos, though on a more sporadic basis than in previous decades.

Spaniards' reaction to the ongoing violence varied with the interests of the policy maker. In Sonora, settlers and resident clergy perceived the peril from the conflicts as far greater than officials in Mexico City saw it. Assessment of the level of threat itself gave rise to further conflict. One such instance of vigorous dispute about the degree of danger is revealed in the following documents from 1771:

A report from the provinces

It is not possible in this brief letter of response to satisfy perfectly the desire of your grace. The 17th of May of the present year [1771] when we departed from the missions of Cucurpe and Opodepe,[10] the most interior and frontier towns of Sonora gentility [paganism], the inhabitants were experiencing the most unfortunate and unhappy times, ever harassed by rebellious Pimas, Seris, and ferocious Apaches. In the month of April when the Expeditionary Troop was arranging its withdrawal and return to Mexico City,[11] a party of Pimas attacked some Spaniards, vecinos, and Indians en route from the goldfields of Cieneguilla[12] to their homes in Opodepe and Nacámeri;[13] the enemy killed four of ours, who were then buried in the church of Opodepe, and two days earlier they buried two others whom the enemies killed near the town of Nacámeri. In the same month of April Pimas attacked and killed two vecinos of the mission and town of Cucurpe near the spring called Arituava[14] who were returning from the same places. On the 24th of May, one day before our arrival at the pueblo of Tónichi,[15] Pimas or Seris killed an Indian [probably an Opatan or Nébome][16] near Tónichi, and in nearby San Antonio de la Huerta[17] they carried off all the livestock, while in Tecoripa[18] they stole the mission oxen.

Even the Expeditionary Troop was not free of attack in those days of rebel invasions. In Carrizal de San Marcial[19] the rebels [presumably Sibúpapas and Seris] mounted a surprise attack on the troop. They stole the troop's herd of horses and even stole the saddled horse of the distinguished Comandante Don Domingo Elizondo.

The enemy Apaches never have been more arrogant and bloody than in those two months of April and May. On the road up and down the Río de Sonora five or six leagues from the town of Ures[20] and twenty or twenty-five leagues from the garrison at Pitic[21] where the troop was stationed, Apaches attacked a platoon of riflemen of the company of Don Antonio Pol, who was escorting the King's herd of horses. The enemies killed the sergeant and two riflemen, carried off two muleteers, and made off with sixty-six mules. At around the same time they [Apaches] assaulted the parish priest of Cuquiárachi who was traveling to administer confession. They killed three of the party and made off with four of his escort and the padre sustained two arrow wounds. A few days earlier they killed three Spaniards who had departed Bacanuchi for the town of Chinapa. In the presidios of Fronteras and Tubac toward the end of April and early May they stole two herds of horses and killed several soldiers and vecinos. Finally, sir, it would be a bothersome narrative to relate all the misfortunes that took place in the Province of Sonora in the referred to months of April and May that were the last of our stay in that Province.

Of the placers and discoveries of gold at Cieneguilla we must relate that the first who made possible this discovery were Spaniards, vecinos, and Indians from the missions and towns of our administration,

> and after three weeks or a month [the prospectors] *came saying they had recovered* [only] *some fifteen pesos, others thirty, some eighty, another one hundred, and some none, one or another lucky one who found one or two grains of sixty and eighty pesos and one of nine marks. When we departed people were returning to their towns because there is no water at Cieneguilla to work the land, not even any to drink. The placer mine of Cornelio, at some distance from Opodepe, has, to our knowledge yielded only a half or one real, that with a mining pan, and for others, nothing. Of Aguas Frías we have no information, nor have we heard during our years of residence, any report of discovery* [of gold] *in our absence. It is true that a lot of gold has been taken from Cieneguilla, but not in the abundance and ease that we have heard about here.* (Translation mine)[22]

Governor Fayni Sets the Record Straight

In late August or early September 1771 two Franciscan priests from the Sonoran missions of Cucurpe and Opodepe arrived in the city of Durango.[23] They met there with the governor of Nueva Vizcaya,[24] Joseph Fayni,[25] probably at his request. Fayni was so taken with what the friars had to say about social conditions in Sonora that he requested them to relate it in the presence of a scribe. First, however, he dictated an introduction to their testimony in which he entreated them to relate

> whether accounts are true of the state of prosperity in Sonora according to pamphlets being circulated in Mexico on the 17th of July 1771. [And] . . . the actual events that have taken place [in Sonora], even if they are not as grand as those painted by the pamphlets now being circulated [in Mexico City]. They would not have escaped your ears and eyes, you being padres on the ground during the time the events actually took place, and it would help me greatly if you would satisfy my desire and inform me about the events in full detail.[26]

The documents refer to the priests as Friars Antonio Canals and Antonio Reyes (who referred to himself as Antonio de los Reyes). They agreed most willingly to Governor Fayni's request. Their testimony appears on the previous page.

Fayni used the priests' dramatic testimony to underscore what he viewed as the disturbing reality of life in Sonora. Their account differed considerably from the glowing conditions described in printed documents then being circulated in Mexico City by high officials, to which Fayni refers. As governor of Nueva Vizcaya, Fayni knew that security in Chihuahua and Durango was tenuous. He often documented the results of Apache and perhaps Comanche raids.[27] He was determined to set the record straight in Mexico City and Havana about the state of affairs in the Northwest, and the report of the Sonorans was most helpful to his cause. Fayni appears to have forwarded the priests' testimony and other documents to Julián Arriaga, minister of the Indies, in Havana. Apart from José de Gálvez, who as visitador (inspector general) reported directly to King Charles III, Arriaga was the top-ranking representative of the king in the New World.

This was not the first time Fayni had gone straight to the top, for in a similar letter (missing) of July 11 to Arriaga he enclosed a testimonial from Pedro Antonio Queipo de Llano, chief magistrate of Chihuahua and also a person of some consequence in Sonora. Queipo de Llano in the missing letter described "the anguish that has been caused by the inexplicable increase of continued outbreaks from barbarians in that part of the land [Sonora] and dreadful damages to miserable mule drivers, vendors of goods and supplies, and other unhappy souls who hoping to find life instead find death."[28]

The document containing the friars' testimony bears a notary's seal, lending an air of authority to the letters and to Fayni himself. His preface further notes the many travails suffered by Sonorans in 1771 due primarily to the "apostate Seris, Piatos, and Sibúpapas[29] who for a long time have afflicted this very province."[30] A third document in the folio is an unsigned summary of the second, perhaps written by Fayni.

The scribe noted that he was preparing copies and reserving the original for Fayni, who apparently sent it to Julián Arriaga. He may also have sent copies to his superiors, including José de Gálvez, the symbol and fomenter of Bourbon reforms in the Americas. In a separate document, Fayni reported an Apache attack near Chihuahua in July 1771 in which several hundred horses were stolen and at least a dozen colonists killed. Clearly Fayni was on a mission to discredit promoters of speculative investment in the Northwest, whom he must have viewed as hucksters.[31] The priests' references to the paucity of gold are aimed at profiteers and speculators who spread tales of gold so abundant that it covered the ground.

In 1765 Gálvez had been named by King Charles III as *visitador general de Nueva España* (inspector general for New Spain). His principal task was simple: enhance revenues into the royal treasury. To accomplish this it was necessary to address directly the impediments to increasing the king's income. One of the chief blockages was the seemingly incessant loss of life and property resulting from Native uprisings and raiding in northwest New Spain—namely, Sonora and Nueva Vizcaya.[32] Once these rebellions were quieted, orderly development could occur, Gálvez believed, especially in the mining sector, which was the most lucrative source of revenue for the Crown.

The documents Fayni forwarded to Arriaga are a direct slap at Gálvez. In a letter written around the same time, Fayni described the losses to Apache attacks in Chihuahua. His language was blunt and his mission was successful. Arriaga ordered the viceroy Marques de Croix to find out what was really happening in Chihuahua, a reality "so opposed to what on these same dates Visitador General Don José de Gálvez is saying about the province of Nueva Vizcaya."[33] The visitador had widely proclaimed that the back of indigenous resistance in Sonora had been broken and orderly capitalist development could now take place, the only hindrance left being the Apache nuisance. The fact that Fayni chose to bypass his immediate superior suggests that the governor, who was widely respected among his contemporaries, smelled a rat and doubted that Gálvez, a known promoter, would take his message seriously. In describing the two dreadful months of 1771, the friars Canals and Reyes highlighted the political and social turmoil in Sonora that Gálvez appeared to be unaware of or chose to gloss over.

The two Franciscans had presided over their missions for less than three years. On Gálvez's orders, Jesuits were expelled from New Spain in 1767 and it was mid-1768 before Franciscan friars, whom the Crown called on to replace the Black Robes, arrived in Sonora. We know little about Friar Canals (or Canales) except that he made his way by land from Mazatlán to Sonora, and by midsummer of 1768 was rather uncomfortably installed as priest at Opodepe.[34] He despised the place and its Indians. He complained bitterly that he spent far too much time in the kitchen supervising cooking and cleaning and had "to see that they wash the meat and remove the worms and moths; otherwise all would arrive scrambled on the plate."[35] He found the Opodepe mission populated mainly by half-breeds who viewed the clergy with contempt and their pronouncements with scorn. Father Canals openly beseeched his betters for help "to get me out of this Purgatory, not to say hell."[35]

Friar Reyes, also known as Friar Antonio de los Reyes, was a prolific writer and forwarded extensive reports to Viceroy Antonio Bucareli in Mexico City in which he noted the deplorable conditions in the formerly prosperous missions and the continuing attacks by Natives, primarily Apaches. He was also appalled by the loss to indigenous communities of the best and most fertile lands as colonists appropriated them.[36] Later he would express outrage at the clumsy and inefficient administrative system the Franciscans had adopted.

José de Gálvez, who had been instrumental in orchestrating the Jesuits' expulsion, had ordered the missions to be stripped of land, limiting their assets to the actual mission buildings. Gálvez ordered the former communal lands of the missions put up for grabs for colonists. Deprived of the income of crops and livestock from mission fields and pastures, the missionaries became desperate for funding to support their continued work among their congregations. Gálvez also split the Sonoran missions into two ecclesiastical provinces. The Pimería Alta, roughly northwestern Sonora, which included the Opatan missions of Cucurpe and Opodepe, was henceforth to report to the Colegio de Santa Cruz de Querétaro, while the remainder of Sonora (including the Opatería minus Cucurpe and Opodepe) would lie under the jurisdiction of the province of Santiago de Jalisco in Guadalajara.[37] This split was based on the ability of the jurisdictions to provide priests to fill the vacancies left by the departed Jesuits, but it proved to be administratively clumsy. The friars Canals and de los Reyes may have thus joined Fayni in having an axe to grind with Gálvez, in their case due to his abolition of missions and his meddling in the missionaries' administration of their Indian affairs.

Friar Reyes a decade later was appointed the first bishop of Sonora, making the story more complicated indeed. More of that below.

Three Decades of Indigenous Conflicts Leading Up to 1771

In 1771 the province of Ostimuri bounded Sonoran territory on the south. Yaquis and Mayos, chronic troublemakers for the Spanish beginning in 1740, lived mostly in Ostimuri.[38] Though they were proving tough adversaries for continued Spanish dominance, at that time they were not *Sonoran* rebels (though from the Mexican viewpoint they would come to be so after independence in 1825, when Ostimuri was dissolved and incorporated into Sonoran territory). The Sonoran frontier in 1771 began in the south roughly at the north and west bank of the Río Yaqui and ended in the north somewhere vaguely near the Gila River. It was bounded on the east, as it is today, in the mid-Sierra Madre by the province of Nueva Vizcaya, which included what are now Chihuahua and Durango, and on the west by the Sea of Cortés.

The indigenous Sonorans involved in challenging Spanish and clerical rule—barbarians, enemies, and rebels as Spaniards labeled them, but undoubtedly champions of freedom, protectors of the land, and patriots in their own eyes—were Apaches, Piatos, Seris, Sibúpapas, and Upper Pimas. Mayos and Yaquis were celebrated fighters and resisters of Ostimuri but were not involved in the incidents recounted during the two months of hostilities in 1771. Conchos, Janos, Jocomes, and Sumas had been spirited fighters located primarily east of the Sierra Madre Occidental. Most of them had been militarily neutralized by the end of the seventeenth century. Opatans, though initially Sonora's largest indigenous group, had not offered organized resistance to the Spaniards since the ill-fated attempts to organize in 1681. Following that debacle, they had offered only sporadic flare-ups of protest in isolated regional rebellions. Opatans were now preoccupied with helping Spaniards ward off Apache attacks that were devastating Opatan towns—the price they seem to have paid for harboring Spaniards with their herds of livestock in their midst.

In the Sonora of 1771, indigenous resistance to Spaniards, though widespread and often violent, was sporadic and disorganized. As we have seen, Sonora escaped the organized violence of the Pueblo Rebellion of 1680, as Spaniards had smashed the supposed Opatan conspiracies in 1681, which, had they gone undetected, could have proved similarly devastating.[39] A revolt of Upper Pimas in 1695 destroyed some villages and saw a priest assassinated, but Spanish authorities rather quickly brought it under control.[40] Beginning in Ostimuri in 1740, three decades of hostilities tested the Spanish will to remain in the region. These uprisings and the violence of the 1770s were thus only the latest episodes in a long history of Native unrest. However, these attacks on the settlers and their associates destabilized Sonoran society, tested the mettle of many Jesuits, and subsequently delayed the religious agenda of the Franciscans who had replaced the recently expelled Jesuits. Worst of all from Gálvez's standpoint, the resistance threatened the king's revenues from gold and silver—his royal fifth of the take and the sales taxes generated by strong economies associated with a thriving mining industry.

Some of the hostile actions of 1771 may have been coordinated, but they were probably mostly guerrilla-type assaults. Some, especially those of the Apaches, can be considered raids whose purpose was to provision Apache bands. Comanches and other Natives well armed with European weapons, including horses, had forced Apaches west of their earlier hunting and dwelling lands. Apaches thus vented their needs on anyone in their path. Other attacks would be considered military or guerrilla resistance (from the indigenous standpoint) or terrorist attacks (from the colonists' standpoint).

Sonora in 1771 was already war-weary from several decades of uprisings and armed attacks. The revolt of 1740 against Spaniards, led primarily by Yaquis, but with broad participation by Mayos and Lower Pimas, had resulted in more than a thousand dead Spaniards and as many as five thousand dead Indians. The roots of the revolt were complex but involved predictable grievances, primarily Spanish appropriation of aboriginal lands, encroachment into fields, and mistreatment of Indians by clerics. The fighting had spilled over from Ostimuri into Sonora, where, in a battle at Tecoripa (in Pima Bajo [Lower Pima] country), the allied indigenous forces had suffered huge losses. Spain's strategic losses were also massive, however. Ostimuri, the mineral- and farm-rich region between the Mayo and Yaqui rivers, was virtually cleared of non-Natives, including priests, and its lucrative mines were shut down.[41] While Spanish authorities had more or less put down the rebellion, there was no decisive defeat, no wholesale surrender of the indigenous forces. Though the fighting ended, the Yaquis and Mayos did not view themselves as vanquished. They would live to fight another day—in the Yaqui uprising of 1825, after they had become annexed into Sonora; in violence that spilled over into the Opatería; and once again in Yaqui-Mayo rebellions in the 1880s.

The Upper Pima uprising of 1751, led by Luis Oacpicagigua, better known as Luis of Sáric, was a brief and ferocious outburst in which more than one hundred Spaniards were killed in the fighting and associated assassinations. It lasted little more than a month. Although the revolt appeared to attract little in the way of widespread support among other Upper Pimas, it made Spaniards jittery and caused them to reconsider their overall policies toward Native peoples. They established the presidio of Tubac to keep an eye on the Pimans as well as the Apaches. Even with the added military presence, Upper Pimas continued sporadic acts of resistance against Spaniards and colonists.[42]

The Mountain Pimas of Ostimuri (what is now eastern Sonora) rebelled in 1769, attacking most towns east of the Río Yaqui—Maicoba, Nuri, Ónavas, Tarachi, and Yécora. It is not clear whether or not their hostilities extended into Sonora, but they were a constant threat at Sonora's eastern borders.[43]

Even more threatening were raids and attacks by Seris and Sibúpapas who holed up in the Cerro Prieto (now the Sierra Libre), a forty-kilometer-long, convoluted, north-south trending volcanic range south of Hermosillo.

The Seris' anti-Spanish hostility had a specific origin: after repeated violent clashes with Spanish forces, many of them had agreed to a truce and had been relocated from their traditional homelands on the coast to the inland Río San Miguel, where they agreed to farm the lands offered to them in return for renouncing raiding. Once the Seris developed the agricultural potential of these farmlands, colonists, who in general mistreated the Seris, found their level, fertile fields much to their liking. In 1748 the colonists managed to have the Seris forcibly evicted and appropriated their lands for themselves. The Seris, never enthusiastic agriculturalists anyway, responded by resuming their raiding on a more intense scale. They found adequate water and edible plants and wildlife in the tortuously rugged Cerro Prieto, where they were joined by an even greater number of Lower Pimas called Sibúpapas. For nearly twenty years, from 1750 to 1769, these temporary allies disrupted commerce along the north-south route of Sonora, attacking from their impregnable redoubts in the Cerro Prieto. Their raids made settled life nearly impossible in the Pitic (Hermosillo) region and on the lower Río Sonora. No traffic in the lower part of the province of Sonora was safe from their attacks. The critically important land routes between the port of Guaymas and the settlements of Pitic and Pópulo on the Río San Miguel became nearly impassable.

The two groups were dislodged only through the largest military campaign ever carried out in Spanish colonial Sonora.[44] The campaign, which lasted three years, from 1767 to 1769, involved more than a thousand troops under the command of General Domingo Elizondo. The general was a favorite of the inspector general, who had ambitious designs for Sonora. After numerous failures and setbacks, Elizondo adopted search-and-destroy tactics and was able to demoralize and eventually dislodge the Seris and Sibúpapas. He undertook lesser campaigns to the north and appeared to have "pacified" aggressive Piatos and Pimans as well. By late 1770 Elizondo was convinced that his campaigns and strategy had ended the threat posed by Sonoran indigenous groups to Spanish domination. In early 1771 he returned with his expeditionary force to Mexico City.[45] The events in late spring of 1771 showed his optimism to be premature.

Apaches were even more of a threat than Seris, who never became nomadic horsemen, as did the Apaches.[46] During the mid-eighteenth century, Apaches demonstrated their capability of raiding nearly anywhere in Sonora and even as far south as Ostimuri, but their actions were most notable in the northern and eastern portions of Sonora. By 1742 they had forced the abandonment of the mission towns of Cuchuta and Teuricachi in the shadow of the presidio of Fronteras.[47] In 1751, in the face of seemingly unending attacks, the Sonoran capital at San Juan Bautista, a mining town near present-day Cumpas, was abandoned after having been a real for nearly a century.[48] Apache attacks during the 1760s forced the abandonment of most of the mines in the northern and eastern portions of the province.[49] At times Apaches joined Seris in attacking Spanish settlements and travelers.[50] Apaches raided Fronteras itself, stealing many horses and cows. As devastating as these attacks were, the worst depredations by Apaches were to come later.

The outbreak of hostilities in early 1771 seemed not to follow any pattern. In March, only a month before the attacks, Elizondo, flush with victory over the Sonoran rebellions, had announced that the province would now enjoy peace.[51] The spate of violence occurred during a time when heated discussions were taking place among Spanish authorities as to how best to treat the supposedly conquered Piatos, Pimans, Sibúpapas, and Seris. Some authorities argued for deportation of any who had been involved in uprisings, a measure the Mexican government adopted over a century later during the Porfiriato.[52] Others wanted them prohibited from owning any sort of arms or livestock. General Elizondo appears to have recommended a more conciliatory course, arguing against confiscating all arms and horses from the vanquished. Such deportations had been one of the bases of Seri uprisings in the first place. Prohibiting them from owning horses would simply encourage them to raid and steal in order to obtain them.

Elizondo's Triumph and Sonoran Unrest

In spite of objections from other Spaniards, Elizondo appears to have stood by his orders for the treatment of conquered indigenous people. He departed from Sonora with his dragoons, arriving at Mexico City on August 12. The viceroy Marques de Croix in Mexico City accepted his recommendations and added that the conquered peoples would be furnished with land and livestock, provided that they in turn accepted a sedentary life and accommodate missionaries.[53] To some extent the Piatos, Pimans, and Sibúpapas agreed to the terms. For the most part, the Seris did not. Once before, they had accepted Spanish promises only to see their land and livelihood stolen by colonists.

After Elizondo's pronouncements and words of magnanimity, the theft of his horse and saddle must have been especially galling. That the priests Canals and Reyes would mention it in their letter underscores the political nature of their testimony. Bringing the rather trivial occurrence to the attention of high officials of the Crown could only underscore the tenuous nature of the so-called peace that Elizondo (and his backers Croix and Gálvez) had claimed to achieve. If the rebels were bold enough to steal the horse and saddle of the commander of the Spanish forces, Sonora could hardly be considered a safe place where the Native peoples had been "pacified."

The events of April and May 1771 in Sonora and those of later months in Chihuahua noted by Fayni do not appear to have shaken the confidence of either Croix or Gálvez, or perhaps they were deaf to them. Gálvez had conceived of Elizondo's costly campaign as part of a general Europeanization of Sonora. Now that the Seris and Sibúpapas had been crushed, he believed the Crown could focus attention on defeating Apaches, and within months Sonora would become safe for investment, development, and full Europeanization. So great was his optimism that on reaching Mexico City in early 1771 he promoted a joint stock company, a partnership of the Crown and private investors who would purchase shares in developing the mineral wealth of Sonora. In July, Croix and Gálvez shored up their sales pitch by publishing the *Brief news of the military expedition to Sonora and Sinaloa, its happy success and the advantageous state in which as a consequence of the expedition both provinces find themselves*.[54] This hyperbolic document announced the Crown's intent to create an expanded line of presidios designed to protect the province from Apache attacks. In it they boasted that no Apache attacks had taken place in Nueva Vizcaya for three months, a claim Fayni disputed and which should have made any potential investor nervous.[55] Indeed, apart from the documents submitted by Fayni, no mention of the numerous hostilities is to be found, suggesting that except for Apache raids, Native resistance was viewed as nothing more than a few brief, isolated incidents, the mischief perpetrated by maverick remnants of indigenous forces. As for the Apaches, the Marques de Croix announced the creation of the post of military comandante inspector to take them on, a task assigned to Hugo O'Conor.[56] O'Conor responded enthusiastically and undertook six years of aggressive pursuit of Apaches, at great expense and with mixed results.

Fayni and the priests Canals and Reyes seemed intent on undermining the optimism of Gálvez and Croix. All three had much closer contact with the realities of life in the Northwest of New Spain than the lofty administrators, and Fayni seemed doggedly determined that the Crown should appreciate the grave risks confronting colonists hoping to settle there and financiers who might be lulled into making bad investments based on inflated optimism and exaggerated advertising. He seemed to be on a personal mission to deflate the wave of speculation fever that Gálvez was hoping to create. Five years later all hell would break loose in Sonora, with brutal attacks by Apaches and ongoing warfare from Seris, vindicating Fayni's pessimism, at least in the short term.

Gálvez's capitalization scheme failed completely. Several years later Viceroy Antonio Bucareli reported that not a single businessman had stepped forward to purchase stock. Whether word of Sonoran hostilities achieved general circulation thanks to Fayni and the priests' documents, or the plan just appeared unsound, no capital was raised and the company never got off the ground.[57] Bucareli was never convinced of the accuracy of Gálvez's view of Sonora. At Arriaga's urging, he took Fayni's warnings seriously and assigned major resources to O'Conor to bolster his anti-Apache campaigns.

The most intriguing aspect of this saga is the role played by Antonio de los Reyes. Reyes composed numerous and lengthy reports on Sonora after his departure from Durango in 1771. In a 1774 *informe* he reported that quite contrary to his earlier (1771) protestation of scant gold to be found in the province:

> It is incredible, Your Excellency, for all who have not experienced it, the immense quantities of gold and silver that have been and continue to be produced in this province of Sonora. One can say without exaggeration that all of its terrain is one continuous mine of silver and fount of gold, commonly called placers.[58]

The indignant cleric of 1771, who had minimized the presence of gold in Sonora, was ordained bishop of Sonora in 1782 with the blessing of José de Gálvez, the very megalomaniac inspector general whose plans for Sonora Reyes the priest had helped undo. But why would Reyes testify before a scribe that promoters had exaggerated the amount of gold in Sonora and then only three years later speak with unmatched exaggeration of the abundance of precious metals as though he were a promoter himself? Reyes proved to be a most ambitious, headstrong, imperious, and vain bishop, and perhaps consistency was not a quality he valued highly.[59]

Ultimately, though, Elizondo, Croix, and Gálvez were proved mostly right. The expedition of 1767–1770 *had* broken the back of Sonoran resistance.

The Apaches were far from vanquished, Seris would reignite their conflict, and the wars of the Yaquis and Mayos would maintain Sonora in ferment for more than another century. In spite of the ferocity of these conflicts, though, the European population would continue to expand. Settlers did manage to survive in great numbers and avoid the dangers of indigenous resistance. The mine at Cieneguilla revived in 1803 in spite of the lack of water, and other gold and silver mines would open or reopen as well. Many Spaniards would become wealthy. The nonindigenous population of Sonora would continue to expand while that of Natives would continue to shrink. By 1800 two-thirds of the inhabitants of Sonora were nonindigenous, a proportion double that of forty years earlier.[60] By that same year missions had all but disappeared and Indians had been mostly relegated to marginal lands near their former fertile milpas.[61]

In the year 2000 aboriginal Sonorans (including Ostimurans) constituted less than 5 percent of Sonora's population.

Today only Seris remain a cohesive indigenous group in the area that was Sonora prior to 1825. They are involved in frequent clashes, some of them armed, with non-Seris, usually over fishing rights in Seri territory and matters relating to Seri sovereignty. In 2005 the federal government dispatched troops to quell the Seris' ongoing armed attempts at asserting their autonomy.

By the year 2000 Triques and Mixtecos from the state of Oaxaca had migrated to Sonora in such numbers that they exceeded both Seris and Guarijíos in population.

Despite weaknesses in the Crown's early plans for making Sonora into a Spanish province, the results after two centuries of occupation vindicated the overall strategy. Native resistance during that period was limited to a few scattered rebellions. Raids from Apaches remained a serious liability, but Apaches for the most part entered Sonora from the north and east and then withdrew. Overall loss of life from armed conflicts remained rather small, especially compared with Ostimuri to the south and the Chihuahuan and Durangan portions of Nueva Vizcaya to the east of the Sierra Madre. Except for Seris, resident Indians in general became Catholics, at least in name, and settlers successfully assumed mastery over the best agricultural lands while Indians were to be found only at the edges of towns and fields and in the areas Spaniards least coveted. (In Sonoran towns the most prestigious and valuable lots are those nearest the church and the plaza.) By the time of Mexican independence, the bulk of Sonoran lands rested in private hands and only a minimal area of useful land remained firmly in indigenous hands. Sonora, more than any other Mexican state, became famous for two introduced European commodities: wheat and beef. Today most Sonorans disdain corn tortillas, preferring those made from white flour and grease, and extol the culinary subtlety of carne asada.

The descriptions of Sonora in 1771 appear to underscore the disappearance of priests as major actors in the dramatic conflicts there. By 1771, Father Januske's impassioned pleas for the removal of settlers' cattle seem quaint, as do the fuming indignations of Father Guerrero concerning his truant Indians and those of Fathers Canal and Molarja about the indignities they had suffered at the hands of apostate Indians north of Arizpe. By 1771 the missions were in the process of being dismantled: in the priestly vacuum between the expulsion of the Jesuits in 1767 and the arrival of the Franciscan replacements the following year, most of the mission communities fell into utter disarray and their buildings showed serious signs of deterioration or complete destruction.[62] The role of priests as a third force in the conflicts of colonial Sonora had mostly come to an end. Jesuits had been harshly punished for their role as a quasi-independent force in the Northwest. The influence of Franciscans over indigenous communities slowly waned as well. In 1827 the Mexican government expelled all Spanish-born priests. Most of these were older clerics who had demonstrated some willingness to defend the Indians of their missions or parishes. With their disappearance, the last vestiges of missions disappeared. Henceforth the notable clashes would take place directly between Indians on the one hand and the settlers, their descendents, and the governments that supported them on the other.

Appendix

The Tuape Indians' Legal Struggle to Regain Their Lands
AHP 318, 1658B, leg. 41

The Tuape Indians' Case

As the file of documents opens, the natives of Tuape, destitute and without an advocate, have appeared before the governor of Nueva Vizcaya, don Enrique Dávila y Pacheco, in Parral, Chihuahua, requesting that he appoint them an attorney to defend their interest. The year is 1658 and Parral is a lengthy journey of many days from tiny Tuape, as the Natives are careful to point out. After the introductory documents, the time shifts backward. I have added to each different narrative the date or approximate date of the deposition or statement to offer the reader a chronological perspective.

July (?), 1658
[In Parral, Chihuahua] Damian Sidaicavit, native governor of the town of Mátape in the province of Sonora and Francisco Huduri and Lorenzo Tenorat residents of said pueblo and natives of the pueblo of Tiape [Tuape]. For ourselves and for the Indian leaders and members of the pueblo, we appear before Your Grace in the best form that our right requires and we state that we have come on foot from our said and faraway towns more than 200 leagues away. We come as miserable, poor men and without any support other than that of Your Grace, requesting justice against the heirs of

General Pedro de Perea, now deceased, so that we can tranquilly enjoy our lands, ancient lands by the river that was near our town of Tuape, lands that he has invaded with his livestock for more than twenty years,[1] and that we be free to use our lands and to have them once again for the reasons and testimony that we present to Your Grace, judging it appropriate for our rights that Your Grace would serve us if Your Grace were to appoint for us a defender, which at this point the natives of this kingdom do not have, so that he can legitimately defend that which we request. We pray that with Your Grace's great Christianity you will do that which we hope. Regarding this we ask and plead that you order that we be provided with a defender and once that is done order him to defend us in keeping with our right and the justice that we request and in everything else.

Damian Sidaicavit, governor.

Parral, July 23, 1658
Order: As presented [the document below] Alférez Diego de Alarreta will be appointed defender of the natives. If he accepts the appointment, the oath will be administered by don Enrique Dávila y Pacheco, knight of the order of Santiago and governor and captain of war of this kingdom of Nueva Vizcaya. Approved and signed. [Signature]

In Parral in the said day, month, and year before the said señor governor and war captain, Diego de Galarreta [Alarreta] appeared and having been notified through the above document, stated that he accepted and will accept the said task of defender and in his acceptance swore to God our Lord and the sign of the cross in the proper form that he would do everything properly and faithfully following his loyal understanding, with no fraud. He stated that he would discern and did discern the assigned task given the power and authority as stated by law, that in every way possible he will represent the case of the said Indians. And he signed as defender. [Signature]

Presentation of Tuape Indians' Case, Perhaps by Pedro Talemuche, Indian Governor of Mátape: A Summary by the Scribe

April 3, 1657
In the real and mines of San Pedro de los Reyes, province of Sonora, third of April, 1657, in the presence of Captain don Francisco Coto, alcalde mayor and war captain of said province for His Majesty. The following made a

presentation: Pedro Talemuche, governor of the pueblo of Mátape and its settlements of Indians, Ygnacio Cabairu and Lorencho Batorochi, both topiles[2] of the settlements of Tuape and Uparo representing the remaining natives and descendents of those pueblos of Tuape and Uparo for whom we[3] certify that they will be and will approve of what we are doing.

We appear before Your Grace and in the best and proper legal form we will make a claim against don Pedro de Perea and Captain Juan de Munguía Villela, husband and his wife, doña Andrea de Perea, as children and heirs of Captain Pedro and doña María de Ibarra, their rightful parents and any other children and heirs. In relating the facts, it is the case that the places called Tuape[4] and Uparo were villages of natives from time immemorial. These villages were populated and settled by us, and our ancestors [but], we now live in the village of Mátape, where we were forced to relocate, having been removed from lands that were and are ours in the aforementioned villages of Tuape and Uparo. It was thus: we never failed to take advantage of the natural possession of our lands in the summer and the irrigation season, holding them as useful and ideal for summer and irrigated planting, lands quiet and peaceful in our possession. And in this state of tranquil and peaceful property of ours, the said Captain Pedro de Perea, who was from this province of Sonora and chief justice there, made and attempted with the [approval of] His Majesty his intention to found a villa[5] in that place. In the meantime he planned to establish a site [in Tuape] and a site as well in the Valle de Sonora that would be his permanent home. He requested such a place and terrain in Tuape, a site for a house, lent to him by the Indians who at the time had planted milpas and bean fields. He [demanded] that [land] under the terms of the said pact [with the Indians] and he built his house right on top of a bean field that had already been planted and was greening, all because he was in a big hurry and could not wait until harvest time arrived. He compensated the Indian from whom he had taken the land by offering him two sacks of beans and promised he would provide him with beans for however long he would live there, and he agreed to pay him each year for the rest of the time he would be at that site, promising that he would give them a certain portion of the yield while he was moving to the site that he would found in the Valley of Sonora. As part of the pact he also gave the owner of the plot some coarse blue cloth, a knife, and an adze. Involved in all this was the sublieutenant Juan de Oliva, who accompanied don Pedro de Perea and with whom Perea founded the said house where he lived with his family, the place now called Nombre de Diós, to which place he introduced many cows, donkeys, and horses. He kept them [the livestock] so that the said Indians, as natural owners of the sites and their town and ancient lands, would quit planting their lands, lands that for their convenience and abundant harvests the Indians could call their own when the lands were in their own hands. During the delay that Captain Perea experienced while moving himself and his family into Sonora, the cattle and horses continued multiplying and invading the Indians' lands. [The same happened with] the servants' families and other persons, from whose presence the Indians received many grave damages and annoyances in their fields that had already been sowed [as well as] in their persons. [For these reasons] they requested the said Captain Perea to allow the said fields and lands to return to their free and unencumbered state, and after his death they asked doña María de Ibarra to do the same [that is, return the land to the Indians]. Pedro de Perea did not agree to that request.

So the Indians were forced to appeal to doña María's sense of justice,[6] since she was in possession of the said house and site of Nombre de Diós. She acknowledged the rights and civil and natural possessions held by the said Tuapes and Uparos to the said lands and terrains of the said pueblos. As legal guardian and teacher and healer of her children [she had power to decide for her children], she, in her part of the legal action, made an agreement with the Indians on the sixteenth of March of 1652 and with Padre Daniel Ángelo [Marras],[7] their missionary and minister, that in order to avoid damages, injuries and annoyances, within the two years from the said date [March 16, 1652], she would vacate the land and leave empty her house of all family as well as all the livestock, all the said lands and limits of Tuape and Uparo. She agreed not to settle or found settlements within two leagues of these said boundaries. Although the said concordia [agreement] declares that the said Indians should build a large house and two smaller ones on the location [probably on the Río Sonora] where said doña María de Ibarra or her designate should indicate and could allow cattle to wander there [the Indians did not agree and] were not obliged to fulfill that part of the concordia due to the damage and injury it would cause them. Still, in order best to comply with the provisions of the agreement, since that time, we[8] have fulfilled and feel obligated to fulfill every part that pertained to us. The two years mentioned in the agreement have long since passed and doña María de Ybarra [Ibarra] died long ago. Upon don Pedro's death, she came to be in charge of said estate of Nombre de Diós. She and her son, during her lifetime, should have fulfilled her part of the said concordia, abandoning the place and removing the said cattle. Maliciously, they [the heirs] have refused to do so. The said cattle are still inflicting grave damages and injuries to the crops that the said Indians have within the said boundaries for which cause they have ceased to plant, much to their grief and the calamities they have suffered as the [heirs] mistreated them as did their slaves and servants in both word and deed. The mistreatment of the Indians has been so great that don Pedro's heirs and servants have lost the respect of our minister, because he defends us and helps us. This great scandal and bad example are just some of the things that we can allege in our favor, things we [consider] having alleged and expressed [in this document].

To Your Grace we ask and beseech that having accepted our version as the truth concerning the part that is so evident, our ownership and the natural right we have to the said lands and boundaries where the said estate of Nombre de Diós is located, that you put pressure on don Pedro de Perea and his heirs to fulfill the terms of the concordia and execute its terms. If they do not fulfill the term of the agreement, we ask you to force them to pay for the time that they have occupied the land, because on our part we are ready to meet the terms of the concordia, by declaring that the said lands and boundaries are ours, that is, those of the said pueblos of Tuape and Uparo. If it is necessary, we request the compensation for any time that may have passed [beyond the terms of the concordia].

To prove our demand, we present the narrative of Padre Lorenzo de Cárdenas, the late minister and missionary who was from the said pueblo of Mátape and the posts of Tuape and Uparo, in which he declares the right that we have to the said lands and the fact of the said concordia. We request the verification of the concordia through the testimony of the witnesses involved in making it. Of course we swear by God in the strongest possible terms that our demand is based on the truth and without any ill will. We plead for justice in any way that will prove our cause and we implore the office of Your Grace. Not knowing how to sign [the document] we ask that our priest, Daniel Ángelo [Marras], minister and missionary of the said town of Mátape and its partido, to sign it. [signed] Daniel Angelo.

Certification by the Scribe Ignacio de Barraiersa

I have seen by the said señor captain and chief justice and declare that the aforementioned papers were presented [as proof] and that he ordered that the opposing parties each receive a copy and that they be summoned to court to argue the [existence and validity] of the concordia and once it is presented, witnesses will certify whether it was genuine. And thus I order and sign=don Francisco Coto=In my presence=Ignacio de Barraiersa=above-named scribe [the symbol "=" appears in the manuscript to separate names].

In the mining town of San Pedro de los Reies [Reyes] on the sixteenth of April 1657. I, the present scribe certified and read the petition addressed to don Pedro de Perea [Jr.] and Captain Juan de Munguía y Villela and they say that they heard the reading and that they asked to receive the documents so that they might properly respond and I certify that they signed—don Pedro de Perea [Jr.]=Juan de Munguía y Villela=Ignacio de Barraiersa=above-named scribe

The Narrative of Padre Lorenzo de Cárdenas, Priest at Mátape[9]

July 10, 1647

Named by the father visitador in fulfillment of the obedience with which his reverence has placed me as the elder missionary in the Aibino mission[10] and the very first minister of that district and the pueblo of Tuape, I declare with emphasis that the lands and the sites that belong to the Indians who were residents of the pueblo of Tuape [still, by right, belong to them]. Although it is true that the said Tuape Indians were relocated to lands of the pueblo of Mátape, it was due to the great injustices they suffered in their ancient homeland of Tuape, including a crippling shortage and drying up of water and disappearance of firewood and for other reasons of advisability and prudence that at the time seemed warranted. The father superior and captain at that time were in charge of the entire province and arranged that the pueblo of Mátape would provide and share with them [the Tuapeños] parcels of irrigable lands where the said Tuapeños in fact managed to plant. Thus they became accustomed to [living and working on] the land they shared with the pueblo of Mátape and were somewhat exempted from part of the work requirement[11] owing to the fact they still had to transport their corn four leagues, the distance from Mátape to their ancient homelands in Tuape.[12] When they could have more comfortably carried their corn [perhaps from Banachari to Mátape instead] the long distance from there to their ancient home in Tuape, even that prudent relocation that finds them well accommodated in Mátape [did not deter them from maintaining their ties to Tuape]. So they cannot be said to have lost the rights to their ancestral lands and possessions that they possessed from the beginning in their old home of Tuape, [including] all the lands that surround and delimit their location in the vicinity in the now empty pueblo of Tuape. In respect to the town, toward the east their lands and possessions ran through all the valleys that run up to the foot and foothills of the sierra on the road to Babuco[13] and some Indians planted even farther inside the sierra in summer in the place with a hot spring about two leagues from old Tuape on the left-hand side on the route to Babuco and the rest of the way north. All those lands belonged to the Indians, those located in the canyons and arroyo bottoms that flow out of Sinbicar, even as far as the great stream of [the Río] Sonora in a place then called Bacoache[14] to which I was called to offer confessions to some sick people and to baptize some young converts. And I saw there [along the way] many milpas planted by Tuapeños who were later baptized after their planting, which they continued to plant each year in that place even after they had been transferred to the pueblo of Mátape. With respect to Tuape, between the north and the east the Tuapeños' lands and possessions run through the valley that begins at the old cattle corral located on a small hill. Through a flat and the location of the corral their lands pass through a mesquite grove and a palm grove until reaching the slope of the very high mountains that fall off straight into [the Río] Sonora. There I saw for the whole length of the valley a large number of irrigated fields up to where the corral was located, and below which grew a grove of white cottonwoods. On the bank of some artesian wells along the slope upward toward the north with respect to the said corral, from which they drew the water and directed it into their irrigation ditches that watered their summer fields, I observed them over the space of more than six years until the Indians were relocated to Mátape. Just because the Spaniards who now live in that site maintain that they have not seen the fields or the irrigation does mean that it was not true. Many living Indians who sowed that said place next to the corral and irrigated with the water from those very same artesian wells can verify that what I said is true. With respect to the old pueblo of Tuape, toward the south their lands and possessions ran a long league all the way up to the ranchería called Banachari. There the Tuapeños planted with irrigation and in summertime[15] for many years even after their migration to Mátape. There, they lacked fields for sowing a little wheat for their padre,[16] because Indians there [at Mátape] had already sowed all the available fields so when they pointed out the land to the padre that now can be seen in the same site at Banachari, it hadn't been planted. All of that land and pasture was in the middle of a pond and a huge swamp full of very tall and thick carrizo[17] and sedges and tules and was fenced in the Mexican [style]. Because that land is in the middle of a hilly area and is fenced[18] all the way around the hill, the runoff of water below the hills and the valley that flows from the north and another from the south, had [naturally been] dammed and diverted so much that it formed a lake deep enough to reach the cinches [of a saddle], and consequently it was impossible to cross it.[19] The pathway instead wandered along the hills above the western bank. That was the state of the parcel of land—it was under water and for that reason it didn't belong to anyone; it was without an owner since the Indians could not plant on it. Instead they planted along the banks around the said pond until with the hard work of their priest [Father Cárdenas himself!] they constructed several canals and irrigation ditches that drained all the water and the pond dried up so that the land could be put to use [for crops]. The priest invested in cattle and brought them to be slaughtered so that the Indians could survive on the meat while they were preparing and planting the fields, just as he had done with wheat in Bacarope and Nácori,[20] and where they planted the orchard in Mátape—all those places had been in the middle of swamps overgrown with thick carrizo. At the site of Banachari after draining it, wheat was planted for more than eight years[21] while the Indians planted their corn.[22] Even after moving to Mátape they went back [to Banachari] to plant by irrigation there because it was closer [to Mátape than to Tuape] but afterward with time and the expansion of the cattle of Captain don Pedro de Perea (may God guard over him in heaven) the livestock began to move toward Banachari [from Tuape], where they liked the forage so much that they grew used to it and became comfortable in the area. The constant presence of the cattle around Banachari produced concern and alarm among the owners and managers of the cattle because of the damage that they were doing [to the crops] in spite of the care the dark-skinned cowboys exercised while they were driving the cattle up toward the high mountains that look out onto [the Río] Sonora, and in spite of the vigilance of the Indians who were guarding the wheat and their own cornfields. The Indians finally became weary of planting only to have the livestock eat their crops and the priest grew exasperated and irritated trying to settle arguments. Disgusted, the Indians ceased planting at the said site of Banachari.

With respect to the last remaining possessions and lands of the old pueblo of Tuape, they run toward the west, and they begin from the same pueblo, up to the abandoned rancherías that they call Uparo and another one nearby that is located on a high and prominent rise toward the west, whose ruined adobe huts can be seen on that same hill from which runs another draw between the north and west, where the Indians would plant many fields in the summer. But in their most important summer fields and those they planted when they also had abundant irrigation, they made many plantings of corn and beans. These begin from the base and lower slopes of a huge bare and round hill. It is large and high and according to [the Indians] it is of the same size as the hill they have named Sunucabit—el cerro de maíz—or as it is said. They deposit[ed] their corn in a granary since they used to harvest so much out of those lands. The lands begin from the same hill or mountain that is situated toward the southern part of that same hill [Sunucabit] on the other side of the arroyo facing the villa that was to be called Nombre de Diós. The summer fields ran on both sides of that same arroyo, until they joined the fields of the Indians of Tiepe [Tuape?], which are downstream on the same arroyo due west. In consequence, because they have such good and sure irrigation for the summer harvests the Tuapeños continued to plant on the said arroyo even after having been moved to the pueblo of Mátape. Toward the east, between Mátape and Bacarope they were provided with summer plots and irrigated land in a variety of places and valleys, principally those at a place called Tanami where in my time they had harvests that were abundant or even better, admired by many and envied by others for the quality of those cultivated lands and crops produced by those very Tuapeño Indians. In spite of them having been given those lands, they [the Tuapeños] did not lose their right and the dominion that they exercised over the lands they left in Tuape, since they are entitled to have possessions in an infinite number of locations and distant places. Some of the others [Spaniards] like don Pedro (may he be in heaven), although he left Basiroa[23] with all his household and family to live in the place called Nombre de Diós, he did not lose his right and dominion that he had over his lands in Basiroa, so the Tuapeños have the same mastery and right over their lands. They include those lands in the very same place and lot where [don Pedro] located and built the flat-roofed house where he lived in the settlement called Nombre de Diós. Don Pedro (may he be in heaven) resolved and settled once and for all to move his family from Basiroa. He came in person, accompanied by his Spanish soldiers, searching all that arroyo downstream [from Tuape] for the purpose of finding some place where he could build his home, not being content with just any place, even the place with the artesian wells, located near what today is the cattle corral. That place was too exposed and lacking in protection. He decided instead to build his house to the north, [text unclear] determined to construct the house in that place, but that house now has guests and only a single convenience—that he was able to channel the water from the irrigation ditch and water right to his kitchen and the patio of his house so that he could plant his orchard without even having to leave his place. On the other hand the prudent caballero realized the drawbacks to the place. It was constricted between the hills on the two sides of the arroyo and was very humid, being close to the stream, and its size was insufficient for the town he hoped to build. He found the place he wanted in the Valley of Sonora and gave it a temporary name that he had borrowed from the Valley [unclear]. Using an interpreter, who was Diego Lirro, a vecino of Pueblo de Álamos,[24] [Pedro de Perea] explained to the Tuape Indians that his [Pedro's] principal intent was not to live and inhabit Tuape permanently but to build a fort in the Valley of Sonora in the great flat that lies beyond the ranchería called Sonora.[25] Around the fort would be houses of the villa that he intended to build. And [with that understanding] he solicited the labor to build in Tuape and to make the place come alive. With that [the temporary nature of his stay in Tuape] in mind he hoped to rent a place for his house where he could for a time lodge his family. In light of all this, to cover the expenses for the construction in the Valley of Sonora he hoped to bring from Basiroa all his livestock, and at the same time to prevent his livestock, in his absence, from wandering away with the wild cows of Basiroa. With these explanations he had all his livestock driven to the plains around Tuape where *ad tempus* he established his ranch with the pact, implicit on the part of Captain don Pedro (may God look after him) and with the tacit assent on the part of the Indians, permitting him temporary [*posuis non rennuendo que ad tempus*] use of their fields and common lands for his cattle. He chose the said lot to build his house at the time that the field [that he chose for a lot] was all planted in a large bean field still in flower, since it was toward the end of the month of September when the crops are not yet ripe. At the same time don Pedro learned that a judge he had summoned [to legalize the arrangement for renting the Tuapeños' land] had arrived at Tuape, but, to his misfortune, the judge abruptly shortened his trip to the villa and departed almost immediately from Tuape [so don Pedro never completed the documents].

    Don Pedro de Perea then traveled to Basiroa, intent upon sending his entire home and family to Tuape and did so. He greatly hoped that the building of the house would have already begun at the time of his departure [for

Basiroa]. So through all these hurried negotiations there was no room for patience and he did not want to hold things up while the said field of beans was maturing and then being harvested. However, the owner of the field and the land around it answered clearly and distinctly that he had no desire to sell, saying that although he was elderly, he had sons and grandsons who would inherit that piece of land to support him with certainty through irrigation, which in it he had, and thus seeing the refusal [with which the Indian spoke] the captain, so as to avoid making things worse or attacking the Indian, agreed with him on two things. First, for the bean field that was green and in flower, he would offer him in dry beans what was growing in the field still unpicked, and so he gave him two full sacks of the beans they call tepary. And because the Indian did not want to sell that land, the least he would do would be to lease the lot for a time so that he could build the house that he hoped to have on that location while over on the Río Sonora he was building another house. In the meantime he would rent that site [from the Indian] and he would give the owner a similar quantity of beans every year and in addition he gave the said Indian two varas of coarse blue cloth, a knife, and an adze. To all of this witnesses were present, none so credible as the lieutenant Juan de Oliva, who in the captain's absence (may he be in heaven) he had named as his lieutenant of justice and war captain and who was present at all the said events and at the clearing of the bean field and the measuring off of the field and the first stones and the foundations of that house which due to the industry, assistance, and energy that he [Juan de Oliva] put into the building of the house, it was finished and occupied in less than three months. And as a person [that is, Juan de Oliva] of such Christianity and a faithful vassal of Your Majesty he will confirm the truth of what I have set forth in all of my statement and information being with the obligation I have as a priest and religious leader even though I am most unworthy to satisfy my conscience and my order of obedience of Your Reverence my father visitador, may God guard him, I beg, from this district of Movas the tenth of July of 1647. Lorenzo de Cárdenas

Statement of María de Ibarra: The Concordia

March 16, 1652

In this town of Mátape on the sixteenth day of the month of March of 1652 Father Daniel Ángelo religious leader of the company of Jesus and minister of the said district in the name of the Indians of the pueblo of Tuape, and its rancherías [and representing the other side], doña María de Ybarra [Ibarra], who was wife of General [sic][26] don Pedro de Perea, deceased. "In my name and in the name of all my children as a tutor and nurse of my said children regarding a dispute that is unresolved between the said parties—Indians and me—concerning the site and territory of what is now called Nombre de Diós. We [that is, the defendants] state that for the road to peace and to resolve the said disagreements, differences, and grievances, we can manage to convene and harmonize in the following manner, and that is to be assured that the said Indians will not pursue the argument and demand that they initiated, nor do they intend to pursue any other and they will leave the said María de Ybarra and her heirs in the said place according to and in such a manner that up until now they have possessed until the time of two years being the end of February of the year 1654 and I, the said María de Ybarra, [agree that] I am obliged to remove from inside the said lands all my house and all the livestock that I can, leaving free and unoccupied the said lands for the said Indians without it being necessary for the said Indians to make a request before any judge but instead that they shall be enabled to enter and possess all the said lands as their very own. In the case that the said María de Ybarra[27] within the two years cannot not remove all of her livestock those that remain can be taken by anyone who can care for them at any time. [After the two years are up] she will remove without damage to the said Indians, in accordance with the pact and conditions, that the said doña María de Ybarra or whoever acquired her right, shall not have any livestock or house within two leagues of the district of Tuape as the Indians shall indicate. About damages the said Indians indicated and that in order to accomplish this, she would abandon and donate the houses she inhabits today as well as the other ranches to the said Indians. [On the other hand] the Indians and the said padre [Daniel Ángelo] in the name of the Indians will be obliged to make and build a house with two rooms on the place that she or whoever carries her office, shall indicate and judge appropriate to which to move her livestock. In order to protect our rights, we ask that a copy of this be given to each of the two parties so that each party will be obligated to fulfill it."

We sign our names being witnesses= Father Pedro Bueno[28] and Melchor de Robles and Pedro González de Betancor=Doña María de Ybarra=Melchor de Robles=Daniel Ángelo=Pedro Bueno

The Father Superior Appoints Padre Daniel Ángelo to be Priestly Advocate for the Indians

March 4, 1657
Pedro Gonzales de Betancor=Juan Antonio de Almazán, witnesses.
I, Pedro Baltasar de Loaisa, monk and believer of the Company of Jesus superior of this mission of San Francisco de Borja do bestow authority onto Padre Daniel Ángelo of the same company so that in the name of the Indians who are petitioners in the abovementioned case, in order for their just demand to be ably presented, that he, as priest and father to the Indians, a people abandoned, shall request before any justice the restoration of the place and lands of Tuape that are now called Nombre de Diós by alleging that they [the lands] have been usurped. In order to accomplish that I give to said father Daniel Ángelo full license and authority, dated in this pueblo of Tónichi the fourth of March 1657 and I signed=Baltasar de Loaysa [Loaisa]

The Scribe Records the Appointment of Juan Franco Maldonado as the Indians' Public Advocate

April 13, 1657
In the real de minas of San Pedro de los Reyes of the province of Sonora on the thirteenth day of April 1657 before Captain don Francisco Coto, chief justice and captain of war of this province of Sonora, for His Majesty there appeared Pedro Tasemuchu, governor of the pueblo of Mátape and its congregated partialities=and Lorenzo Batorocho=Ignacio Cabairu=topiles of the partiality of the pueblo of Tuape and Uparo=and Lorenzo Taghumunibuce=and Francisco Dochisguari=natives of the said partiality.[29] And for language the said Francisco Dochisguari belongs to a nation that speaks the Mexican language[30] and that in it [that language] he explained to Juan de Loia, a distinguished Spaniard, who is able to understand the Mexican language, what the Indians wished to hand over. [Juan de Loia] said that [the Indians] said that they [the present Indians], acting in the name of all the Indians of the aforementioned partiality [Tuape and Uparo], through this legal document grant power of attorney to Juan Franco Maldonado, citizen of this said real, especially so that in the name of the Indians he can further the dispute and cause that they have lodged with Alcalde Mayor [Francisco Coto] against don Pedro de Perea [Jr.] and his children and the heirs of Captain don Pedro de Perea and doña María de Ybarra their parents, concerning the lands and

boundaries of the said places of Tuape and Uparo where they had the [previously] referred to ranch of large livestock that they called Nombre de Diós, that they [the children and heirs of Pedro de Perea] should abandon and leave free those lands for the reasons and causes that their demand states and in the said dispute that he [Juan Franco Maldonado] carry out the petitioned requirements, verifications, and information and proofs; present witnesses, papers, and written records; make sworn statements; articulate counter arguments, setting aside those that are necessary; request terms, judicial orders, sentences, interlocutories, and definitive conclusions, accepting those in their favor, and appealing and arguing those that may be against them; challenge witnesses for the other side; and make the strongest and most effective judicial and extrajudicial[31] cases that may be in their favor to the best of his ability at present. In order to [accomplish] everything that has been mentioned and [all that pertains] to it [the Indians] bestow on him [Juan Franco Maldonado] all legal authority with freedom to do what is necessary to administer the case and further the cause of the Indians.

Being witnesses=Juan Mora=and Matías de Loia=and Lorenzo de Ortega present. I, the present scribe, give faith that I know the [Indians that gave power of attorney], and they stated that they do not know how to sign their names. At their request a witness signed the document in their name and the said interpreter swore that he had interpreted faithfully and he signed [the document]=don Francisco Coto=by his order=Ignacio de Barraiersa=scribe named=Juan de Loia=Lorenzo de Ortega

Juan Franco Maldonado Advocates for the Tuapeños

April 30, 1657
In the real de minas of San Francisco de los Reyes, province of Sonora and Nueva Andalucía[32] on the thirtieth day of April, 1657, in the presence of Captain don Francisco Coto, chief justice and war captain of the said province by His Majesty, Juan Franco Maldonado presented the following in the name of the governor of the pueblo of Indians of Mátape and its partialities and of the Indians of Tuape and Uparo and in virtue of his power in the dispute against don Pedro de Perea [Jr.] and the Captain Juan Munguía de Villela as the husband of doña Andrea de Ybarra and the rest of the children and heirs of General don Pedro de Perea and doña María de Ybarra, parent and in-laws of the above mentioned, over the site and ranch that they now

call Nombre de Diós that is in the possession of said don Pedro de Perea [Jr.]. Responding to the contrary petition the nineteenth of the present month[33] and year according to what it [the contrary petition] says, I say that Your Grace as competent and legal judge with knowledge of this cause should order exactly as it is petitioned [as the Indians request] in the demand of my aforementioned clients. Briefly and summarily the case is a simple one, based on the nature of the transaction, the accord that the said doña María de Ybarra made in favor of said Indians. In that document she acknowledges that the natives have populated lands and sites of Tuape and Uparo from time immemorial and that those same natives now residing at the pueblo of Mátape are the plaintiffs and are Tuapeños and descendents of the Tuapeños. Even though they did move and reside there at Mátape, they did not lose their natural right to possession of said lands, nor can their right have expired by any passage of time, even though they may not have planted and enjoyed the use of their land, as they always had in the past.

It is clear [from doña María's point of view][34] that the said concordia [to which she agreed] is null and void for the reasons that they [the Indians] allege because doña María de Ybarra at the time when she made it was a widow and the legal guardian of her aforementioned children and their possessions, and she has the greatest interest in the ranch that General don Pedro de Perea left behind, and even if [she had the control] of all [the hacienda] she did not consider it of sufficient value, compared with what she had given him, a large dowry, as everybody knows, including much silver and jewelry. The hacienda did not satisfy her expectations, based upon the amount that she had given [as a dowry] to don Pedro. She is also dissatisfied with the agreement that don Pedro made with the Indians. She, being informed of all [the transactions] by persons of total honesty, Christianity, and experience, without other persons or their interests interfering, as owner and mistress of her own actions, concluded that as things were, her children and heirs could not even claim the house, though if she had sold it, the ranch, and livestock, they could then have [claimed a share of her estate]. [She could have sold the estate because] she viewed all of these possessions as her personal property.

Further, as it is alleged in the [Indians'] demand, it is obvious that they [don Pedro and heirs] never acquired possession of said sites, since they [don Pedro and family] inhabited them only on the loan basis until he could build in the Valley of Sonora, where he was supposed to found the villa and the dwellings that were never built. Besides, with the authority that the said General don Pedro de Perea chief justice and captain of war of this province of Sonora, without there being anyone opposing him, kept and continued to keep the said livestock ranch in those sites much to the detriment of the Indians. As subjects of the said general [the Indians] through their ministers reminded him that he was violating their agreement, but he took no action until they, my clients, submitted a demand before the judge and it was after that that they made the said concordia. The terms of the concordia were defined as has been referred. However, up to that time the commission[35] that [the Crown] had bestowed on don Pedro required him to fulfill [its provisions] in the stated time and to adhere to the protocols, formalities, and proper steps that the ordinances spell out for founding towns and the foundations for establishing cattle haciendas. And even a person who has enough express authority to do so [found the towns, and so forth], such as a lieutenant of the governor, whatever foundation he may make, it must be established within the time limits of his charter. For that reason the charter that don Pedro and his men brought here is null and void and without effect. It is not pertinent to state that because of the meritorious service performed by said General don Pedro de Perea for Your Majesty in pacifying and conquering in this province, that he should be able to own and possess the said places and ranch. Even if Your Majesty wishes to remunerate him, it should certainly be your will that it not be to the detriment of third parties and even worse, people utterly powerless and without the ability to defend themselves as is the case with the Indians and the said cattle ranch. [The ranch buildings] should be maintained there [as a payment] for the damages and losses the said native Indians have suffered from them [the Spaniards] where, as everyone knows, they have planted their subsistence crops both for their livestock and for their slaves and servants of the ranch. Having that in mind, and the other things are favorable to my clients I beg to Your Grace that you order and execute the said concordia, strongly reaffirming its validity, ordering its current occupants and livestock expelled from the said ranch and lands and boundaries, so that the Indians can freely enjoy their traditional lands and that they be turned over free of damage, harassment, and the vexations that they continually receive. I ask you to provide justice and signed documents, in which you certify the necessary orders.=Juan Franco Maldonado—I have seen in this charter[36] that what is contained in it is contrary to the [original?] charter made by Your Majesty to don Pedro de Perea as is stated in its titles, by don Juan de Peralta, chief justice and war captain and lieutenant of the governor and former captain of this province [appointed] by Your Majesty.[37] I ordered and order that they gather before a competent judge and thus he ordered and signed=don Francisco Coto=before me Ignacio de Barraiersa=scribe named.

May 15, 1657

In the said real de minas the fifteenth day of May, in the said year (1657) I the present scribe read and notified Juan Franco Maldonado in the presence of witnesses the above auto in his person who stated that he heard the reading of the document and would respond as soon as possible for his clients. The witnesses were don Juan de Berdigel and Francisco Roldán, in which I give faith and signed=Juan Franco Maldonado=before me=Ignacio de Barraiersa=scribe named.

June 1, 1658

Finding: In the real de minas of San Pedro de los Reies and Sonora on the first day of June, 1658, in the presence of captain and chief justice Andrés Pérez Lora appeared Juan Franco Maldonado with a petition that he presented on behalf of the Native Indians of the pueblo of Mátape as solicitor and defender. In the claim that he had submitted against don Pedro de Perea [Jr.], praying as asked in name of the said Indians a judgment in the said dispute, it being convenient for the rights of the party he represents. It was analyzed, admitted, and proven. It was ordered that it be provided as requested. The decree [the judgment] was transcribed and transferred to the letter and it filled eight sheets minus one-half sheet and I certify and give faith as a receiving justice [judge pro tem], because the original judge was not present. [The requested document] is correct faithfully and legally derived from the original with neither more nor less words or issues than those mentioned in the original. And in order to certify that this is the truth give faith, being witnesses Bernardo de Lora and Tomás de Mendosa who attended [the proceedings] agree that it is correct—[signed] Andres Pérez Lora, testigo, Bernardo de Lora, Thomas [sic] de Mendosa who were in attendance.

June 1, 1658

In the real de minas of San Pedro de los Reyes in Sonora on the first day of June of 1658 Juan Franco Maldonado appeared with a petition that he presented as defender and solicitor for the Indian natives of Mátape and Tuape, requesting as the solicitor that for the rights of his clients it would be useful if the court were to provide him some of the documents that the other side, don Pedro de Perea [Jr.] had presented to the captain and chief justice who at that time was don Francisco Coto and having been decreed according and as he requests, it was said Captain don Francisco Coto whose presence was required in this part [of the proceedings] because the documents of the other side were not turned over to the archive, and he [Coto, after being summoned] responded that he had turned over the originals to the contrary party [who is] don Pedro de Perea [Jr.]. [Coto delivered this document] by petition as is stated and attached to the judgments and titles because they were personal titles to the said lands and other grants made on behalf of his [don Pedro Junior's] father General don Pedro de Perea, which he [Coto] certifies and declares under oath of and to the Cross that they turned over [to him] and reside in his possession and in order to certify that it is the truth, I authorize by my hand along with the signature of Captain Francisco Coto as judge pro tem because [Coto as] the original judge was not present. In the presence of two witnesses, who are Bernardo de Lora and Tomás de Mendoza, citizens of this mining town=Judge: Andres de Lora, Francisco Coto (retired judge summoned to the case), Bernardo de Lora, Thomás de Mendoza.

Final Concordia, September 4, 1658, Parral

In the Office of General don Enrique Dávila y Pacheco, Governor of Nueva Vizcaya

Don Pedro de Perea [Jr.] as the elder to my brother don Tomás de Perea to whose guardianship I was assigned by the justice of Sonora and by the end and death of my parents, General don Pedro de Perea and doña María de Ybarra and the same in the name and with the legal power of attorney of Captain Juan de Munguía husband and with the person of doña Andrea de Perea, my sister, and that of Domingo de Apresta, husband of doña Josefa de Ybarra, my sister, we are all heirs of our said parents, now deceased, through which powers I now present in the proper form.

And I, Diego de Alarreta, as defender of the Indians and natives of the pueblo of Mátape and of the old [sites] of Tuape and Uparo as the place of contention. We appear before Your Grace and I say that the said don Pedro de Perea, for me and for him that on behalf of the said Indians and natives, there has been a complaint lodged and, in response, that [he states] we will vacate the lands and sites that we have populated with livestock in the province of Sonora that is called Nombre de Diós and in the light of the high cost of adjudication and in order to make things right for the Indians who do so much wish to reclaim their lands. To maintain peace and harmony and attending to a proposal of last year 16[57?], as it was agreed to by the said doña María de Ybarra, now the deceased mother, and on the part of the Indians of Mátape and natives of Tuape that is the place under consideration before Your Grace, on behalf of both parties in the dispute we are in agreement and in concert with the natives and their advocate is in agreement with me in this manner:

I, said Pedro de Perea, for myself and for the said name, will vacate and empty the said place called Nombre de Diós, which is where at the present time we have built houses of our homestead and the corrals for the livestock that belongs to us. The old place [where the natives lived] was named Tuape and adjacent to it were the lands of Uparo and Vanantian with the arable lands. And we are to depart (leaving to the Indians all harvested crops, houses with all that is built in the said place), vacating up to the final water hole that is located in a mesquite grove about two leagues more or less from the said place, on the same roadway that leads from the old site of Tuape to the [Río] Sonora. I will remove from the said place all of my livestock and in [another location] the Indians will be required to build us a single house with rooms for living and for our servants. It will be in a place from which and without breaking the agreement, we will manage our livestock that have spread all over the range, promising to exercise caution on our part, that the said cows will not enter their fields in the time when they are planted. As for what is required of the said Indians, I, Diego de Alarreta, as their advocate, having communicated with Damian, the governor of the pueblo of Mátape and with Francisco Huduri and Torim Otenoro, residents of said pueblo and natives of Tuape, that seeing how they came from Tuape, I read them the contents [of the concordia] and they were most pleased and after discussing the matter they obligated themselves to construct the said house with rooms as referred to in the place so declared as the home of don Pedro and his people, in return for the houses and other buildings that they graciously leave behind in the site of Tuape and Nombre de Diós, therefore, through the arrangements to which we agree under the law, we, Pedro de Perea for me and in the name of my people and that of the said Diego de Alarreta, as the advocate, and for that which pertains to each [party] in the present [concordia], to settle the said disagreement and in order to bring the blessing of peace, it be enforced and executed, forever precluding the possibility that someone might claim to have been cheated or damaged. And thus we commit ourselves by signature of both parties.

Signed: Diego de Alarreta==Pedro de Perea

Notes

INTRODUCTION

1. Secular clergy were those priests appointed by a bishop and not pertaining to or under the hierarchical control of any religious order.
2. Until 1664 the Crown restricted the priests to Iberian ethnicity, fearing that priests of other national extraction might not exhibit exemplary loyalty to the Crown. At that time, the shortage of clerics led to the lifting of the ban.
3. See Bernardo García Martínez, "La creación de Nueva España," in *Historia general de México* (Mexico City: El Colegio de México, 2000), 261–65.
4. See, for example, Herbert E. Bolton, *Rim of Christendom: A Biography of Eusebio Francisco Kino, Pacific Coast Pioneer* (Tucson: University of Arizona Press, 1984).
5. Useful and readily available sourcebooks in English include the following: Edward Spicer, *Cycles of Conquest* (Tucson: University of Arizona Press, 1962); Father Andrés Pérez de Ribas, *History of the Triumphs of Our Holy Faith Amongst the Most Barbarous and Fierce Peoples of the New World*, trans. and ed. Daniel Reff, Maureen Ahern, and Richard Danford (Tucson: University of Arizona Press, 1999); Robert West, *Sonora: Its Geographical Personality* (Austin: University of Texas Press, 1993); and Father Ignaz Pfefferkorn, *Sonora: A Description of the Province*, trans. and annot. Theodore E. Treutlein (Tucson: University of Arizona Press, 1989). For a history of Nueva Vizcaya, see Oakah Jones, *Los Paisanos: Spanish Settlers on the Northern Frontier of New Spain* (Norman: University of Oklahoma Press, 1996). For readers of Spanish, the following is comprehensive, though it lacks an index: *Historia general de Sonora*, vol. 2, coord. Sergio Calderón Valdés (Hermosillo, Mexico: Gobierno del Estado de Sonora, 1985). For archaeological history, Carroll Riley's *Becoming Aztlán: Mesoamerican Influences in the Greater Southwest, AD 1200–1500* (Salt Lake City: University of Utah Press, 2005) is a well-written description of pre-Columbian peoples of the region and their interconnections.
6. David J. Weber, *The Spanish Frontier in North America* (New Haven, CT: Yale University Press, 1992), 78–80, 112; based on Lino Gómez Canedo, *Evangelización*

y conquista: Experiencia franciscana en hispanoamérica (Mexico City: Editor Porrúa, 1977).
7. The ten tribute-free years were specified in the Laws of the Indies. *Recopilación de Leyes de los Reinos de las Indias*, ed. S. Lyman Tyler (Salt Lake City: University of Utah, American West Center, 1980), book 6, title 5, law 3, 145.
8. A useful map of the route can be found in Carl Sauer, *Road to Cíbola*, Ibero-American 3 (Berkeley: University of California Press, 1932).
9. I derived most of the historical material in these paragraphs from the writings of Pérez de Ribas, *History of the Triumphs*. Later Jesuit scholars questioned whether some of his references were accurate but seem to agree that they were for the most part, i.e., John Bannon, *The Mission Frontier in Sonora, 1620–1687* (Saint Louis: Catholic Historical Society, 1955). Bannon himself was a Jesuit apologist.
10. Pérez de Ribas, *History of the Triumphs*, 335–45, 412–14.
11. Gerard Decorme, *La obra de los jesuitas mexicanos durante la época colonial, 1552–1767* (Mexico City: José Porrua e hijos, 1941), 2:41ff.
12. Padre Méndez reported (Pérez de Ribas, *History of the Triumphs*, 288) that he baptized 3,100 infants in the first fifteen days of his entrada, but of these, five hundred died of disease.
13. Pérez de Ribas describes the missionizing among the Mayos (*History of the Triumphs*, 285–99) and the Yaquis (335–55).
14. Cáhita is the language group that includes the Mayo and Yaqui languages.
15. Jones, *Los Paisanos*, 177. That number included missions among the Mayos, Nébomes, and Yaquis, who were located in Ostimuri, now part of Sonora.
16. George Hammond and Agapito Rey, *Narratives of the Coronado Expedition, 1540–1542* (Albuquerque: University of New Mexico Press, 1940), 250.
17. David Yetman, *The Ópatas: In Search of a Sonoran People* (Tucson: University of Arizona Press, 2010), 227–30.
18. *Historia general de Sonora*, 90–91.
19. Cited in J. Rodney Hastings, "People of Reason and Others: The Colonization of Sonora to 1767," *Arizona and the West* 3 (1961): 330.
20. Sergio Ortega Noriega, "El sistema de misiones jesuíticas, 1591–1699," in *Tres siglos de historia sonorense (1530–1830)*, ed. S. Ortega Noriega and Ignacio de Río (Mexico City: Instituto de Investigaciones Históricas, UNAM, 1993), 68.
21. Oakah Jones, *Nueva Vizcaya: Heartland of the Spanish Frontier* (Albuquerque: University of New Mexico Press, 1988), 85.
22. AHP 318 1718A. Visita de la Provincia de Sonora practicada por el gobernador del Reyno.
23. See, for example, Steven LeBlanc, *Prehistoric Warfare in the American Southwest* (Salt Lake City: University of Utah Press, 1999).
24. The province of Sonora in colonial times was separate from the province of Ostimuri, which included lands east and south of the Río Yaqui and north and west of the Río Mayo. Within Ostimuri lay most Mayo and Yaqui territory, lands

of the Guarijíos of the Sierra Madre, parts of the Opatería, and a large portion of Jova lands as well. The boundaries of Sonora of the time make for some awkward inclusions and exclusions in these essays. I have chosen to cross boundaries from time to time rather than adopt strict geographical limits. I have not considered the dynamics of Mayos and Yaquis as part of this book, however, even though Yaqui lands included parts of Sonora north and east of the Río Yaqui. The history of these two peoples is perhaps the most important dynamic in the history of present-day Sonora but has been treated widely elsewhere.

25. Carl Sauer, *Aboriginal Population of Northwestern Mexico*, Ibero-American 10 (Berkeley: University of California Press, 1935).

26. The difference between Lower Pimas and Mountain Pimas is confusing. I find that Timothy Dunnigan provides the most useful distinction (Timothy Dunnigan, "Lower Pima," in *Handbook of North American Indians*, ed. Alfonso Ortiz [Washington, D.C.: Smithsonian Institution, 1983], 10:217). He includes all Pima speakers south of the Pima pueblo of Nacámeri on the Río San Miguel as Lower Pimas, meaning that both Lower Pimas of Ónavas on the Río Yaqui, whose language was thoroughly documented (Campbell Pennington, ed., *Vocabulario en la lengua névome* [Salt Lake City: University of Utah Press, 1975]), and Mountain Pimas of such settlements as Maicoba and Yécora should be considered Lower Pimas. Most researchers refer to Mountain Pimas as those living in the Sierra Madre to the east of the Río Yaqui, while Lower Pimas include those of Ónavas, Movas, and Nuri on the east bank of the Yaqui or its eastern tributaries, and the Ures on the Río Sonora. Nébomes, also considered Lower Pimas, lived in the villages of San José de Pimas, Suaqui Grande, and Tecoripa. During the late seventeenth and eighteenth centuries, Spaniards also referred to the latter as Sibúpapas, although this reference may have been limited to an apostate group of Lower Pimas from those villages that joined Seris in the Sierra Libre in the mid-eighteenth century. Thus Lower Pimas, Mountain Pimas, Nébomes, Sibúpapas, and Ures all spoke closely related dialects of a common language related to, but distinct from, contemporary Pima/Papago, or O'odham. Present-day O'odhams report that they can converse with Pimans of Yécora and Maicoba, but only with difficulty. Linguists today refer to the aboriginal distribution of Piman languages as the Tepiman Corridor. It stretched in a continuous band from north of Phoenix to the state of Durango in Mexico.

27. River Pimas, who refer to themselves as Akimel O'odham, were highly successful farmers who lived primarily along the Gila and Salt Rivers in what is now Arizona. Sobaípuris farmed along the San Pedro River, also in Arizona. Many Pimans who lived in Sonora inhabited regions with less reliable water for irrigation.

28. This "belt" connected Tepiman speakers from the Akimel O'odham on the Gila and Salt Rivers in Arizona to the Tepehuanes of Durango. See David Shaul and Jane Hill, "Tepimans, Yumans, and other Hohokam," *American Antiquity* 63 (1998): 375–96.

29. A comprehensive history and description of Seris is Richard Felger and Mary Beck Moser, *People of the Desert and Sea* (Tucson: University of Arizona Press, 1985).
30. Jack Forbes, "The Janos, Jocomes, Mansos and Sumas Indians," *New Mexico Historical Review* 32 (1957): 324. Forbes believed the Jocomes to be (Chiricahua) Apaches. Shaul (in Yetman, *The Ópatas*, 269) disagrees.
31. See also *Historia general de Sonora*, 93.
32. Thomas Hinton, *A Survey of Indian Assimilation in Eastern Sonora*, Anthropological Paper 4 (Tucson: University of Arizona Press, 1959), 18.
33. See Shaul in Yetman, *The Ópatas*, 269.
34. Mary Beck Moser and Stephen Marlett, *Comcáac quih yaza quih hant ihíp hac: Diccionario Seri-Español-Inglés* (Mexico City: Plaza y Valdés Editores, 2005), 14.
35. Shaul in Yetman, *The Ópatas*, 69–70, 271.
36. Juan Ortiz Zapata, "Relación de 1678," Archivo Histórico de Hacienda (Mexico City), Leg. 26.
37. Pérez de Ribas, *History of the Triumphs*, 185.
38. R. H. Barlow, transcriber, *La relación de Sahuaripa de 1778* (Mexico City: Memorias de la Academia Mexicana de la Historia, 1947), 83.
39. Baltasar Obregón, *Historia de los descubrimientos de Nueva España* (Seville, Spain: Ediciones Alfar, 1997), 158.
40. Juan Nentvig, *Rudo ensayo: Descripción geográfica, natural y curiosa de la provincia de Sonora* (Mexico City: Instituto Nacional de Antropología e Historia, 1977), 72.
41. Obregón, *Historia de los descubrimientos*, 149; Adolph Bandelier, *Final Report of Investigations Among the Indians of the Southwestern United States, 1880–1885*, Archaeological Institute of America Papers, American Series 3 (Cambridge, MA: Archaeological Institute of America, 1890–1892), 58.
42. See William Doolittle, *Pre-Hispanic Occupance in the Valley of Sonora, Mexico: Archaeological Confirmation of Early Spanish Reports* (Tucson: University of Arizona Press, 1988); also Pedro de Castañeda in Hammond and Rey, *Coronado Expedition*, 250.
43. For an excellent summary of these encounters, see David Wilcox, "The Tepiman Connection: A Model of Mesoamerican-Southwestern Interaction," in *Ripples in the Chichimec Sea: New Considerations of Southwestern-Mesoamerican Interactions*, ed. Frances Joan Mathien and Randall H. McGuire (Carbondale: Southern Illinois University Press, 1986).
44. Several of these encounters are described in Ernest Burrus, *Kino and Manje, Explorers of Sonora and Arizona* (Saint Louis: Jesuit Historical Institute, 1971).
45. West, *Sonora*, 46–48.
46. See AHP 318 1715:14. Complaint of Padre Daniel Januske of insolence of Grijalva brothers and mistreatment of Indians in chapter 6, below. Numerous ranches dotted the valley of the Río Moctezuma by this time. That of General José Zubiate dated from around 1700 (Francisco Almada, *Diccionario de historia, geografía, y biografía sonorenses* [Hermosillo, Mexico: Gobierno del Estado de Sonora, 1990], 742). It was

vast and could have come into his possession only by a grant from the Crown. By 1700 Zubiate was running large herds in the vicinity of Nacozari. Cattle ranches were located in the vicinity of most, if not all, mines (*Historia general de Sonora*, 95).
47. Bannon, *Mission Frontier*, 102.
48. Pérez de Ribas wrote repeatedly of the evils of polygamy and the rejoicing of priests when Indians renounced the practice. See especially Pérez de Ribas, *History of the Triumphs*, 229.
49. AHH Temporalidades 0017:62. February 1722. Letter from Caitano Guerrero to padre provincial.
50. Concerning the involvement of the mission of Mátape in commerce with miners, see West, *Sonora*, 59; Charles Polzer, "The Evolution of the Jesuit Mission System in Northwestern New Spain, 1600-1767" (PhD diss. 444, University of Arizona, 1972b), 73, 164.
51. See Fay Jackson Smith, *Captain of the Phantom Presidio* (Spokane, WA: Arthur H. Clark, 1993) for an extensive discussion of the corruption in the Fronteras or Corodéhuachi Presidio.
52. See AHH 278, letter to Joseph Rodríguez Gallardo, 1742, describing the abandonment of two Ópata towns due to Apaches. Also, Juan Nentvig (*Rudo ensayo*, 109-10) in 1764 described the abandonment of Sonoran mines and mining towns due to Apache depredations.
53. Bill Lockart, "Prehistoric Confusion: A Cultural Comparison of Manso, Suma, and Jumano Indians of the El Paso del Norte," *Journal of the Southwest* 39 (1997): 181.
54. A key study in understanding the Gálvez reforms is Luis Navarro García, *Don José de Gálvez y la comandancia general en las provincias internas* (Seville, Spain: Escuela de Estudios Hispano-Americanos de Sevilla, 1964); a comprehensive summary of the campaign against the rebellious Pimans and Seris is Thomas Sheridan, *Empire of Sand: The Seri Indians and the Struggle for Spanish Sonora, 1645-1803* (Tucson: University Arizona Press, 1999). AGI (Guadalajara 513, diario of Hugo Oconor, 87, 1773) contains lively descriptions of Oconor's expeditions against Apaches.
55. For a description of this historical process, see Saúl Gerónimo Romero, *De las misiones a los ranchos y haciendas: La privatización de la tenencia de la tierra en Sonora, 1740-1860* (Hermosillo, Mexico: Gobierno del Estado de Sonora, 1991); also Yetman, *The Ópatas*, 194-201.
56. AHES Tomo 60, Exp. 5 037933. 21 diciembre 1836. Letter from Juzgado de Paz Juan Antonio Bustamante to the Gobernador del Estado.
57. I must interject a brief word about antecedents for these essays. I recall in the early 2000s being most impressed by an article I ran across on the colonization of Sonora written in 1961 by the historian and later distinguished climatologist J. Rodney Hastings, whom I had known for his writings on climate and vegetation. I wish I had had a chance to discuss my viewpoint with Rodney, whose considerable archival skills were exceeded by his geographical sophistication and his profound understanding of the relationships among people, climate, vegetation,

and history. I have had the luxury of being able to locate and pore over some manuscripts that were unavailable to him but that have been made available to me thanks to the prodigious efforts at microfilming the archives at Parral, Chihuahua, by Charles DiPeso and his associates (Archivo Histórico de Parral, AHP) and in Mexico City by the team led by Charles Polzer and his associates (Archivo General de la Nación, AGN, and Archivo Histórico de Hacienda, AHH). These microfilmed documents are now available at the University of Arizona. Due to the lasting contributions of DiPeso and Polzer and their associates, I have been able to locate many of the primary sources that Hastings lacked. I thank Rodney and his brilliant collaborator, Ray Turner, for establishing for me once and for all the unbreakable link between history and the land.

CHAPTER ONE

1. I wish to acknowledge the considerable assistance I received from Carlos del Cairo and Rodrigo Rentería in translating and interpreting the documents in the lengthy folio from 1658, located in the Archivo Histórico de Parral, that forms the basis of this article. Much of the essay was published in the *Journal of the Southwest* 53 (Spring 2011): 33–86.
2. AHP 318, 1658B, Leg. 41.
3. The year 1637 seems plausible for the founding of Tuape. Juan de Oliva, one of Pedro de Perea's original settlers, testified in 1649 that he had lived in the region for twelve years, which would establish 1637 as the date for the first settlement in Sonora. AHP 318, 1649A, Leg. 14, relación de alcalde mayor Simón Lazo de la Vega, 1649.
4. García Martínez, "Nueva España," 261–65.
5. See, for example, David Yetman, "*Ejidos*, Land Sales, and Free Trade in Northwest Mexico: Will Globalization Affect the Commons?" *Journal of American Studies* 41 (2000): 211–34.
6. In early colonial times, Sonora did not include the lands of Mayos and Yaquis or those of other indigenous groups living east of the Río Yaqui and south of the Río Aros, all of which lay in the province of Ostimuri.
7. The town of Corazones was first named by Cabeza de Vaca in 1536. Coronado's expedition possibly passed through the same place in 1540. Sauer, *Road to Cíbola*, 14–38.
8. Obregón, *Historia de los descubrimientos*, 155. Natives tipped the arrows with poison produced from the sap of *yerba la flecha*, *Sebastiania bilocularis* S. Watson. As late as the 1680s, native leaders encouraged rebels to engage Spanish forces in the hills or in their homes, where the bow and arrow were more effective in combat than firearms. See AGI Escribanía 400 C, 173.
9. The ten tribute-free years were specified in the Laws of the Indies. *Recopilación*, book 6, title 5, law 3, 145.

10. Both Jesuits and Franciscans considered the work requirement imposed on Indians to constitute their tithe. José Refugio de la Torre Curiel, "Conquering the Frontier: Contests for Religion, Survival, and Profits in Northwestern Mexico, 1768–1855" (PhD diss., University of California at Berkeley, 2005), 157.
11. AGN Misiones 26 f129v, January 1653, Gerónimo de la Canal letter to padre provincial. But see also AHP 318, 1649A, Leg. 14, relación de alcalde mayor Simón Lazo de la Vega, 1649. Father Gerónimo de la Canal ran into stiff and reasoned resistance to his evangelizing. When all else failed, he called in a military strike. In writing of his experiences he does not mention the huge military backup he required. The military leader involved, Simón Lazo de la Vega, alcalde mayor of Sonora, wrote an extended description of the incident.
12. For a summary of the dates in which missions were founded, see Spicer, *Cycles of Conquest*; Yetman, *The Ópatas*; and Paul Roca, *The Paths of the Padres Through Sonora* (Tucson: Arizona Pioneers' Historical Society, 1967).
13. For a detailed history of Nueva Vizcaya, see Jones, *Nueva Vizcaya*.
14. Jones, *Nueva Vizcaya*, 85.
15. In addition to the material derived from the AHP 1658B, sources on Pedro de Perea used for this article include the following: Almada, *Diccionario*; Pérez de Ribas, *History of the Triumphs*; Decorme, *La obra de los jesuitas mexicanos*; Luis Navarro García, *Sonora y Sinaloa en el siglo XVII* (Seville, Spain: Escuela de Estudios Hispano-Americanos de Sevilla, 1967); West, *Sonora*; *Historia general de Sonora*; Juan Mateo Manje, *Luz de tierra incógnita*, vol. 2 (Tucson: Arizona Silhouettes, 1954); and Francisco Zambrano, *Diccionario bio-bibliográfico de la Compañía de Jesús en México*, vol. 4 (Mexico City: Editorial Jus, 1961). Further material is contained in the translation of a document purportedly written by Father Pedro Pantoja, perhaps in the late 1660s, and translated by Charles Polzer ("The Franciscan Entrada into Sonora 1645–1652: A Jesuit Chronicle," *Arizona and the West* 14 [1972a]: 253–72). For the Coronado expedition, the source is Richard Flint, *Great Cruelties Have Been Reported: The 1544 Investigation of the Coronado Expedition* (Dallas: Southern Methodist University Press, 2002).
16. Navarro García, *Sonora y Sinaloa*, 249.
17. Pérez de Ribas, *History of the Triumphs*, 143; Navarro-García describes Martínez de Hurdaide as "piadoso y justiciero" (*Sonora y Sinaloa*, 248).
18. Gómez Canedo, *Evangelización y conquista*, 74–82.
19. Pérez de Ribas suggests that Captain Perea failed to provide protection for a priest threatened by dissident Nébomes. See Pérez de Ribas, *History of the Triumphs*, 406. Juan Mateo Manje also describes the exploits of Pedro de Perea in *Luz de tierra incógnita*, 279–82.
20. See Thomas Barnes, Thomas Naylor, and Charles Polzer, *Northern New Spain: A Research Guide* (Tucson: University of Arizona Press, 1981), 13.
21. Pedro was required to finance his own army—the Crown merely provided him with a license, which he may have been required to purchase, and stipulated

requirements. The government had no interest in financing operations like Pedro's but was quite willing to endorse the entradas, sensing benefit from mining and further penetration into gentile territory. See Matthew Restall, *Seven Myths of the Spanish Conquest* (Oxford: Oxford University Press, 2003), 65–67.

22. Almada, *Diccionario*, 176.
23. Not an easy task. Most ambitious Spaniards preferred the more benign climate and proven mineralization of central Mexico. Many Spaniards recruited for New Mexico abandoned their posts, hightailing it back south when the realities of life there became clear. Pedro de Perea must have lured them to Sonora with tales of mineral riches and warm winters, probably glossing over the six-month-long summers and false reports of silver deposits. See Weber, *The Spanish Frontier*, 89–90.
24. John Kessell, *Pueblos, Spaniards, and the Kingdom of New Mexico* (Norman: University of Oklahoma Press, 2008), 46.
25. Jones, *Los Paisanos*, 181.
26. Zambrano, *Diccionario bio-bibliográfico*, 672–78. See also Decorme, *La obra de los jesuitas mexicanos*, 263.
27. Such is the claim of Fray A. Nuñez, "Carta edificante histórico-curiosa, escrita desde la misión de Santa María de Baserac en los fines de Sonora" (special collections, University of Arizona Library, 1777).
28. See Manje, *Luz de tierra incógnita*, 280–82; also Polzer, "Fransciscan Entrada." In this article, Polzer translated a *relación*, which he attributed to Padre Pedro Pantoja, *padre visitador* on the Río Sonora during this period. The author attributes the Franciscan entrada to Pedro's machinations, through which the friars were led to believe that they were being officially invited to evangelize that part of the world. I suspect that the relación is a diplomatic attempt to gloss over what must have been some angry exchanges between members of the two orders.
29. Navarro García, *Sonora y Sinaloa*, 253.
30. Pradeau and Burrus, "Historia de las misiones sonorenses y sus pueblos de visita" (doc. ined., special collections, University of Arizona Library, 1965). Navarro García (*Sonora y Sinaloa*) assigns the above date of Pedro's death. Almada (*Diccionario*) maintains that he died in 1644. In the manuscript translated in Polzer ("Franciscan Entrada"), the author, perhaps Padre Pedro Pantoja, says that he (Pantoja) administered last rites to Pedro in 1645. However, his relación was written as much as forty years later and contains several important errors.
31. See Polzer, "Franciscan Entrada," 271. Polzer believes the relación was written by Father Pantoja himself, between 1666 and 1684.
32. See also the map in *Historia general de Sonora*, 81.
33. Polzer, "Franciscan Entrada," 264.
34. For an extended description of the damage that cattle inflicted on a Sonoran indigenous community, see also chapter 6 (AHP 318 1715B, 125). Complaint of Daniel Januske of insubordination. See also chapter 7.
35. West, *Sonora*, 47.

36. Pantoja (?) in Polzer ("Franciscan Entrada," 270) asserts that María de Ibarra died in Banámichi.
37. See Daniel Reff, *Disease, Depopulation, and Culture Changes in Northwestern New Spain, 1518-1764* (Salt Lake City: University of Utah Press, 1991), 255-57. In 2002 unirrigated farmland in the United States yielded 30-50 bushels per acre (bpa) of wheat, while unirrigated cornfields yielded 127-150 bpa. Irrigating wheat (including inputs) increases yield to about 71 bpa, while corn rises to 169 bpa. Source: 2002 Census of Agriculture, U.S. Dept. of Agriculture Statistics Service.
38. Polzer, "Jesuit Mission System," 168.
39. Daniel Ángelo Marras was priest at Mátape from 1653 until 1681. He was known as an energetic and entrepreneurial priest of doubtful religiosity. See *Historia general de Sonora*, 71 and Navarro García (*Sonora y Sinaloa*), 217-23.
40. The languages spoken in missions in the Opatería are listed in annual reports (*anuas*) submitted by the Jesuits to their overseers. Only a few were comprehensive, but these were quite specific. One such document was written by Padre Juan Ortiz Zapata in 1678 ("Relación de 1678").
41. Campbell Pennington, "Cultura de los eudeve del noroeste de México," *Noroeste de México* 6 (1982): 9-34.
42. *Recopilación*, book 6, title 3, law 1, 108; law 11, 113. An instructive example of the stern prohibition on Indians' venturing away from missions can be found in AHP 318, 1707 N12. Father Miguel Guerrero Villaseca, the priest at Bacadéhuachi, managed to have a squadron from the presidio at Janos carry out a sweep of Sonoran mining locations, forcibly gathering Indians who had abandoned the mission at Bacadéhuachi without the priest's authorization. See chapter 5.
43. Almada, *Diccionario*, 176.
44. Navarro García, *Sonora y Sinaloa*, 223.
45. Susan Deeds, "Rendering unto Caesar: The Secularization of Jesuit Missions in Mid-Eighteenth-Century Durango" (PhD diss., University of Arizona, 1981), 22.
46. *Recopilación*, 114-16.
47. Polzer, "Jesuit Mission System," 73, 164. Marras sidestepped the Jesuit prohibition on ownership of enterprises (especially mining) by placing all the commercial holdings under the Colegium of Mátape, the school for neophytes. Under the influence of the polemics of Bartolomé de las Casas, the Crown had forbidden Spaniards to enslave Indians. The embargo did not apply to Africans, however, and the use of African slave labor continued in Mexico and in Sonora well into the nineteenth century. That religious orders might own slaves may seem surprising but it was by no means unusual. Both Carmelite and Benedictine monasteries maintained establishments for breeding slaves in the state of Río de Janeiro in colonial Brazil (Miguel Carneiro de Cunha, "Silences of the Law: Customary Law and Positive Law on the Manumission of Slaves in 19th Century Brazil," *History and Anthropology* 1 [1985]: 432). On the other hand, Jesuits provided Indians of Paraguayan and Bolivian missions with firearms and training in their use to fend off Portuguese slave raiders.

48. Cárdenas mentioned the diversions of water at Tuape used primarily to irrigate Pedro de Perea's orchards. Similarly, Father Januske (chapter 6) lamented the defoliation of his fruit trees by cattle. The Bohemian Jesuit Pfefferkorn criticized the Natives' lack of interest in cultivating the orchards (Pfefferkorn, *Sonora: A Description*, 74). To date no fruit trees have been domesticated from wild Sonoran plants.
49. María Valle de Borrero Silva, "La administración de Sonora: Los alcaldes mayores en la primera mitad del siglo XVIII," *Temas Americanistas* 21 (2008): 53.
50. See Restall, *Seven Myths*, 66.
51. Nicolas de La Fora, *Relación del viaje que hizo a los presidios internos situados en la frontera de la America septentrional* (Mexico City: Editorial Pedro Robredo, 1939), 136.
52. José Refugio de la Torre Curiel, "Patriotas en conflicto: Rebeliones, disputas por tierras y sospechas de infidencia entre los Ópatas de Sonora a principios del siglo XIX," in *Los grupos nativos del septentrión novohispano ante la independencia de México, 1810–1847*, coord. Martha Ortega Soto, Danna Legin Rojo, and María Estela Báez-Villaseñor (Mexico City: Korph Lithograpikz Editorial, 2010), 221–33. Primary sources: Archivo de la Real Audiencia de Nueva Galicia (ARAG), Biblioteca Pública del estado de Jalisco. Primary Ramo Civil, 427-11-6947, fs. 3–4 and forward; also ARAG, Ramo Civil, 424-1-6888, f. 190, 20, 44–45, 69; 120140, 36–37, 151, 164–65, 167.
53. Aleš Hrdlička, "Notes on Indians of Sonora, México," *American Anthropologist* 6 (1904): 51–89.
54. Nancy Farriss, *Maya Society Under Colonial Rule* (Princeton, NJ: Princeton University Press, 1984), 283.
55. AHP 318, 1655A G8. Juicio de residencia de Juan Munguía de Villela. The proceedings in this document take place in San Juan Bautista.
56. The supposed "American Dream," or owning a house, is a contrived concoction of the housing industry in the United States. The original significance can more appropriately be attributed to the hopes of Spanish settlers in the Americas. These are admirably described in García Martínez, "Nueva España," 261–64.
57. Ibid., 217–23.
58. Reff, *Culture Changes in Northwestern New Spain*, 226.
59. AGN Misiones 26 f129v; January 1653. Letter from Gerónimo de la Canal. Father Canal in reporting his missionary work in the region made no mention of the military intervention that shored up the Jesuits' flagging and failing evangelization.
60. AHP 318, 1649A, Leg. 14.
61. Pantoja (?) in Polzer, "Franciscan Entrada," 272.
62. AHP 318, 1655A G8. The actual date of the folio is 1659. See Almada, *Diccionario*, 434, concerning the founding of the town of Santa Cruz.
63. I have calculated this population change from a census reported by Pedro Tamarón y Romeral, bishop of Nueva Vizcaya, who visited the region in 1759–1760

and recorded the population of Indians and vecinos for every settlement in the Opatería (Pedro Tamarón y Romeral, *Demostración del vastísimo obispado de la Nueva Vizcaya—1765* [Mexico City: Editores Porrúa e hijos, 1937]).

64. Missions were far more than the mere buildings or settlements in which religious rites were carried out. Missions constituted a geographical area over which priests exercised authority. Within those areas they were vested with nearly absolute power.

65. Pradeau and Burrus, "Historia de las misiones," under biography of Pedro Bueno.

66. AGI, Patronato, 232, Ramo 3rd. 3e, 2nd part, 1–14. Cited in Navarro García, *Sonora y Sinaloa*, 204.

67. AHH Temporalidades Leg. 325, 67, 69, 70, 71. Daniel Marras's response to charges brought by Spanish settlers and miners. The harshest charges were those of Sonoran alcalde mayor Dicastillo, which Marras goes to great and dubious lengths to refute.

68. Navarro García, *Sonora y Sinaloa*, 206.

69. For a description of the dismantling of missions, see Romero, *La Privatización*.

CHAPTER TWO

1. Much of the information in this paragraph is derived from Charles Polzer's translation of a document entitled "The relation of what occurred in the dispute between the Society of Jesus and the religious of Saint Francis" (Polzer, "Franciscan Entrada," 263–78). Polzer (269) suggests that the manuscript (AHH Temporalidades, Leg. 1126, exp. 2) dated from between 1666 and 1684 and the probable author was Father Pedro Pantoja himself. If so, and Polzer's reasons were well taken, it is a most self-serving history, a virtual hagiography of Father Pantoja. Other information in this section came from Pérez de Ribas, *History of the Triumphs*, and Spicer, *Cycles of Conquest*.

2. Whether Father Canal and other priests (apart from Padre Bartolomé Castaño) were conversant in Native languages is difficult to assess. Some authors attribute rigid language proficiency requirements to Jesuit missionaries. For example, "In no case could the vice-provincial allow a missionary to become a full-fledged Jesuit by pronouncing his final vow until his fluency was approved" (John Augustine Donohue, *After Kino: Jesuit Missions in Northwestern New Spain, 1711–1767* [Saint Louis: Jesuit Historical Institute, 1969], 44). The practice in the field was far less rigorous than this, however, and later Jesuits lamented many priests' inability to deliver sermons in the language of their congregation. See Manuel Aguirre, S. J. Report on Sonoran Missions and priests' ability to deliver sermons in the Indians' language, 1764. AHH Leg. 17, Temporalidades, Leg. 0017 no. 022–24.

3. AGN Misiones 26:129–31, 1653. Report of Gerónimo de la Canal. Father Canal composed his report (memoirs) in 1653, seven years after the events he describes. Cucubazunuchi (or Cucubazunichi) does not appear in any reference books or

maps that I have seen. However, the village by the name of Bacanuchi still exists in the region, roughly the same distance north of Arizpe as the latter is from Sinoquipe, and that may have been the place to which Father Canal had been directed, Cucubazunuchi.
4. Cristóbal Cañas, *Estado de la Provincia de Sonora, julio de 1730*. Documentos para la historia de México, 3a serie, 1835–1857, transcribed, with notes by Flavio Molina Molina (Hermosillo, Mexico: Diócesis de Sonora, 1978).
5. If Father Canal spoke any Teguima at all, he could hardly have spoken it with any degree of fluency. The thought of the priest attempting to describe the tortures of hell in an alien language to an uninterested or skeptical people paints a ludicrous picture.
6. Once again we must question how this conversation took place between two people speaking mutually unintelligible languages.
7. AGN Missiones 26:135V–137V, 1653.
8. Almada (*Diccionario*, 80) believes this to be the case.
9. It is possible that Padre Pantoja, in spite of his long years in the Río Sonora Valley, had been misinformed, or that perhaps Pedro de Perea had boasted of an achievement that had never happened. To my knowledge, the only other mention of such an expedition came from Juan de Oliva, one of Pedro's officers and another member of the original party. The testimony of these two soldiers interviewed by Simón Lazo de la Vega suggests that both had previous military experience in the two offending villages, so the expedition may indeed have taken place.
10. AHP 318, 1649A 14.
11. Polzer, "Franciscan Entrada." If the author of the document was in fact Pantoja, the padre visitador gave himself another nice pat on the back. Describing himself, he wrote that "Pantoja acted as interpreter. It was he who made the arrangements because the Indians [of Teuricachi] understood him quite well; he knew the language with complete fluency, breadth, and elegance. He had composed a grammar and a vocabulary, and had written many sermons" (277). If this was not mostly hot air, it meant that Pantoja was fluent in Teguima but not necessarily in the Pima tongues or in Eudeve, an important language in the region. The paragraph cited should also be interpreted as a slap in the face of the Franciscans, who were not noted for their linguistic competence, as Pantoja took care to emphasize in the article.
12. AHP 318, 1649A 14. Letter to Simón Lazo de la Vega from Ignacio Molarja. *Tlátole*, an Aztec term, was a rousing speech or harangue delivered to Native Americans by other Native Americans, usually as a means of firing them up to commit anti-Spanish acts. The term appears throughout literature of the colonial period. Spaniards came to assume that any Indian issuing tlátoles was inciting Natives to riot, and so Spanish authorities outlawed tlátoles and suspected treason of anyone accused of delivering them.
13. AHP 318, 1649A 14. Report of Simón Lazo de la Vega, August 1649 and thereafter.

This folio contains a series of documents dictated by Captain Lazo, letters to him from the priests, and depositions of vecinos. The pages are not numbered, which makes specific citations difficult.

14. Almada (1990, 131) attributes to Miguel de Casanova the identity of the Natives of Cucuribasca and Buchibacuachi as Pimas Altos. I interpret Casanova's references differently. Polzer ("Franciscan Entrada"), West (*Sonora*, 46), and others also identify the peoples of the two pueblos as Hímeris (or Pimas Altos), but a careful reading of the documents makes it clear that the Natives of the two rebellious towns, though often allied with the Hímeris, were of different ethnicity.

    The fact that two soldiers, veterans of Pedro de Perea's entrada, were witnesses to the military sophistication of the Indians of the two villages suggests that perhaps Pedro de Perea had, in fact, led an unsuccessful campaign against them.

15. Juan de Oliva, who oversaw the construction of Pedro's house at the ranch called Nombre de Diós at Tuape, would have accompanied Pedro de Perea on any military campaign. If Pedro had indeed vanquished the peoples of the two pueblos, Oliva would likely have made a reference to the conquest in his testimony. While Oliva has seen the people and appears to be familiar with the villages, he does not speak of any military history with them. I surmise that Pedro may have led a small expedition against one or both of the towns, but the result was inconclusive.

    The military expedition against the two villages took place in 1649. If Juan de Oliva meant that he had been in the region for twelve years, that would make 1637 the arrival of Pedro de Perea's men at Tuape.

16. For a description of the military experience of settlers, see Restall, *Seven Myths*, 27–43.
17. Cynics might point out that this generosity on the priests' part dealt in booty that was the result of Indian labor. The ethnicity of the servants is unstated.
18. Paul Roca, *The Paths of the Padres Through Sonora* (Tucson: Arizona Pioneers' Historical Society, 1967), 151–52.
19. Lest the reader question the use of torture by Spaniards, see chapter 3.
20. We can only conjecture just how the three priests could have known that Padre Huter would be available. Perhaps they had already had discussions with the visitador Pedro Pantoja, who, although not present at the battle, was certainly still in the region (in addition to being padre visitador, he was priest at the mission of Baviácora on the Río Sonora)—witness his signing off on Captain Lazo's version of the events as presented to the priests in Santiago at the conclusion of the military campaign.
21. Relación in Polzer, "Franciscan Entrada," 265.
22. AHH Leg. 26. Report of Padre Juan Ortiz Zapata, "Relación de 1678," 286, 304.
23. Polzer, "Franciscan Entrada," 260.
24. Ibid.
25. Cortés formed alliances with a long list of Indian *señorios* (small governments or city-states), but it was primarily Tlaxcala that provided him with an army that did

most of the fighting (and destruction) against the Aztecs. For an excellent description of the process and function, see *Historia general de México* (Mexico City: El Colegio de México, 2000), 239–40. A sustained discussion in English is available in Hugh Thomas, *Conquest: Montezuma, Cortés, and the Fall of Old Mexico* (New York: Simon and Schuster, 1993). An account of the alliance between the Tlaxcalans and Spaniards from a Native viewpoint can be found in Fray Diego Durán, *The History of the Indies of New Spain* (Norman: University of Oklahoma Press, 1994), 522–27. Nuño de Guzmán also employed indigenous forces in his destruction of Michoacán and a host of other Indian nations in Nueva Galicia. Pérez de Ribas describes the use of Mayos to attack Yaquis, their ancient enemies.

26. Polzer, "Franciscan Entrada," 274.

CHAPTER THREE

1. AGN Misiones 26, 135v–137v, 1653. Report of Gerónimo de la Canal. He refers to the region around Teuricachi as "la frontera de sumas de el norte." After some skirmishes in which several Sumas were shot to death, Father Canal claimed they requested baptism and settled at the mission of Óputo.
2. Of the many extended accounts and discussions in English of the Great Northern Revolt, as the Pueblo Revolt is more accurately described, I have found the most readable to be Kessell, *Pueblos, Spaniards*. Also useful in understanding the uprising is David J. Weber, ed., *What Caused the Pueblo Revolt of 1680?* (New York: Bedford/St. Martin's Press, 1999).
3. AGI Guadalajara 138, fol. 177. Report of virrey (viceroy) Conde de Paredes. (At times the voice of the report changes, but it generally appears to be that of Conde de Paredes.) Legajo 138 contains several reports of the uprising, some of them in great detail.
4. Ibid., fol. 276.
5. AGI Guadalajara 318, rollos 1 and 2, contain several accounts of the revolt, several of them derived from the same original. One of the most readable can be found on rollo 2, 286ff.
6. Ibid., rollo 2, 183.
7. Ibid., 182ff.
8. Ibid., 281, 752.
9. Ibid., 281v.
10. Ibid., 186.
11. Kessell, *Pueblos, Spaniards*, 125, 133.
12. The pueblos were divided from within and under assault from without by both Apaches and Utes. Their armed resistance was spotty and poorly coordinated. Indian losses were considerable. See Kessell, *Pueblos, Spaniards*, 139, 153–55.
13. Bautista is often spelled Bauptista or even Baptista. I have chosen to incorporate the most common spelling of the town's name in this essay.

14. AGI Guadalajara 138, pieza 3, microfilm rollo 2, 274–78. Navarro García unearthed the document.
15. Ibid., 276v.
16. Ibid., 274.
17. Navarro García (*Sonora y Sinaloa*, 266, 275) considered the Janos, Jocomes, and Sumas (and other nomadic tribes) to be closely related Athapaskans. More recent scholarship has led to the abandonment of this position. Forbes (*Janos, Jocomes*) considered Janos and Sumas to be one and the same.
18. AGI Guadalajara 138, 276.
19. Almada, *Diccionario*, 222.
20. AGI Guadalajara 138, 276.
21. To their dismay, Spaniards learned that in terms of loyalty they could not distinguish between infidel and Christianized Indians. They would learn in Sonora that most of the leaders of the conspiracy were closely linked to the missions and were considered Christians by their priests, some of them devout. Several of the accused pointed to their deep involvement in mission religious activities.
22. AGI Guadalajara 138, 30–35.
23. Bolton, *Rim of Christendom*, 74–75, 87–91.
24. Jesuits questioned the Franciscan policy of not learning Native languages. See Polzer, "Franciscan Entrada," 277ff, cited in chapter 1, above.
25. Spicer, *Cycles of Conquest*, 232.
26. The identity of Necuas remains elusive. Apart from the manuscript under consideration, I have not discovered other references to them. Peoples of that name survive in northern Baja California, but their relationship to any peoples of Nueva Vizcaya is unsubstantiated.
27. AGI Guadalajara 138, 30–35.
28. Quintero, it appears, was an avaricious settler who allowed his cattle to invade Indian fields and devour their crops. He became a vocal advocate of fierce punishment of insolent Indians. See Navarro García, *Sonora y Sinaloa*, 272.
29. AGI Escribanía 400 C, Cuaderno 2. Autos originales que se fulminaron por el Gen. Lázaro Berdugo y Don Francisco Cuerbo en el tiempo que administraron justizia en la provincia de Sonora; sobre la conspirazión de los yndios de dicha provinzia. July 1681. This section is alternately numbered 122–201 and is available at AGI in microfilm, rollo 2, under Escribanía 400 C.
30. The ethnic and linguistic identity of Jocomes remains obscure. Forbes (*Janos, Jocomes*) believed them, along with Sumas and Janos, to be Athapascan speakers. David Shaul (in Yetman, *The Ópatas*, 65 fn), however, after a review of all available literature, finds ethnic and linguistic identification of these peoples to be inconclusive.
31. AGI Escribanía 400 C, Cuaderno 2, 123.
32. The narrative yields no description of the jail or prison. We can only assume that it was a small, thick-walled adobe building with only one entrance and tiny windows, if it had any windows at all.

33. This was possibly a slap at the Jesuits, since it suggested that the missions were places that sheltered or nurtured anti-Spanish intrigue and that the priests were given to mollycoddling Indians.
34. AGI Escribanía 400 C, Cuaderno 2, 133.
35. The reference to walls is intriguing. *Reales* were often wide-open towns, but this suggests that vecinos were concerned about security from Indian raids and had erected what was at least a semblance of a protective wall around the settlement. San Juan Bautista was founded in 1657, so in a couple of decades its importance seems to have risen and the revenues from silver mining were sufficient to finance a wall. The town lasted about ninety years as capital of Sonora before being abandoned in favor of San Miguel Horcasitas on the lower Río San Miguel.
36. AGI Escribanía 400 C, Cuaderno 2, 136.
37. Ibid., 173–74.
38. The chronology of Jaure's testimony is confusing. In the folio of Escribanía 400 C in the Archivo General de Indias, his testimony rests in a different archive located much later in the file, yet his testimony was taken on July 7, 1681, while Verdugo was closing up his case in Chinapa. It does not fit gracefully into the other depositions taken under Verdugo's auspices, yet for consistency it must be included in the order in which I have placed it.
39. AGI Escribanía 400 C, Cuaderno 2, 173.
40. Ibid., 145.
41. Ibid., 155.
42. Luis Navarro García, an eminent historian from Seville, makes no mention of the Spaniards' use of torture in his discussion of these incidents. The documents reveal torture to be highly refined and widely applied.
43. While Bacobichi figures prominently in the interrogations in the manuscript, I have been unable to locate it. It is probably a synonym for Bacoachi. Other writers have made reference to it, but if it was a different pueblo its location remains unknown. If it is a now-defunct pueblo, it probably lay somewhere between Cuquiárichi on the Río Cuquiárichi and Bacoachi on the Río Sonora, some forty kilometers to the southwest.
44. The manuscript reads (p. 156) "Badequachi," which I interpret as Bacoachi. Native names for towns gave Spanish scribes fits.
45. AGI Escribanía 400 C, Cuaderno 2, 178.
46. Ibid., 179.
47. A description of the events from the standpoint of the priest of Bacadéhuachi would be instructive at this point. It has not yet turned up.
48. AGI Escribanía 400 C, Cuaderno 2, 181. This may be the same Francisco Banasuri who was arrested in October in Cuquiárichi. The scribe wrote down what he heard.
49. This is geographically confusing. Lorenzo Quintero owned a mine in Tepache and lived there with his wife. His servant, Javier, apparently from Chinapa, had given him early information about the conspiracy, which Quintero had then reported

to Lázaro Verdugo in San Juan Bautista in early July. The witness who referred to Javier lived in Bacadéhuachi, a considerable distance from Tepache. The connection does not emerge from the extant documents.

50. AGI Escribanía 400 C, Cuaderno 2, 194.
51. Ibid., 389.
52. *Arcabuzeados*; citation is translated from AGI Escribanía 400 C, Cuaderno 2, 402.
53. Ibid.
54. Possibly viewed from the other side of the river. Bacerac and Bavispe lie on the west bank of the Río Bavispe, and Guachinera is situated well to the west of where the river enters the canyon country of the Sierra Madre. To reach Bacerac from Guachinera, one must climb through steep mountains or cross the river twice. The execution squadron must have crossed the river once, well upstream from Bacerac, then found the river had risen before crossing at Bacerac. The trail probably passed through Tamichopa, which lies on the northeast bank of the river some fifteen kilometers southeast of Bacerac. That may have been the location of the execution.
55. AHP 318, 1681A, 4.
56. Ibid.
57. Almada, *Diccionario*, 182.
58. AGI Escribanía 400 C, Cuaderno 2, 352.
59. Ibid., 347.
60. Ibid., 339–64.
61. AGI Escribanía de Camera 400 C, Cuaderno 4, fols 3–4. This section is also located on microfilm reel 2, 339–406. However, the alternate numbering that Navarro García used is 1–68 (each page bears at least two numbers).
62. AGI Escribanía 400 C, Cuaderno 4, fols 3–4, 40. This may represent the earliest extant reference to Ópatas.
63. *Segua* means "flower" in Teguima, as well as in Cáhita. The name used here may have been a pseudonym.
64. Spaniards discovered among the Ópata a complicated system of kin and marriage relationships. The most prominent of these was the *noragua*, or godbrother. Noragua was different from the Spanish compadre, since the bond appears to have been cemented independent of relationship to children. Men became noraguas through an elaborate ritual. Thereafter the bond was irrevocable, the tie between them so powerful that Jesuits noted that there was nothing a man would not do for his noragua. Jean Johnson, *The Ópata: An Inland Tribe of Sonora* (Albuquerque: University of New Mexico Press, 1950), 30.
65. AGI Escribanía 400 C, Cuaderno 4, 3–4, 346, 347, 348.
66. Ibid., 365–405.
67. *Sebastiania bilocularis*, a plant in the spurge family that is common in much of the Opatería. The earliest Spanish arrivals in the region found to their displeasure that Indians used arrows tipped with the poison to great effect. The tubes to which

Quintero was referring were probably hollow sections of the stalk of a cane grass, *Phragmites australis*.
68. AGI Escribanía 400 C, Cuaderno 4, 3–4, 354.
69. Ibid., 362.
70. Ibid., 365.
71. Finished as well were any thoughts of organized pan-Opatan resistance. The only interruption in the general peace within the Opatería for the next 125 years was a minor tremor in the east. In 1696 a small group of Opatans led by an Opatan named Pablo Quihui, a newly converted Catholic of Bacerac, and, it appears, a veteran of the conspiracy of 1681, made a short-lived attacked on Spanish holdings. Quihui proclaimed that the Opatan allegiance to Spaniards had gained them nothing. His reasoning for taking up arms is difficult to quarrel with: the Opatans' lands had become overrun with Spaniards who stole the best fields and pastures and forced Opatans into slavery in their own lands. Spaniards made Opatans fight the Apaches and eastern tribes, the only result being that the Apaches viewed them, the Opatans, as an enemy. In spite of lofty promises, their "friends" the Spaniards did more damage than their enemies, the Apaches. Better to join with the Conchos and Jocomes against the Spaniards, he proclaimed. Spaniards captured and executed his top leaders. Quihui himself was killed by a lightning strike near Janos and his "uprising" fizzled to an end. See Francisco Javier Alegre, *La historia de la compañía de Jesús en Nueva España* (Mexico City: Impresa J. M. Lara, 1841–1842), 2:130–31.
72. For a more extended discussion of Ópata ethnicity, see my remarks and those of linguist David Shaul in Yetman, *The Ópatas*, 64–79.
73. AGI Escribanía 400 C, 1684, 205–58.
74. Ibid., 122.
75. Ibid. Report from Matheo Verdugo, January 1682.

CHAPTER FOUR

1. Much of this article appeared in the *Journal of Arizona History* (Autumn 2004): 291–306. I wish to acknowledge the assistance of Abigail Sotelo in translating and interpreting the archival documents of this case. In late 2009, some four years after she and I worked through the file from the Parral archives that formed the basis for this article, I discovered through a Google search that a Mexican researcher had discovered the same file in the Parral archives and had published a similar article in Spanish in 2001. Dr. José Mirafuentes Galván appears to have had access to documents that were missing from the microfilms I consulted. His article bears reading. The citation is José Mirafuentes Galván, "Los maleficios de Don Marcos Humuta," *Estudios de historia novohispana* 25 (2001): 117–54.
2. Manje, *Luz de tierra incógnita*, 171.
3. Susan Deeds, *Defiance and Deference in Mexico's Colonial North: Indians Under*

Spanish Rule in Nueva Vizcaya (Austin: University of Texas Press, 2003), 98, 104; Noemí Quezada, "The Inquisition's Punishment of Curanderos," in *Cultural Encounters: The Impact of the Inquisition in Spain and the New World*, ed. M. E. Perry and A. J. Cruz (Berkeley: University of California Press, 1991), 35–37; Bolton, *Rim of Christendom*, 12, 21; Cynthia Radding, *Entre el desierto y la sierra: Las naciones O'odham y Teguima de Sonora, 1530–1840* (Mexico City: Instituto Nacional Indigenista, 1995), 99. Radding cites the example of a mid-eighteenth-century Arizpe priest who determined that sorcerers had harmed two fellow priests. He had Ópatas arrested for the crime. Archives of the colonial era in northwest Mexico are replete with Europeanized accounts of sorcerers and sorcery. Reports decreased as the colonial period waned.
4. Pérez de Ribas, *History of the Triumphs*, 96.
5. Malcolm Ebright and Rick Hendricks, *The Witches of Abiquiu* (Albuquerque: University of New Mexico Press, 2006), 163.
6. Harry Crosby, *Antigua California: Mission and Colony on the Peninsular Frontier, 1697–1768* (Albuquerque: University of New Mexico Press, 1994), 209. Crosby contends that Baja California Jesuits "did not overreact to the threat of former shamans living among their neophytes. No mission policy dictated their ostracism or punishment, as long as they were discreet and did not openly question a missionary's authority."
7. AHH Temporalidades Leg. 0278 No. 14. 1740. An Ópata curandero from Soyopa was detained in Ónavas, a Nébome (Mountain Pima) town, for having cured a local Indian woman by removing three bones from her stomach. Under orders from the mission priest, the Ópata was arrested and sentenced to receive one lash from every resident of the mission. After the punishment, he was reported to have fled back northward into Ópata country. Curandismo is often still practiced in both indigenous and mestizo communities of northwestern Mexico, usually in cases where the afflicted person cannot afford allopathic treatment, or where such treatment has proven ineffective. The manuscripts of the case discussed above are classified as AHP 318, 1704B, 15–81 in the University of Arizona Library's microfilm section.
8. Cañas, *Estado de la Provincia*, 5.
9. AHP 318, 1703, 31. Criminal case against Mateo, a Sonoran Indian.
10. Among educated Spaniards, belief in witchcraft varied from person to person. Governor Córdoba's sentence suggests he was a believer. He was in good company. In the mid-eighteenth century a priest in Abiquiu, New Mexico, accused *Genízaros* (Hispanicized Indians) of placing a hex on him and called for them to be prosecuted criminally. His accusations of witchcraft and those of many others arose at a time when Abiquiu was under relentless attacks from Comanches, which created an atmosphere of fear and accusations in the pueblo. The case became hugely complicated (see Ebright and Hendricks, *The Witches of Abiquiu*).
11. Around 1906, Tamichopa became a colony of Kickapoos, an Algonquin tribe.

When oil was discovered under their Oklahoma land, the U.S. government made an agreement with Mexico to provide them with land along the Río Bavispe. Although they have lost their indigenous language, Kickapoos ("Kikapus" in Spanish) still tend their modest farms in Tamichopa and collect a small check each month from the U.S. government. The Río Bavispe originates in the Sierra Madre of northwestern Chihuahua and flows north in extreme eastern Sonora until it encounters the massive Sierra San Luis. It passes through a fault zone for about forty kilometers, then turns generally south, flowing past the mission towns of Óputo (now Villa Hidalgo) and Guásavas. Roughly forty-five kilometers south of Guásavas, it is joined by the Río Aros from the east to form the Río Yaqui. The towns of Bacerac and Bavispe are located adjacent to the river. Guachinera stands on a bluff above a tributary of the Bavispe.

12. The name Ópata appears increasingly after the 1690s and becomes widespread in documents, especially following the publication in 1702 of a Teguima grammar by the Jesuit Father Natal Lombardo of Arivechi. It was printed in book form and entitled *El arte de la lengua teguima vulgarmente llamada Opata*. See Yetman and Shaul in Yetman, *The Ópatas*, 64–79.

13. Wick Miller, "Uto-Aztecan Languages," in *Handbook of North American Indians*, ed. Alfonso Ortiz (Washington, D.C.: Smithsonian Institution, 1983), 10:113–24. David Shaul (2008 personal communication) places Opatan (Teguima and Eudeve) in its own branch of the Uto-Aztecan northern languages. Nueva Vizcaya included the province of Sonora until 1734, hence the repeated references in the documents to Bacerac being part of Nueva Vizcaya.

14. Nuñez, "Carta edificante."

15. The community dynamics that led to the accusations must have involved matters unrelated to sorcery or witchcraft. That is to say, it was probably not a matter of professional jealousy among practitioners. The documentary record, though extensive, provides almost no insight into social conditions in the Bavispe communities at the turn of the eighteenth century.

  I would not have come upon this group of documents were it not for the database provided in the Arizona State Museum's Documentary Relations of the Southwest. A note in the database by Tom Barnes brought them to my attention.

16. A vecino vouched for Marcos's literacy. But if Marcos was literate, he was barely so. Vecinos were usually considered *gente de razón* (people of reason) and their testimony would have been carefully heard in a case such as this.

17. One Juan Moreno appears in the proceedings of 1707 described in chapter 5. It is possible that he is the same Moreno who appears here. He is apparently the owner of a small mine.

18. It seems odd that the two accusers would acknowledge that they were curanderos, since this sort of practice was frowned upon and often punished by the priests.

19. The handwriting on the letter is that of an experienced scribe. While it is possible that Marcos wrote it himself, it is highly doubtful, given the wording and the

stylized cursive penmanship. Marcos's signature is written in the jerky script of a person carefully moving pen across paper.

20. The mission priests invested the traditional governors with considerable power. This was an important tool in protecting the clerics from being inundated with requests to settle mundane disputes and rule on a huge variety of matters. As we have seen in chapters 2 and 3, military officers felt free to remove governors from office and bestow the canes of office on more sympathetic sorts, though this practice could lead to great dissension as well. However, the office of *gobernador tradicional* was clearly of Spanish origin and thus could arouse resentment among indigenous people, who might be inclined to identify the governor with things Spanish.

21. Two hundred lashes was a standard severe penalty. See chapter 3.

22. In the meantime, Captain General Miguel de Abajo apparently was transferred, as his signature no longer appears on the documents, while that of Francisco Pacheco y Zavallos becomes more prominent.

23. This was common procedure in ecclesiastical crimes, and perhaps in civil crimes as well. Apparently, women found guilty of crimes were infrequently incarcerated. Where imprisonment was inappropriate, they were usually referred to religious authorities for further indoctrination.

24. Pérez de Ribas, *History of the Triumphs*, 96–97, 414–15.

25. Yetman, *The Ópatas*, 56–57.

26. Cañas, *Estado de la Provincia*.

27. See the remarks of Padre José Torral in Ernest Burrus and Felix Zubillaga, eds., *Misiones mexicanas de la Compañía de Jesús, 1618–1745* (Madrid: Ediciones José Porrua Turanza, 1982), 122–23, 136; Padre Carlos Roxas, Report on the Mission of Arizpe, Bancroft Library M-M 1714.

28. Johnson, *The Ópata*, 42–43; Crosby, *Antigua California*, 38, 208.

29. Pérez de Ribas, *History of the Triumphs*, 374–75. For a detailed description, see *Historia general de Sonora*, 55–56.

30. For a contemporary analysis of the events in Salem, see Mary Beth Norton, *In the Devil's Snare: The Salem Witchcraft Crisis of 1692* (New York: Alfred A. Knopf, 2002).

31. The Inquisition was never active in Nueva Vizcaya, so its proceedings were unavailable. The thoroughness with which representatives of the Crown investigated the Bacerac matter indicates that it held high priority with them.

32. Carlos de Roxas, "Report on the Mission of Arizpe," Bancroft Library, University of California, Berkeley, M-M 1714, 1744; Pfefferkorn, *Sonora: A Description*, 226–27.

33. Pfefferkorn, *Sonora: A Description*, 227. His caustic (and insightful) remarks probably reflect the fall from fashion among some priests of accusations of sorcery (but clearly not the power of the devil). Sorcery was still perceived as a problem in Jesuit missions during the mid-eighteenth century. See AHH Temp. Leg 0278, 14,

1740. Accusations of witchcraft. See also AGN Provincias Internas 33:524–44, 1793. Report of the danger from sorcerers, Barbastro to Revillagigedo.
34. Yetman, *The Ópatas*, 199–200.
35. William Merrill, *Rarámuri Souls: Knowledge and Process in Northern Mexico* (Washington, D.C.: Smithsonian Institution Press, 1988), 132–34. Merrill describes the widespread belief in the power of sorcerers among the Rarámuri (Tarahumara). In the mid-1980s I visited a curandero in the Mayo town of Los Buayums, Sonora. A town resident was a curandero certified as such by Mayo authorities in the Mayo administrative center of Etchojoa, Sonora. The fellow produced for me a printed list of services he could perform. Included were dehexing automobiles, horses, houses, and outbuildings, and reversing hexes imposed by other practitioners.

The practice of exorcism continues among some religious groups.

Late in the twentieth century an American priest became embroiled in an argument in a Sonoran village with the exchequer of the keys to the town's colonial era church. When she refused to open the church for him, the priest placed a hex on the entire town. So great was the consternation of the citizenry that another priest from Arizona found it necessary to visit the town and remove the hex.

CHAPTER FIVE

1. *Recopilación*.
2. *Recopilación*, book 6, title 3, law 1, 108; law 11, 113.
3. Daniel Reff, Maureen Ahern, and Richard Danford (*History of the Triumphs*, 393 fn) note that an early priest reported that Nébomes and Opatans in the southern Opatería lived in "ninety large rancherías or towns." In parts of the Opatería, village life was the rule. Elsewhere reduction was necessary. Pérez de Ribas (*History of the Triumphs*, 389) noted of the "Aivino [Opatan], the Sisibotari [Opatan], the Batuco [Opatan], the Ures [Piman], and finally, the Sonora [Opatan] nation . . . These nations have been *reduced* to about twenty pueblos" (italics mine). In other words, the scattered population of the region had been concentrated in twenty pueblos. He also notes that reduction was not necessary in the area of Sahuaripa, since towns already existed there. Towns were noted along the Río Sonora in the mid-sixteenth century by Obregón (*Historia de los descubrimientos*, 157). Spicer (*Cycles of Conquest*, 95) reports that "by 1646 forty Opata rancherías were reduced . . . [to] two churches at Oposura and Cumpas."
4. Pérez de Ribas in Reff, Ahern, and Danford, *History of the Triumphs*, 470.
5. The ten tribute-free years provision was specified in the Laws of the Indies. *Recopilación*, book 6, title 5, law 3, 145. Under the Jesuits' tenure, no Indians of the Northwest would pay taxes, even after 140 years of mission activity.
6. *Recopilación*, book 6, title 3, law 36, 87.
7. *Recopilación*, book 6, title 3, law 10, and title 15, laws 1–15.

8. *Recopilación*, book 6, title 3, law 18, 116. This proscription was enforced in apparent contradiction of the *Recopilación*, book 6, part 1, law 12, 76, which states that "Indians may move from one location to another." By 1787 the Laws had been modified to read "The Commander General of Internal Provinces shall take the necessary measures to ensure that the Indians do not leave their towns without fulfilling their communal work and planting their own fields before being allowed to depart for work in the mines, and then only with a written permit to leave and in the company of a justice of the peace from the town . . ." AGI Guadalajara 559, 28 de febrero 1787. Council of the Indies Custodio.
9. AHP 318, 1707 N12. This folio consists of thirty-two double pages. It is incomplete, lacking the concluding autos (orders) that contained the governor's verdict.
10. Manje, *Luz de tierra incógnita*, 171.
11. At this time, Sahuaripa, Arivechi, Tacupeto, and Quimbunazorra were all parts of Ostimuri, not of Sonora, and hence under the jurisdiction of the alcalde mayor of Ostimuri, Blás Ezquerr (thus he spells his own name as witnessed by his repeated signature on documents). Other sites that Domínguez visited, including Cumpas, Aguaje, Pópulo, and Opodepe, were located in Sonora.
12. Franciscans welcomed the military reconquest of New Mexico in 1692 and in subsequent years. In Texas, Indians abandoned Spanish missions for French settlements in 1717 when the French offered them trade goods such as blankets, firearms, and metal utensils. This led the Franciscan priests to demand from the Crown a squadron of soldiers to burn down the Indians' houses of pagan worship, force them back to the Franciscans' missions, and prevent them from fleeing once again (Weber, *The Spanish Frontier*, 186).
13. AHP 318, 1707 N 14. According to Manje, Domínguez treated him badly, dragging him out of his home in Bacanuchi on the upper Río Sonora, leaving his wife and children behind without explanation and without protection, placing him in handcuffs, and forcing him to ride a mule (and not a horse, of which he had many) all the way to Parral. Manje was absolved when Jesuits dropped the charges but continued to involve himself in the controversy between Jesuits and civil authorities.
14. This folio contains references to several mines that flourished in the early eighteenth century but have long since disappeared. The size of the mining towns is difficult to estimate from the information provided. Most of the details of Quimbunazorra's location (and its spelling) must be derived from these documents, which make it clear that the mine and mining town were located in the vicinity of Arivechi in the Tacupeto district. The contemporary village of Valle de Tacupeto is located some thirty kilometers south of Sahuaripa on the Arroyo Sahuaripa.
15. In his book *Luz de tierra incógnita*, Juan Matheo Manje mentions (134) that he and Father Eusebio Kino were accompanied on one of their exploratory journeys up the Santa Cruz River to the Gila River by one Antonio Ortiz, resident

soldier of San Juan Bautista. I have not managed to determine whether or not this is the same Antonio Ortiz de Cortés who figures prominently in this narrative. However, since Captain Domínguez also arrested Manje on the same expedition in which he arrested Ortiz de Cortés, it seems quite plausible that they were one and the same person.

16. In this case, the term *hacienda* refers to a mine with its small smelter or roaster.
17. Having mine workers and servants in debt to their masters or bosses was commonplace at the time. These sorts of debts were seldom paid off and the Indians simply became peons whose debts were perpetual. See West, *Sonora*, 51.
18. For a description of the mining town of Aguaje, see Donald Garate, *Juan Bautista de Anza: Basque Explorer in the New World, 1693–1740* (Reno: University of Nevada Press, 2003), 54–70.
19. AHP 318, 1708 G30. Causa criminal contra gobernador de los jobas.
20. These same charges have for decades been leveled against Mexico's federal judicial police, who respond only to the president of the republic and are widely viewed as roving, lawless brigands.
21. AHP 318, 1708 G30. This folio contains several documents that pertain to Asencio Domínguez's roundup of runaways and appear to be a continuation of his reports from the previous year.
22. AHP 318, 1708 G30.
23. Ibid.
24. This folio reveals the effectiveness of mail service in northwestern Mexico in the eighteenth century. The couriers who delivered letters were probably well-trained Indians—Ópatas and perhaps even Tarahumaras—who were renowned even then for their ability to run for many hours at a stretch without stopping. The rapidity of mail delivery is impressive, especially given the convoluted topography and great distances involved in northeastern Sonora and western Chihuahua. Same-day delivery was apparently available between Bacanora and Sahuaripa and Sahuaripa and Batuc. With nonstop runners offering express service, delivery from Sahuaripa to and from Parral may have been possible in a week.
25. Jovas were a Uto-Aztecan-speaking group from extreme eastern Sonora who appear to have migrated to the Sahuaripa and Bacanora areas sometime after the arrival of the Jesuits. In contact times they appear to have lived in small groups or clans in remote canyons of the Sierra Madre of eastern Sonora and eschewed village life. They were reported to have raided Spanish and Opatan settlements in the mid to late seventeenth century, including attacks on Bacadéhuachi and Nácori Chico. Opatans sometimes enslaved them. Their language is only remotely related to Opatan, probably having closer affinities to Tarahumara. Jovas were generally weaker militarily than the dominant Teguimas (Ópatas) of the region and far less is known about them than the Teguimas. At the time of these documents, though, Jovas must have constituted a majority in Sahuaripa, since the traditional governor of Sahuaripa was a Jova. The small town of Pónida, two kilometers north of

Arivechi, some twenty-five kilometers south of Sahuaripa, is still recognized in Sonora as a Jova town, even though the last Native speaker died in the latter part of the twentieth century.
26. This suggests that Father Guerrero and his predecessors had done a poor job of indoctrination.
27. Although both Quimbunazorra and Pibipa are included in Sonoran territory today, they lie east of the Río Yaqui and thus in the eighteenth century they were included in the province of Ostimuri.
28. The shipping route of the equipment is not specified in the documents. Transportation by cart from the port of Guaymas would have been much simpler and faster than overland—across the Sierra Madre—from forges in Parral. The first one hundred miles northward from Guaymas up the valley of the Río Mátape is mostly flat or rolling, with only one low pass before arriving at Batuc. Eastward from Batuc to Sahuaripa and Arivechi, however, the terrain is mountainous and would have made for slow and difficult shipping.
29. Simón García uses the figure of "150 leagues," most probably to dramatize the injustice he faced in the court proceedings. That estimate was hardly an exaggeration, and the convoluted terrain made the distance ever so much more difficult.
30. This was a bloody insurrection of Indians, primarily Pimas Bajos, who had grown weary of the damage to their crops by livestock and the general abuses of their land tenure associated with the arrival of vecinos. In addition to destroying Tacupeto, the rebels virtually obliterated the nearby town of Onapa in the Sahuaripa Valley. See Navarro García, *Sonora y Sinaloa*, 291–93.
31. At the time, the annual stipend for a priest was 350 pesos.
32. AHP 318, 1708 G30, 24.
33. See Alegre, *La historia de la compañía*, 2:130–31. See also chapter 3, note 67.

CHAPTER SIX

1. Radding, *Entre el desierto*, 164. See also AHP 318, 1718A, 101, order of governor forbidding outsiders to enter missions.
2. Bannon, *Mission Frontier*, 59.
3. Januske had previously been priest in the Piman mission of Tubutama, where he narrowly escaped an attempt at assassination in the Piman uprising of 1695. Prior to that, he had been a missionary among the Tarahumaras. See Bolton, *Rim of Christendom*, 270, 296–97.
4. The exact number of lashes was supposedly established by regulation, but the priests retained discretion to vary the number. Five lashes may seem like a draconian punishment for something as apparently trivial as failure to attend Mass, but in comparison with other punishments, it was rather light. In the case of Marcus Humuta (see chapter 4), those who accused him falsely were sentenced to one hundred lashes in one case, and fifty in another. The governor of Nueva Vizcaya in

1718 ordered a punishment of two hundred lashes for anyone carrying on business in Indian pueblos without authorization, though it is not clear that anyone ever received that punishment (AHP 318, 1718A, 101).

Even these punishments were not especially heavy sentences compared to those elsewhere. João José Reis, in his detailed study of the revolt of Muslim slaves and freemen in Brazil in 1835, documented punishments of up to twelve hundred lashes. These were administered in doses of no more than fifty lashes per day, after which a doctor would examine the patient and recommend when he or she could withstand the next dose of flogging. The procedure would thus continue until the specified number had been administered. Although the recipients of such torture died from the lashes from time to time, authorities and slave owners had an interest in punishing, but not killing, the victim, since slaves represented an economic investment, and if they died from the lashing, the sentence would not be very distinguishable from a death sentence. João José Reis, *Slave Rebellion in Brazil* (Baltimore: Johns Hopkins University Press, 1993), 215–23.

5. AHP 318, 1715, 14. Complaint of Padre Daniel Januske of insolence of Grijalva brothers and mistreatment of Indians.
6. Vecinos frequently complained that the priests treated Indians as slaves while at the same time forbidding vecinos and miners to employ them for wages.
7. Outsiders were generally forbidden to enter mission lands without the permission of the priest.
8. AHH Temporalidades Leg. 325-36. July 27, 1713. Letter from Daniel Januske to Padre Provincial Francisco Xavier de Mora.
9. AHH Temporalidades 278 2:1723; Daniel Januske, report on the present state of the missions of this province, 11.
10. AHH Temporalidades Leg. 325-36:12.
11. AHP 318, 1718A. Inspection of Sonora by Inspector Bezerra Nieto.
12. Also spelled "Zubiate." Both spellings are commonly used, but the folio uses "Subiate," and I have followed suit. Almada (*Diccionario*) presents a lengthy biographical sketch of Subiate but fails to mention any of the protracted controversy surrounding his cattle and the damage they wreaked on the crops of Sonoran Indians.
13. See letter from Nícolas de Oro. AHH Temporalidades Leg. 0325:33, ca. September 13, 1713.
14. In this case, according to Padre Nícolas de Oro, the alcalde mayor who witnessed the corralled cattle was Domingo Picado Pacheco, who perhaps was filling in for the ailing Pacheco y Zevallos, or perhaps was serving as full-fledged alcalde. Donald Garate, however, refers to Picado Pacheco as *sargento de armas de Sonora*, not alcalde mayor, even though Picado Pacheco refers to himself in these documents as alcalde mayor (Garate, *Juan Bautista de Anza*, 101). While it seems odd that the priest would err in referring to a Spanish authority's title, this may be the case here. Still, Picado Pacheco seems to have believed he had the alcalde's authority

to fine Padre Januske for allowing Indians of Cumpas and Oposura to run up debts when they left the mission to work for the vecinos and appears to have ordered his scribe to state his title as alcalde mayor, so he was at least claiming to be the alcalde and operating out of Opodepe. Throughout this confusion, I have not been able to determine precisely who was the alcalde mayor of Sonora in 1713. Januske implies that it was Pacheco y Zevallos, and, indeed, the folio contains signed letters from him. However, other documents suggest it was Picado Pacheco, or even someone else. It may be that in the earlier months of 1713 Picado Pacheco was alcalde, but the position reverted (or was presented) to Pacheco y Zevallos by midsummer of 1713.

15. AHP 0325:33, section 3. Padre Januske refers to the "long absence of said General Alcalde Mayor don Domingo Picado" and suggests interim strategies for dealing with the livestock destruction.
16. AHH Temporalidades Leg. 0325:032–036, 1713. Letter from Daniel Januske to padre provincial and responses from José Subiate. These folios contain several letters from Januske in which he rails against the settlers' mistreatment of Indians.
17. Januske specifically mentions ranchers other than Subiate in his correspondence found in AHH Temporalidades Leg. 0325:32 and 33, April–September 1713.
18. Historical drought records show 1715 to have been a drought year in the American Southwest and northwest Mexico, followed by 1716, which was a year of severe drought. See Dale Brenneman, "Climate of Rebellion: The Relationship Between Climate Variability and Indigenous Uprisings in Mid-Eighteenth-Century Sonora" (PhD diss., University of Arizona, 2004).
19. AHH Temporalidades 325:036, July 1713.
20. AHH Temporalidades 325:32. Letter from Padre Luís Pinelli to Padre Provincial Mathías Ginó, October 29, 1709.
21. "*Embusteros y chichimecas*."
22. AHP 318, 1715B, 125:6f.
23. AHP 318, 1715B, 125:33ff.
24. Almada, *Diccionario*, 742.
25. Donohue, *After Kino*, 22. This claim seems somewhat implausible, given the years of running battle between the two. If Donohue is correct, Januske's protests against Subiate's abuses must have been insincere.
26. AHH Temporalidades 325:32, 19 (italics mine).
27. Ibid., 20.
28. Bolton, *Rim of Christendom*, 498.
29. Charles Polzer, *Kino Guide II: His Missions—His Monuments* (Tucson: Southwestern Mission Research Center, 1982), 10.
30. Garate, *Juan Bautista de Anza*, 74.
31. AHP 318, 1715B, without number, September 15, 1715 or 1716.
32. Almada, *Diccionario*, 46–48. Almada devotes three pages to Álvarez Tuñón's notoriously corrupt career. For an extensive description of his administration of the presidio of Fronteras, see Smith, *Captain of the Phantom Presidio*.

33. Borrero Silva, "La administración de Sonora," 62.
34. Ibid., 110.
35. We cannot discount the additional possibility that among the violators were some of Álvarez Tuñon's personal enemies.
36. AHP 318, 1718A, 101. Governor's order that no Spaniards will enter Indian pueblos.
37. Daniel Januske, report on the present state of the missions of this province, 1723. AHH 278 2:11.

CHAPTER SEVEN

1. Much of this article originally appeared under the title "Sonora in 1771: Hard Times or an Investor's Paradise?" in the *New Mexico Historical Review* 80, no. 4 (2005): 379–96.
2. Hastings, "People of Reason and Others."
3. An excellent account of the value to the Crown of Opatan fighters is found in José Rodríguez Gallardo, "Informe de Sinaloa y Sonora, August 12, 1750," MS 218, special collections, University of Arizona Library, 110 (section 16). Letter to Lt. Col. Diego Ortiz y Parilla, March 16, 1750.
4. Spicer, *Cycles of Conquest*, 125.
5. Yetman, *The Ópatas*, 93.
6. Spicer, *Cycles of Conquest*, 106–8.
7. Bernard Fontana, "History of the Papago," in *Handbook of North American Indians*, ed. Alfonso Ortiz (Washington, D.C.: Smithsonian Institution, 1983), 10:137.
8. Kieran McCarty, "Franciscan Beginnings on the Arizona-Sonora Desert, 1767–1770" (PhD diss., Catholic University of America, 1973), 154.
9. *Historia general de Sonora*, 216–19.
10. The trip from northern Sonora to Durango required about three months. During the rainy season many arroyos were impassable and roads were washed out. Priests would also take a day or two to rest and recover at missions along the route.
11. The expeditionary force led by Captain Domingo Elizondo charged with dislodging Seris and Sibúpapas from the Sierra Libre (Cerro Prieto).
12. Cieneguilla was one of the most productive gold strikes in Mexico's Northwest. It is located in especially inhospitable desert some fifty kilometers southeast of Pitiquito. A soldier searching for a rebellious Seri struck gold in February 1771. Word spread quickly and by June two thousand prospectors were digging for gold. Cieneguilla had become the largest town in Sonora. By 1772 the population reached seven thousand, at least a half of whom were Indians, many of them veteran miners from such depleted ore bodies as San Antonio de la Huerta. The easily accessible gold suddenly petered out and it became a veritable ghost town. A second strike occurred nearby in 1803 and by 1805 Cieneguilla once again boasted

a large population of five thousand. However, there was no water to support the population, to irrigate farmland, or to assist in placer mining. It was necessary to haul the ore on foot for many kilometers to a spring where it could be panned. The summers were insufferable and unrelentingly hot. Once the visible gold ran out, the town was once again abandoned. See *Historia general de Sonora*, 277–79, and Navarro García, *Don José de Gálvez*, 254. Enough placer gold remains in the area, however, that local prospectors occasionally make rich finds. One storeowner in Pitiquito in the 1990s reported financing the construction and opening of a business with proceeds from his gold prospecting.

13. Nacámeri, renamed Rayón in 1825, was an Upper Pima town on the Río San Miguel. It is now a prosperous but isolated town of fifteen hundred.
14. A small village along the railroad near Trincheras. It appears to have been abandoned.
15. A village on the east bank of the Río Yaqui, some three kilometers north of the Highway 17 bridge over the river. It was an important town in eastern Sonora until the mid-twentieth century.
16. Nébomes were Pima speakers who lived south of the Opatería in such present-day villages as Ónavas, Movas, and Yécora. They came to be known as Lower Pimas, Mountain Pimas, and some of them as Sibúpapas.
17. A mining boomtown on the west bank of the Río Yaqui some six kilometers north of Tónichi.
18. A Nébome or Sibúpapa town on Arroyo Tecoripa, a tributary of the Río Yaqui. Mexico Highway 17 passes through Tecoripa.
19. A town on the Río Mátape some seventy kilometers northeast of Empalme Bay near Guaymas, where the Río Mátape empties into the bay. San Marcial was often an incarceration point for rebellious Sibúpapas. Today it is a tiny, somnolent hamlet on a seldom-visited dirt road.
20. A former capital of Sonora, now upstream (northeast) from Hermosillo about sixty kilometers. Ures is a bustling and handsome small town of five thousand inhabitants.
21. Pitic was an important settlement of Spaniards (military and civilian) and relocated Seris. Its location is now within the limits of the Sonoran capital city of Hermosillo.
22. The account of Friars Canales and Reyes. AGI 512, Durango, 11 July 1771. Notarized document.
23. Cucurpe and Opodepe were Eudeve (Opatan) towns that still flourish on the Río San Miguel, which lies east of Mexico Route 15 and roughly parallels it south of Santa Ana nearly to Hermosillo, where it joins the Río Sonora.
24. Nueva Vizcaya originally included Sonora as well as Chihuahua and Durango.
25. Or Faini.
26. AGI Guadalajara 512, 1771. Preface to notarized document, Joseph Fayni.
27. Athapaskan-speaking Apaches were nomads of the western plains until they

learned the use of horses in the late seventeenth century. This technological innovation increased their mobility and their range and they expanded their territory westward and southwestward. In the mid-eighteenth century they were forced even farther west under pressure from Uto-Aztecan-speaking Comanches. Comanches were better versed in the use of firearms, and their military threat forced Apaches to abandon their traditional hunting grounds and resulted in an increase in Apache raiding in Arizona, Chihuahua, and Sonora. Veronica Tiller, "Jicarilla Apache," in *Handbook of North American Indians*, ed. Alfonso Ortiz (Washington D.C.: Smithsonian Institution, 1980), 10:447–50. Comanches became feared raiders as far west as western tributaries of the Río Grande and well into Nueva Vizcaya. For a more systematic study of Comanches, see Stanley Noyes, *Los Comanches: The Horse People, 1751–1845* (Albuquerque: University of New Mexico Press, 1993).
28. AGI Guadalajara 512. See below.
29. Archival documentation of the correct pronunciation of this group's name is unclear. The late Franciscan historian Friar Kieran McCarty assured me that the antepenultimate accent is correct.
30. AGI Guadalajara 512, Durango, 11 July 1771. Quoted from the letter, Fayni to Julián Arriaga. Piatos were Upper Pimas living in the vicinity of Pitiquito and Caborca. AGI Guadalajara 512, Durango, 4 September 1771. Testimony of Friars Canales and Reyes suggests that the name is a contraction of Pimas Altos. Other writers distinguish between Pimans and Piatos. Sibúpapas were a group of Nébomes or Lower Pimas who lived in the towns of Cumuripa, San José de Pimas, Suaqui Grande, and Tecoripa, but were mostly from Suaqui. Although their language has no discernable connection with Seri, the two groups formed an alliance and proved to be devastatingly competent raiders.
31. Navarro García, *Don José de Gálvez*, 202.
32. Another impediment to increased rationalization of the economy was the system of missions to Indians administered by the Jesuits. While some missions generated a surplus, most were barely self-sufficient and thus contributed nothing to the regional economy. Gálvez decided that the mission system must go. But that is a different and better-known story.
33. Navarro García, *Don José de Gálvez*, 204.
34. Friar Kieran McCarty has admirably documented the arrival of Franciscans in Sonora. Kieran McCarty, *A Spanish Frontier in the Enlightened Age: Franciscan Beginnings in Sonora and Arizona, 1767–1770* (Washington, D.C.: Academy of American Franciscan History, 1981).
35. John Kessell, *Friars, Soldiers, and Reformers: Hispanic Arizona and the Sonora Mission Frontier, 1767–1856* (Tucson: University of Arizona Press, 1976), 43.
36. Antonio de los Reyes, 1772. Report 1772. Transcribed and translated by Kieran McCarty. MS 227, special collections, University of Arizona Library. "The good lands, which lie some distance to the north, have been appropriated and settled by

twelve or thirteen white families, who are established on a ranch, properly called 'El Realito.'"
37. AGI Guadalajara 559. This *signatura* is dedicated to Galvez's proposed ecclesiastical administrative changes. The Franciscan archives from that period still remain in Guadalajara in the great church of Zapopan. My repeated attempts to gain access to those documents have been futile. The archives from Querétaro are now housed in the Franciscan convent at Celaya, Guanajuato, and are readily accessible to scholars.
38. Both groups were well represented as laborers in mines throughout the region, however. West, *Sonora*, 66.
39. Navarro García, *Sonora y Sinaloa*, 265.
40. For a somewhat fanciful account of the rebellion from a Jesuit standpoint, see Bolton, *Rim of Christendom*, 288–314.
41. The most comprehensive accounts of the revolt of 1740 are found in Luis Navarro García, *La sublevación del Yaqui de 1740* (Seville, Spain: Escuela de Estudios Hispano-Americanos de Sevilla, 1966); and Edward Spicer, *The Yaquis: A Cultural History* (Tucson: University of Arizona Press, 1980), 39–50. Navarro García comments on the uprising: "The rebellion of the Yaquis and their allies in 1740 placed in danger Spanish domination, and therefore the civilizing and evangelizing efforts that in that remote Northwest were developing" (1). The indigenous people would undoubtedly have agreed. Endangering Spanish domination seemed to have been precisely their aim. They might have taken serious issue with Navarro García as to what constituted "civilizing" and "evangelizing," however.
42. For a detailed description of the Pima Uprising of 1751, see Spicer, *Cycles of Conquest*, 129–30.
43. *Historia general de Sonora*, 215.
44. For a comprehensive account of the Spanish campaign against the Seris, including transcriptions of all extant archival sources, see Sheridan, *Empire of Sand*, 1999.
45. AGI Guadalajara 512, Durango, 4 September 1771. Testimony of Friars Canales and Reyes.
46. Traditional Seri lands lie along the coast of the Gulf of California from Guaymas north to near Puerto Peñasco and inland until they encounter Piman lands. Their territory is too dry for livestock except for feral burros; hence the Seris never became horsemen.
47. AHH 278:20, 1742; anonymous letter to Inspector José Rodríguez Gallardo.
48. Spicer, *Cycles of Conquest*, 238.
49. Nentvig (*Rudo ensayo*) states the following (translation mine):

> The old mine of Nacozari, at 14 leagues north of Cumpas is very rich but much reduced by the depredations of Apaches. There is only one vecino left . . . plus a few close to razón and a few Ópatas. There are many good mines in the direction of all winds, but they are little and

poorly worked due to the risk run to those who work the mines, of Apache attacks. To the north were two other mines, Chunerovavi at five leagues, with rich gold and silver and mine smelters ... whose lands, with the smelters ... [were] ... abandoned the 5th of March of 1742 when the nearby mine of Aguaje was attacked by Apaches. The latter was maintained, even as late as 1744, when it was attacked for a second time by Apaches, resulting in the death of various Christians and the burning of houses, and remains abandoned even today. The same is the case with the *Viejo* mine of Nacozari, deserted since 1742. The mine of Peña ..., that of Hacienda Vieja ... that of Barrigón, all depopulated due to the cruelty of the Apaches a few years earlier, not for lack of precious metal ... among others the Pinal (silver and gold ...) and Huacal, somewhat more distant. Closer by, the Pinal mine was the old town of Toaportzi; San Juan del Río, deserted due to said enemy, along with another near Óputo, called Nori.

It seems ironic that Spaniards, who inflicted the most ghastly of punishments—including carefully administered torture—on Indians who insisted on maintaining their freedom from Spanish incursion, would steadfastly accuse Apaches and others of cruelty. See also Weber, *The Spanish Frontier*, 206.

50. Spicer, *Cycles of Conquest*, 239.
51. Navarro García, *Don José de Gálvez*, 183.
52. The Porfiriato refers to the time of the dictatorship of Porfirio Díaz, roughly 1880–1910.
53. Navarro García, *Don José de Gálvez*, 184–85.
54. This printed pamphlet survives in excellent condition in the Archivo de Indias in Seville. It might be construed as the forerunner of promotional real estate pamphlets.
55. The source of this material is Navarro García, *Don José de Gálvez*. The work is directly derived from archival sources, primarily the Archivo de Indias in Seville.
56. Navarro García, *Don José de Gálvez*, 201–4. See also AGI Guadalajara 513, Diario of Hugo Oconor, 87, 1773. O'Conor was apparently appointed with a nudge from his uncle, Alejandro O'Reilly, governor of Louisiana and a distinguished general. O'Conor proved to be an indefatigable and canny opponent of the Apaches. As commander of the northern forces he adopted a strategy of pursuing them with large numbers of troops, including a preponderance of indigenous enemies of the Apaches, especially Opatans, embarking on long, exhausting campaigns. He experienced some success, but not as much as he believed. After his death in 1779, Apache attacks in Sonora and Nueva Vizcaya resumed with a vengeance. For his diaries translated into English, see Donald Cutter, ed., *The Defenses of Northern New Spain: Hugo O'Conor's Report to Teodoro de Croix, July 22, 1777* (Dallas: Southern Methodist University Press, 1994).

57. Navarro García, *Don José de Gálvez*, 203.
58. AGI Guadalajara 586 LC 105-1-24, 1774. Informe del estado de las misiones. Manuscript edited and transcribed by Friar Kieran McCarty.
59. For accounts of Reyes and his activities, see Albert Stagg, *The First Bishop of Sonora: Antonio de los Reyes, O.F.M.* (Tucson: University of Arizona Press, 1976); Almada, *Diccionario*; and Polzer, *Kino Guide*.
60. Peter Gerhard, *The Northern Frontier of New Spain* (Princeton, NJ: Princeton University Press, 1982), 285.
61. Romero (*La privatización*) describes the gradual disappearance of mission lands in favor of private estates.
62. Fernando Ocaranza, *Los franciscanos en las provincias internas de Sonora y Ostimuri* (Published by the author, 1930), 220.

APPENDIX

1. The first page of the folio is undated, but since it refers to the appearance of the Tuapeños and Matapeños in Parral, Nueva Vizcaya, and preceded the findings of the court, the date is probably July 1658. It is difficult to establish that Pedro de Perea loosed his livestock in Tuape by 1638, so the reference to twenty years may be incorrect.
2. A topile was a constable appointed by a priest. Topiles also assisted traditional governors in community matters.
3. In the manuscript here and elsewhere, the narrating voice changes from third person to first person plural to reflect the voices of the Indians.
4. The scribe routinely spells the town "Toapa."
5. A villa is a town recognized as such by the Crown. Pedro de Perea's orders from the Crown included constructing a villa, though its location was left up to him.
6. Alternately, "seek the services of a justice of the peace."
7. Daniel Ángelo Marras (1629–1689) was priest of the mission of Mátape from 1653 to 1681.
8. Here the narrative switches again from the third person to the first person.
9. Lorenzo de Cárdenas (1596–1656) was mission priest at Mátape beginning in 1630. His deposition occurred at least ten years prior to the findings in this case and appears to have been taken in Movas, on the Río Chico, a tributary on the east bank of the Río Yaqui. The scribe consistently refers to Mátape as Matapa.
10. Aibino refers to the ecclesiastical district in which Mátape, Nácori Grande, and Pueblo de Álamos were located. The pre-Columbian settlement of Aibino was the site of the first conversions to Christianity by Jesuits in the Opatería.
11. Probably a reference to mandatory work on mission lands for the benefit of the mission. Under the mission system Indians were required to work two to three days a week on mission fields or other projects. The priests at their discretion could relieve subjects of the requirement.

12. The geography here is most confused. Mátape lies over one hundred kilometers to the southeast of Tuape, roughly twenty-five leagues, not sixteen kilometers (four leagues). It is hard to believe that the Tuapeños would have carried their grain for storage all the way from Mátape to Tuape or vice versa.
13. The places that Father Cárdenas mentions in this section do not appear on any contemporary maps of the Río San Miguel or Mátape regions. Banachari was apparently the site of a mine located not far from Mátape, perhaps south of the Río Sonora west of Puerta del Sol.
14. The present town of Bacoachi lies on the upper Río Sonora more than seventy kilometers to the northeast of Tuape, so Father Cárdenas was in a good position to see a lot of country and observe human activity during his journey there.
15. Father Cárdenas contrasts (inconsistently) *milpas de aguas* and *milpas de verano*. The former term appears to refer to irrigated fields that can produce two crops a year or one crop in a dry year, the latter to rain-fed fields that usually produce only in summertime, or not at all during drought.
16. Priests were accustomed to eating bread made of wheat flour. Their hunger for that grain imparted a high priority to raising wheat on mission fields. Priests often justified the sizeable Indian labor invested in raising the newly introduced crop by proclaiming wheat an alimentary boon to the Indians.
17. Bamboo-like cane grass (*Phragmites australis*).
18. The fencing would have been of thorny brush woven among wooden stakes, based upon a technique imported from Mesoamerica, hence the reference to "Mexican." Wire fences were not available for at least two centuries and barbed wire did not become generally available in Mexico until well into the twentieth century. Prior to the European introduction of livestock, Indians had no reason to build fences except as boundary markers.
19. The dam may have been a natural impoundment, or Spaniards may have dammed the watercourse to form a stock tank. The text does not make it clear.
20. Bacarope does not appear on contemporary maps. Nácori Grande, a few kilometers from Mátape, was a visita of Mátape. Father Cárdenas is giving himself and the Jesuits a pat on the back as well as pointing out the claimed advantages that Europeans in general and Jesuits in particular had bestowed upon the peoples of the Northwest by introducing European grains and fruit trees.
21. Under the mission work obligation, Indians were required to plant wheat for the priests.
22. Ecologists now would deplore these "reclamation" activities, the priest's directives for draining the wetlands so that he and his colleagues could have their wheat. Intentionally eliminating swamps, lagoons, and cienegas undoubtedly led to the overall drying up of the region and was probably a contributing factor to later famines that in turn led to rebellions against the Spanish presence. The wetlands and constantly flowing springs were also prime habitat for game. Draining and drying them led to a decrease in huntable food.

23. Basiroa is a Cáhita-speaking location on the Río Cuchujaqui, which drains from near Álamos, Sonora, into the Río Fuerte in Sinaloa.
24. Pueblo de Álamos, roughly twenty kilometers northwest of Mátape, was a visita of that mission.
25. This may be the earliest archival reference to a place called Sonora. The valley and river were known by the name far earlier (also by the name *Señora*), but this reference indicates that both may have derived their names from the ranchería named here.
26. Throughout much of the document, the scribe refers to don Pedro de Perea as "General," despite his having only the rank of captain. He uses the officer title to distinguish don Pedro de Perea, the father, from don Pedro de Perea, the son.
27. The change from the first person to the third appears to be the result of the scribe's copying of earlier documents and forming one consistent narrative.
28. Pedro Bueno was a Jesuit priest stationed at Mátape, apparently jointly with Daniel Ángelo Marras. Ideally, each mission would house two priests.
29. Such a listing of the indigenous (probably Eudeve) names rarely occurs in documents from the colonial era. The first names are uniformly Spanish, in keeping with colonial laws that mandated each Native to be bestowed with a Spanish name on being baptized.
30. The scribe lumps all Native languages under the term "Mexican," a term usually reserved for Nahuatl, the Aztec language. Eudeve is a Uto-Aztecan language, i.e., distantly related to Nahuatl, which Juan de Loia may have spoken and understood. Just how well he understood Eudeve is not clear.
31. The surprising term *extrajudicial* seems to refer to procedures beyond the normal legal proceedings, such as bribery, extortion, and blackmail. If so, it is an early documentary acknowledgment of the corruption that always plagued the Spanish judicial system.
32. Pedro de Perea had received authorization from the governor of Nueva Vizcaya to call his new territory Nueva Andalucía after Pedro's birthplace in Spain (Almada, *Diccionario*, 494). The name never took hold, probably due to Pedro's early demise and the disfavor into which he fell, and this is a rare case of the use of Pedro's megalomaniac title for Sonora, more than a decade after his death.
33. The document referred to here does not appear in the folio.
34. The most plausible interpretation of this section is that María de Ibarra regretted having made the concordia (accord), since it would leave her with a far smaller estate than what she brought as a dowry to her marriage with Pedro de Perea. Even though she had agreed to vacate Tuape after two years, she now saw the agreement as a commitment made by her husband years earlier that was not to her benefit and was thus null and void. It does not appear plausible that Juan Francisco Maldonado would himself argue that the concordia is null and void, since he calls upon the alcalde mayor to enforce its provisions and expel all of Pedro's heirs and his livestock.

35. This is an apparent reference to the commission, or merced, that Pedro de Perea obtained from the governor of Nueva Vizcaya naming him alcalde mayor of Sonora, with the provision that he found a villa within four years, and so forth. The advocate is arguing that because Pedro did not fulfill the requirements, he had no authority to found the villa or to commandeer lands from the Indians, i.e., whatever authority he might have had expired when the four-year requirement for founding a villa expired, somewhere around the mid-1640s.
36. This may be a reference to a second "commission," or merced, rescinding the first and removing Pedro de Perea as alcalde mayor due to his misdeeds, and replacing him with Juan de Peralta, who would serve as alcalde mayor from 1645 to 1648. This formal notice appeared in the Opatería in early 1645. Pedro de Perea had died the previous autumn and thus never received the notification of his expulsion. While the wording of his discharge appears to be lost, Almada believes that it was issued at least in part due to Pedro's failure to comply with the initial requirements of the commission. Pedro seems to have anticipated his ouster and appointed an interim replacement, who, in turn, was ousted when Juan de Peralta was named.
37. Meaning the second merced, which vacated the first.

Glossary

convoco: insurrectionary or subversive meeting of Natives; often a clandestine setting for the delivery of tlátoles

fiscal: functionary of a mission, usually assistant to the traditional Native governor, perhaps subordinate to a topile

gobernador: traditional governor; in colonial Sonora, an Indian official, usually appointed by a mission priest, called upon to represent his people and to carry out orders of the priests or other Spanish officials. Priests and military officers bestowed ceremonial canes of office upon the governors.

milpa: cornfield, often including beans and squash

Opatans: indigenous people of northeastern Sonora linked by the affinity of their languages

Opatería: land of the Opatans, the northeast quadrant of the present state of Sonora

tlátole: (Náhuatl) harangue; insurrectionary message; a call to arms

topile: functionary of a mission, usually assistant to the traditional governor

vecino: a Spanish settler, often provided by the Crown with land for farming or raising cattle

References

AGI—Archivo General de Indias, Seville.
AGN—Archivo General de la Nación, Mexico City.
AHES—Archivo Histórico del Estado de Sonora.
AHH—Archivo Histórico de Hacienda, Mexico City.
AHP—Archivo Histórico de Parral, Chihuahua.

Alegre, Francisco Javier. 1841–1842. *La historia de la compañía de Jesús en Nueva España.* Vols. 2–3. Mexico City: Impresa J. M. Lara.

Almada, Francisco. 1990. *Diccionario de historia, geografía, y biografía sonorenses.* Hermosillo, Mexico: Gobierno del Estado de Sonora.

Bandelier, Adolph. 1890–1892. *Final Report of Investigations Among the Indians of the Southwestern United States, 1880–1885.* Archaeological Institute of America Papers, American Series 3. Cambridge, MA: Archaeological Institute of America.

Bannon, John. 1955. *The Mission Frontier in Sonora, 1620–1687.* Saint Louis: Catholic Historical Society.

Barlow, R. H., transcriber. 1947. *La relación de Sahuaripa de 1778.* Mexico City: Memorias de la Academia Mexicana de la Historia, Tomo 6-N. 1:60–89.

Barnes, Thomas, Thomas Naylor, and Charles Polzer. 1981. *Northern New Spain: A Research Guide.* Tucson: University of Arizona Press.

Bolton, Herbert E. 1984. *Rim of Christendom: A Biography of Eusebio Francisco Kino, Pacific Coast Pioneer.* Tucson: University of Arizona Press.

Borrero Silva, María Valle de. 2008. "La administración de Sonora: Los alcaldes mayores en la primera mitad del siglo XVIII." *Temas Americanistas* 21:48–65.

Brenneman, Dale. 2004. "Climate of Rebellion: The Relationship Between Climate Variability and Indigenous Uprisings in Mid-Eighteenth-Century Sonora." PhD diss., University of Arizona.

Burrus, Ernest. 1971. *Kino and Manje, Explorers of Sonora and Arizona.* Saint Louis: Jesuit Historical Institute.

Burrus, Ernest, and Felix Zubillaga, eds. 1982. *Misiones mexicanas de la Compañía de Jesús, 1618–1745.* Madrid: Ediciones José Porrua Turanza.

Cañas, Cristóbal. 1730. *Estado de la Provincia de Sonora, julio de 1730.* Documentos para la historia de México, 3a serie, 1835–1857. Transcribed, with notes by Flavio Molina Molina, 1978. Hermosillo, Mexico: Diócesis de Sonora.

Carneiro de Cunha, Manuel. 1985. "Silences of the Law: Customary Law and Positive Law on the Manumission of Slaves in 19th Century Brazil." *History and Anthropology* 1:427–43.

Crosby, Harry. 1994. *Antigua California: Mission and Colony on the Peninsular Frontier, 1697–1768*. Albuquerque: University of New Mexico Press.

Cutter, Donald, ed. 1994. *The Defenses of Northern New Spain: Hugo O'Conor's Report to Teodoro de Croix, July 22, 1777*. Dallas: Southern Methodist University Press.

Decorme, Gerard. 1941. *La obra de los jesuitas mexicanos durante la época colonial, 1552–1767*. Vol. 2. Mexico City: José Porrua e hijos.

Deeds, Susan. 1981. "Rendering unto Caesar: The Secularization of Jesuit Missions in Mid-Eighteenth-Century Durango." PhD diss., University of Arizona.

———. 2003. *Defiance and Deference in Mexico's Colonial North: Indians Under Spanish Rule in Nueva Vizcaya*. Austin: University of Texas Press.

de la Torre Curiel, José Refugio. 2005. "Conquering the Frontier: Contests for Religion, Survival, and Profits in Northwestern Mexico, 1768–1855." PhD diss., University of California at Berkeley. UMI Microfilm 321-0558.

———. 2010. "Patriotas en conflicto: Rebeliones, disputas por tierras y sospechas de infidencia entre los Ópatas de Sonora a principios del siglo XIX." In *Los grupos nativos del septentrión novohispano ante la independencia de México, 1810–1847*. Martha Ortega Soto, Danna Legin Rojo, and María Estela Báez-Villaseñor, coordinadoras, 201–33. Mexico City: Korph Lithograpikz Editorial.

Donohue, John Augustine. 1969. *After Kino: Jesuit Missions in Northwestern New Spain, 1711–1767*. Saint Louis: Jesuit Historical Institute.

Doolittle, William. 1988. *Pre-Hispanic Occupance in the Valley of Sonora, Mexico: Archaeological Confirmation of Early Spanish Reports*. Tucson: University of Arizona Press.

Dunnigan, Timothy. 1983. "Lower Pima." In *Handbook of North American Indians*, edited by Alfonso Ortiz, 10:217–29. Washington, D.C.: Smithsonian Institution.

Durán, Fray Diego. 1994. *The History of the Indies of New Spain*. Norman: University of Oklahoma Press.

Ebright, Malcolm, and Rick Hendricks. 2006. *The Witches of Abiquiu*. Albuquerque: University of New Mexico Press.

Farriss, Nancy. 1984. *Maya Society Under Colonial Rule*. Princeton, NJ: Princeton University Press.

Felger, Richard, and Mary Beck Moser. 1985. *People of the Desert and Sea*. Tucson: University of Arizona Press.

Flint, Richard. 2002. *Great Cruelties Have Been Reported: The 1544 Investigation of the Coronado Expedition*. Dallas: Southern Methodist University Press.

Fontana, Bernard. 1983. "History of the Papago." In *Handbook of North American Indians*, edited by Alfonso Ortiz, 10:137–38. Washington, D.C.: Smithsonian Institution.

Forbes, Jack. 1957. "The Janos, Jocomes, Mansos and Sumas Indians." *New Mexico Historical Review* 32:319–34.

Garate, Donald. 2003. *Juan Bautista de Anza: Basque Explorer in the New World, 1693-1740*. Reno: University of Nevada Press.

García Martínez, Bernardo. 2000. "La creación de Nueva España." In *Historia general de México*, 237-306. Mexico City: El Colegio de México.

Gerhard, Peter. 1982. *The Northern Frontier of New Spain*. Princeton, NJ: Princeton University Press.

Gómez Canedo, Lino. 1977. *Evangelización y conquista: Experiencia franciscana en hispanoamérica*. Mexico City: Editor Porrúa.

Greenleaf, Richard. 1969. *Mexican Inquisition of the Sixteenth Century*. Albuquerque: University of New Mexico Press.

Hammond, George, and Agapito Rey. 1940. *Narratives of the Coronado Expedition, 1540-1542*. Albuquerque: University of New Mexico Press.

Hastings, J. Rodney. 1961. "People of Reason and Others: The Colonization of Sonora to 1767." *Arizona and the West* 3:321-40.

Hastings, J. Rodney, and Raymond Turner. 1965. *The Changing Mile*. Tucson: University of Arizona Press.

Hinton, Thomas. 1959. *A Survey of Indian Assimilation in Eastern Sonora*. Anthropological Paper 4. Tucson: University of Arizona Press.

Historia general de México. 2000. Mexico City: El Colegio de México.

Historia general de Sonora. 1985. Vol. 2. Sergio Calderón Valdés, coordinator. Hermosillo, Mexico: Gobierno del Estado de Sonora.

Hrdlička, Aleš. 1904. "Notes on Indians of Sonora, México." *American Anthropologist* 6:51-89.

Johnson, Jean. 1950. *The Ópata: An Inland Tribe of Sonora*. Albuquerque: University of New Mexico Press.

Jones, Oakah. 1988. *Nueva Vizcaya: Heartland of the Spanish Frontier*. Albuquerque: University of New Mexico Press.

———. 1996. *Los Paisanos: Spanish Settlers on the Northern Frontier of New Spain*. Norman: University of Oklahoma Press.

Kessell, John. 1976. *Friars, Soldiers, and Reformers: Hispanic Arizona and the Sonora Mission Frontier, 1767-1856*. Tucson: University of Arizona Press.

———. 2008. *Pueblos, Spaniards, and the Kingdom of New Mexico*. Norman: University of Oklahoma Press.

La Fora, Nicolas de. 1939. *Relación del viaje que hizo a los presidios internos situados en la frontera de la America septentrional*. Mexico City: Editorial Pedro Robredo.

LeBlanc, Steven. 1999. *Prehistoric Warfare in the American Southwest*. Salt Lake City: University of Utah Press.

Lockart, Bill. 1997. "Prehistoric Confusion: A Cultural Comparison of Manso, Suma, and Jumano Indians of the El Paso del Norte." *Journal of the Southwest* 39:113-49.

Manje, Juan Matheo. 1954. *Luz de tierra incógnita*. Vol. 2. Tucson: Arizona Silhouettes.

McCarty, Kieran. 1973. "Franciscan Beginnings on the Arizona-Sonora Desert, 1767-1770." PhD diss., Catholic University of America.

―――. 1981. *A Spanish Frontier in the Enlightened Age: Franciscan Beginnings in Sonora and Arizona, 1767-1770*. Washington, D.C.: Academy of American Franciscan History.
Merrill, William. 1988. *Rarámuri Souls: Knowledge and Process in Northern Mexico*. Washington, D.C.: Smithsonian Institution Press.
Miller, Wick. 1983. "Uto-Aztecan Languages." In *Handbook of North American Indians*, edited by Alfonso Ortiz, 10:113-24. Washington, D.C.: Smithsonian Institution.
Mirafuentes Galván, José Luis. 2001. "Los maleficios de Don Marcos Humuta." *Estudios de historia novohispana* 25:117-54.
Molina Molina, Flavio, transcriber. 1978. *Estado de la Provincia de Sonora, julio de 1730*, by Cristóbal Cañas, 1730. Documents para la historia de México, 3a serie, 1835-1857. Hermosillo, Mexico: Diócesis de Sonora.
Moser, Mary Beck, and Stephen Marlett. 2005. *Comcáac quih yaza quih hant ihíp hac: Diccionario Seri-Español-Inglés*. Mexico City: Plaza y Valdés Editores.
Navarro García, Luis. 1964. *Don José de Gálvez y la comandancia general en las provincias internas*. Seville, Spain: Escuela de Estudios Hispano-Americanos de Sevilla.
―――. 1966. *La sublevación del Yaqui de 1740*. Seville, Spain: Escuela de Estudios Hispano-Americanos de Sevilla.
―――. 1967. *Sonora y Sinaloa en el siglo XVII*. Seville, Spain: Escuela de Estudios Hispano-Americanos de Sevilla.
Nentvig, Juan. (1764) 1977. *Rudo ensayo: Descripción geográfica, natural y curiosa de la provincia de Sonora*. Mexico City: Instituto Nacional de Antropología e Historia.
Norton, Mary Beth. 2002. *In the Devil's Snare: The Salem Witchcraft Crisis of 1692*. New York: Alfred A. Knopf.
Noyes, Stanley. 1993. *Los Comanches: The Horse People, 1751-1845*. Albuquerque: University of New Mexico Press.
Nuñez, A. 1777. "Carta edificante histórico-curiosa, escrita desde la misión de Santa María de Baserac en los fines de Sonora." Special collections, University of Arizona Library.
Obregón, Baltasar. 1997. *Historia de los descubrimientos de Nueva España*. Seville, Spain: Ediciones Alfar.
Ocaranza, Fernando. 1933. *Los franciscanos en las provincias internas de Sonora y Ostimuri*. Published by the author.
Ortega Noriega, Sergio. 1993. "El sistema de misiones jesuíticas, 1591-1699." In *Tres siglos de historia sonorense (1530-1830)*, edited by S. Ortega Noriega and Ignacio de Río, 41-94. Mexico City: Instituto de Investigaciones Históricas, UNAM.
Pennington, Campbell, ed. 1975. *Vocabulario en la lengua névome*. Salt Lake City: University of Utah Press.
―――. 1982. "Cultura de los eudeve del noroeste de México." *Noroeste de México* 6:9-34. A publication of the Instituto Nacional de Antropología e Historia, Secretaría de Educación Pública.
Pérez de Ribas, Andrés. (1645) 1999. *History of the Triumphs of Our Holy Faith Amongst*

the Most Barbarous and Fierce Peoples of the New World. Translated and edited by Daniel Reff, Maureen Ahern, and Richard Danford. Tucson: University of Arizona Press.

Pfefferkorn, Ignaz. 1989. *Sonora: A Description of the Province*. Translated and annotated by Theodore E. Treutlein. Tucson: University of Arizona Press.

Polzer, Charles. 1972a. "The Franciscan Entrada into Sonora 1645–1652: A Jesuit Chronicle." *Arizona and the West* 14:263–78.

———. 1972b. "The Evolution of the Jesuit Mission System in Northwestern New Spain 1600–1767." PhD diss. 444, University of Arizona.

———. 1982. *Kino Guide II: His Missions—His Monuments*. Tucson: Southwestern Mission Research Center.

Pradeau, Alberto Francisco, and Ernest Burrus. 1965. "Historia de las misiones sonorenses y sus pueblos de visita." Doc. ined. Special collections, University of Arizona Library.

Quezada, Noemí. 1991. "The Inquisition's Punishment of Curanderos." In *Cultural Encounters: The Impact of the Inquisition in Spain and the New World*, edited by M. E. Perry and A. J. Cruz. Berkeley: University of California Press.

Radding, Cynthia. 1995. *Entre el desierto y la sierra: Las naciones O'odham y Teguima de Sonora, 1530–1840*. Mexico City: Instituto Nacional Indigenista.

———. 1997. *Wandering Peoples: Colonialism, Ethnic Spaces, and Ecological Frontiers in Northwestern Mexico, 1700–1850*. Durham, NC: Duke University Press.

Recopilación de Leyes de los Reinos de las Indias. (1681) 1980. (The Indian cause in the Spanish laws of the Indies.) Edited by S. Lyman Tyler. Salt Lake City: University of Utah, American West Center.

Reff, Daniel. 1991. *Disease, Depopulation, and Culture Changes in Northwestern New Spain, 1518–1764*. Salt Lake City: University of Utah Press.

Reff, Daniel, Maureen Ahern, and Richard Danford, trans. and eds. 1999. *History of the Triumphs of Our Holy Faith Amongst the Most Barbarous and Fierce Peoples of the New World*, by Andrés Pérez de Ribas, 1645. Tucson: University of Arizona Press.

Reis, João José. 1993. *Slave Rebellion in Brazil*. Baltimore: Johns Hopkins University Press.

Restall, Matthew. 2003. *Seven Myths of the Spanish Conquest*. Oxford: Oxford University Press.

Riley, Carroll. 2005. *Becoming Aztlán: Mesoamerican Influences in the Greater Southwest, AD 1200–1500*. Salt Lake City: University of Utah Press.

Roca, Paul. 1967. *The Paths of the Padres Through Sonora*. Tucson: Arizona Pioneers' Historical Society.

Rodríguez Gallardo, José. 1750. "Informe de Sinaloa y Sonora, August 12, 1750." MS 218. Special collections, University of Arizona Library.

Romero, Saúl Gerónimo. 1991. *De las misiones a los ranchos y haciendas: La privatización de la tenencia de la tierra en Sonora, 1740–1860*. Hermosillo, Mexico: Gobierno del Estado de Sonora.

Sauer, Carl. 1932. *Road to Cíbola*. Ibero-American 3. Berkeley: University of California Press.
———. 1935. *Aboriginal Population of Northwestern Mexico*. Ibero-American 10. Berkeley: University of California Press.
Shaul, David, and Jane Hill. 1998. "Tepimans, Yumans, and other Hohokam." *American Antiquity* 63:375–96.
Sheridan, Thomas. 1999. *Empire of Sand: The Seri Indians and the Struggle for Spanish Sonora, 1645–1803*. Tucson: University Arizona Press.
Smith, Fay Jackson. 1993. *Captain of the Phantom Presidio*. Spokane, WA: Arthur H. Clark.
Spicer, Edward. 1962. *Cycles of Conquest*. Tucson: University of Arizona Press.
———. 1980. *The Yaquis: A Cultural History*. Tucson: University of Arizona Press.
Stagg, Albert. 1976. *The First Bishop of Sonora: Antonio de los Reyes, O.F.M.* Tucson: University of Arizona Press.
Tamarón y Romeral, Pedro. 1937. *Demostración del vastísimo obispado de la Nueva Vizcaya—1765*. Introduction by Vito Alessio Robles. Mexico City: Editores Porrúa e hijos.
Thomas, Hugh. 1993. *Conquest: Montezuma, Cortés, and the Fall of Old Mexico*. New York: Simon and Schuster.
Tiller, Veronica. 1980. "Jicarilla Apache." In *Handbook of North American Indians*, edited by Alfonso Ortiz, 10:447–50. Washington D.C.: Smithsonian Institution.
Weber, David J. 1992. *The Spanish Frontier in North America*. New Haven, CT: Yale University Press.
———, ed. 1999. *What Caused the Pueblo Revolt of 1680?* New York: Bedford/St. Martin's Press.
West, Robert. 1993. *Sonora: Its Geographical Personality*. Austin: University of Texas Press.
Wilcox, David. 1986. "The Tepiman Connection: A Model of Mesoamerican-Southwestern Interaction." In *Ripples in the Chichimec Sea: New Considerations of Southwestern-Mesoamerican Interactions*, edited by Frances Joan Mathien and Randall H. McGuire. Carbondale: Southern Illinois University Press.
Yetman, David. 2000. "*Ejidos*, Land Sales, and Free Trade in Northwest Mexico: Will Globalization Affect the Commons?" *Journal of American Studies* 41(2/3): 211–34.
———. 2010. *The Ópatas: In Search of a Sonoran People*. Tucson: University of Arizona Press.
Zambrano, Francisco. 1961. *Diccionario bio-bibliográfico de la Compañía de Jesús en México*. Vol. 4. Mexico City: Editorial Jus.
Zapata, Juan Ortiz. 1678. "Relación de 1678." Archivo Histórico de Hacienda (Mexico City). Leg. 26. Also found in Documentos para la historia de México, Tercera Serie.

Index

Achero, Juan, 125, 126
Aconchi, 55, 56, 60, 64, 135, 180
Agramont y Arce, Francisco, 76–78
Aguaje, 149–50
Akimel O'odham, 14
Alarreta, Diego de, 211, 227–28
alcalde mayor, 6, 10, 12, 20, 31, 35, 41–42, 48–49, 55, 60, 81, 100, 101, 109, 121, 132, 145, 148, 149, 156, 161, 166, 172, 174, 177, 179, 182, 184, 189–92, 211, 222, 234, 235, 238
Alejo, 148, 153, 162
Alesa, Marcos de, 109
Almagro, Andrés de, 113
Álvarez y Tuñón, Alcalde Mayor, 20, 190–93, 255
ambas majestades, conflict of, 4, 11–12
Ángelo, Daniel. *See* Marras, Padre Daniel Ángelo
Apaches, 14, 22, 24, 56, 75, 80, 82, 85, 91, 95, 108, 120–21, 232, 233, 242, 246, 257–60; attacks on Spaniards by, 22, 23, 187, 196, 197, 199, 202, 203–8
Apresta, Domingo de, 227
Archivo de Indias, Sevilla, 2
Argüelles, Andrés de, 193
Arituava, 197
Arivechi, 147, 150, 248, 252, 253
Arizona, 5, 14, 22, 49, 93, 127, 231
Arizpe, 15, 17, 29, 33, 48, 55–59, 61–62, 64, 66, 68–70, 81, 89, 108, 118, 138, 209, 240
Arriaga, Julián, 199–200, 207, 258
Arroyo Sahuaripa, 147

Atondo, Governor Ysidro, 79–80, 116
Ayeta, Fray Francisco de, 74–78
Aztecs, 3, 69, 242

Babico, 216
Bacadéhuachi, 20, 97–103, 106–7, 111, 120, 122, 127, 131, 132, 140, 144–65, 174, 244–45, 252
Bacanora, 154, 252
Bacanuchi, 147, 197, 240, 251
Bacarope, 217, 218
Bacerac (Santa María), 19, 82, 93, 104, 106, 108, 110, 121, 124–37, 245, 246, 248–49
Bacoachi (Bacobatzi), 58, 72, 82–91, 94–95, 101, 118, 175, 216, 244, 262
Bacobichi, 93, 94, 108, 118, 244
Baduqui, Francisco, 94–95
Baduqui, Miguel, 129–35
Bagueri, Juan, 105
Ballesteros, Pedro de, 183, 186–87, 192
Bamocho, 82
Banachari, 36, 37, 50, 215–17, 262
Banámichi, 32, 34, 35, 38, 55, 64, 237
Banasuri, 93, 98, 109–10, 120, 244
Bandelier, Adolph, 16, 232
Banichuri. *See* Banasuri
Bannon, John, S. J., 168–69
Baroyeca, 156
Barraiersa, Ignacio de, 43, 214–15, 223, 226
Basiroa, 32, 49, 218–20, 263
Batuc, 15, 39, 64–65, 152, 252–53
Baviácora, 55, 58, 63, 64, 69, 241; traditional governor of, 63
Bavispe (San Miguel), 82, 93–97, 100,

102, 104, 106–8, 110, 111, 120–21, 127–29, 245, 248
Bezerra Nieto, Antonio, 12–13, 146, 254
Bolton, Herbert, 188
Bourbon reforms, 199
Bucareli, Viceroy Antonio, 200, 207
Buchibacuachi, 58, 63–66, 70, 241
Bueno, Padre Pedro, 221

Cabeza de Vaca, Álvar Núñez, 15, 234
Cadereita, Governor, 31
Cáhita (language group), 8, 128, 230, 245, 263
Caiso, Juan, 88, 118
Cajeme (municipality and Yaqui warrior), 25
California, 79
Canal, Padre Gerónimo de, 17, 48, 49, 54–71, 145, 235, 238–39; defeated in debate by Indian, 57; threatened by Indians, 58
Canals, Fray Antonio, 198, 200, 201, 206
Cananea, 82
Canari, Lucas, 93, 96, 102, 105–6, 120
Cañas, Padre Cristóbal, 56, 135, 240, 247
Cárdenas, Padre Lorenzo de, 36, 37, 39–42, 44–45, 50, 52, 180, 214, 215, 217, 238, 261–62
Carretas, 96, 108, 121, 130
Casanova y Ami, Miguel de, 61
Casas Grandes, 74–75, 91
Castaño, Padre Bartolomé, 55, 56
Celeste, Padre Carlos, 118
Cerro Prieto, 203, 204
Charles III, King, 199
chichimec, 106
Chiguari, Christóbal, 102, 105
Chihuahua, 12, 22, 26, 43, 56, 74, 77, 80, 91, 96, 102, 120, 125–28, 130, 133, 134, 147, 157–58, 172, 185, 189, 192–93, 199, 200–201, 206, 208, 210, 248, 252, 257, 258, 266
Chinapa, 63–65, 67, 69, 71, 72, 81–91, 93–95, 100, 108–9, 118
Chinarras, 80

chupando (ritual smoking), 85, 86, 91, 95, 98, 101, 108–10, 118, 197, 244
Cieneguilla, 197–98, 208, 256
Ciudad Obregón, Sonora, 25
Cocoba, Cristóbal, 99–100
Cocomaques, 13
colonos, 32, 41
Comanches, 202
Comcáac. *See* Seris
Comprehensive Ordinances of 1573, 3
Conchos, 10, 14–15, 22, 72, 80, 102, 106, 120, 126, 202, 246
concordia (legal agreement), 45–46, 49, 213–15, 220, 224–25, 227–28, 263
Conde de Peredes, Viceroy, 75
conflicts among Indians, 7, 202
convoco, 81, 86, 89, 91–92, 96, 97, 99, 100, 104, 108, 112–13, 117, 120, 263
Corazones, founded by Coronado, 28
Córdoba, Governor. *See* Fernández de Córdoba, Governor Juan
Corodéhuachi, 22, 127, 233
Coronado Expedition, 5, 11, 28, 64
Cortés, Hernán, 69
Coto, Francisco, 39, 42, 44–45, 50, 211, 215, 222–23, 226–27
Covarrubias, Padre Joseph de, 99, 102
Croix, Marquis de, 200, 205–6
Crown (king), Spanish: backing Pedro de Perea, 27; conflicting motives of, 27; effects of Pueblo Rebellion on, 76; imposition of taxes and tithes, 29, 47; promotion of mining, 10; ten-year limit on missions, 29; value of settlers to, 2, 27
Cuchuta, 82, 109, 110, 111, 115, 205
Cucubazunuchi, 55, 57, 239–40
Cucuribasca, 58, 63–67, 69, 70, 82, 241
Cucurpe, 15, 91, 196–98, 201, 257
Cuervo y Valdez, Francisco, 81, 100–121; applying torture, 103; ordering executions, 105
Culiacán, Sinaloa, 5
Cumpas, 35, 63, 64, 66, 86, 127, 133, 149, 160, 169–71, 175–76, 179–82, 184–89

Cuquiárichi, 82–84, 86–87, 90–95, 98, 101, 104, 108–11, 115, 118, 244
curanderos, 19, 124, 133, 135–40, 247–48, 250
curandismo. See curanderos

Dávila, Padre Luis, 99
Dávila y Pacheco, Governor Enrique, 26, 28, 45, 210–11, 227
de Abajo, Miguel, 129, 131, 133
de la Cruz, Mateo, 125, 137
de la Torre, Nicolás, 132
demanda (legal challenge), 41
de Rojas, Padre Carlos, 138
Dicastillo, Gregorio López, 50–51, 172
Dimara, Pablo, 82–86, 88–89, 94, 120
Dimare, 65–66
Dimigra, Antonio, 83–85
disease: effect on Natives of Northwest Mexico, 7–9
Doheme (Eudeve), 15
Domínguez, Captain Acensio, 145–67, 173
Dominican Order, 123
Douglas, Arizona, 22, 127
drought, 21, 36, 175, 179, 181, 184, 188–89, 255
Duque de Linares, Viceroy, 191, 193
Duqui, Joseph, 99
Durango, 6, 12, 23, 30, 198–99, 201, 207, 231; governor of, 23, 199
Duro, Fray Marcos, 128

ecclesiastical immunity, 109
Ecocore, 65–66
El Fuerte Presidio, Sinaloa, 29, 59, 116
Elizondo, Domingo, 197, 204–7, 256
El Paso, 74, 75, 77
Escorza, Juan Bautista, 76, 78–79, 90, 92, 95, 97–104, 106–8, 111, 116, 119; orders executions of Opatans, 99–102, 116
Estrella, Padre Antonio, 104–5
Eudeve(s), 3, 9, 13, 15, 27, 29, 37, 41, 52, 64, 80, 120, 237, 240, 248, 257; as a creole language, 15; use of poisoned arrows, 29
Ezquerr, Blás, 145, 156–60, 162, 251

Fain de Mendizábel, Pedro, 187–88
Farris, Nancy, 46
Fayni, Joseph, 23, 198–201, 206–7, 257–58
Féliz, Sebastián, 159–60
Fernández de Córdoba, Governor Juan, 126–27, 133–34, 146–47, 150–57, 159–62, 165–66, 247
Figueroa, Padre Gerónimo, 33
Figueroa, Salvador de, 183, 186–87
Franciscans, 1, 2, 5, 9, 10, 23–24, 28–29, 33–34, 41, 52, 55, 58, 64, 68, 73, 78–79, 121, 128, 138, 196, 198, 200–202, 209, 230, 235, 237–43, 251; accept invitation of Pedro de Perea to Sonora, 33, 41, 58; conflict with Jesuits in Sonora, 33–34, 68; killed in Pueblo Rebellion, 73, 79
frijolar, 21, 40, 176
Fronteras, 22, 83, 127, 129, 133, 167, 190, 197, 205, 233, 255

Gálvez, José de, 23, 199–202, 206–7, 233, 257–58; campaign against rebellious Indians, 23, 199–202; reforms of, 23
Gándara, Juan, 45–46
García, Padre Cristóbal, 68
García, Simón, 147–67; possessions listed, 157–58
García de la Serna, Domingo, 150
García de Salcedo, Jose, 51
Gila River, 16, 201
González, Father Manuel, 144
governor, traditional Indian, 63, 85, 91, 93, 96, 98, 100, 102, 105–6, 107, 110, 120, 125–28, 133–36, 151, 155, 163, 182, 211, 212, 249, 261
Grijalva, Bernardo, 170, 177–79, 183, 190
Grijalva, Juan, 170–73, 177, 179, 180–85, 192, 232, 254
Guachinera (San Juan), 82, 86, 93, 99–106, 108–11, 120, 127, 129, 131, 245, 248

Guadalajara, 182, 201; Audiencia of, 50–51, 166, 170
Guásavas (Guásabas, Huásabas), 78, 89, 90–91, 99–100, 102, 108, 112–13, 127, 148–49, 248
Guaymas, 14, 157
Guerrero, Padre Caitano, 20
Guerrero Villaseca, Padre Miguel, 20, 122, 140, 144–54, 161, 164, 169
Gulf of California, 14
Gutiérrez de la Cruz, Juan, 104
Guzmán, Diego de, 5
Guzmán, Nuño de, 5

Havana, 141, 166, 199
hechiceros (sorcerers), 19, 123–25, 130–33, 135, 136, 138
Hermosillo, 149–50, 203–4
Hia'Ched O'odham, 13
Hímeris, 13, 56, 60, 64, 68, 195, 241
History of the Triumphs of Our Holy Faith, 123
Hoguez y San Martín, Manuel (de), 148–49, 192
Hohokams, 16
Hrdlička, Aleš, 46
Huásabas. *See* Guásavas
Humuta, Marcos, 19, 128–38
Hurdaide, Captain Martínez de, 7–9, 29, 30, 70, 235; military expeditions of, 8–9, 29
Huter, Padre Juan de, 67–68

Ibarra, Andrea de, 43
Ibarra, Josefa de, 40, 43, 45
Ibarra, María de, 35, 38, 43, 212–13, 220, 221–24, 227–28, 263
Indians: abused by settlers, 167–94; arming of, 63–64; attacks on Spaniards, 22; conflicts among, 7; effect of livestock on, 21; mission labor requirement, 143; punishments for failure to attend Mass, 144, 169; vulnerability to drought, 21
Inquisition, 124

inspections, Spanish government, 12
irrigation, 37, 38
Isleta Pueblo, 74, 77

Jalisco, 6
Janos (Indians), 10, 14, 15, 22, 56, 72, 77, 80, 82, 85–86, 95–97, 108, 120–21, 202, 232, 237, 243, 246
Janos (settlement, presidio), 12, 121, 146, 165
Januske, Padre Daniel, 21, 168–94, 195, 209, 232, 236, 238, 253–55
Jaure, Javier, 89, 90, 120
Javier, 81–83, 87, 98, 244
Jesuits, 1–13, 18–24, 28–42, 44–59, 67–72, 79, 101, 104–5, 109, 122–25, 128–29, 135–38, 141–42, 145–47, 152–55, 166, 168–69, 172–73, 178, 181, 185, 188–90, 194, 196, 200–202, 209, 230, 232, 235, 238, 239, 243, 244–45, 247–51, 258; as advocates for Indians, 40–41; conflict with Franciscans in Sonora, 33–34, 41; conflicts with miners, 48, 50–51, 143, 168; conflicts with settlers, 50, 168, 172; conflicts with soldiers, 101, 145–67; doctrines, 142; in Durango, 6; expulsion of, 23–24, 51–52, 196, 200; goals of in Mexico's Northwest, 29; importance of Indians to, 2; as legal advisors to Indians of Tuape, 27–53; as merchants, 48, 50; as missionaries to Northwest Mexico, 3–10; need for Indian labor, 11; Order as an instrument of the Crown, 4, 28, 42; punishment of Indians, 169; resistance from Natives to, 6; and sorcerers, 122–125, 135–36; utopian goals of, 29; *visitador*, 11
Jocomes, 10, 14, 15, 22, 56, 72, 80, 82, 86, 95–97, 108, 120–21
joint-stock company, 206
Jojoí, Ignacio, 91–94, 109–10, 120
Jovas, 9, 13, 14, 16, 97, 151–56, 163–66, 231, 252, 253
Jumanos, 10

Jumari, Gerónimo, 89, 113–14
Juraque, Juan, 112–14
Juras, Ignacio, 86, 88
justicias (judges), 20

Kino, Padre Eusebio, 3, 144–47, 155, 173, 188–89, 251

ladino, 81. *See also* Javier
La Fora, Nicolás de, 45
Laws of the Indies (*Recopilación*), 24, 31, 32, 37, 41, 115, 141–42, 144, 148, 174, 230, 234, 235, 250–51; prohibitions against wandering, 143; regulations applied to Indians, 141–42, 148; ten-year grace period for conversion, 4, 10, 32, 142
Lazo de la Vega, Captain Simón, 17, 35, 48, 59–71, 82, 234, 240–41
Leal, Padre Antonio, 109
Lira, Juan de, 99
livestock, effect on Indians of, 12, 16, 21, 40, 47, 111–12, 168–95; destruction of springs, 179–81; destruction of crops in Tuape, 34, 38, 40
Loaisa, Padre Pedro Baltasar de, 222
Loia, Juan de, 222
López de Trujillo, Juan, 158
Luis of Sáric, 203

Magdalena, Sonora, 33
Maiboca, Juan, 99, 102
Maicoba, 161, 164, 203
Maldonado, Juan Franco, 39–40, 44, 222–23, 225–26, 263
Malleus Maleficarum, 123
manantial, 35
Manje, Juan Mateo, 122, 144–45, 147, 155, 166, 173–74, 178, 232
Manso, Fray Tomás, 128
Mansos, 10
manuscripts, challenges in reading, 43–44
Marras, Padre Daniel Ángelo, 37, 39–40, 42, 50–51, 213–14, 237, 239, 261, 263

Mass: attendance required of Indians, 18
Mátape, 10, 15, 20, 29, 36–43, 48, 50, 52, 127, 210–12, 214–18, 220, 222–24; as regional economic center, 42, 48, 50
mayordomo, 20
Mayos, 6–8, 24, 29, 128, 150, 201–3, 230–31, 234, 242; language of, 14, 127
Méndez, Father Pedro de, 8
mercedes (land grants), 18
Meresichi, 46
Mexico, conquest of, 69
Mexico City, 48, 49, 55, 59, 77, 166, 204, 206
milpa, 21, 34, 39, 88, 99, 112, 173–74, 176, 181, 183, 186–87, 193, 208, 212, 216, 262, 265
miners, 11, 62; accusations against Jesuits, 11; need for Indian labor, 11–12, 48, 143, 147; attracted to Opatería, 17
mines: attraction to Indians, 20, 143; disruptions to missions, 21; importance to the Crown, 10; labor shortages in, 143, 147; in New Spain, 10, 48; regulations of, 10
mining. *See* mines
missions, 6, 9–12, 15, 18–19, 21, 23–24, 26, 28, 36, 37, 47–48, 50, 53, 54, 64, 66, 68–70, 72, 118, 121–22, 127, 138, 140, 142–43, 146–48, 153–54, 168, 172–74, 176, 188–89, 194, 196–98, 200–201, 208–9, 230, 235, 237, 239, 243, 244, 251, 253; demise of, 23, 53
Mixtecos, 208
Moctezuma, 25, 133, 148–49, 169
Molarja, Padre Ignacio, 58, 59, 62, 66, 71, 209, 240
Montefrío, Padre Egidio de, 66
Montesclaros (Fort), 5, 7–8
Montoya, Pedro de, 87, 90, 94–96
Mora, Padre Francisco Xavier, 177–78
Morales, Antonio, 132
Moreno, Bérnave Felizardo, 114–15
Moreno, Juan, 129, 148
Moreno, Padre from Moctezuma, 25

Mountain Pimas, 13, 22, 161, 165, 231, 253, 257
Movas, Sonora, 39, 43, 220, 231, 157, 220, 231, 257, 261
Muguaqui, 110
Munguía de Villela, Juan, 38, 40, 42–43, 45, 49, 212, 215, 223, 227, 238

Nacámeri, 64, 157, 197, 231
Nacatóbari, 62, 65, 76, 78, 95
nacimiento (spring), 35
Nácori Chico, 97, 103, 106–7, 144–45, 153, 155, 217, 252, 261
Nacozari, 17, 18, 72, 82–83, 86, 88, 90, 108, 116, 175, 184, 233, 259, 260
Navarro García, Luis, 2, 39, 120, 233, 235–36, 243–45, 253, 257–59
Nébomes, 9, 13, 15–16, 29, 70, 197, 230–31, 235, 247, 250, 257–58
Necuas, 80, 243
New Mexico, 3, 9, 18, 22, 28, 30–33, 42, 47–49, 55, 61, 69, 72–81, 91–92, 98, 111, 116, 120, 124, 128, 166, 175, 188, 199–200, 206
New Spain, 23, 30, 52, 69, 73, 166
Nombre de Diós, ranch, 32, 35, 38, 39, 43, 45, 212, 218, 221–24, 227, 228
noragua, 110
Nueva Andalucía, 31, 34, 223, 263
Nueva Vizcaya, 12, 26, 30, 33, 69, 72, 76–77, 79, 80, 124, 126, 159, 164, 174, 189, 191, 194–95, 198–201, 206, 208, 211, 227, 229
Nuri, 203

Oacpicagigua, Luis (Luis of Sáric), 203
Ob (Mountain Pimas), 13, 161, 164
Obregón, Baltazar, 16
O'Conor, Hugo, 206
Oera, 16
Oliva, Juan de, 48–49, 61, 212, 220, 234, 240
Onapa, 176
Ónavas, 14, 43, 203
O'odham, 6

Ópata-Cahitan language group, 14, 15, 37, 68, 128
Ópatas (Opatans), 2, 13, 15, 24, 48, 68–69, 120, 124, 126, 128, 135, 138, 150, 186, 230, 232–33, 235, 238, 243, 245–50, 259, 267; conspiracies of 1681, 18, 72–121; demographics, 13; as townspeople, 10, 16; as warriors, 15, 16, 24, 121
Opatería, 2, 3, 9, 14–18, 22, 28, 30, 46, 48, 54, 70, 72, 77, 82, 89, 92, 95, 108, 109, 112, 116, 119–20, 127–28, 135, 137–38, 142, 168, 169, 176, 201, 203, 231, 237, 239, 245–46, 250, 257, 261; epidemic diseases in, 48; Indian attacks on Spaniards in, 22; prehistoric conflicts in, 16, 70; similarity in climate to Spain, 30
Opodepe, 45–46, 64, 150, 196–98, 200–201, 251, 255, 257
Oposura, 25, 63, 64, 67, 133, 169, 173–74, 176, 179, 181–89, 192, 250, 255
Oro, Padre Nicolás de, 174
Ortiz de Cortés, Juan Antonio, 148–67, 251–52
Ostimuri, 6, 24, 29, 81, 120, 145, 149, 156, 158, 176, 185, 201–4, 208, 230, 234, 251, 253
Otermín, Governor Antonio de, 73, 75–79, 92

Pacheco (y Zavallos), Francisco, 111, 113–15, 119, 132–34, 137, 172–74, 177–78, 181–82, 184–86, 189, 249, 255; applying torture, 114
padre visitador, 34. See also *visitador*
Pantoja, Padre Pedro, 34, 55, 58–60, 63, 68–70, 235–40
Papagóchic (Chihuahua), 134
Parral (Chihuahua), San José de, 12, 20, 26, 27, 30–31, 40, 42–45, 59, 74–75, 82, 125, 127, 133–34, 145–46, 150, 152, 155–60, 166, 172–74, 182, 189, 191, 210–11, 227, 234, 246, 251–53; effect of Pueblo Rebellion on, 75; gold discoveries at, 30

Peralta, Juan, 225, 264
Peralta, Pedro de, 83, 90–92, 94, 106, 119
Perea, Captain Pedro de, 11, 17, 26–53, 54, 55, 58, 60–62, 68, 128, 169, 211–15, 217, 219, 221, 222–28, 234–36, 240–41, 261, 263–64; appointment as alcalde mayor de Sonora, 31; death of, 33–34, 38; Jesuit suspicion of, 31; mistreatment of Indians by, 33–35, 37–38; recruitment of New Mexicans as settlers by, 32
Perea, Pedro de, Junior, 35, 38, 40, 43, 45–46, 62, 215, 222–24, 226–28
Perea, Thomas de, 43
Pérez de Ribas, Padre Andrés, 123, 230, 232–35, 239, 242, 247, 249–50
Pérez Lora, Andrés, 226
Pfefferkorn, Ignaz, 138, 229
Phillip II, king of Spain, 141
Piatos, 13, 196, 199, 202, 204–5, 258
Pibipa, 148, 152, 156, 157, 253
Picado Pacheco, Domingo, 174–75, 178, 254–55
Pícolo, Padre Francisco María, 147, 151–55, 162, 164–65
Picundo, Captain Pascual, 129–33
Pimas, 3, 9, 13–16, 22–23, 29, 33, 39, 56, 60, 64, 68–69, 82, 108, 120, 128, 146, 150, 161, 165, 172, 176, 195–97, 202–5, 231–33, 240–41, 247, 250, 253, 257–59; attacks on Spaniards by, 22, 23, 108; languages of, 14, 56, 127
Pimas Altos, 82, 241, 258
Pimas Bajos, 9, 39, 64, 161, 176, 196, 203, 253
Pimería, Pimería Alta, 15, 30, 172, 201
Pinelli, Padre Luis, 180
Pitic, 197, 204, 257
Pol, Antonio, 197
Polici, Padre Horacio, 7, 19, 128–31, 134, 137, 203
polygamy, 19, 142, 233
Polzer, Charles, S. J., 68, 70, 189, 233–43
Pópulo, 150
presidios, corruption in, 22

priests: and Indian polygamy and sorcery, 18; use of the lash by, 20, 169, 171; and wandering Indians, 19, 141–44
prospectors, 10, 11, 28, 198, 256–57
Pueblo de Álamos, 219
Pueblo Indians, 74, 75, 77, 120
Pueblo Rebellion of New Mexico, 18, 72–74, 89, 98, 119, 137, 202

quadrilla (work gang), 147–50
Queipo de Llano, Pedro Antonio, 199
Querétaro, Colegio de Santa Cruz de, 201
Quiburi, 82, 93
Quigue, Francisco, 85–88, 91, 93–94, 118
Quihui, 167
Quimbunazorra (San Juan de la Cueva de), 147, 150–52, 156–61, 163, 251, 253
Quintero, Lorenzo, 81–83, 98, 112–15, 243, 244, 246

Ramírez del Prado, Captain Alonzo, 59
Ramos, José, 97
ranching, disruption to missions and Indians, 21, 34, 168–94
real (mining town), 10
reduccion[es] (reduction[s]), 4, 18, 37, 52, 141–43, 250
Reff, Daniel, 48
repartimiento, 143, 167
requerimiento, 61, 65
residencia (evaluation of term of office), 42, 67, 121, 238
Reyes, Fray Antonio (de los), 198, 200–201, 206–7, 211, 215, 257, 258, 259, 261
Río Bavispe, 10, 19, 30, 33, 58, 82, 93, 96, 97, 100, 102, 104, 106–8, 127–28, 245, 248
Río Chico, 39, 43, 261
Río de la Concepción, 14
Río Fronteras, 58
Río Fuerte, 5, 7, 8, 13, 29, 32, 59, 263
Río Grande, 19, 73, 77
Río Mátape, 10, 127
Río Mayo, 156

Río Moctezuma, 10, 15, 17, 33, 35, 127, 186, 188–89, 232
Río Sahuaripa, 10. *See also* Arroyo Sahuaripa
Río San Miguel, 26, 27, 30, 31–33, 35–36, 40–41, 48, 49, 54, 60, 91, 127, 150, 204, 231, 244, 257, 262
Río Sonora, 6, 10, 14, 16, 17, 28, 29–30, 32–33, 35–42, 44, 47, 49, 54–71, 81, 84–85, 89, 125, 127, 142, 147, 175, 180, 195, 197, 204, 213, 216–27, 220, 228, 231, 236, 240, 244, 250–51, 257, 262
Río Yaqui, 9–10, 29, 43, 157, 201, 203, 230–31, 234, 248, 253, 257, 261
rivers, absence of east of Sierra Madre, 5
Romero, Joseph, 183, 186–87, 192
Romo de Vivar, José, 117–20
royal fifth, 10, 12, 47, 202

Sagori, Juan, 98, 100
Sahuaripa, 9, 14, 16, 62, 106, 147–48, 151–56, 161–66, 176
Salem, Massachusetts, 136
Salt River, 16
San Antonio de la Huerta, 197
San Antonio Mine, 157–58
San Francisco de Borja, 222
San Juan Bautista, 17, 35, 47, 72, 76–81, 86, 90–91, 100, 106, 108, 111, 113–14, 116, 121, 145, 148, 149, 172, 174, 184–87, 205, 238, 244, 245, 252
San Juan y Santa Cruz, Manuel, 189–91, 193–94
San Marcial, Carrizal de, 197, 257
San Martin, Padre Juan, 152
San Pedro de los Reyes, Real de, 35, 43, 47, 211, 215, 222, 223, 226
Santa Cruz, 188
Santa Fe, New Mexico, 73, 75
Santiago, Real de, 6, 35, 47, 48, 60–62, 65, 241
Santiago de Jalisco, Franciscan province of, 201
Sarina, Andrés, 105
Sea of Cortés, 201

second Opatan conspiracy, 108, 115
Segua, Simón, 110
Seguida, María, 128–35
Seris, 3, 12–14, 22–24, 29, 150, 195–97, 199, 202–8, 231, 232, 233, 256, 257, 259; attacks on other Indians, 13; on Spaniards, 22, 23, 24, 202–8; language as an isolate, 14; resistance to reduction, 14
Serva, Santo Tomás de, 107
settlers: appropriation of land by, 47; attracted to the Opatería by precious metals, 17; conflicts with Jesuits, 50–51, 173, 167–94; corruption among, 12, 167–94; disputes with Indians, 20, 167–94; introduction of livestock by, 47, 167–94; need for food supply, 11; value to the Crown of, 2
Shaul, David, 15
Sibúpapas, 13, 197, 199, 202–6, 231, 256
Sidaicavit, Damian, 210–11, 228. *See also* Sidaycavit, Damian
Sidaycavit, Damian, 26. *See also* Sidaicavit, Damian
Sierra Libre, 203
Sierra Madre, 5, 9, 10, 14, 26, 30, 108, 127, 201, 202, 208
Sinaloa, 80
Sino, Pablo, 105
Sinoquipe, 55, 56, 58, 64, 68, 174
Sisibatori(s), 9
Sivacome Muchica, Francisco, 102–3, 105
Sivacume, Thomás, 186–87
Sobaípuris, 13, 93
Sodora, Francisco, 102, 103, 105
soldiers: as representatives of the king, 4; as settlers, 2
Sonora, 2, 3, 5, 6, 9, 10, 11, 12, 14, 15, 24, 27, 30, 43, 117, 147, 172, 185, 197, 225–26, 227; effect of Pueblo Rebellion on, 18, 75; depopulation due to Indian attacks, 23, 195–208; founding of, 27 passim; Valley of, 66, 212, 219, 224
Sonora (mine), 151
sorcerers (*hechiceros*), 19, 123 passim, 155

Suárez, Fray Juan, 68
Subiate, Joseph de, 149–50, 172, 174–94, 254–55
Sumas, 10, 14, 22, 72, 77, 80, 82, 85–86, 91, 93, 96, 108, 120–21, 202; disappearance of, 23; language of, 15; uprising of 1684, 121; warlike tendencies of, 14, 22, 23, 121, 161
Sunucabit, 218
Suri, Diego, 82–85, 88–89, 92, 94, 120

Tacupeto, 160–61, 176
Taname, 218
Tánori, Juan, 153–55
tapisque (tepisque), 101
Tarachi, 203
Tarahumaras, 10, 33, 128
Tasay, Pedro, 102, 105
Tebidéhuachi, 82, 85, 111, 115, 120
Tecoripa, 14, 203
Teguima(s), 3, 13, 14, 15, 29, 37, 55, 64, 69, 120, 125, 128; origin of name, 15; use of poisoned arrows, 29
Tenochtitlán, 3, 69
Tepache, 18, 72, 76, 82, 89, 92, 95, 97, 111–13, 161
Tepehuanes, 6, 10; resistance to Jesuits, 6
Tepiman languages, 14, 15
tequío (work requirement), 167
Terrenate, 82
terrenos baldíos (unoccupied lands), 40
Teuricachi (Turicachi), 77, 82, 108, 109–10, 113, 115, 116
"The Bishop," 148–49
tlátoles, 59, 63, 81, 83–89, 92, 95–100, 104, 106, 110, 112–14, 117, 143
Tlaxcala, 69
Tohono O'odham, 13, 14
Tonibabi, 148
Tónichi, 43, 157, 197, 222, 257
topile, 84, 97, 101, 105, 107
torture applied, 93, 95–96, 98, 102–3, 114, 119
Tosocomache, cave of, 108, 118–19
Triques, 208

Tuape, 15, 17, 26, 27–53, 54, 169, 210–28; destruction of wetlands in, 36; planting crops around, 36
Tubac, 197, 203
Tubutama, 14, 172
Turoque, Ignacio, 85, 88
typhus, 45

Uchacari, 108
Úparo, 37, 38, 211–20
Ures, 14, 36
Uro, Juan, 101–3, 105
Uto-Aztecan, 14, 15

Valencia, Captain Pedro de, 92, 97, 111–13
Valenzuela, 174
vecinos, 13, 49, 62, 171
Vega, Captain Simón Lazo de la. *See* Lazo de la Vega, Captain Simón
Verdugo, Lázaro, 76, 78–102, 109, 118–19, 121; orders executions of Opatans, 88, 90, 116
Verdugo de Chávez, Matheo, 109, 121
villa, 11, 31–32; requirements for creation of, 32–33
visitador, 11, 20. *See also padre visitador*
vizcocho (hardtack), 62

wetlands, destruction of, 36
wheat, 209; planting of in Tuape, 36, 42, 49
wine, prohibition of sales to Indians, 143
witchcraft, 124, 145

Yaquis, 6, 7, 15, 29, 70, 150, 201–3; language of, 14, 128; wars of, 23–25, 203
Ybarra, María de. *See* Ibarra, María de
Yécora, 14, 160, 164, 203
yerba la flecha (arrow poison), 112–14

Zambrano, Captain Gerónimo de, 164
Zapata, Padre Ortiz, 11, 68, 69
Zuaques, 8
Zubiate, Joseph de. *See* Subiate, Joseph de

www.ingramcontent.com/pod-product-compliance
Lightning Source LLC
Chambersburg PA
CBHW020943230426
43666CB00005B/147